The Native Tribes of Central Australia

Spencer Baldwin and F. J. Gillen

London

1899

TO
A. W. HOWITT
AND
LORIMER FISON
WHO LAID THE FOUNDATION OF OUR
KNOWLEDGE OF AUSTRALIAN ANTHROPOLOGY
THIS WORK IS DEDICATED BY THE AUTHORS

Preface

IN the following pages we have endeavoured to set forth an account of the customs and social organisation of certain of the tribes inhabiting Central Australia.

It has been the lot of one of us to spend the greater part of the past twenty years in the centre of the continent, and as sub-protector of the Aborigines he has had exceptional opportunities of coming into contact with, and of gaining the confidence of, the members of the large and important Arunta tribe, amongst whom he has lived, and of which tribe both of us, it may be added, are regarded as fully initiated members.

In the month of July, 1894, we met at Alice Springs, when the scientific expedition organised by Mr. W. A. Horn, of Adelaide, visited that part of the continent, and it was then that one of us gave to Dr. E. C. Stirling, the anthropologist of the expedition, notes which have since been published in the anthropological section of the report on the work of the expedition. This report included the results of the information gained up to that time with regard to the Central tribes, and in respect to certain points, we have, to some extent, had to traverse the same ground in order to make our account as complete as possible; but it was very evident that in regard to the customs and organisation of the tribe we were then only on the threshold of the inquiry, and at a subsequent time we determined to carry on the work.

During the summer of 1896–7, the natives gathered together at Alice Springs to perform an important series of ceremonies, constituting what is called the Engwura, and this, which occupied more than three months, we witnessed together. The series of ceremonies then enacted enabled us not only to gain a knowledge of, and an insight into the meaning of certain of them, which until then had not been seen by Europeans, but also served to indicate lines of inquiry along which further investigation would prove to be of value.

In addition to the investigation of various customs, such as those connected with initiation and magic, we have paid special attention to the totemic system and to matters concerned with the social organisation of the tribes. In connection especially with the totemic system, we desire to emphasize the fact that, whilst there is some degree of uniformity in regard to customs amongst the series of tribes inhabiting the continent, there is also, as might be expected, very considerable diversity. The physical conditions of the continent are such that groups of tribes inhabiting various regions have been, to a large extent, isolated from one another for a long period of time and have undoubtedly developed along different lines. The result is that, in respect to the totemic system, for example, groups of tribes differ from one another to a large extent, and the customs of no one tribe or group can be taken as typical of Australia generally in, at most, anything but broad outline.

The question of the social organisation of the Australian tribes and the significance of the "terms of relationship" have given rise to a considerable amount of difference of opinion, and into these we have inquired as carefully as possible. The result of our work is undoubtedly to corroborate that of Messrs. Howitt and Fison in regard to these matters.

We have endeavoured to set forth the results of our investigations so that the reader may see, on the one hand, the actual facts, and on the other, the conclusions at which, in certain cases, we have arrived after a consideration of these.

As it has been our main object to write simply an account of the Central tribes, we have not referred to the work of other authors, except so far as it was directly concerned with the tribes investigated. The work by Mr. W. E. Roth on the Aborigines of North-West Central Queensland reached us when our manuscript was written, and we have added references to it chiefly in the form of footnotes. Mr. Roth's work bears more closely upon certain parts of ours than that of any other author does, and is in some respects, especially in connection with the system of organisation, the most detailed account yet published of any Australian tribe, and we gladly take this opportunity, as fellow-workers in the same field, of expressing our high appreciation of his work.

The time in which it will be possible to investigate the Australian native tribes is rapidly drawing to a close, and though we know more of them than we do of the lost Tasmanians, yet our knowledge is very incomplete, and unless some special effort be made, many tribes will practically die out without our gaining any knowledge of the details of their organisation, or of their sacred customs and beliefs.

We have, in conclusion, the pleasant duty of acknowledging the assistance received from various friends. To Mr. C. E. Cowle and Mr. P. M. Byrne, both of whom, from long residence amongst them, are well acquainted with the natives, we are indebted in various ways for the most cordial assistance, and to Mr. Cowle one of us owes the opportunity of traversing certain parts of the interior which would otherwise have been inaccessible to him.

To Mr. C. Winnecke we are especially indebted. There is no one who has a fuller knowledge of the topography of Central Australia, and this knowledge he most generously and freely placed at our disposal, drawing up for us the two maps on which are indicated the localities of the principal spots associated with the traditions of the Arunta natives. It will be understood that these maps are not intended to indicate our present knowledge of the geographical features of Central

Australia, all except the more important ones being purposely omitted.

We have to thank Mr. W. A. Horn and Dr. E. C. Stirling for permission to utilize certain drawings illustrative of native rock paintings which were originally made to illustrate Dr. Stirling's anthropological report dealing with the Arunta tribe.

Finally, we have to express our deep sense of the obligation under which we lie to Dr. E. B. Tylor and Mr. J. G. Frazer. It need hardly be pointed out how much we are indebted to their work as indicating to us lines of inquiry, but in addition to this we have received from them the most cordial personal encouragement and help. They have most kindly read through the proofs—indeed to Mr. Frazer we are deeply indebted for the final revision of these, and in offering them our warmest thanks, we venture to express the hope that the work may prove to be worthy of the interest which they have taken in it.

MELBOURNE, *March*, 1898.

Chapter I Introduction

Nature of the country occupied by the natives—Distribution of the natives in local groups—Names given to the local groups—Local Totemic groups—The Alatunja or head man of each group and his powers—The position of Alatunja a hereditary one—Strong influence of custom—Possibility of introduction of changes in regard to custom—Councils of old men—Medicine men—Life in camp—Hunting customs—Food and method of cooking—Tracking powers—Counting and reckoning of time—General account of the more common weapons and implements—Clothing—Fighting—Local Totemic groups—Variation in customs amongst different Australian tribes—Personal appearance of the natives—Cicatrices—Measurements of the body—Moral character—Infanticide—Twins—Dread of evil magic.

THE native tribes with which we are dealing occupy an area in the centre of the Australian continent which, roughly speaking, is not less than 700 miles in length from north to south, and stretches out east and west of the transcontinental telegraph line, covering an unknown extent of country in either direction. The nature of the country varies much in different parts of this large area; at Lake Eyre, in the south, it is actually below sea-level. As we travel northwards for between 300 and 400 miles, the land gradually rises until it reaches an elevation of 2,000 feet; and to this southern part of the country the name of the Lower Steppes may appropriately be given. Northwards from this lies an elevated plateau forming the Higher Steppes, the southern limit of which is roughly outlined by the James and Macdonnell ranges, which run across from east to west for a distance of 400 miles.

The rivers which rise in the Higher Steppes find their way to the south, passing through deep gaps in the mountain ranges and then meandering slowly across the Lower Steppes until they dwindle away and are lost amongst the southern sandy flats, or perhaps reach the great depressed area centreing in the salt bed of Lake Eyre.

Away to the south and west of this steppe land lies a vast area of true desert region, crossed by no river courses, but with mile after mile of monotonous sand-hills covered with porcupine grass, or with long stretches of country where thick belts of almost impenetrable mulga scrub stretch across.

We may first of all briefly outline, as follows, the nature of the country occupied by the tribes with which we are dealing. At the present day the transcontinental railway line, after running along close by the southern edge of Lake Eyre, lands the traveller at a small township called Oodnadatta, which is the present northern terminus of the line, and lies about 680 miles to the north of Adelaide. Beyond this transit is by horse or camel; and right across the centre of the continent runs a track following closely the course of the single wire which serves to maintain, as yet, the only telegraphic communication between Australia and Europe. From Oodnadatta to Charlotte Waters stretches a long succession of gibber[1] plains, where, mile after mile, the ground is covered with brown and purple stones, often set close together as if they formed a tesselated pavement stretching away to the horizon. They are formed by the disintegration of a thin stratum of rock, called the Desert Sandstone, which forms the horizontal capping of low terraced hills, from which every here and there a dry watercourse, fringed with a thin belt of mulga-trees, comes down on to the plain across which it meanders for a few miles and then dies away.

The only streams of any importance in this part of the country are the Alberga, Stevenson, and Hamilton, which run across from the west and unite to form the Macumba River, which in times of flood empties itself into Lake Eyre. It is only very rarely that the rainfall is sufficient to fill the beds of these three streams; as a general rule a local flood occurs in one or other of them, but on rare occasions a widely distributed rainfall may fill the creeks and also the Finke river, which flows south from the Macdonnell range, which lies away to the north. When such a flood does occur—and this only takes place at long and irregular intervals of time—then the ordinary river beds are not deep enough to hold the body of water descending from the various ranges in which the tributary streams take their rise. Under these conditions the flood waters spread far and wide over the low-lying lands around the river courses. Down the river beds the water sweeps along, bearing with it uprooted trees and great masses of *débris*, and carving out for itself new channels. Against opposing obstacles the flood wrack is piled up in heaps—in fact, for months afterwards *débris* amongst the branches of trees growing in and about the watercourses indicates the height reached by the flood. What has been for often many months dry and parched-up land is suddenly transformed into a vast sheet of water. It is only however a matter of a very short time; the rainfall ceases and rapidly the water sinks. For a few days the creeks will run, but soon the surface flow ceases and only the scattered deeper holes retain the water. The sun once more shines hotly, and in the damp ground seeds which have lain dormant for months germinate, and, as if by magic, the once arid land becomes covered with luxuriant herbage. Birds, frogs, lizards and insects of all kinds can be seen and heard where before everything was parched and silent. Plants and animals alike make the most of the brief time in which they can grow and reproduce, and with them it is simply a case of a keen struggle, not so much against living enemies, as against their physical environment. If a plant can, for example, before all the surface moisture is exhausted, grow to such a size that its roots can penetrate to a considerable distance below the surface to where the sandy soil remains cool, then it has a chance of surviving; if not, it must perish. In just the same way amongst animals, those which can grow rapidly, and so can, as in the case of the frogs, reach a stage at which they are able to burrow while the banks of the waterhole in which they live are damp, will survive.

It is difficult to realise without having seen it the contrast between the Steppe lands of Australia in dry and rainy seasons. In the former the scene is one of desolation; the sun shines down hotly on stony plains or yellow sandy ground, on which grow wiry shrubs and small tussocks of grass, not closely set together, as in moister country, but separated from one another, so that in any patch of ground the number of individual plants can be counted. The sharp, thin shadows of the wiry scrub fall on the yellow ground, which shows no sign of animal life except for the little ant-hills, thousands of whose occupants are engaged in rushing about in apparently hopeless confusion, or piling leaves or seeds in regular order around the entrance to their burrows. A "desert oak"[2] or an acacia-tree may now and then afford a scanty shade, but for weeks together no clouds hide the brightness of the sun by day or of the stars by night.

Amongst the ranges which rise from the Higher Steppes the scenery is of a very different nature. Here, wild and rugged quartzite ranges, from which at intervals rise great rounded bluffs or sharply outlined peaks, reaching in some instances a height of 5,000 feet, run roughly parallel to one another, east and west, for between 300 and 400 miles. These ridges are separated from one another by valleys, varying in width from 200 or 300 yards to twenty miles, where the soil is hard and yellow and the scrub which thinly covers it is just like that of the Lower Steppes. The river courses run approximately north and south, and, as the watershed lies to the north of the main ranges, they have to cut at right angles across the latter. This they do in gorges, which are often deep and narrow. Some of them, except at flood times, are dry and afford the only means of traversing the ranges; others are constantly filled with water which, sheltered from the heat of the sun, remains in the dark waterholes when elsewhere the watercourses are quite dry. The scenery amongst the ranges is by no means devoid of beauty. The rugged red rocks, with here and there patches of pines or cycads, or stray gum-trees with pure white trunks, stand out sharply against the clear sky. In the gorges the rocks rise abruptly from the sides of the waterpools, leaving often only a thin strip of blue sky visible overhead. In some cases the gorge will run for half a mile across the range like a zigzag cleft not more than ten or twelve feet wide.

In addition to the Steppe lands there lies away to the south and west the true desert country where there are no watercourses other than the very insignificant ones which run for at most a mile or two across the sandy flats which surround the base of isolated hills such as Mount Olga or Ayers Rock. In this region the only water is to be found in rock holes on the bare hills which every now and then rise out above the sand-hills and the mulga-covered flats. Nothing could be more dreary than this country; there is simply a long succession of sand-hills covered with tussocks of porcupine grass, the leaves of which resemble knitting-needles radiating from a huge pin-cushion, or, where the sand-hills die down, there is a flat stretch of hard plain country, with sometimes belts of desert oaks, or, more often, dreary mulga scrub. In this desert country there is not much game; small rats and lizards can be found, and these the native catches by setting fire to the porcupine grass and so driving them from one tussock to another; but he must often find it no easy matter to secure food enough to live upon. In times of drought, which very frequently occur, the life of these sand-hill blacks must be a hard one. Every now and then there are found, right in the heart of the sand-hills, small patches of limestone, in each of which is a deep pit-like excavation, at the bottom of which there may or may not be a little pool of water, though such "native wells," as they are called, are of rare occurrence and are the remnants of old mound springs. More likely than not, the little water which one does contain is foul with the decaying carcase of a dingo which has ventured down for a drink and has been too weak to clamber out again. The most characteristic feature of the desert country, next to the sand-hills, are the remains of what have once been lakes, but are now simply level plains of glistening white salt, hemmed in with low hills covered with dreary scrub. Around these there is no sign of life, and the most perfect silence reigns.

Such is the general nature of the great area of Steppe and desert land inhabited by the Central Australian natives. In times of long-continued drought, when food and water[3] are both scarce, he has to suffer privation; but under ordinary circumstances, except in the desert country, where it can never be very pleasant, his life is by no means a miserable or a very hard one. Kangaroo, rock-wallabies, emus, and other forms of game are not scarce, and often fall a prey to his spear and boomerang, while smaller animals, such as rats and lizards, are constantly caught without any difficulty by the women, who also secure large quantities of grass seeds and tubers, and, when they are in season, fruits, such as that of the quandong or native plum.

Each of the various tribes speaks a distinct dialect, and regards itself as the possessor of the country in which it lives. In the more southern parts, where they have been long in contact with the white man, not only have their numbers diminished rapidly, but the natives who still remain are but poor representatives of their race, having lost all or nearly all of their old customs and traditions. With the spread of the white man it can only be a matter of comparatively a few years before the same fate will befall the remaining tribes, which are as yet fortunately too far removed from white settlements of any size to have become degraded. However kindly disposed the white settler may be, his advent at once and of necessity introduces a disturbing element into the environment of the native, and from that moment degeneration sets in, no matter how friendly may be the relations between the Aborigine and the new-comers. The chance of securing cast-off clothing, food, tobacco, and perhaps also knives and tomahawks, in return for services rendered to the settler, at once attracts the native into the vicinity of any settlement however small. The young men, under the new influence, become freed from the wholesome restraint of the older men, who are all-powerful in the normal condition of the tribe. The strict moral code, which is certainly enforced in their natural state, is set on one side, and nothing is adopted in place of it. The old men see with sorrow that the younger ones do not care for the time-honoured traditions of their fathers, and refuse to hand them on to successors who, according to their ideas, are not worthy to be trusted with them; vice, disease, and difficulty in securing the natural food, which is driven away by the settlers, rapidly diminish their numbers, and when the remnant of the tribe is gathered into some mission station, under conditions as far removed as they can well be from their natural ones, it is too late to learn anything of the customs which once governed tribal life.

Fortunately from this point of view the interior of the continent is not easily accessible, or rather its climate is too dry and the water supply too meagre and untrustworthy, to admit as yet of rapid settlement, and therefore the natives, in many parts, are practically still left to wander over the land which the white man does not venture to inhabit, and amongst them may still be found tribes holding firmly to the beliefs and customs of their ancestors.

If now we take the Arunta tribe as an example, we find that the natives are distributed in a large number of small local groups, each of which occupies, and is supposed to possess, a given area of country, the boundaries of which are well known to the natives. In speaking of themselves, the natives will refer to these local groups by the name of the locality which each of them inhabits. Thus, for example, the natives living at Idracowra, as the white men call it, will be called *ertwa Iturkawura opmira*, which means men of the Iturkawura camp; those living at Henbury on the Finke will be called *ertwa Waingakama opmira*, which means men of the Waingakama (Henbury) camp. Often also a number of separate groups occupying a larger district will be spoken of collectively by one name, as, for example, the groups living along the Finke River are often spoken of as Larapinta men, from the native name of the river. In addition to this the natives speak of different divisions of the tribe according to the direction of the country which they occupy. Thus the east side is called *Iknura ambianya*, the west side *Aldorla ambianya*, the south-west *Antikera ambianya*, the north side *Yirira ambianya*, the south-east side *Urlewa ambianya*. *Ertwa iknura ambianya* is applied to men living on the east, and so on.

Still further examination of each local group reveals the fact that it is composed largely, but not entirely, of individuals who describe themselves by the name of some one animal or plant. Thus there will be one area which belongs to a group of men who call themselves kangaroo men, another belonging to emu men, another to Hakea flower men, and so on, almost every animal and plant which is found in the country having its representative amongst the human inhabitants. The area of country which is occupied by each of these, which will be spoken of as local Totemic groups, varies to a considerable extent, but is never very large, the most extensive one with which we are acquainted being that of the witchetty grub people of the Alice Springs district. This group at the present time is represented by exactly forty individuals (men, women, and children), and the area of which they are recognised as the proprietors extends over about 100 square miles. In contrast to this, one particular group of "plum-tree" people is only, at the present day, represented by one solitary individual, and he is the proprietor of only a few square miles.

With these local groups we shall subsequently deal in detail, all that need be added here in regard to them is that groups of the same designation are found in many parts of the district occupied by the tribe. For example, there are various local groups of kangaroo people, and each one of these groups has its head man or, as the natives themselves call him, its Alatunja.[4] However small in numbers a local group may be it always has its Alatunja.

Within the narrow limits of his own group the local head man or Alatunja takes the lead; outside of his group no head man has of necessity any special power. If he has any generally-recognised authority, as some of them undoubtedly have, this is due to the fact that he is either the head of a numerically important group or is himself famous for his skill in hunting or fighting, or for his knowledge of the ancient traditions and customs of the tribe. Old age does not by itself confer distinction, but only when combined with special ability. There is no such thing as a chief of the tribe, nor indeed is there any individual to whom the term chief can be applied.

The authority which is wielded by an Alatunja is of a somewhat vague nature. He has no definite power over the persons of the individuals who are members of his group. He it is who calls together the elder men, who always consult concerning any important business, such as the holding of sacred ceremonies or the punishment of individuals who have broken tribal custom, and his opinion carries an amount of weight which depends upon his reputation. He is not of necessity recognised as the most important member of the council whose judgment must be followed, though, if he be old and distinguished, then he will have great influence. Perhaps the best way of expressing the matter is to say that the Alatunja has, *ex-officio*, a position which, if he be a man of personal ability, but only in that case, enables him to wield considerable power not only over the members of his own group, but over those of neighbouring groups whose head men are inferior in personal ability to himself.

The Alatunja is not chosen for the position because of his ability; the post is one which, within certain limits, is hereditary, passing from father to son, always provided that the man is of the proper designation—that is, for example, in a kangaroo group the Alatunja must of necessity be a kangaroo man. To take the Alice Springs group as an example, the holder of the office must be a witchetty grub man, and he must also be old enough to be considered capable of taking the lead in certain ceremonies, and must of necessity be a fully initiated man. The present Alatunja inherited the post from his father, who had previously inherited it from his father. The present holder has no son who is yet old enough to be an Alatunja, so that if he were to die within the course of the next two or three years his brother would hold the position, which would, however, on the death of this brother, revert to the present holder's son. It of course occasionally happens that the Alatunja has no son to succeed him, in which case he will before dying nominate the individual whom he desires to succeed him, who will always be either a brother or a brother's son. The Alatunjaship always descends in the male line, and we are not aware of anything which can be regarded as the precise equivalent of this position in other Australian tribes, a fact which is to be associated with the strong development of the local groups in this part of the continent.

The most important function of the Alatunja is to take charge of what we may call the sacred store-house, which has usually the form of a cleft in some rocky range, or a special hole in the ground, in which, concealed from view, are kept the sacred objects of the group. Near to this store-house, which is called an *Ertnatulunga*, no woman, child, or uninitiated man dares venture on pain of death.

At intervals of time, and when determined upon by the Alatunja, the members of the group perform a special ceremony, called *Intichiuma*, which will be described later on in detail, and the object of which is to increase the supply of the animal or plant bearing the name of the particular group which performs the ceremony. Each group has an *Intichiuma* of its own, which can only be taken part in by initiated men bearing the group name. In the performance of this ceremony the Alatunja takes the leading part; he it is who decides when it is to be performed, and during the celebration the proceedings are carried out under his direction, though he has, while conducting them, to follow out strictly the customs of his ancestors.

As amongst all savage tribes the Australian native is bound hand and foot by custom. What his fathers did before him that he must do. If during the performance of a ceremony his ancestors painted a white line across the forehead, that line he must paint. Any infringement of custom, within certain limitations, is visited with sure and often severe punishment. At the same time, rigidly conservative as the native is, it is yet possible for changes to be introduced. We have already pointed out that there are certain men who are especially respected for their ability, and, after watching large numbers of the tribe, at a time when they were assembled together for months to perform certain of their most sacred ceremonies, we have come to the conclusion that at a time such as this, when the older and more powerful men from various groups are met together, and when day by day and night by night around their camp fires they discuss matters of tribal interest, it is quite possible for changes of custom to be introduced. At the present moment, for example, an important change in tribal organisation is gradually spreading through the tribe from north to south. Every now and then a man arises of superior ability to his fellows. When large numbers of the tribe are gathered together—at least it was so on the special occasion to which we allude—one or two of the older men are at once seen to wield a special influence over the others. Everything, as we have before said, does not depend upon age. At this gathering, for example, some of the oldest men were of no account; but, on the other hand, others not so old as they were, but more learned in ancient lore or more skilled in matters of magic, were looked up to by the others, and they it was who settled everything. It must, however, be understood that we have no definite proof to bring forward of the actual introduction by this means of any fundamental change of custom. The only thing that we can say is that, after carefully watching the natives during the performance of their ceremonies and endeavouring as best we could to enter into their feelings, to think as they did, and to become for the time being one of themselves, we came to the conclusion that if one or two of the most powerful men settled upon the advisability of introducing some change, even an important one, it would be quite possible for this to be agreed upon and carried out. That changes have been introduced, in fact, are still being introduced, is a matter of certainty; the difficulty to be explained is, how in face of the rigid conservatism of the native, which may be said to be one of his leading features, such changes can possibly even be mooted. The only possible chance is by means of the old men, and, in the case of the Arunta people, amongst whom the local feeling is very strong, they have opportunities of a special nature. Without belonging to the same group, men who inhabit localities close to one another are more closely associated than men living at a distance from one another, and, as a matter of fact, this local bond is strongly marked—indeed so marked was it during the performance of their sacred ceremonies that we constantly found it necessary to use the term "local relationship." Groups which are contiguous locally are constantly meeting to perform ceremonies; and among the Alatunjas who thus come together and direct proceedings there is perfectly sure, every now and again, to be one who stands pre-eminent by reason of superior ability, and to him, especially on an occasion such as this, great respect is always paid. It would be by no means impossible for him to propose to the other older men the introduction of a change, which, after discussing it, the Alatunjas of the local groups gathered together might come to the conclusion was a good one, and, if they did so, then it would be adopted in that district. After a time a still larger meeting of the tribe, with head men from a still wider area—a meeting such as the Engwura, which is described in the following pages—might be held. At this the change locally introduced would, without fail, be discussed. The man who first started it would certainly have the support of his local friends, provided they had in the first instance agreed upon the advisability of its introduction, and not only this, but the chances are that he would have the support of the head men of other local groups of the same designation as his own. Everything would, in fact, depend upon the status of the original proposer of the change; but, granted the existence of a man with sufficient ability to think out the details of any change, then, owing partly to the strong development of the local feeling, and partly to the feeling of kinship between groups of the same designation, wherever their local habitation may be, it seems quite possible that the markedly conservative tendency of the natives in regard to customs handed down to them from their ancestors may every now and then be overcome, and some change, even a radical one, be introduced. The traditions of the tribe indicate, it may be noticed, their recognition of the fact that customs have varied from time to time. They have, for example, traditions dealing with supposed ancestors, some of whom introduced, and others of whom changed, the method of initiation. Tradition also indicates ancestors belonging to particular local groups who changed an older into the present marriage system, and these traditions all deal with special powerful individuals by whom the changes were introduced. It has been stated by writers such as Mr. Curr "that the power which enforces custom in our tribes is for the most part an impersonal one."[5] Undoubtedly public opinion and the feeling that any violation of tribal custom will bring down upon the guilty person the ridicule and opprobrium of his fellows is a strong, indeed a very strong, influence; but at the same time there is in the tribes with which we are personally acquainted something beyond this. Should any man break through the strict marriage laws, it is not only an "impersonal power" which he has to deal with. The head men of the group or groups concerned consult together with the elder men, and, if the offender, after long consultation, be adjudged guilty and the determination be arrived at that he is to be put to death—a by no means purely hypothetical case—then the same elder men make arrangements to carry the sentence out, and a party, which is called an *"ininja,"* is organised for the purpose. The offending native is perfectly well aware that he will be dealt with by something much more real than an "impersonal power."[6]

In addition to the Alatunja, there are two other classes of men who are regarded as of especial importance; these are the so-called "medicine men," and in the second place the men who are supposed to have a special power of communicating with the *Iruntarinia* or spirits associated with the tribe. Needless to say there are grades of skill recognised amongst the members of these two classes, in much the same way as we recognise differences of ability amongst members of the medical profession. In subsequent chapters we shall deal in detail with these three special types; meanwhile in this general *résumé* it is sufficient to note that they have a definite standing and are regarded as, in certain ways, superior to the other men of the tribe. It may, however, be pointed out that, while every group has its Alatunja, there is no necessity for each to have either a medicine or an *Iruntarinia* man, and that in regard to the position of the latter there is no such thing as hereditary succession.

Turning again to the group, we find that the members of this wander, perhaps in small parties of one or two families, often, for example, two or more brothers with their wives and children, over the land which they own, camping at favourite spots where the presence of waterholes, with their accompaniment of vegetable and animal food, enables them to supply their wants.[7]

In their ordinary condition the natives are almost completely naked, which is all the more strange as kangaroo and wallaby are not by any means scarce, and one would think that their fur would be of no little use and comfort in the winter time, when, under the perfectly clear sky, which often remains cloudless for weeks together, the radiation is so great that at night-time the temperature falls several degrees below freezing point. The idea of making any kind of clothing as a protection against cold does not appear to have entered the native mind, though he is keen enough upon securing the Government blanket when he can get one, or, in fact, any stray cast-off clothing of the white man. The latter is however worn as much from motives of vanity as from a desire for warmth; a *lubra* with nothing on except an ancient straw hat and an old pair of boots is perfectly happy. The very kindness of the white man who supplies him, in outlying parts, with stray bits of clothing is by no means conducive to the longevity of the native. If you give a black fellow, say a woollen shirt, he will perhaps wear it for a day or two, after that his wife will be adorned with it, and then, in return for perhaps a little food, it will be passed on to a friend. The natural result is that, no sooner do the natives come into contact with white men, than phthisis and other diseases soon make their appearance, and, after a comparatively short time, all that can be done is to gather the few remnants of the tribe into some mission station where the path to final extinction may be made as pleasant as possible.

If, now, the reader can imagine himself transported to the side of some waterhole in the centre of Australia, he would probably find amongst the scrub and gum-trees surrounding it a small camp of natives. Each family, consisting of a man and one or more wives and children, accompanied always by dogs,[8] occupies a *mia-mia*, which is merely a lean-to of shrubs so placed as to shield the occupants from the prevailing wind, which, if it be during the winter months, is sure to be from the south-east. In front of this, or inside if the weather be cold, will be a small fire of twigs, for the black fellow never makes a large fire as the white man does. In this respect he certainly regards the latter as a strange being, who makes a big fire and then finds it so hot that he cannot go anywhere near to it. The black fellow's idea is to make a small fire such that he can lie coiled round it and, during the night, supply it with small twigs so that he can keep it alight without making it so hot that he must go further away.

Early in the morning, if it be summer, and not until the sun be well up if it be winter, the occupants of the camp are astir. Time is no object to them, and, if there be no lack of food, the men and women all lounge about while the children laugh and play. If food be required, then the women will go out accompanied by the children and armed with digging sticks and *pitchis*,[9] and the day will be spent out in the bush in search of small burrowing animals such as lizards and small marsupials. The men will perhaps set off armed with spears, spear-throwers, boomerangs and shields in search of larger game such as emus and kangaroos. The latter are secured by stalking, when the native gradually approaches his prey with perfectly noiseless footsteps. Keeping a sharp watch on the animal, he remains absolutely still, if it should turn its head, until once more it resumes its feeding. Gradually, availing himself of the shelter of any bush or large tussock of grass, he approaches near enough to throw his spear. The end is fixed into the point of the spear-thrower, and, aided by the leverage thus gained, he throws it forward with all his strength. Different men vary much in their skill in spear-throwing, but it takes an exceptionally good man to kill or disable at more than twenty yards. Sometimes two or three men will hunt in company, and then, while one remains in ambush, the others combine to drive the animals as close as possible to him. Euros[10] are more easily caught than kangaroos, owing to the fact that they inhabit hilly and scrub country, across which they make "pads," by the side of which men will lie in ambush while parties of women go out and drive the animals towards them. On the ranges the rock-wallabies have definite runs, and close by one of these a native will sit patiently, waiting hour by hour, until some unfortunate beast comes by.

In some parts the leaves of the pituri plant (*Duboisia Hopwoodii*) are used to stupefy the emu. The plan adopted is to make a decoction in some small waterhole at which the animal is accustomed to drink. There, hidden by some bush, the native lies quietly in wait. After drinking the water the bird becomes stupefied, and easily falls a prey to the black fellow's spear. Sometimes a bush shelter is made, so as to look as natural as possible, close by a waterhole, and from behind this animals are speared as they come down to drink. It must be remembered that during the long dry seasons of Central Australia waterholes are few and far between, so that in this way the native is aided in his work of killing animals. In some parts advantage is taken of the inquisitive nature of the emu. A native will carry something which resembles the long neck and small head of the bird and will gradually approach his prey, stopping every now and then, and moving about in the aimless way of the bird itself. The emu, anxious to know what the thing really is, will often wait and watch it until the native has the chance of throwing his spear at close quarters. Sometimes a deep pit will be dug in a part which is known to be a feeding ground of the bird. In the bottom of this a short, sharply-pointed spear will be fixed upright, and then, on the top, bushes will be spread and earth scattered upon them. The inquisitive bird comes up to investigate the matter, and sooner or later ventures on the bushes, and, falling through, is transfixed by the spear. Smaller birds such as the rock pigeons, which assemble in flocks at any waterhole, are caught by throwing the boomerang amongst them, and larger birds, such as the eagle-hawk, the down of which is much valued for decorating the body during the performance of sacred ceremonies, are procured by the same weapon.

It may be said that with certain restrictions[11] which apply partly to groups of individuals and partly to individuals at certain times of their lives, everything which is edible is used for food.[12] So far as cooking is concerned, the method is primitive. Many of the vegetables such as the Irriakura (the bulb of *Cyperus rotundus*), may be eaten raw, or they may be roasted in hot ashes. Very often large quantities of the pods of an acacia will be gathered and laid on the hot ashes, some of which are heaped up over them, and then the natives simply sit round, and "shell" and eat the seeds as if they were peas—in fact they taste rather like raw green peas. Perhaps the most standard vegetable diet of the natives in this part of the Centre is what is called by the natives in the north of the Arunta, Ingwitchika, and by white men usually Munyeru. This is the seed of a species of Claytonia. The women gather large quantities and winnow the little black seeds by pouring them from one *pitchi* into another so that the wind may carry off the loose husks, or else, taking some up in their hands, they blow the husks away. When freed from the latter, they are placed on one of the usual grinding stones and then ground down with a smaller stone held in the hand. Water is poured on every now and then, and the black, muddy-looking mixture tumbles over the side into a receptacle, and is then ready for eating either raw or after baking in the ashes. Munyeru seems to take the place amongst these tribes of the Nardoo (the spore cases of *Marsilea quadrifolia*) which is a staple article of food in the Barcoo district and other parts of the interior of Australia.

In the case of animals the larger ones are usually cooked in more or less shallow pits in the ground. An opossum is first of all disembowelled, the wool is then plucked off with the fingers and the body placed on the hot ashes. A rock wallaby is treated in much the same way, except that the hair is first singed off in the fire and then the skin is scraped with a piece of flint. The ashes are heaped up over the body, which, when partly cooked, is taken out and an incision made in each groin; the holes fill and refill with fluid, which is greatly appreciated and drunk up at once. The animal is then divided up, the flint at the end of the spear-thrower being used for this purpose. When cooking an Echidna the intestines are first removed. Then a small hole is dug, the bottom is sprinkled with water, and the animal placed in it. The back is covered with a layer of moist earth or sand, which is removed after about a quarter of an hour, and hot ashes substituted, which are removed after a few minutes. The skin with the quills is next cut off with a flint, and the body is then placed amongst hot ashes till cooked.

When a euro or kangaroo is killed, the first thing that is always done is to dislocate the hind-legs so as to make the animal what is called *atnuta* or limp. A small hole is cut with a flint in one side of the abdomen, and after the intestines have been pulled out, it is closed up with a wooden skewer. The intestines are usually cooked by rolling them about in hot sand and ashes, any fat which may be present being carefully removed, as it is esteemed a great delicacy. One of the first things to be done is to extract the tendons from the hind limbs. To do this the skin is cut through close to the foot with the sharp bit of flint which is attached to the end of the spear-thrower. A hitch is next taken round the tendon with a stick, and then, with one foot against the animal's rump, the man pulls until the upper end gives way. Then the loose end is held in the teeth, and, when tightly stretched, the lower end is cut through with the flint and the tendon thus extracted is twisted up and put for safe keeping beneath the waist girdle, or in the hair of the head just behind the ear. These tendons are of great service to the natives in various ways, such as for attaching the barbed points on to the ends of the spears, or for splicing spears or mending broken spear-throwers. Meanwhile a shallow pit, perhaps one or two feet deep, has been dug with sticks, and in this a large fire is made. When this burns up, the body is usually held in the flames to singe off the fur, after which it is scraped with a flint. Sometimes this part of the performance is omitted. The hind legs are cut off at the middle joint and the tail either divided in the middle or cut off close to the stump. When the fire has burnt down the animal is laid in the pit on its back with its legs protruding through the hot ashes, which are heaped up over it. After about an hour it is supposed to be cooked, and is taken off, laid on green boughs so as to prevent it from coming in contact with the earth, and then cut up, the hind legs being usually removed first. In some parts where the fur is not singed off, the first thing that is done after removing the body from the fire is to take off the burnt skin. The carver assists himself, during the process of cutting the body up into joints, to such dainty morsels as the heart and kidneys, while any juice which accumulates in the internal cavities of the body is greedily drunk.

When cooking an emu the first thing that is done is to roughly pluck it; an incision is then made in the side and the intestines withdrawn, and the inside stuffed with feathers, the cut being closed by means of a wooden skewer. A pit is dug sufficiently large to hold the body and a fire lighted in it, over which the body is held and singed so as to get rid of the remaining feathers. The legs are cut off at the knee joint, and the head brought round under one leg, to which it is fastened with a wooden skewer. The ashes are now removed from the pit, and a layer of feathers put in; on these the bird is placed resting on its side; another layer of feathers is placed over the bird, and then the hot ashes are strewn over. When it is supposed to be cooked enough, it is taken out, placed on its breast, and an incision is made running round both sides so as to separate the back part from the under portion of the body. It is then turned on to its back, the legs taken off and the meat cut up.

The tracking powers of the native are well-known, but it is difficult to realise the skill which they display unless one has seen them at work.[13] Not only does the native know the track of every beast and bird, but after examining any burrow he will at once, from the direction in which the last track runs, tell you whether the animal is at home or not. From earliest childhood boys and girls alike are trained to take note of every track made by every living thing. With the women especially it is a frequent amusement to imitate on the sandy ground the tracks of various animals, which they make with wonderful accuracy with their hands. Not only do they know the varied tracks of the latter, but they will distinguish those of particular men and women. In this respect the men vary greatly, a fact which is well known to, and appreciated by, those in charge of the native police in various parts of the interior of the continent. Whilst they can all follow tracks which would be indistinguishable to the average white man, there is a great difference in their ability to track when the tracks become obscure. The difference is so marked that while an ordinary good tracker will have difficulty in following them while he is on foot, and so can see them close to, a really good one will unerringly follow them up on horse or camel back.[14] Not only this, but, strange as it may sound to the average white man whose meals are not dependent upon his ability to track an animal to its burrow or hiding place, the native will recognise the footprint of every individual of his acquaintance.

Whilst in matters such as tracking, which are concerned with their everyday life, and upon efficiency in which they actually depend for their livelihood, the natives show conspicuous ability, there are other directions in which they are as conspicuously deficient. This is perhaps shown most clearly in the matter of counting. At Alice Springs they occasionally count, sometimes using their fingers in doing so, up to five, but frequently anything beyond four is indicated by the word *oknira*, meaning much or great. One is *nintha*, two *thrama* or *thera*, three *urapitcha*, four *therankathera*, five *theranka-thera-nintha*. Time is counted by "sleeps" or "moons," or phases of the moon, for which they have definite terms: longer periods they reckon by means of seasons, having names for summer and winter. They have further definite words expressing particular times, such as morning before sunrise (*ingwunthagwuntha*), evening (*ungwūrila*), yesterday (*abmirka*), day before yesterday (*abmirkairprina*), to-morrow (*ingwuntha*), day after to-morrow (*ingwunthairprina*), in some days (*ingwunthalkura*), in a short time (*ingwunthaunma*), in a long time (*ingwuntha arbarmaninja*).[15] It may also be said that for every animal and plant which is of any service to them, and for numberless others, such as various forms of mice, insects, birds, &c., amongst animals, and various kinds of shrubs and grasses amongst plants, they have distinctive names; and, further still, they distinguish the sexes, *marla* indicating the female sex, and *uria* the male. In many respects their memory is phenomenal. Their mental powers are simply developed along the lines which are of service to them in their daily life.

However, to return to the native camp once more. If we examine their weapons and implements of various kinds, that is those usually carried about, they will be found to be comparatively few in number and simple. A woman has always a *pitchi*, that is a wooden trough varying in length from one to three feet, which has been hollowed out of the soft wood of the bean tree (*Erythrina vespertilio*), or it may be out of hard wood such as *mulga* or eucalypt. In this she carries food material, either balancing it on her head or holding it slung on to one hip by means of a strand of human hair or ordinary fur string across one shoulder. Not infrequently a small baby will be carried about in a *pitchi*. The only other implement possessed by a woman is what is popularly called a "yam stick," which is simply a digging stick or, to speak more correctly, a pick. The commonest form consists merely of a straight staff of wood with one or both ends bluntly pointed, and of such a size that it can easily be carried in the hand and used for digging in the ground. When at work, a woman will hold the pick in the right hand close to the lower end, and, alternately digging this into the ground with one hand, while with the other she scoops out the loosened earth, will dig down with surprising speed. In parts of the scrub, where live the honey ants, which form a very favourite food of the natives, acre after acre of hard sandy soil is seen to have been dug out, simply by the picks of the women in search of the insect, until the place has just the appearance of a deserted field where diggers have, for long, been at work "prospecting." Very often a small *pitchi* will be used as a shovel or scoop, to clear the earth out with, when it gets too deep to be merely thrown up with the hand, as the woman goes on digging deeper and deeper until at last she may reach a depth of some six feet or even more. Of course the children go out with the women, and from the moment that they can toddle about they begin to imitate the actions of their mother. In the scrub a woman will be digging up lizards or honey ants while close by her small child will be at work, with its diminutive pick, taking its first lessons in what, if it be a girl, will be the main employment of her life.

So far as clothing is concerned, a woman is not much encumbered in her work. She usually wears around her neck one or more rings, each of which is commonly formed of a central strand of fur string, round which other strands are tightly wound till the whole has a diameter varying from a quarter to half an inch. The two ends of the central strand are left projecting so that they can be tied behind the neck, and the ring thus made is thickly coated with grease and red ochre. A similar kind of ring is often worn on the head[16] and, amongst the younger women especially, instead of, or perhaps in addition to, the hair neck ring, there may be worn a long string of the bright red beads of the bean tree. Each bead is bored through with a fire stick, and the pretty necklet thus made hangs round the neck in several coils, or may pass from each shoulder under the opposite arm pit.

North of the Macdonnell Ranges the women wear small aprons formed of strands of fur string suspended from a waist string, and on the forehead they often wear an ornament composed of a small lump of porcupine-grass resin, into which are fixed either a few kangaroo incisor teeth or else a number of small bright red seeds. A short strand of string is fixed into the resin and by means of this the ornament is tied to the hair, so that it just overhangs the forehead.

The men's weapons consist of shield, spears, boomerang and spear-thrower, all of which are constantly carried about when on the march. The shields, though they vary in size, are of similar design over practically the whole Central area. They are uniformly made of the light wood of the bean tree, so that their actual manufacture is limited to the more northern parts where this tree grows. The Warramunga tribe are especially noted for their shields, which are traded far and wide over the Centre. Each has a distinctly convex outer and a concave inner surface, in the middle of which a space is hollowed out, leaving a bar running across in the direction of the length, which can be grasped by the hand.

In the Ilpirra, Arunta and Luritcha tribes the ordinary spear is about ten feet, or somewhat less, in length; the body is made of Tecoma wood and the tip of a piece of *mulga*, which is spliced on to the body and the splicing bound round with tendon. Close to the sharp point a small curved barb is attached by tendon, though in many this barb is wanting. A rarer form of spear is made out of heavier wood, such as the desert oak (*Casuarina Descaineana*), and this is fashioned out of one piece and has no barb.

The spear-thrower is perhaps the most useful single thing which the native has. It is in the form of a hollowed out piece of *mulga* from two feet to two feet six inches in length, with one end tapering gradually to a narrow handle, and the other, more suddenly, to a blunt point, to which is attached, by means of tendon, a short, sharp bit of hard wood which fits into a hole in the end of a spear. At the handle end is a lump of resin into which is usually fixed a piece of sharpedged flint or quartzite, which forms the most important cutting weapon of the native.

The boomerangs are not like the well-known ones which are met with in certain other parts and which are so made that when thrown they return to the sender. The Central Australian native does not appear to have hit upon this contrivance, or, at least, if he ever possessed any such, the art of making them is now completely lost; his boomerang has a widely open curve, and the flat blade lies wholly in one plane.

In addition to these weapons a man will probably carry about with him a small wallet which is made simply of part of the skin of some animal, or perhaps of short strips of bark tied round with fur string. In this wallet he will carry a tuft or two of feathers for decoration, a spare bit or two of quartzite, a piece of red ochre, a kind of knout which has the form of a skein of string, and is supposed, by men and women alike, to be of especial use and efficacy in chastising women, and possibly he will have some charmed object, such as a piece of hair cut from a dead man's head and carefully ensheathed in hair or fur string. If the man be old it is not at all unlikely that he will have with him, hidden away from the sight of the women, a sacred stick or bull-roarer, or even a sacred stone.

In the south of the Arunta tribe the women weave bags out of string made of fur or vegetable fibre, in which they carry food, &c., but these are not found in the northern parts.

One of the most striking and characteristic features of the Central Australian implements and weapons is the coating of red ochre with which the native covers everything except his spear and spear-thrower.

As regards clothing and ornament, the man is little better off than the woman. His most constant article is a waist belt made of human hair—usually provided by his mother-in-law. On his forehead, stretched across from ear to ear, is a *chilara* or broad band made of parallel strands of fur string, and around his neck he will have one or more rings similar to those worn by the women. His hair will be well greased and also red-ochred, and in the Luritcha and Arunta it may be surmounted by a pad of emu feathers, worn in much the same way as a chignon, and tied on to the hair with fur string. If he be at all vain he will have a long nose-bone ornament, with a rat-tail or perhaps a bunch of cockatoo feathers at one end, his *chilara* will be covered with white pipeclay on which a design will be drawn in red ochre, and into either side of his chignon will be fastened a tuft of white or brightly-coloured feathers. His only other article of clothing, if such it can be called, is the small public tassel which, especially if it be covered with white pipeclay, serves rather as an ornament than as a covering.

Such are the ordinary personal belongings of the natives which they carry about with them on their wanderings.

Each local group has certain favourite camping grounds by the side of waterholes, where food is more or less easily attainable, and in spots such as these there will always be found clusters of *mia-mias*, made of boughs, which are simply replaced as the old ones wither up, or when perhaps in the hot weather they are burnt down.

When many of them are camped together it can easily be seen that the camp is divided into two halves, each separated from the other by some such natural feature as a small creek, or very often if the camping place be close to a hill, the one half will erect its *mia-mias* on the rising, and the other on the low ground. We shall see later that in the case of the Arunta tribe, for example, all the individuals belong to one or other of the four divisions called Panunga, Bulthara, Purula and Kumara, and in camp it will be found that the first two are always separated from the last two.

During the day-time the women are sure to be out in search of food, while the men either go out in search of larger game, or else, if lazy and food be abundant, they will simply sleep all day, or perhaps employ their time in making or trimming up their weapons. When conditions are favourable every one is cheerful and light-hearted, though every now and then a quarrel will arise, followed perhaps by a fight, which is usually accompanied by much noise and little bloodshed. On such occasions, if it be the women who are concerned, fighting clubs will be freely used and blows given and taken which would soon render *hors de combat* an ordinary white woman, but which have comparatively little effect upon the black women; the men usually look on with apparent complete indifference, but may sometimes interfere and stop the fight. If, however, two men are fighting, the mother and sisters of each will cluster round him, shouting at the top of their voices and dancing about with a peculiar and ludicrous high knee action, as they attempt to shelter him from the blows of his adversary's boomerang or fighting club, with the result that they frequently receive upon their bodies the blows meant for the man whom they are attempting to shield.

As a general rule the natives are kindly disposed to one another, that is of course within the limits of their own tribe, and, where two tribes come into contact with one another on the border land of their respective territories, there the same amicable feelings are maintained between the members of the two. There is no such thing as one tribe being in a constant state of enmity with another so far as these Central tribes are concerned. Now and again of course fights do occur between the members of different local groups who may or may not belong to the same or to different tribes.

We have already spoken of the local groups as being composed mainly of individuals each of whom bears the name of some animal or plant; that is each such group consists, to a large extent, but by no means exclusively, of men and women of, what is commonly spoken of as, a particular totem. The question of totems amongst these tribes will be dealt with in detail subsequently, what we desire to draw attention to here is simply the fact that, in these tribes, there is no such thing as the members of one totem being bound together in such a way that they must combine to fight on behalf of a member of the totem to which they belong. If, for example, a large number of natives are gathered together and a fight occurs, then at once the Panunga and Bulthara men on the one hand, and the Purula and Kumara on the other hand, make common cause. It is only indeed during the performance of certain ceremonies that the existence of a mutual relationship, consequent upon the possession of a common totemic name, stands out at all prominently. In fact it is perfectly easy to spend a considerable time amongst the Arunta tribe without even being aware that each individual has a totemic name, whilst, on the other hand, the fact that every individual belongs to one or other of the divisions, Panunga, Purula, etc., is soon apparent. This is associated with the fact that in these tribes, unlike what obtains in so many of the tribes whose organisation has hitherto been described, the totem has nothing whatever to do with regulating marriage, nor again does the child of necessity belong either to its mother's or its father's totem.

In many works on anthropology it is not unusual to see a particular custom which is practised in one or more tribes quoted in general terms as the custom of "the Australian native." It is, however, essential to bear in mind that, whilst undoubtedly there is a certain amount in common as regards social organisation and customs amongst the Australian tribes, yet, on the other hand, there is great diversity. Some tribes, for example, count descent in the maternal line, others count it in the paternal line; indeed, it is not as yet possible to say which of these methods is the more widely practised in Australia. In some tribes totems govern marriage, in others they have nothing to do with the question. In some tribes a tooth is knocked out at the initiation rite, in others the knocking out of the tooth may be practised, but is not part of the initiation rite, and in others again the custom is not practised at all. In some tribes the initiation rite consists in circumcision and perhaps other forms of mutilation as well; in others this practice is quite unknown. In some tribes there is a sex totem, in others there is no such thing; and in isolated cases we meet with an individual totem distinct from the totem common to a group of men and women.

When the great size of the land area occupied by the Australian tribes is taken into account, such diversity in custom and organisation is not to be wondered at. When, if ever, we gain an adequate knowledge of the various tribes still left, it may be possible to piece the whole together and to trace out the development from a common starting-point of the various customs and systems of organisation met with in different parts of the continent. At the present time we can perhaps group the tribes into two or three large divisions, each possessing certain well-marked features in common, such as counting descent in the maternal or paternal line as the case may be, but beyond this, as yet, we cannot go.[17]

In the matter of personal appearance, whilst conforming generally to the usual Australian type of features, there is very considerable difference between various individuals. In the matter of height, the average of twenty adult males measured by us, was 166.3 cm. The tallest was 178.2 cm., and the shortest 158.2 cm. The average of ten adult females was 156.8 cm.; the tallest was 163 cm., and the shortest was 151.5 cm. The average chest measurement of the same twenty men was 90.33 cm.; the greatest being 97 cm., and the least 83 cm.

In some the pronounced curve of the nose gave superficially a certain Jewish aspect, though in many this curve was completely wanting, and in all the nasal width was very considerable, the spreading out of the lobes being certainly emphasised by the practice of wearing a nose-bone. In the twenty males the average width was 4.8 cm. and the length 5.1 cm.; in the ten females the average width was 4.3 cm. and the length 4.6 cm. The greatest width in any male was 5.4 cm. and the least 3.9 cm.; the length of the former was 5.2 cm., and of the latter 4 cm. The greatest length was 6.2 cm., and in this case the width was 4.9 cm., which represents the greatest variation measured as between the length and width, the latter in some few cases (five out of the thirty) slightly exceeding the length. The root of the nose is depressed and the supra-orbital ridges very strongly marked. The buccal width is considerable, averaging 5.8 cm. in the males and 5.4 cm. in the females. The greatest width in the males is 6.5 cm. and in the females 6 cm., the least width being respectively 5.3 cm. and 4.7 cm. The lips are always thick.

In colour the Central Australian, though usually described as black, is by no means so. Out of the twenty males examined all, save one, corresponded as closely as possible with the chocolate-brown which is numbered 28 on Broca's scheme,[18] the odd one was slightly lighter. The only way in which to judge correctly of the colour is to cut a small square hole in a sheet of white paper and to place this upon the skin; unless this is done there is a tendency on first inspection to think that the tint is darker than it really is. To ascertain the tint two or three parts of the body were tested, the chest, back and legs. It must be remembered that the Central Australian native is fond of rubbing himself over with grease and red ochre, especially at times when ceremonies are being performed, but we do not think that in the individuals examined this interfered materially with the determination, the colour of all the individuals and of the various parts tested being strikingly uniform. While at work we always had two or three of them together, and they could always detect the patch of colour on the plate which corresponded to that of the skin examined. The women, with one exception, corresponded in colour to number 29, the odd one being of the darker shade, number 28, like the men. The new-born child is always of a decidedly lighter tint, but it rapidly darkens after the first day or two. A half-caste girl at Alice Springs corresponded to number 21 in colour, and the offspring, a few months old, by a white man of a half-caste woman in the southern part of the tribe, was undistinguishable in colour from the average English child of the same age.

The hair of the head is always well developed in the males, though, owing to certain customs which will be described later, and which necessitate the periodical cutting off of the hair, the amount on the head of any individual is a variable quantity. When fully developed it falls down over the shoulders in long and very wavy locks. As a general rule it is shorter than this, but it always appears to be more or less wavy, though the fondness of the natives for smearing it over with grease and red ochre frequently results in the production of tangled locks, in each of which the component hairs are matted together, whereas in the natural state they would simply form a wavy mass. The beard is usually well-developed, and better so amongst the Arunta, Ilpirra, and Luritcha than amongst the northern tribes, such as the Warramunga and Waagi, where the whiskers are usually but comparatively poorly developed. The beard is usually frizzy rather than wavy, and in some instances this feature is a very striking one; but we have never, amongst many hundred natives examined, seen one which could be called woolly. The colour, except amongst the older men who have reached an age of, so far as can be judged, fifty or sixty years, when the hair becomes scanty and white, is usually jet black, though the presence of abundant red ochre may, at first sight, cause it to appear to be of a more brownish hue, and occasionally it is of a dark brown tint rather than jet black. Amongst the children there are now and then met with some whose hair is of a decidedly lighter colour, but the lightness is confined to the tips, very rarely reaching to the roots, and with the growth of the individual it usually, but not always, assumes the normal dark colour. The legs and arms usually have a thin coating of short, crisp, black hair, and sometimes the whole body may be covered with hair, the most extreme development of which was seen in the case of one of the oldest men, where, as the hair was white with age, it stood out in strong contrast to the dark skin; but, as a rule, the hairs on the general surface of the body are nothing like so strongly developed as in the case of the average Englishman, and are not noticeable except on close examination.

The method of treatment of the hair varies in different tribes and produces a marked difference in the appearance of the face. In all the tribes living between Charlotte Waters in the south and Tennant Creek in the north the men, at puberty, pull out the hairs on the forehead, causing this to look much more lofty and extensive than it is in reality. Each hair is separately pulled out, and over the part thus artificially made bare the *chilara* or forehead band is worn. The remaining hair is tightly pulled back and usually bound round with fur string, and is often in the Arunta and Luritcha tribes surmounted by the emu-feather chignon already referred to. In the Urabunna tribe away to the south of Charlotte Waters the hair is often enclosed in a net-like structure. In the Warramunga tribe the older men, but only those who have reached an age of about forty years, pull the hairs out of the upper lip, a custom never practised in the more southern tribes.

Amongst the women the hair is generally worn short,[19] which is closely associated with the fact that, at times, each woman has to present her hair to the man who is betrothed to her daughter, for the purpose of making him a waist-belt. The body is usually smooth with, at most, a development of very fine short hairs only perceptible on close examination, and there may be occasionally a well-marked development of hair on the lip or chin, which is especially noticeable in the old women, some of whom are probably fifty years of age and have reached a stage of ugliness which baffles description.

A very striking feature of both men and women are the body scars which are often spoken of as tattoo marks, a name which, as Dr. Stirling says, "is unfortunate and should be abandoned, as the scars in question with which the bodies of Australian natives are generally decorated differ entirely from the coloured patterns produced by the permanent staining of the tissue with pigments to which the term tattoo mark ought to be limited."[20]

Every individual has a certain number of these scars raised on his body and arms, but very rarely on the back. As is well known, they are made by cutting the skin with a piece of flint, or, at the present day, glass is used when obtainable, and into the wound thus made ashes are rubbed or the down of the eagle-hawk, the idea being, so they say, to promote healing, and not, though the treatment probably has this effect, to aid in the raising of a scar. In some cases they may stretch right across the chest or abdomen. As a general rule the scars are both more numerous and longer on the men than on the women, but no definite distinction can be drawn in this respect; the absolutely greatest number of scars noticed being on a woman on whom there were forty roughly parallel cicatrices between the navel and a point just above the breasts. Very frequently, on the other hand, the scars are limited on a woman to one or two which unite the breasts across the middle line. The cicatrices in the region of the breast usually stand out most prominently, the most marked ones having an elevation of 15 mm. and a width of 20 mm. In addition to these roughly horizontal bands, which are always made in greater or lesser number, others may be present which we may divide into three series, (*a*) a few usually curved bands on the scapular region which are not often met with; (*b*) a series of usually paired short bands leading off on either side obliquely across the chest to the shoulder; (*c*) bands on the arms. In some cases these may be vertically disposed, in others horizontally, and in others we find some of one form and some of the other. In all of them again there is no distinction to be drawn between men and women. Occasionally the cicatrices on the arm will be as prominent as those on the body, but usually they are less so.

There is, apart from ornament, no special meaning, so far as their form or arrangement is concerned, to be attached at the present day to these cicatrices, nor could we discover anything in their customs and traditions leading to the belief that they had ever had any deeper meaning.[21] Vague statements have been made with regard to marks such as these, to the effect that they indicate, in some way, the particular division of the tribe to which each individual belongs. Amongst the tribes from Oodnadatta in the south, to Tennant Creek in the north, they certainly have no such meaning, and we are very sceptical as to whether they have anywhere in Australia; they are so characteristic of the natives of many parts, that the idea of their having a definite meaning is one which naturally suggests itself; but at all events, so far as the tribes now dealt with are concerned, they have no significance at the present day as indicative of either tribal, class, or totemic group.

In addition to these every man will be marked usually on the left shoulder, but sometimes on the right as well, with irregular scars which may form prominent cicatrices, and are the result of self-inflicted wounds made on the occasion of the mourning ceremonies which are attendant upon the death of individuals who stand in certain definite relationships to him, such, for example, as his *Ikuntera* or father-in-law, actual or tribal. Not infrequently the men's thighs will be marked with scars indicative of wounds inflicted with a stone knife during a fight.

Just like the men, the women on the death of certain relatives cut themselves, and these cuts often leave scars behind. Sometimes writers have described these scars and treated them as evidence of the cruel treatment of the women by the men, whereas, as a matter of fact, by far the greater number of scars, which are often a prominent feature on a woman's body, are the indications of self-inflicted wounds, and of them she is proud, as they are the visible evidence of the fact that she has properly mourned for her dead.

Not infrequently platycnemia, or flattening of the tibial bones, is met with, and at times the curious condition to which Dr. Stirling has given the name of Camptocnemia. The latter consists in an anterior curvature of the tibial bone and gives rise to what the white settlers have, for long, described by the very apt term "boomerang-leg." To what extent either or both of these conditions are racial or pathological it seems difficult to say, and for a full description of them the reader is referred to Dr. Stirling's report.[22]

As a general rule both men and women are well nourished, but naturally this depends to a large extent on the nature of the season. When travelling and hungry the plan is adopted of tightening the waistbelt, indeed this is worn so tight that it causes the production of a loose flap of skin, which is often a prominent feature on the abdomens of the older men. Though the leg is not strongly developed, so far as size is concerned, still it is not always so spindle-shaped as is usually the case amongst Australian natives, and the muscles are as hard as possible, for the black fellow is always in training. The calf is decidedly thin, the average of the twenty men, in circumference in its widest part, being 31.5 cm., and of the ten women, 29.8 cm.

The hands are decidedly small, the large span of the men averaging 16.8 cm. and of the women, 15.6 cm. Only three of the men measure over 18 cm., and one measuring 22 cm. was of very exceptional size for a native. The smallest measures 15.3 cm.

For the measurements of the head reference must be made to the appendix; here it must suffice to say that the average cephalic index of the twenty men is 74.5, and that of the ten women, 75.7. These are, of course, the measurements in the living subject; but, even if we allow for the two units which Broca concluded should be subtracted from the index of the living subject to get that of the cranium,[23] they are still relatively high as compared with the index of 71.5, which may be regarded as about the average index for Australian skulls. It must also be noted that there is great variability amongst the different individuals, the minimum measurement of the males being 68.8 lying at the extreme of dolichocephalic skulls, while the maximum of 80.55 is just within the limit of sub-brachicephalic skulls. In the females the smallest index is 73.88, and the largest 80.7. It must also be remembered that, owing to constant rubbing of the head with grease and red ochre, which mat the hairs together and form a kind of coating all round their roots, there is considerable difficulty experienced in bringing the instrument into contact with the actual scalp, and that this difficulty has of course to be encountered twice in the measurement of the transverse diameter. Making all allowances, there remains the strongly marked variation which undoubtedly exists amongst the various individuals.

We may, in general terms, describe the Arunta native as being somewhat under the average height of an Englishman. His skin is of a dark chocolate colour, his nose is distinctly platyrhinic with the root deep set, his hair is abundant and wavy, and his beard, whiskers and moustache well-developed and usually frizzled and jet black. His supra-orbital ridges are well-developed, and above them the forehead slopes back with the hair removed so as to artificially increase its size. His body is well formed and very lithe, and he carries himself gracefully and remarkably erect with his head thrown well back.

Naturally, in the case of the women, everything depends upon their age, the younger ones, that is those between fourteen and perhaps twenty, have decidedly well-formed figures, and, from their habit of carrying on the head *pitchis* containing food and water, they carry themselves often with remarkable grace. As is usual, however, in the case of savage tribes the drudgery of food-collecting and child-bearing tells upon them at an early age, and between twenty and twenty-five they begin to lose their graceful carriage; the face wrinkles, the breasts hang pendulous, and, as a general rule, the whole body begins to shrivel up, until, at about the age of thirty, all traces of an earlier well-formed figure and graceful carriage are lost, and the woman develops into what can only be called an old and wrinkled hag.

In regard to their character it is of course impossible to judge them from a white man's standard. In the matter of morality their code differs radically from ours, but it cannot be denied that their conduct is governed by it, and that any known breaches are dealt with both surely and severely. In very many cases there takes place what the white man, not seeing beneath the surface, not unnaturally describes as secret murder, but, in reality, revolting though such slaughter may be to our minds at the present day, it is simply exactly on a par with the treatment accorded to witches not so very long ago in European countries. Every case of such secret murder, when one or more men stealthily stalk their prey with the object of killing him, is in reality the exacting of a life for a life, the accused person being indicated by the so-called medicine man as one who has brought about the death of another man by magic, and whose life must therefore be forfeited.[24] It need hardly be pointed out what a potent element this custom has been in keeping down the numbers of the tribe; no such thing as natural death is realised by the native; a man who dies has of necessity been killed by some other man, or perhaps even by a woman, and sooner or later that man or woman will be attacked. In the normal condition of the tribe every death meant the killing of another individual.

Side by side, however, with this crude and barbarous custom we find others which reveal a more pleasing side of the native character. Generosity is certainly one of his leading features. He is always accustomed to give a share of his food, or of what he may possess, to his fellows. It may be, of course, objected to this that in so doing he is only following an old established custom, the breaking of which would expose him to harsh treatment and to being looked upon as a churlish fellow. It will, however, hardly be denied that, as this custom expresses the idea that in this particular matter every one is supposed to act in a kindly way towards certain individuals, the very existence of such a custom, even if it be only carried out in the hope of securing at some time a *quid pro quo*, shows that the native is alive to the fact that an action which benefits some one else is worthy of being performed. And here we may notice a criticism frequently made with regard to the native, and that is that he is incapable of gratitude. It is undoubtedly true that the native is not in the habit of showing anything like excessive gratitude on receiving gifts from the white man, but then neither does he think it necessary to express his gratitude when he receives a gift from one of his own tribe. It is necessary to put one's self into the mental attitude of the native, and then the matter is capable of being more or less explained and understood. It is with him a fixed habit to give away part of what he has, and he neither expects the man to whom he gives a thing to express his gratitude, nor, when a native gives him anything, does he think it necessary to do so himself, for the simple reason that giving and receiving are matters of course in his everyday life; so, when he receives anything from a white man, he does not think it necessary to do what he neither does nor is expected to do, in the case of his fellow-tribesmen. It does not occur to him that an expression of gratitude is necessary. On the other hand he parts, as a matter of course, and often for the merest trifle (not only what is a trifle to us, but also to him), with objects which have cost him much labour to produce, but which a white man perhaps takes a fancy to. That he is, in reality, incapable of the feeling of gratitude is, so far as our experience goes, by no means true. It may be added that, taking all things into account, the black fellow has not perhaps any particular reason to be grateful to the white man, for it must be remembered that his feelings are concerned with the group rather than with the individual. To come in contact with the white man means that, as a general rule, his food supply is restricted, and that he is, in many cases, warned off from the water-holes which are the centres of his best hunting grounds, and to which he has been accustomed to resort during the performance of his sacred ceremonies; while the white man kills and hunts his kangaroos and emus he is debarred in turn from hunting and killing the white man's cattle. Occasionally the native will indulge in a cattle hunt; but the result is usually disastrous to himself, and on the whole he succumbs quietly enough to his fate, realising the impossibility of attempting to defend what he certainly regards as his own property.

With regard to their treatment of one another it may be said that this is marked on the whole by considerable kindness, that is, of course, in the case of members of friendly groups, with every now and then the perpetration of acts of cruelty. The women are certainly not treated usually with anything which could be called excessive harshness. They have, as amongst other savage tribes, to do a considerable part, but by no means all, of the work of the camp, but, after all, in a good season this does not amount to very much, and in a bad season men and women suffer alike, and of what food there is they get their share. If, however, rightly or wrongly, a man thinks his wife guilty of a breach of the laws which govern marital relations, then undoubtedly the treatment of the woman is marked by brutal and often revolting severity. To their children they are, we may say uniformly, with very rare exceptions, kind and considerate, carrying them, the men as well as the women taking part in this, when they get tired on the march, and always seeing that they get a good share of any food. Here again it must be remembered that the native is liable to fits of sudden passion, and in one of these, hardly knowing what he does, he may treat a child with great severity. There is no such thing as doing away with aged or infirm people; on the contrary such are treated with especial kindness, receiving a share of the food which they are unable to procure for themselves.

Infanticide is undoubtedly practised, but, except on rare occasions, the child is killed immediately on birth, and then only when the mother is, or thinks she is, unable to rear it owing to there being a young child whom she is still feeding, and with them suckling is continued for it may be several years. They believe that the spirit part of the child goes back at once to the particular spot from whence it came, and can be born again at some subsequent time even of the same woman. Twins, which are of extremely rare occurrence, are usually immediately killed as something which is unnatural but there is no ill-treatment of the mother, who is not thought any the less of, such as is described as occurring in the case of certain West African peoples by Miss Kingsley. We cannot find out what exactly lies at the root of this dislike of twins in the case of the Arunta and other tribes. Dr. Fison once suggested that it might be due to the fact that the idea of two individuals of the same class being associated so closely was abhorrent to the native mind, that it was, in fact, looked upon much in the light of incest. In the case of the twins being one a boy and the other a girl, this might account for it, but when they both are of the same sex it is difficult to see how any feeling of this kind could arise. Possibly it is to be explained on the simpler ground that the parent feels a not altogether unrighteous anger that two spirit individuals should think of entering the body of the woman at one and the same time, when they know well that the mother could not possibly rear them both, added to which the advent of twins is of very rare occurrence, and the native always has a dread of anything which appears strange and out of the common. In connection with this it may be added that on the very rare occasions on which the child is born at a very premature stage as the result of an accident, nothing will persuade them that it is an undeveloped human being; they are perfectly convinced that it is the young of some other animal, such as a kangaroo, which has by some mistake got inside the woman.[25]

On rare occasions, at all events amongst the Luritcha tribe, children of a few years of age are killed, the object of this being to feed a weakly but elder child, who is supposed thereby to gain the strength of the killed one.

When times are favourable the black fellow is as light-hearted as possible. He has not the slightest thought of, or care for, what the morrow may bring forth, and lives entirely in the present. At night time men, women and children gather round the common camp fires talking and singing their monotonous chants hour after hour, until one after the other they drop out of the circle, going off to their different camps, and then at length all will be quiet, except for the occasional cry of a child who, as not seldom happens, rolls over into the fire and has to be comforted or scolded into quietness.

There is, however, in these, as in other savage tribes, an undercurrent of anxious feeling which, though it may be stilled and, indeed, forgotten for a time, is yet always present. In his natural state the native is often thinking that some enemy is attempting to harm him by means of evil magic, and, on the other hand, he never knows when a medicine man in some distant group may not point him out as guilty of killing some one else by magic. It is, however, easy to lay too much stress upon this, for here again we have to put ourselves into the mental attitude of the savage, and must not imagine simply what would be our own feelings under such circumstances. It is not right, by any means, to say that the Australian native lives in constant dread of the evil magic of an enemy. The feeling is always, as it were, lying dormant and ready to be at once called up by any strange or suspicious sound if he be alone, especially at night time, in the bush; but on the other hand, just like a child, he can with ease forget anything unpleasant and enter perfectly into the enjoyment of the present moment. Granted always that his food supply is abundant, it may be said that the life of the Australian native is, for the most part, a pleasant one.

In common with all other Australian tribes, those of the Centre have been shut off from contact with other peoples, and have therefore developed for long ages without the stimulus derived from external sources. It is sometimes asserted that the Australian native is degenerate, but it is difficult to see on what grounds this conclusion is based. His customs and organisation, as well as his various weapons and implements, show, so far as we can see, no indication of any such feature. It may be said that, as far as we are yet acquainted with their customs, the various tribes may be regarded as descended from ancestors who observed in common with one another certain customs, and were regulated by a definite social system which was at one time common to them all. In course of time, as they wandered over the continent and became divided into groups, locally isolated to a large extent from one another, these groups developed along different lines. It is true that there has not been any strongly marked upward movement, but on the other hand, with possibly a few exceptions which might have been expected to occur now and again in particular cases such as that of the Kulin tribe, instanced by Mr. Howitt, any movement which there has been in social matters has been clearly in the direction of increasing their complexity, and there is, at all events, no evidence of the former existence of any stage of civilisation higher than the one in which we now find them.

Chapter II

The Social Organisation of the Tribes

Division of the tribe into two exogamous intermarrying groups—Remarks on "group-marriage"—Terms of relationship—The latter are not in these tribes "terms of address," the object of which is the avoidance of the use of personal names—There are no terms of relationship in English which convey the same meaning as do those of Australian natives—Organisation of the Urabunna tribe—Marriage regulated by totem—Absence of individual marriage, and the existence of a form of group-marriage—Terms of relationship—Arrangement of the classes so as to allow of counting descent in either the maternal or paternal line—Organisation of the Arunta tribe—Marriage is not regulated by totem—Terms of relationship amongst the Arunta, Luritcha, Kaitish and Warramunga tribes—Details with regard to the terms of relationship in the Arunta tribe—Particular terms applied to father-in-law, &c.—Restrictions with regard to elder and younger sisters—The class divisions of the Ilpirra, Kaitish, Iliaura, Waagai, Warramunga, Bingongina and Walpari tribes—Distinct names for males and females in the last three.

THE fundamental feature in the organisation of the Central Australian, as in that of other Australian tribes, is the division of the tribe into two exogamous inter-marrying groups. These two divisions may become further broken up, but even when more than two are now present we can still recognise their former existence.

In consequence of, and intimately associated with, this division of the tribe, there has been developed a series of terms of relationship indicating the relative status of the various members of the tribe, and, of necessity, as the division becomes more complex so do the terms of relationship.

In the tribes with which we are dealing we can recognise at least two important types which illustrate different grades in the development of the social organisation. The first of these is found in the Urabunna tribe, the second in the Arunta, Ilpirra, Kaitish, Waagai, Warramunga, Iliaura, and Bingongina tribes.

The less complex the organisation of the tribe the more clearly do we see evidence of what Messrs. Howitt and Fison have called, in regard to Australian tribes, "group marriage." Under certain modifications this still exists as an actual custom, regulated by fixed and well-recognised rules, amongst various Australian tribes, whilst in others the terms of relationship indicate, without doubt, its former existence. As is well known, Mr. McLennan held that the terms must have been invented by the natives using them merely for the purpose of addressing each other or as modes of salutation. To those who have been amongst and watched the natives day after day, this explanation of the terms is utterly unsatisfactory. When, in various tribes, we find series of terms of relationship all dependent upon classificatory systems such as those now to be described, and referring entirely to a mutual relationship such as would be brought about by their existence, we cannot do otherwise than come to the conclusion that the terms do actually indicate various degrees of relationship based primarily upon the existence of inter-marrying groups. When we find, for example, that amongst the Arunta natives a man calls a large number of men belonging to one particular group by the name "Oknia" (a term which includes our relationship of father), that he calls all the wives of these men by the common name of "Mia" (mother),[26] and that he calls all their sons by the name of "Okilia" (elder brother) or "Itia" (younger brother), as the case may be, we can come to no other conclusion than that this is expressive of his recognition of what may be called a group relationship. All the "fathers" are men who belong to the particular group to which his own actual father belongs;

all the "mothers" belong to the same group as that to which his actual mother belongs, and all the "brothers" belong to his own group.

Whatever else they may be, the relationship terms are certainly not terms of address, the object of which is to prevent the native having to employ a personal name. In the Arunta tribe, for example, every man and woman has a personal name by which he or she is freely addressed by others—that is, by any, except a member of the opposite sex who stands in the relationship of "Mura" to them, for such may only on very rare occasions speak to one another.[27] When, as has happened time after time to us, a native says, for example, "That man is Oriaka (a personal name), he is my Okilia," and you cannot possibly tell without further inquiry whether he is the speaker's blood or tribal brother—that is, the son of his own father or of some man belonging to the same particular group as his father—then the idea that the term "Okilia" is applied as a polite term of address, or in order to avoid the necessity of using a personal name, is at once seen to be untenable.

It is, at all events, a remarkable fact that (apart from the organisation of other tribes, in respect of which we are not competent to speak, but for which the same fact is vouched for by other observers) in all the tribes with which we are acquainted, all the terms coincide, without any exception, in the recognition of relationships, all of which are dependent upon the existence of a classificatory system, the fundamental idea of which is that the women of certain groups marry the men of others. Each tribe has one term applied indiscriminately by the man to the woman or women whom he actually marries and to all the women whom he might lawfully marry—that is, who belong to the right group—one term to his actual mother and to all the women whom his father might lawfully have married; one term to his actual brother and to all the sons of his father's brothers, and so on right through the whole system. To this it may be added that, if these be not terms of relationship, then the language of these tribes is absolutely devoid of any such.[28]

A great part of the difficulty in understanding these terms lies in the fact that we have amongst ourselves no terms which convey the same idea of relationship as do those of savage peoples. When once, for example, the term "Mia," used amongst the Arunta tribe, has been translated by the English term "mother," an entirely wrong impression is apt to to conveyed. Mia does include the relationship which we call mother, but it includes a great deal more, and to the Arunta native the restriction of the term as used in English is as incomprehensible as apparently the extension of the term is to white men who are not accustomed to the native use. To understand the native it is simply essential to lay aside all ideas of relationship as counted amongst ourselves. They have no words equivalent to our English words father, mother, brother, &c. A man, for example, will call his actual mother "Mia," but, at the same time, he will apply the term not only to other grown women, but to a little girl child, provided they all belong to the same group. We have, for example, asked a fully grown man who the little child was with whom he was playing, and have received the answer that it was so and so, mentioning her personal name, and that she was his Mia. Her own personal name he would use in speaking both to her and to us, but the term Mia expressed the relationship in which she stood to him.

We have dwelt somewhat at length upon this because so distinguished a writer as Mr. McLennan and others who, accepting his dictum, have dealt with the subject, have attempted to disprove the supposition that any such group relationship is actually expressed in the terms of relationship used by the Australian natives. For this reason we have, as carefully and minutely as possible, and without prejudice in favour of one theory or the other, examined into the social organisation of the tribes with which we have come into contact. The conclusion to which we have come is that we do not see how the facts, which will now be detailed and upon a consideration of which this conclusion is based, can receive any satisfactory explanation except on the theory of the former existence of group marriage, and further, that this has of necessity given rise to the terms of relationship used by the Australian natives. As will be seen, group marriage, in a modified but yet most unmistakable way, occurs as an actual system in one of the tribes with which we are dealing.

We may now pass on to consider first the organisation of the Urabunna tribe, as this represents a less complex condition than the second type which is met with in the Arunta and other tribes.

In reference to the names to apply to the various divisions of the tribe, we have felt considerable difficulty, and have decided that as such terms as phratry, gens, clan, &c., have all of them a definite significance, and, as applied to Australian tribes, may be misleading, it is better to use the term class as applying to the two main exogamous intermarrying groups, each of which forms a moiety of the tribe, and the term sub-class as applying to the divisions of the class. We therefore use these terms with this significance.[29]

The Urabunna organisation appears to be, if not identical with, at least very closely similar to, that of the Dieri tribe, whose territory adjoins it on the south, and which has been dealt with previously by Mr. Howitt[30] The whole tribe is divided up into two exogamous intermarrying classes, which are respectively called Matthurie and Kirarawa, and the members of each of these again are divided into a series of totemic groups, for which the native name is Thunthunnie. A Matthurie man must marry a Kirarawa woman, and not only this, but a man of one totem must marry a woman of another totem, certain totems being confined to each of the exogamous classes. Thus a dingo marries a waterhen, a cicada a crow, an emu a rat, a wild turkey a cloud, a swan a pelican, and so on.[31]

The organisation can be shown as represented in the following table, only a limited number of the totems being indicated:—

Class.	Totem.
Matthurie	Wild duck (Inyarrie).
	Cicada (Wutnimmera).
	Dingo (Matla).
	Emu (Warraguti).
	Wild turkey (Kalathurra).
	Black swan (Guti), &c.
Kirarawa	Cloud (Kurara).
	Carpet snake (Wabma).
	Lace lizard (Capirie).
	Pelican (Urantha).
	Water hen (Kutnichilli).
	Crow (Wakala), &c.

Descent is counted through the mother, both as regards class and totem, so that we can represent marriage and descent as counted in the Urabunna tribe by the following diagram, in which the letter *f* indicates the female and the letter *m* the male.

m. Dingo Matthurie marries
f. Water-hen Kirarawa

m. Water-hen Kirarawa marries   f. Water-hen Kirarawa marries
f. Dingo Matthurie   m. Dingo Matthurie
m. or f. Dingo Matthurie   m. or f. Water-hen Kirarawa

There are still further restrictions to marriage than those which merely enact that a dingo man must marry a water-hen woman, and it is here that we are brought into contact with the terms of relationship. Enquiring into case after case you meet constantly, in this matter of restriction in regard to marriage, with the reply that though a particular woman belongs to the right totem into which a man must marry, yet there is a further restriction preventing marriage in this particular case. For example, not every dingo may marry a particular water-hen woman. To a dingo man all water-hen women are divided into four groups, the members of which respectively stand to him in the relationship of (1) *Nowillie* or father's sisters; (2) *Biaka*, children or brothers' children; (3) *Apillia*, mother's younger brothers' daughters; (4) *Nupa*, mother's elder brothers' daughters. It will of course be understood that a mother's brother's child is identical with a father's sister's child, and that the fathers and brothers may be either blood or tribal.

We can, amongst the individuals named, distinguish women of three different levels of generation; the *Nowillie* belong to that of the father and to still older generations; the *Biaka* to younger ones and the *Apillia* and *Nupa* to the same generation as the individual concerned. A man can only marry women who stand to him in the relationship of *Nupa*, that is, are the children of his mother's elder brothers blood or tribal, or, what is the same thing, of his father's elder sisters. The mother of a man's *Nupa* is *Nowillie* to him, and any woman of that relationship is *Mura* to him and he to her, and they must not speak to one another. In connection with this it must be remembered that it is not necessary for the woman to actually have a daughter for her to be *Nowillie* and so *Mura* to the man, the very fact that she was born a sister of his father places her in this relationship. In the same way *Nupa*, the term applied to a woman with whom it is lawful for a man to have marital relations, and which is thus the term applied to a wife, cannot, strictly speaking, be regarded as at all the equivalent of the latter term. It is applied indiscriminately by a dingo man to each and every member of a group of water-hen women with one or more of whom he may perhaps actually have marital relations, but with any one of whom it is lawful and possible for him to do so. When we say possible for him to have such marital relations, we mean that any one of those women might be assigned to him, as they all, in fact, stand to him in the relationship of potential wives.

The word *Nupa* is without any exception applied indiscriminately by men of a particular group to women of another group, and *vice versa*, and simply implies a member of a group of possible wives or husbands as the case may be.

While this is so, it must be remembered that in actual practice each individual man has one or perhaps two of these *Nupa* women who are specially attached to himself and live with him in his own camp. In addition to them, however, each man has certain *Nupa* women, beyond the limited number just referred to, with whom he stands in the relationship of *Piraungaru*.[32] To women who are the *Piraungaru* of a man (the term is a reciprocal one), the latter has access under certain conditions, so that they may be considered as accessory wives.

The result is that in the Urabunna tribe every woman is the special *Nupa* of one particular man, but at the same time he has no exclusive right to her as she is the *Piraungaru* of certain other men who also have the right of access to her. Looked at from the point of view of the man his *Piraungaru* are a limited number of the women who stand in the relationship of *Nupa* to him. There is no such thing as one man having the exclusive right to one woman; the elder brothers, or *Nuthie*, of the latter, in whose hands the matter lies, will give one man a preferential right, but at the same time they will give other men of the same group a secondary right to her. Individual marriage does not exist either in name or in practice in the Urabunna tribe.

The initiation in regard to establishing the relationship of *Piraungaru* between a man and a woman must be taken by the elder brothers, but the arrangement must receive the sanction of the old men of the group before it can take effect. As a matter of actual practice, this relationship is usually established at times when considerable numbers of the tribe are gathered together to perform important ceremonies, and when these and other matters of importance which require the consideration of the old men are discussed and settled. The number of a man's *Piraungaru* depend entirely upon the measure of his power and popularity; if he be what is called "*ūrkū*," a word which implies much the same as our word "influential," he will have a considerable number, if he be insignificant or unpopular, then he will meet with scanty treatment.

A woman may be *Piraungaru* to a number of men, and as a general rule men and women who are *Piraungaru* to one another are to be found living grouped together. A man may always lend his wife, that is, the woman to whom he has the first right, to another man, provided always he be her *Nupa*, without the relationship of *Piraungaru* existing between the two, but unless this relationship exists, no man has any right of access to a woman. Occasionally, but rarely, it happens that a man attempts to prevent his wife's *Piraungaru* from having access to her, but this leads to a fight and the husband is looked upon as churlish. When visiting distant groups where, in all likelihood, the husband has no *Piraungaru*, it is customary for other men of his own class to offer him the loan of one or more of their *Nupa* women, and a man, besides lending a woman over whom he has the first right, will also lend his *Piraungaru*.

All the children of women who are *Nupa* to any man, whether they are his special *Nupas*, or *Piraungaru*, or *Nupa* women with whom he has no marital relations, call him *Nia*, and he calls them *Biaka*. Whilst naturally there is a closer tie between a man and the children of the women who habitually live in camp with him, still there is no name to distinguish between the children of his special *Nupa* and those of any other woman to whom he is *Nupa*, but with whom he has no marital relations. All *Biaka*, or children of men who are at the same level in the generation and belong to the same class and totem, are regarded as the common children of these men, and in the same way the latter are regarded collectively by the *Biaka* as their *Nia*.

It will thus be seen that in the Urabunna tribe we have apparently an organisation closely similar to that described by Mr. Howitt as occurring in the Dieri tribe with which it is associated locally. It will also be evident that in both these tribes there is what can only be described as a modified form of group-marriage, the important features of which may be summarised as follows. We have:—

>   1.   A group of men all of whom belong to one moiety of the tribe who are regarded as the *Nupas* or possible husbands of a group of women who belong to the other moiety of the tribe.
>   2.   One or more women specially allotted to one particular man, each standing in the relationship of *Nupa* to the other, but no man having exclusive right to any one woman, only a preferential right.
>   3.   A group of men who stand in the relationship of *Piraungaru* to a group of women selected from amongst those to whom they are *Nupa*. In other words, a group of women of a certain designation are actually the wives of a group of men of another designation.

A curious feature in the social organisation of the Urabunna tribe is the restriction in accordance with which a man's wife must belong to what we may call the senior side of the tribe so far as he himself is concerned. He is only *Nupa* to the female children of the elder brothers of his mother, or what is exactly the same thing, to those of the elder sisters of his father. It follows from this that a woman is only *Nupa* to men on the junior side of the tribe so far as she is concerned. This marked distinction between elder and younger brothers and sisters is a striking feature, not only in tribes such as the Urabunna, in which descent is counted in the female line, but also in tribes such as the Arunta in which descent is counted in the male line.

If we draw up a genealogical tree in the Urabunna tribe, placing the elder members on the left side and the younger members on the right side, then every woman's *Nupa* lies to the right, and every man's to the left side of his or her position in the genealogical tree.

The following table gives the terms of relationship as they exist amongst the Urabunna tribe. It will be seen that we have given three columns of names, (1) the native names, (2) the exact equivalent of the native names in our English terms, and (3) the English terms included wholly or partly in the native terms. In this way it will be seen, for example, that there are no native words at all equivalent to our English terms cousin, uncle, aunt, nephew; in fact, as we have said before, unless all ideas of terms of relationship as counted amongst ourselves be abandoned, it is useless to try and understand the native terms. No native can understand how we can possibly apply the same term cousin to children of the brothers of a father and at the same time to children of the sisters of a father. In the same way it will be seen that a brother's children are perfectly distinct from those of a sister; if I am, say a crow man, then my brothers' children are born cicadas and my sisters' children are born crows. As my own children are cicadas, I naturally have a term in common between them and the cicada offspring of my brothers, and quite a different term for the crow children of my sisters.

It will be seen on examining the table that no man or woman applies the same name to, for example, both a crow and a cicada, and further still, that all the names are applied to groups of individuals all of whom stand in a definite relationship to the individual by whom the term is used. In addition to the table we have also drawn up a genealogical tree which will perhaps aid in explaining what is without doubt a somewhat intricate subject, and in the table we have numbered each individual, and taking a particular individual have represented in tabular form the names which he applies to the other members of the group so as to include and illustrate all the various terms as used.[33]

TABLE OF RELATIONSHIP TERMS.

URABUNNA TRIBE.

Native Terms; actual Relationship expressed in English Terms.		English Terms, included wholly or partly in the Native Terms.
Nia	Father	Father.
Kawkuka	Father's brothers, blood and tribal	Uncle.
	Mother's brothers, blood and tribal	Uncle.
	Wife's father	Father-in-law.
	Husband's father	
Luka	Mother	Mother.
Namuma	Mother's elder sisters, blood and tribal	Aunt.
	Mother's younger sisters, blood and tribal	Aunt.
Nowillie	Father's sisters, blood and tribal	Aunt.
	Grandmother on father's side, blood and tribal	Grandmother.
	Husband's mother	Mother-in-law.
	Wife's mother.	
Biaka	Sons	Son.
	Daughters	Daughter.
	Brother's sons and daughters, blood and tribal	Nephew and niece.
Thidnurra	Sister's sons and daughters, blood and tribal	Nephew and niece.
Nuthie	Elder brother	Brother.

	Father's elder brothers' sons, blood and tribal	Cousin.
Kakua	Elder sisters	Sister.
	Father's elder brothers' daughters, blood and tribal	Cousin.
Kupuka	Younger brothers	Brother.
	Father's younger brothers' sons, blood and tribal	Cousin.
	Younger sisters	Sister.
	Father's younger brothers' daughters, blood and tribal	Cousin.
Wittewa	Father's younger sisters' sons	Cousin.
	Sisters' husbands, blood and tribal	Brother-in-law.
	Wife's brother	
Nupa	Father's elder sisters' daughters, blood and tribal	Cousin.
	Wife	Wife.
	Husband	Husband.
Apillia	Husband's sisters, blood and tribal	Sister-in-law.
	Father's younger sisters' daughters	Cousin.
Kadnini	Grandfather on father's side, blood and tribal	Grandfather.
	Grandmother on mother's side, blood and tribal	Grandmother.
	Son's children	Grandchildren.
Thunthi	Grandfather on mother's side, blood	Grandfather.

and tribal
Daughter's children. Grandchildren.

If we take the man numbered 25 in the genealogical tree we shall find that he applies the following names to the various individuals represented. It will be noticed that in connection with the woman numbered 14 we have given a separate branch line of descent, so as to be able to indicate the grandparents on the maternal as well as the paternal side.

The man numbered 25 applies the following names to the various individuals:—

Kadnini, to the individuals numbered	1,	2,	b,	53,	54.
Nowillie, to the individuals numbered	3,	5,	9,	17.	
Thunthi, to the individuals numbered	a,	4,	55,	56.	
Nia, to the individuals numbered	6,	7,	8,	18.	
Kawkuka, to the individuals numbered	10,	12,	16.		
Luka,[34] to the individuals numbered	13,	14.			
Namuma, to the individuals numbered	11,	15.			
Wittewa, to the individuals numbered	19,	30,	32,	37,	40.
Apillia,[35] to the individuals numbered	31,	33,	39.		
Nupa,[36] to the individuals numbered	20,	36,	38.		
Kakua, to the individuals numbered	22,	24.			
Nuthie, to the individuals numbered	21,	23.			
Kupuka, to the individuals	26,	27,	28,	29,	34, 35.

numbered						
Biaka, to the individuals numbered	41,	42,	45,	46,	47,	48.
Thidnurra, to the individuals numbered	43,	44,	49,	50,	51,	52.

It may perhaps be wondered how the natives themselves become acquainted with what is to the average white man so apparently elaborate and even, at first sight, complicated, a scheme. In the first place it is not in reality so complicated as it appears, and if we lay aside all pre-conceived ideas of relationship and remember that the terms are constantly being used by the natives who live, so to speak, surrounded with object lessons in the form of the members of the local group, then the difficulty largely vanishes. Another thing to be remembered is that the relationship of one native to another is one of the most important points with which each individual must be acquainted. There are certain customs which are enforced by long usage and according to which men and women of particular degrees of relationship may alone have marital relations, or may not speak to one another, or according to which one individual has to do certain things for another, such as providing the latter with food or with hair, as the case may be, and any breach of these customs is severely punished. The elder men of each group very carefully keep alive these customs, many of which are of considerable benefit to themselves, and when, as at any important ceremony, different groups are gathered together, then matters such as these are discussed, and in this way a knowledge of the various relationships is both gained and kept alive. When a man comes from a distant group, unless he be well known to the group into which he has come, the old men talk the matter over and very soon decide as to his standing.

It sometimes happens, in fact not infrequently, that a man from the neighbouring Arunta tribe comes to live amongst the Urabunna. In the former where it adjoins the latter there are four sub-classes, *viz.*, Bulthara and Panunga, Kumara, and Purula, and in addition descent is counted in the male line. Accordingly the men of the Bulthara and Purula classes are regarded as the equivalents of the Matthurie moiety of the Urabunna tribe, and those of the Panunga and Kumara classes as the equivalents of the Kirarawa. In just the same way a Matthurie man going into the Arunta tribe becomes either a Bulthara or Purula, and a Kirarawa man becomes either a Panunga or a Kumara man. Which of the two a Matthurie man belongs to, is decided by the old men of the group into which he goes. Sometimes a man will take up his abode permanently, or for a long time, amongst the strange tribe, in which case, if it be decided, for example, that he is a Bulthara, then his children will be born Panunga, that is they belong to his own adopted moiety. He has, of course, to marry a Kumara woman, or if he be already provided with a wife, then she is regarded as a Kumara, and if he goes back into his own tribe then his wife is regarded as a Kirarawa and the children also take the same name.

This deliberate change in the grouping of the classes and sub-classes so as to make them fit in with the maternal line of descent or with the paternal, as the case may be, will be more easily understood from the accompanying table.

Arunta.	*Urabunna arrangement of the Arunta sub-classes.*	
Bulthara moiety A	Bulthara	moiety A (Matthurie).
Panunga	Purula	
Kumara moiety B	Panunga	moiety B (Kirarawa).
Purula	Kumara	

The working out of this with the result that the children belong to the right moiety of the tribe into which the man has gone may be rendered clear by taking one or two particular examples.

Suppose that a Matthurie man goes into the Arunta tribe, then he is told by the old men of the group into which he has gone that he is, say, a Bulthara. Accordingly he marries a Kumara woman (or if, which is not very likely, he has brought a woman with him, then she is regarded as a Kumara) and his children will be Panunga, or, in other words, pass into the father's moiety as the sub-classes are arranged in the Arunta, but not into that of the mother as they are arranged amongst the Urabunna.

Again, suppose a Purula man from the Arunta tribe takes up his abode amongst the Urabunna. He becomes a Matthurie, and as such must marry a Kirarawa (or if married his wife is regarded as such). His children are Kirarawa, which includes the sub-class Kumara into which they would have passed in the Arunta tribe, and to which they will belong if ever they go into the latter.

These are not merely hypothetical cases but are, in the district where the two tribes come in contact with one another, of by no means infrequent occurrence; and, without laying undue stress upon the matter, this deliberate changing of the method of grouping the sub-classes so as to allow of the descent being counted in either the male or female line according to the necessity of the case, is of interest as indicating the fact that the natives are quite capable of thinking such things out for themselves. It is indeed not perhaps without a certain suggestiveness in regard to the difficult question of how a change in the line of descent might possibly be brought about.

We may now turn to the consideration of the Arunta tribe in which descent is counted in the male line, and we may regard the Arunta as typical of the large group of tribes inhabiting the centre of the continent from Lake Eyre in the south to near Port Darwin in the north, in which descent is thus counted. The tribes with the classificatory systems of which we have knowledge are the Arunta, Ilpirra, Iliaura, Kaitish, Walpari, Warramunga, Waagai, and Bingongina, which occupy a range of country extending from the latitude of Macumba River in the south to about that of Powell's Creek in the north, that is over an area measuring from north to south some seven hundred and seventy miles (Fig. 1).

In regard to the organisation of the Arunta tribe, with which we shall now deal in detail, it may at the outset be mentioned that the existence of four sub-classes in the southern part of the tribe, and of eight in the northern, appears at first sight to indicate that in the latter the organisation is more complex. In reality, though without having distinct names applied to them, each one of the four sub-classes met with in the south is actually divided into two. The four are Panunga and Bulthara, Purula and Kumara; the first two forming one moiety of the tribe, and the latter two forming another. In camp, for example, the Panunga and Bulthara always camp together separated from the Purula and Kumara by some natural feature such as a creek. The Panunga and Bulthara speak of themselves as *Nakrakia*, and of the Purula and Kumara as *Mulyanuka*—the terms being reciprocal. Further details with regard to this, and evidence of this division into two moieties, are given in connection with the discussion of the Churinga and totems, and in the account of the Engwura.

The marriage system is, in broad outline, omitting at present certain details which will be referred to shortly, as follows. A Bulthara man marries a Kumara woman and their children are Panunga; a Purula man marries a Panunga woman and their children are Kumara; a Panunga man marries a Purula woman and their children are Bulthara; a Kumara man marries a Bulthara woman and their children are Purula.

This may be graphically expressed following Mr. Howitt's plan (as already done by Dr. Stirling) in the following way.[37]

Males.	*Females.*
Panunga	Kumara
Bulthara	Purula
Purula	Bulthara
Kumara	Panunga

In these diagrams the double arrow indicates the marriage connections and the single ones point to the name of the class of the children.

As a matter of fact these diagrams as they stand, though perfectly correct in stating, for example, that a Panunga man marries a Purula woman, are incomplete in that they do not show the important point that to a Panunga man the Purula women are divided into two groups the members of one of whom stand to him in the relationship of *Unawa* whom he may marry, while the members of the other stand in the relationship of *Unkulla* whom he may not marry. This fact is one of very considerable importance. Each of the four sub-classes is thus divided into two, the members of which stand respectively in the relationship of *Ipmunna* to each other. We can represent this graphically as follows, taking, for the sake of simplicity, only two sub-classes, the divisions of one being represented by the letters A and B, and of the other by the letters C and D.

Sub-class.	*Division.*	*Division.*	*Sub-class.*
Panunga	A	C	Purula
	B	D	

A stands in the relationship of *Unawa* to C, *Ipmunna* to B, and *Unkulla* to D. In other words a woman who is *Unkulla* to me is *Ipmunna* to my wife. All women of group C (myself belonging to A), my wife calls sisters—*Ungaraitcha* if they be elder sisters, and *Itia* if they be younger sisters; and all of them stand in the relationship of *Unawa* to myself; but the other Purula women whom my wife calls *Ipmunna* are *Unkulla* to me and I may not marry them.

It is somewhat perplexing after learning that a Panunga man must marry a Purula woman to meet with the statement, when inquiring into particular cases, that a given Panunga man must not marry a particular Purula woman, but in the northern part of the tribe matters are simplified by the existence of distinct names for the two groups; the relationship term of *Ipmunna* still exists, but if I am, for example, a Panunga man, then all my *Ipmunna* men and women are designated by the term *Uknaria*, and in the following tables the eight divisions are laid down, and it will be noticed that the old name is used for one-half and a new name adopted for the other.

(Unclear:)Panunga	Panunga	Purula	Purula
	Uknaria	Ungalla	
Bulthara	Bulthara	Kumara	Kumara
	Appungerta	Umbitchana	

The double arrows indicate the marriage connections.

This division into eight has been adopted (or rather the names for the four new divisions have been), in recent times by the Arunta tribe from the Ilpirra tribe which adjoins the former on the north, and the use of them is, at the present time, spreading southwards. At the Engwura ceremony which we witnessed men of the Ilpirra tribe were present, as well as a large number of others from the southern part of the Arunta amongst whom the four new names are not yet in use.

We have found the following table of considerable service to ourselves in working as, by its means, the various relationships fall into regular arrangement and can be readily indicated.

1	2	3	4
Panunga	Purula	Appungerta	Kumara
Uknaria	Ungalla	Bulthara	Umbitchana
Bulthara	Kumara	Uknaria	Purula
Appungerta	Umbitchana	Panunga	Ungalla

This table was drawn up in the first instance in order to show the marriage relationships and the divisions into which the children pass. Thus, reading across the page, men of the sub-classes shown in column 1 must marry women of the sub-classes shown in column 2. For example, a Panunga man marries a Purula woman, an Uknaria man an Ungalla woman, and so on. Column 3 in the same way indicates their children, those of a Panunga man and a Purula woman being Appungerta, those of an Uknaria man and an Ungalla woman being Bulthara, &c. In the same way if a man of one of the sub-classes in column 2 marries a woman in one of those in column 1, then their children are as represented in column 4. That is, a Purula man marries a Panunga woman and their children are Kumara, and so on.

When, however, we came to deal with the various terms of relationship used in the tribe, we found that they also fell into orderly arrangement in the table, and could be easily shown by means of it.

It will be seen from the table that, as compared with the Urabunna tribe, marriage appears to be very much more restricted, because a man may only marry a woman who belongs to one of eight divisions into which the whole is divided. In the Arunta tribe, however, as will be described in the chapter dealing with the totems, there is, unlike most Australian tribes, no restriction whatever, so far as the totems are concerned. It may therefore be, perhaps, a matter of doubt as to how far the totems of the Arunta are the exact equivalents of those yet described as existing amongst other Australian tribes. Every Arunta native thinks that his ancestor in the Alcheringa[38] was the descendant of the animal or plant, or at least was immediately associated with the object the name of which he bears as his totemic name. In many Australian tribes it seems to be a general custom that a man must not eat or injure his totem, whereas amongst the Arunta there are special occasions on which the totem is eaten, and there is no rule absolutely forbidding the eating of the totem at other times, though it is clearly understood that it must only be partaken of very sparingly. However, though the totems of the Arunta are in certain respects unlike those yet described in other Australian tribes, still there can be no doubt but that they are correctly designated by this name, the most important feature in which they differ from those of other parts of Australia being that they have no reference to customs concerning marriage.

In the Arunta tribe, unlike the Urabunna, there is, as soon as marriage has taken place, a restriction, except on certain special occasions which are subsequently described, of a particular woman to a particular man, or rather, a man has an exclusive right to one special woman though he may of his own free will lend her to other men.

Despite this fact, there is no term applied to a woman who is thus the peculiar property of one man, the woman is simply spoken of as *Unawa* to the man in just the same way in which all the other women are who belong to the group from which the man's wife must come. The terms of relationship are not individual terms, but, just as in the Urabunna and other tribes in some of which we have a form of group marriage existing as an actual institution at the present day, the terms are group terms. To take an example—a Panunga man will have some special woman allotted to him as an individual wife, but the only term which he applies to her is *Unawa*, and that term he also applies to all the women of her group, each of whom might lawfully have been allotted to him. She is one out of a group of potential wives. When, again, a man lends his wife, he only does so to a member of his own group, that is to a man to whom, without having been allotted to him, the woman stands in the relationship of *Unawa* just as she does to the man to whom she has been allotted. In the southern part of the tribe, where only the four divisions exist, a Panunga man will not lend his *Unawa* to a man who belongs to the half of the Panunga to which he himself does not belong, that is he will not lend her to an *Ipmunna* man but only to men who are *Okilia* or *Itia* to him; and in the same way he will only have lent to him a Purula woman to whom he is *Unawa* and not one to whom he is *Unkulla*. In the northern division the original Panunga is divided up into Panunga and Ungalla, and here a Panunga man only lends his wife to a Panunga, an Ungalla to an Ungalla, and so on. In this northern part in must be remembered that the Panunga men are the exact equivalents to another Panunga man of the *Okilia* and *Itia*, that is the tribal brothers of the southern part, while the Ungalla correspond to the *Ipmunna*.

The same group terms are applied in all other cases. Thus a man calls his own children *Allira*, and applies the same term to all his blood and tribal brothers' children, while all his sisters' children are *Umba*. If, again, I am a Panunga man, then my wife is Purula, and her actual father is a Kumara man. Not only do I call this particular man *Ikuntera* or father-in-law, but, where the eight divisions are in force, I apply the same name to all Kumara men. They are one and all the fathers of women whom it is lawful for me to marry.

That this group relationship is actually recognised is made clear by a variety of facts. If, for example, one of my *Ikuntera* dies, it is my duty to cut my shoulders with a stone knife as a mark of sorrow. If I neglect to do this, then any one of the men who are *Ikuntera* to me has the right to take away my wife and give her to some other man to whom she is *Unawa*. I have not only, supposing it to be the actual father of my wife who has died, neglected to do my duty to him, but I have offended the group collectively, and any member of that group may punish me. Again, if I am out hunting and have caught game, and while carrying this home to my camp I chance to meet a man standing to me in the relationship of *Ikuntera*, I should at once have to drop the food, which, from the fact of its having been seen by any one member of that group, has become tabu to me.

In just the same way amongst the women we see clear instances of customs founded on the existence of group relationship. When a child dies not only does the actual *Mia*, or mother, cut herself, but all the sisters of the latter, who also are *Mia* to the dead child, cut themselves. All women call their own children *Umba*, and apply precisely the same term to the children of their sisters, blood and tribal.

The tables which follow give the terms of relationship existing amongst the Arunta, Luritcha, Kaitish and Warramunga, and, in the case of the Arunta, we have drawn up a genealogical tree and, taking a man and his alloted *Unawa*, have arranged in tabular form the various terms which they respectively apply to other individuals, whose relationship to them can be seen on the tree.

For the purpose of comparison we have made the genealogical tree identical with that used in the case of the Urabunna tribe, the individuals being numbered alike on both trees.

TABLE OF RELATIONSHIP TERMS.
ARUNTA TRIBE.

Native Terms.	Actual Relationship expressed in English Terms.	English Terms, included wholly or partly in the Native Terms.
Oknia	Father	Father.
	Father's brothers, blood and tribal	Uncle.
Gammona	Mother's brothers, blood and tribal	Uncle.
Mia	Mother	Mother.
	Mother's sisters, blood and tribal	Aunt.
Uwinna	Father's sisters, blood and tribal	Aunt.
Allira (man speaking)	Sons	Son.
	Daughters	Daughter.
	Sons and daughters of brothers, blood and tribal	Nephew and niece.
Allira (woman speaking)	Sons and daughters of brothers, blood and tribal	Nephew and niece.
Umba (man speaking)	Sons and daughters of sisters, blood and tribal.	Nephew and niece.
Umba (woman speaking)	Sons and daughters	Son.
	Sons and daughters of sisters, blood and tribal	Daughter.
		Nephew and niece.
Okilia	Elder brothers	Brother.
	Sons of father's elder brothers, blood and	Cousin.

Itia (Witia)	tribal Younger brothers	Brother.
	Sons of father's younger brothers, blood and tribal	Cousin.
Ungaraitcha	Elder sisters	Sister.
	Father's elder brother's daughters, blood and tribal	Cousin.
Itia (Quitia)	Younger sisters	Sister.
	Father's younger brothers' daughters, blood and tribal	Cousin.
Unkulla	Father's sisters' sons and daughters, blood and tribal	Cousin.
Unawa (man speaking)	Wife	Wife.
	Brothers' wives, blood and tribal	Sister-in-law.
Unawa (woman speaking)	Husband	Husband.
	Sisters' husbands, blood and tribal	Brother-in-law.
Umbirna (male speaking)	Wife's brother	Brother-in-law.
	Sisters' husbands, blood and tribal	
Intinga (female speaking)	Husband's sisters, blood and tribal	Sister-in-law.
Ilchella (female speaking)	Father's sisters' daughters, blood and tribal	Cousin.
Arunga	Grandfather, father's side	Grandfather.
	Grandchild (son's child)	Grandchild.
Chimmia	Grandfather, mother's side	Grandfather.

	Grandchild (daughter's child)	Grandchild.
Aperla	Grandmother, father's side	Grandmother.
	Grandchild	Grandchild.
Ipmunna	Grandmother, mother's side	Grandmother.
Ikuntera (man speaking)	Wife's father, blood and tribal	Father-in-law.
Mura (man speaking)	Wife's mother, blood and tribal	Mother-in-law.
	Wife's mother's brothers, blood and tribal	
Mura (woman speaking)	Husband's mothers, blood and tribal	Mother-in-law.
	Husband's mother's brothers, blood and tribal	
Nimmera (woman speaking)	Husband's father, blood and tribal	Father-in-law.

TABLE OF RELATIONSHIP TERMS.
LURITCHA TRIBE.

Kartu	Father.	Father.
	Father's brothers, blood and tribal	Uncle.
Gammeru	Mother's brothers, blood and tribal	Uncle.
Yaku	Mother.	Mother.
	Mother's sisters, blood and tribal	Aunt.
Kurntili	Father's sisters, blood and tribal	Aunt.
Katha	Sons	Son.
	Brother's sons, blood and tribal	Nephew.
Urntali	Daughters	Daughter.
	Brother's daughters, blood and tribal	Niece.
Ukari	Sister's sons	Nephew
	Sister's daughters, blood and tribal	Niece.
Kurta	Elder brother	Brother.
	Father's elder brothers' sons, blood and tribal	Cousin.
Mirlunguna	Younger brother	Brother.
	Father's younger brothers' sons, blood and tribal	Cousin.
	Younger sister	Sister.
	Father's younger brothers' daughters, blood and tribal	Cousin.
Kangaru	Elder sister	Sister.
	Father's elder brothers' daughters, blood and tribal	Cousin.
Watchira	Mother's brothers' sons, blood and tribal	Cousin.
Narunpa	Mother's brothers' daughters, blood and tribal	Cousin.

Kuri	Husband	Husband.
	Husband's brothers, blood and tribal	Brother-in-law.
	Wife	Wife.
	Wife's sisters, blood and tribal	Sister-in-law.
Maruthu	Sister's husband, blood and tribal	Brother-in-law.
	Wife's brother, blood and tribal	
Sthoarinna	Husband's sisters, blood and tribal	Sister-in-law.
	Brother's wife, blood and tribal	
Sthamu	Grandfather, father's side	Grandfather.
	Grandfather's brothers, father's side	
Chimpa	Grandfather, mother's side	Grandfather.
	Grandfather's brothers, mother's side	
Kammi	Grandmother, father's side	Grandmother.
	Grandmother's sisters, father's side	
Kapirli	Grandmother, mother's side	Grandmother.
	Grandmother's sisters, father's side	
Waputhu (man speaking)	Wife's father	Father-in-law.
	Wife's father's brothers, blood and tribal	
Gammeru (woman speaking)	Husband's father	Father-in-law.
	Husband's father's brothers, blood and tribal	
Mingai (woman speaking)	Husband's mother	Mother-in-law.
	Husband's mother's sisters,	

Umarri	Wife's mother, blood and tribal	Mother-in-law.
	Wife's mother's sisters, blood and tribal	
	Daughter's husband	Son-in-law.
	Daughter's husband's brothers, blood and tribal	

TABLE OF RELATIONSHIP TERMS.

KAITISH TRIBE.

Native Terms.	Actual Relationship expressed in English Terms.	English Terms, included wholly or partly in the Native Terms.
Akaurli[39]	Father	Father.
	Father's brothers, blood and tribal	Uncle.
Anillia	Mother's brothers, blood and tribal	Uncle.
Arungwa[40]	Mother	Mother.
	Mother's sisters, blood and tribal	Aunt.
Okulli	Father's sister	Aunt.
Atumpirri	Son	Son.
	Daughter	Daughter.
	Brother's sons and daughters	Nephew and niece.
Artwalli	Sisters' sons and daughters	Nephew and niece.
Alkiriia	Elder brother	Brother.
	Father's elder brothers' sons	Cousin.
Achirri	Younger brother	Brother.
	Father's younger brothers' sons	Cousin.
	Father's younger brothers' daughters	
Arari	Elder sister	Sister.
	Father's elder brothers' daughters	Cousin.
Atinkilia	Mother's brothers' daughters	Cousin.
Auillia	Mother's brothers' sons.	Cousin.

Umbirniia	Husband	Husband.
	Wife	Wife.
	Husband's brothers, blood and tribal	Brother-in-law.
	Sister's husband	
	Wife's brothers, blood and tribal	
Untingiia	Husband's sister	Sister-in-law.
Ilchelii (woman speaking)	Father's sisters' daughters	Cousin.
Arungiia	Grandfather, father's side	Grandfather.
	Grandfather's brothers, father's side	
Atchualli	Grandfather, mother's side	Grandfather.
	Grandfather's brothers, mother's side	
Apirli	Grandmother, father's side	Grandmother.
	Grandmother's sisters, father's side	
Aanya or Atmini	Grandmother, mother's side	Grandmother.
	Grandmother's sisters, mother's side	
Ertwali	Wife's father	Father-in-law.
	Wife's father's brothers	
	Husband's father	Father-in-law.
	Husband's father's brothers	
Erlitchi	Husband's mother	Mother-in-law.
	Husband's mother's sisters.	
	Wife's mother	Mother-in-law.
	Wife's mother's sisters.	

TABLE OF RELATIONSHIP TERMS.
WARRAMUNGA TRIBE.

Gampatcha[41]	Father	Father.
	Father's brothers, blood and tribal	Uncle.
Namini	Mother's brothers, blood and tribal	Uncle.
Kurnandi[42]	Mother	Mother.
	Mother's sisters, blood and tribal	Aunt.
Pinari	Father's sisters, blood and tribal	Aunt.
Kartakitchi	Sons	Son.
	Daughters	Daughter.
	Brother's sons and daughters	Nephew and niece.
Klukulu	Sister's son or daughter	Nephew and niece.
Papirti	Elder brother	Brother.
	Father's elder brother's sons	Cousin.
Kukatcha	Younger brother	Brother.
	Father's younger brother's sons.	Cousin.
	Younger sister	Sister.
	Father's younger brother's daughters	Cousin.
Kapurlu	Elder sister	Sister.
	Father's elder brother's daughters	Cousin.
Wankili	Mother's brothers' sons or daughters	Cousin.
Kullakulla	Husband	Husband.
	Husband's brothers, blood and tribal	Brother-in-law.

	Wife	Wife.
	Wife's sisters, blood and tribal	Sister-in-law.
Kallakalla	Sister's husband	Sister-in-law.
	Wife's brothers, blood and tribal	Brother-in-law.
	Husband's sisters, blood and tribal	
Lina (woman speaking)	Father's sisters' daughters	Cousin.
Kangwia	Grandfather, father's side	Grandfather.
	Grandfather's brothers, father's side	
Tapertapu	Grandfather, mother's side	Grandfather.
	Grandfather's brothers, mother's side	
Turtundi	Grandmother, mother's side	Grandmother.
	Grandmother's sisters, mother's side	
Kulukulu	Wife's father	Father-in-law.
	Wife's father's brothers	
	Husband's father	
	Husband's father's brothers	
Unnyari	Husband's mother	Mother-in-law.
	Husband's mother's sisters	
	Wife's mother	Mother-in-law.
	Wife's mother's sisters	
Namini	Daughter's husband	Son-in-law.
	Daughter's husband's brothers.	

If we take the man numbered 25 on the genealogical tree, which, it may be said, applies to both the Ilpirra and Arunta tribes, with slight variation in the names, we shall find that he applies the following names to the individuals indicated by their respective numbers. It will be noticed that two small branch lines are added to show descent in the maternal line.

The man numbered 25 applies the following names to the various individuals:—

Arunga, to the individuals numbered	1, 53, 54.
Aperla, to the individuals numbered	3.
Oknia, to the individuals numbered	6, 7, 8.
Uwinna, to the individuals numbered	5, 9.
Chimmia, to the individuals numbered	a, 55, 56
Ipmunna, to the individuals numbered	b, c, 34, 35.
Unkulla, to the individuals numbered	d, 19, 20, 30, 31.
Ikuntera, to the individuals numbered	10.
Umba, to the individuals numbered	11, 43, 44, 49, 50.
Mia, to the individuals numbered	13, 14, 15, 51.
Gammona, to the individuals numbered	12, 16, 52.
Mura, to the individuals numbered	17, 18.
Okilia, to the individuals numbered	21, 23.
Ungaraitcha, to the individuals numbered	22, 24.
Witia, to the individuals numbered	26, 28.
Quitia, to the individuals numbered	27, 29.
Allira, to the individuals numbered	41, 42, 45, 46, 47, 48.
Unawa, to the individuals numbered	32, 36, 38, 39.
Umbirna, to the individuals numbered	33, 37, 40.

The woman numbered 38 applies the following names to the various individuals:—

Arunga, to the individuals numbered 4.
Aperla, to the individuals numbered 2, 53, 54.
Oknia, to the individuals numbered 10.
Uwinna, to the individuals numbered 11.

Chimmia, to the individuals numbered	c.							
Ipmunna, to the individuals numbered	a,	d,	19,	20,	30,	31,	55,	56.
Unkulla, to the individuals numbered	34.							
Nimmera, to the individuals numbered	6,	7,	8.					
Umba, to the individuals numbered	5,	9,	41,	42,	45,	46,	47,	48.
Mia, to the individuals numbered	17.							
Gammona, to the individuals numbered	18.							
Mura, to the individuals numbered	12,	13,	14,	15,	16.			
Okilia, to the individuals numbered	37.							
Ungaraitcha, to the individuals numbered	36.							
Witia, to the individuals numbered	40.							
Quitia, to the individuals numbered	33,	39.						
Allira, to the individuals numbered	43,	44,	49,	50.				
Unawa, to the individuals numbered	21,	23,	25,	26,	28.			
Ilchella, to the individuals numbered	b,	35.						
Intinga, to the individuals numbered	22,	24,	27,	29.				

A comparison of the terms of relationship here set forth with those in use amongst other tribes, which have been described by Messrs. Howitt and Fison, and more recently and in most valuable detail by Mr. Roth, will serve to show how widely a similar series of terms is in use amongst the various Australian tribes.

We will further exemplify the system by taking a man of one particular group and describe in detail the various relationships which exist between him and other members of the tribe. These and all details given have been derived from various individuals and families, and have been corroborated time after time.

After ascertaining the various relationships we found that they could be represented graphically and in orderly arrangement by means of the table already employed, and, as we have found this table of the greatest service to ourselves in dealing with this somewhat intricate subject, we will make use of it here.

TABLE I.

1	2	3	4
(Unclear:)Panunga	Purula	Appungerta	Kumara
Uknaria	Ungalla	Bulthara	Umbitchana
Bulthara	Kumara	Uknaria	Purula
Appungerta	Umbitchana	Panunga	Ungalla

The brackets signify groups, the members of which are mutually *Ipmunna* to each other.

Column 3 are the children of men of column 1 and of women of column 2. This applies to groups on the same horizontal line in the table. Thus an Appungerta is the child of a Panunga man and a Purula woman; a Panunga is the child of an Appungerta man and an Umbitchana woman. The same remark applies to all the other relationships indicated; thus a Panunga man is *Gammona* to a Kumara.

Column 4 are the children of men of column 2 and of the women of column 1.
A man of column 1 is *Unawa* to a woman of column 2 and *vice versa*, and *Umbirna* to a man of column 2. A woman of column 2 is *Intinga* to a woman of column 1, and *vice versa*.
Column 1 contains men who are *Gammona* of men and women of column 4.
Column 4 contains men who are *Ikuntera* or *Umba* of men, and *Nimmera* of women, of column 1.
Column 2 contains men who are *Gammona* of men and

women of column 3.

Column 3 contains men who are *Ikuntera* or *Umba* of men, and *Nimmera* of women, of column 2.

Men and women of columns 3 and 4 stand mutually in the relationship of *Unkulla* or *Chimmia*.

Women of columns 3 and 4 stand mutually in the relationship of *Ilchella*.

TABLE II.

1	2	3	4
Panunga	Purula	Appungerta	Kumara
Uknaria	Ungalla	Bulthara	Umbitchana
Bulthara	Kumara	Uknaria	Purula
Appungerta	Umbitchana	Panunga	Ungalla

In column 1 the larger and smaller brackets on the right side indicate the relationship of *Uwinna*, the overlapping brackets on the left indicate that of *Mura*. In column 4 the reverse holds true, the brackets on the left indicate the relationship of *Uwinna*, and those on the right side that of *Mura*.

Taking now the case of an individual member of a particular group, we may describe as follows the various relationships in which he stands with regard to the other members of the tribe. We will suppose that this particular individual is an Appungerta man living in the northern part of the tribe where the division into eight groups exists, and we will suppose him to be speaking—

If I am an Appungerta man then—
My father is a Panunga.
All Uknaria are *Ipmunna* to him and *Mura* to me—that is, I may not speak to them if they be women. The daughters of Ungalla men and Uknaria women are Umbitchana and *Unawa* to me—that is, they are women whom I may lawfully marry, and one or more of whom are allotted to me as wives. The

mother of the woman who is allotted to me is my *Tualchamura*.

The sons of Uknaria women, that is the brothers of my *Unawa*, are *Umbirna* to me; so that Umbitchana men are *Umbirna* to Appungerta men, and *vice versa*.

I call my father *Oknia*.

All men whom my father calls *Okilia*, elder brothers, or *Witia*, younger brother, are Panunga, and they are *Oknia* to me. I call his *Okilia*, *Oknia aniaura*, and his *Itia*, *Oknia alkulla*.

My *Oknia's* sisters are Panunga, and they are *Uwinna* to me. That is, Panunga women are *Uwinna* to Appungerta men.

All women whom my wife calls *Ungaraitcha*, elder sisters, or *Quitia*, younger sisters, are Umbitchana, and they also are *Unawa* to me.

All women whom my wife calls *Ipmunna* are Kumara, and they are *Unkulla* to me.

Speaking as an Arunta man living in a part where only four sub-classes are recognised, all the women of my wife's class, who in this case would be Kumara, I myself belonging to the Bulthara, are divided into two sets, the members of one of whom are *Unawa* to me, so that I can marry them; while the members of the other are *Unkulla*, whom I may not marry. The latter are *Ipmunna* to my wife. I can only marry a woman who stands in the relationship of daughter to the women of the half of my father's class to which he does not belong— that is, who are *Ipmunna* to him.

My *Ipmunna* are Bulthara.

My *Unkulla* women are Kumara, and they must marry Bulthara men, and their children are *Mura* to me. That is, the relationship of *Mura* arises from the marriage of male *Ipmunna* and female *Unkulla*. This is an important relationship, as a *Mura* woman is the mother of my wife.

My *Umbirna* are Umbitchana men, who are the sons of Uknaria women—that is, of my female *Mura*.

My *Ungaraitcha*, elder sisters, and *Quitia*, younger sisters, are Appungerta, and are *Unawa* to my *Umbirna*, who are Umbitchana men.

The children of my *Ungaraitcha* and *Quitia* are Ungalla. I call them *Allira* and they call me *Gammona*—that is, Appungerta men are *Gammona* to Ungalla men and women.
My own and my brother's children are *Allira* to me, and I am *Oknia* to them. My mother is Purula. She calls her elder sisters *Ungaraitcha* and her younger ones *Quitia*. I call them all *Mia*. That is, Purula women are *Mia* to Appungerta men. Her elder sisters I call *Mia apmarla*, and her younger sisters *Mia alkulla*.[43]

Speaking again as an Arunta man only recognising four sub-classes the women of the class to which my mother belongs are divided into two groups, the members of one of which have the relationship of *Mia* to me and those of the other that of *Umba*.

The children of the *Okilia* of my *Oknia*, that is my father's elder brothers' children, will be Appungerta as I am, and they will be according to sex, my *Okilia*, elder brothers, or *Ungaraitcha*, elder sisters.
The children of my *Oknia's Ungaraitcha* and of his *Quitia* are Kumara, and are *Unkulla* to me and *Ipmunna* to my wife.
The children of my *Oknia's Okilia* call me *Witia* or younger brother, and the children of my *Oknia's Witia* call me *Okilia*, and I call them *Witia*.
The children of my *Okilia* and *Witia*, that is of my elder and younger brothers, call me *Oknia*, just as my own children do, and I call them *Allira*, and they are Panunga.
The children of my *Ungaraitcha* and *Quitia*, that is of my sisters, I call *Umba*, and they are Ungalla.

That is, once more speaking as an Arunta man recognising only four sub-classes, my own and my brother's children go into the same sub-class as that to which my father belongs, whilst my sister's children go into the sub-class to which my mother belongs, but into the half of it to which she does not belong. That is, relations whom we class together as nephews or nieces as the case may be, are either, in respect to a man,

Allira, that is, brother's children, or *Umba*, that is, sister's children. It will be noted that the terms *Allira* and *Umba* are applied to individuals of both sexes, so that each of them includes individuals whom we call nephews or nieces.

My male *Allira's* children are Appungerta, and are *Arunga* to me and I to them, the term being a reciprocal one.
My *Allira* are Panunga and my *Umba* are Ungalla, and these two are *Unkulla* to each other.
My *Allira* call my *Ungaraitcha* and *Quitia*, that is, my elder and younger sisters, *Uwinna*. That is, Appungerta women are *Uwinna* to Panunga men and women.
The children of my female *Allira*, that is of my daughters, are Kumara, and they are *Chimmia* to me and I to them. The term *Chimmia* expresses the relationship of grandfather or grandchild on the mother's side, just as the term *Arunga* expresses the same on the father's side.
My male *Chimmias'* male children will be Purula and *Gammona* to me, that is they are the blood and tribal brothers of my *Mias*.
My male *Chimmias'* female children will be Purula and *Mia* to me.
The children of my female *Chimmia* are Uknaria and are *Mura* to me, and they are the *Mias* of my wife.
My sisters are Appungerta and the daughters of my father's sisters are Kumara, and therefore stand in the relationship of *Ilchella* to each other; the relationship of *Ilchella* only exists between women. That is, if I am an Appungerta man, then my father's sister's sons and daughters will be Kumara and *Unkulla* to me. If I am an Appungerta woman then my father's sister's daughters will be *Ilchella* to me.
My mother's mother is Bulthara and is *Ipmunna* to me.
My father's mother is Umbitchana and *Aperla* to me.
There are certain differences in the terms used if a woman be speaking which may be noted here. Thus, if I am an Appungerta woman, then I call my own and my sister's children *Umba*, but I call my brother's *Allira*.

I apply the term *Urumpa* to brothers and sisters collectively and also to men and women who are *Unkulla* to me.

The sisters of my husband are Umbitchana, and are *Intinga* to me and *Unawa* to my brothers.

The daughters of my father's sisters are Kumara and *Ilchella* to me.

The sons of my father's sisters are Kumara and are *Unkulla* to me.

My husband's father is Ungalla, and I call him and he calls me *Nimmera*; the same term applies to all men whose sons are born *Unawa* to me.

There is a special term *Tualcha* which is applied in the case of three particular relationships, or rather is added to the usual one in order to show the existence of a special connection between the individuals concerned.[44] Thus, every man calls the members of a particular group by the name of *Ikuntera* or father-in-law, but the particular one whose daughter has actually been assigned to him—whether he has married her or not has nothing to do with the case—he calls *Ikuntera-tualcha*. He may have other wives, but unless the mutual agreement was made between his and the girl's father that he should have the girl to wife, then the father of the latter is not spoken of as *Tualcha*. In the same way the special *Mura* woman to whose daughter a man is betrothed in his *Mura-tualcha*, and, lastly, the individual who is *Ikuntera-tualcha* to one man, is *Unkulla-tualcha* to the father of the latter. If, for example, I am an Appungerta man, then my *Ikuntera-tualcha* is an Ungalla man, and he is *Unkulla-tualcha* to my father.

It will be noticed that distinct names are given to elder and younger brothers and elder and younger sisters. Thus not only are my elder sisters in blood called *Ungaraitcha*, but the daughters of women whom my mother calls *Ungaraitcha* are *Ungaraitcha* to me, and those of women whom my mother called *Quitia* are *Quitia* to me. There are, however, certain exceptions to this which are of interest as showing the influence of counting descent in the male line. Not infrequently two brothers in blood will marry two sisters in blood. When this takes place the usual plan is for the elder brother to marry the elder sister; should, however, the elder sister marry the younger brother, then seniority is counted in the male line. In this case the sons and daughters of the younger daughter are the elder brothers and sisters of those of the elder sister.

A curious custom exists with regard to the mutual behaviour of elder and younger sisters and their brothers. A man may speak freely to his elder sisters in blood, but those who are tribal *Ungaraitcha* must only be spoken to at a considerable distance. To younger sisters, blood and tribal, he may not speak, or at least, only at such a distance that the features are indistinguishable. A man, for example, would speak to his tribal *Ungaraitcha* or elder sister at a distance of say forty yards, but he would not address his *Quitia* or younger sisters unless they were at least 100 yards away. At night-time *Ungaraitcha* and *Quitia* may go to their brother's camp, and if he be present they may, sitting in the darkness where their faces are not distinguishable, converse with his *Unawa* or wife. We cannot discover any explanation of this restriction in regard to the younger sister; it can hardly be supposed that it has anything to do with the dread of anything like incest, else why is there not as strong a restriction in the case of the elder sisters? That there is some form of tabu, or, as the Arunta natives call it, *ekirinja*, in regard to the younger sister is shown also by the fact that a man can never inherit the Churinga of a deceased younger sister, but always inherits, on the other hand, those of a deceased elder sister.

In the tables which follow, we give the intermarrying groups of seven other tribes corresponding to those of the Arunta tribe; those of the Ilpirra are identical with the latter, which indeed, have been derived in their present form from the Ilpirra tribe. In all cases, men of column 1 marry women of column 2, and their children are as arranged in column 3; men of column 2 marry women of column 1, and their children are represented in column 4.

In the case of three tribes, Warramunga, Bingongina and Walpari, the system becomes still further complicated by the addition of distinct names for females. These names are those printed in brackets. In these cases a man of column 1, marries a woman of column 2, whose name is in brackets, and their children are shown in column 3. In the Warramunga tribe, for example, a Thapanunga man marries a Naralu, and their children, if males, are Thapungerta, and if females, Napungerta. In the same way a Chupilla man marries a Napanunga woman, and their children, if males, are Thakomara, if females, Nakomara.

The tables are arranged so that the equivalent groups in the various tribes can be seen at a glance. An Ilpirra Panunga man visiting the Waagi is regarded as a Pungarinju, and amongst the Bingongina he is a Tchana. An Ilpirra Purula woman amongst the Iliaura is regarded as an Upilla, and amongst the Bingongina as a Nala, and so on.

TABLE III
(i) ILPIRRA TRIBE.

1	2	3	4
Panunga	Purula	Appungerta	Kumara
Uknaria	Ungalla	Bulthara	Umbitchana
Bulthara	Kumara	Uknaria	Purula
Appungerta	Umbitchana	Panunga	Ungalla

(ii) KAITISH TRIBE.

1	2	3	4
Apanunga	Purula	Appungerta	Akomara
Uknaria	Thungalla	Kabidgi	Umbitchana
Kabidgi	Akomara	Uknaria	Purula
Appungerta	Umbitchana	Apanunga	Thungalla

(iii) ILIAURA TRIBE.

1	2	3	4
Apanunga	Upilla	Appungerta	Akumara
Uknaria	Thungalla	Appitchara	Umbitchana
Appitchara	Akumara	Uknaria	Upilla
Appungerta	Umbitchana	Apanunga	Thungalla

(iv) WAAGAI TRIBE.

1	2	3	4
Pungarinju	Ikumaru	Wairgu	Kingelu
Bilyarinthu	Chamerameru	Bliniwu	Nurrithu
Bliniwu	Kingelu	Bilyarinthu	Ikumaru
Wairgu	Nurrithu	Pungarinju	Chamerameru

(v) WARRAMUNGA TRIBE.

1	2	3	4
Thapanunga (Napanunga)	Chupilla (Naralu)	Thapungerta (Napungerta)	Thakomara (Nakomara)
Chunguri (Namagili)	Thungalli (Nungalli)	Kabidgi (Nalchari)	Chambein (Lambein)
Kabidgi (Nalchari)	Thakomara (Nakomara)	Chunguri (Namagili)	Chupilla (Naralu)
Thapungerta (Napungerta)	Chambein (Lambein)	Thapanunga (Napanunga)	Thungalli (Nungalli)

(vi) BINGONGINA TRIBE.

1	2	3	4
Tchana (Nana)	Chula (Nala)	Thungarri (Nungarri)	Chimara (Nemara)
Chimita (Namita)	Chungalla (Nungalla)	Thalirri (Nalyirri)	Chambechina (Nambechina)
Thalirri (Nalyirri)	Chimara (Nemara)	Chimita (Namita)	Chula (Nala)
Thungarri (Nungarri)	Chambechina (Nambechina)	Tchana (Nana)	Chungalla (Nungalla)

(vii) WALPARI TRIBE.

1	2	3	4
Chapanunga (Napanunga)	Chupilla (Napula)	Chapungarta (Napungarta)	Chakuma (Nakuma)
Chunguri (Namilpa)	Chungalla (Nungalla)	Chapatcha (Napatcha)	Champechinpa (Nambechinpa)

Chapatcha	Chakuma	Chunguri	Chupilla
(Napatcha)	(Nakuma)	(Namilpa)	(Napula)
Chapungarta	Champechinpa	Chapanunga	Chungalla
(Napungarta)	(Nambechinpa)	(Napanunga)	(Nungalla)

Chapter III

Certain Ceremonies Concerned with Marriage Together with a Discussion Regarding the Same.

Marriage ceremony in the northern Arunta and Ilpirra tribes—Ceremony in the southern Arunta—Ceremony in the Kaitish, Warramunga, Iliaura, Waagai, Bingongina, Walpari and Luritcha tribes—On these occasions men standing in a definite relationship to the woman have access to her—Ceremonies are of the nature of those described by Sir John Lubbock as indicative of "expiation for marriage"—To be regarded as rudimentary customs—Sexual license during corrobborees in the Arunta, Kaitish, Iliaura and Warramunga tribes—This is not, strictly speaking, the lending of wives, as it is obligatory—Feeling of sexual jealousy not strongly enough developed amongst these tribes to prevent the occurrence of general intercourse or lending of wives—The putting of a man to death for wrongful intercourse is no proof of the existence of sexual jealousy—Term lending of wives restricted to private and voluntary lending by one man to another—Discussion of certain parts of Westermarck's criticism of the theory of promiscuity so far as concerns the tribes now dealt with—Customs at marriage and at certain other times afford evidence of the former existence of a time when there existed wider marital relations than now obtain.

WHILST under ordinary circumstances in the Arunta and other tribes one man is only allowed to have marital relations with women of a particular class, there are customs which allow, at certain times, of a man having such relations with women to whom at other times he would not on any account be allowed to have access. We find, indeed, that this holds true in the case of all the nine different tribes with the marriage customs of which we are acquainted, and in which a woman becomes the private property of one man.

The following is the custom amongst the Arunta and Ilpirra tribes. When a girl arrives at marriageable age, which is usually about fourteen or fifteen, the man to whom she has been allotted speaks to his *Unkulla* men, and they, together with men who are *Unkulla* and *Unawa* to the girl, but not including her future husband, take her out into the bush and there perform the operation called *Atna-ariltha-kuma* (*atna*, vulva; *kuma*, cut.[45] The operation is conducted with a stone knife and the operator who is, except in the southern Arunta, a man who is *Ipmunna* to the girl, carries with him one of the small wooden Churinga called *Namatwinna* with which before operating he touches the lips of the vulva, so as to prevent too great a loss of blood. When the operation has been performed, the *Ipmunna, Unkulla* and *Unawa* have access to her in the order named. This ceremony is often performed during the progress of an Altherta or ordinary corrobboree when, during the day time, the men habitually assemble at the corrobboree ground. When it is over the woman's head is decorated, by the *Ipmunna* man who operated, with head bands and tufts of *Alpita*,[46] the neck with necklaces, the arms with bands of fur string, and her body is painted all over with a mixture of fat and red ochre. Thus decorated, she is taken to the camp of her special *Unawa* by the men who have taken part in the ceremony and who have meanwhile painted themselves with charcoal.[47] On the day following the husband will most likely—though there is no obligation for him to do so—send her to the same men, and after that she becomes his special wife, to whom no one else has right of access; though at times a man will lend his wife to a stranger as an act of courtesy, always provided that he belongs to the right class, that is, to the same as himself. After wearing the decorations for a few days, the woman returns them to her *Ipmunna* man.

By reference to the tables already given, it will be clearly seen that on this occasion men of forbidden groups have access to the woman. Suppose, for example, that she is a Purula. Her proper *Unawa* will be a Panunga man, and such an one is normally the only one with whom she may have marital relations. The woman's *Ipmunna* is an Ungalla man, that is, a man who belongs to her own moiety of the tribe; her *Unkulla* are Uknaria, that is, they belong to the half of her husband's class into which she may not marry. In addition to these forbidden men, there are the *Unawa* or men who are her lawful husbands, so far as their class is concerned, but whose general right of access to her is lost when she is allotted to some special individual amongst them.

In the southern Arunta the operation is performed by a man who is *Nimmera* to the woman, that is, a man of the same class as the father of her future husband. For example, if she be again a Purula the man will be a Bulthara. The ceremony is performed when a considerable number of men are together in camp, and the details vary somewhat from those in the northern part. A brother of the woman who has been told by the man that he, the latter, intends to claim his alloted *Unawa* takes the initiative and tells those who are not participating in the ceremony to remain in camp. Individuals who stand in the relationship to her of *Mia, Oknia, Okilia, Ungaraitcha, Gammona, Ipmunna* and the particular *Unawa* to whom she is allotted, sit down in camp, the woman being amongst them. Then a man who is *Nimmera* to her comes up behind, and, touching the woman on the shoulder, tells her to follow him. He goes away accompanied by perhaps two other *Nimmera*, one or two who are *Unkulla* to her, and one or two who are *Unawa*, that is, are of the same class as her future husband. After the ceremony has been performed, she is decorated and brought back to the camp, and told to sit down immediately behind her special *Unawa* whom, after a short time, she accompanies to his camp. That night he lends her to one or two men who are *Unawa* to her, and afterwards she belongs exclusively to him.

Amongst the Kaitish tribe the operation is performed by an *Arari* or elder sister of the woman, and men of the following relationship have access in the order indicated. *Atmini*, the equivalents of the *Ipmunna* amongst the Arunta; *Atinkilia* mothers' brothers' sons; *Alkiriia* and *Achirri*, elder and younger brothers (but not in blood); *Gammona* and *Umbirniia* the equivalent of the *Unawa* amongst the Arunta. It will be seen that in the Kaitish tribe, the usual restrictions are even more notably broken than in the Arunta, for right of access is granted to men who are tribal brothers.

Amongst the Warramunga tribe the operation is performed either by a man who is *Turtundi*, the equivalent of *Ipmunna* in the Arunta, or, as amongst the Kaitish, by an elder sister. Men of the following relationship subsequently have access in the order named. *Turtundi* or *Ipmunna*; *Wankili*, father's sisters' sons; *Papirti* and *Kukatcha*, elder and younger brothers (not in blood); *Kullakulla*, the equivalents of the *Unawa* in the Arunta.

Amongst the Iliaura tribe the operation is performed by an *Ipmunna* man and the following, using the equivalent terms of the Arunta, have access in the order named; *Ipmunna, Unkulla, Okilia, Itia*, and *Unawa*.

In the Waagai and Bingongina tribes the ceremony is the same as in the Warramunga.

In the Walpari tribe the ceremony, as amongst the southern Arunta, is performed by a man who belongs to the same class as the woman's father-in-law, and is called *Kulkuna*; and men of the following relationship have access in the order named. *Kulkuna; Thathana*, the equivalents of the *Ipmunna; Wankillina* or mothers' brothers' sons; *Papertina* and *Kukernina*, elder and younger brothers; and *Kullakulla*, the equivalents of the *Unawa* of the Arunta.

In the Luritcha tribe the operation is performed by a man who is *Sthamu* to the woman, that is, grandfather on the father's side; and men of the following relationship have access in the order named—*Sthamu; Watchira*, mothers' brothers' sons; *Ukari*, sisters' sons; *Kuri*, the equivalents of the *Unawa* of the Arunta.

It will be seen that in the nine tribes referred to there is a substantial agreement in the ceremonies concerned with marriage. It must of course be understood that they refer to the marriage of men and women who have been allotted to one another in one or other of the various ways which obtain amongst the tribes dealt with. In all these tribes we find that individual marriage exists, though in none of them is there a special term applied to the special wife, apart from the general one given in common to her and other women of her group whom it is lawful for a man to marry and outside of whom he may not marry.

In each tribe, again, we find at this particular time when a woman is being, so to speak, handed over to one particular man, that special individuals representing groups with which at ordinary times she may have no intercourse, have the right of access to her. In the majority of tribes, even tribal brothers are included amongst them. The individuals who are thus privileged vary from tribe to tribe, but in all cases the striking feature is that, for the time being, the existence of what can only be described as partial promiscuity can clearly be seen. By this we do not mean that marital rights are allowed to any man, but that for a time such rights are allowed to individuals to whom at other times the woman is *ekirinja*, or forbidden. The ceremonies in question are of the nature of those which Sir John Lubbock has described as indicative of "expiation for marriage," and it is at least very probable that the customs are to be regarded as pointing back to the former existence of an exercise of wider marital rights than those which now obtain in the various tribes. They may in fact be best described as rudimentary customs in just the same way in which we speak of rudimentary structures amongst animals and plants. Just also as the latter are regarded as representative of parts which were once functional in ancestral forms, so also may we regard these rudimentary customs as lingering relics of a former stage passed through in the development of the present social organisation of the various tribes in which they are found.

In addition to the ceremonies which are concerned with marriage, there is another custom of somewhat the same nature, to which reference may be made here. In the eastern and north-eastern parts of the Arunta, and in the Kaitish Iliaura, and Warramunga tribes, considerable license is allowed on certain occasions, when a large number of men and women are gathered together to perform certain corrobborees. When an important one of these is held, it occupies perhaps ten days or a fortnight; and during that time the men, and especially the elder ones, but by no means exclusively these, spend the day in camp preparing decorations to be used during the evening. Every day two or three women are told off to attend at the corrobboree ground, and, with the exception of men who stand in the relation to them of actual father, brother, or sons, they are, for the time being, common property to all the men present on the corrobboree ground. In the Arunta tribe the following is exactly what takes place: a man goes to another who is actually or tribally his son-in-law, that is, one who stands to him in the relationship of *Gammona*, and says to the latter: "You will take my *Unawa* into the bush[48] and bring in with you some *undattha altherta*" (down used for decorating during ordinary corrobborees). The *Gammona* then goes away, followed by the woman who has been previously told what to do by her husband. This woman is actually *Mura* to the *Gammona*, that is, one to whom under ordinary circumstances he may not even speak or go near, much less have anything like marital relations with. After the two have been out in the bush they return to the camp, the man carrying *undattha* and the woman following with green twigs, which the men will wear during the evening dance, tied round their arms and ankles. There will be perhaps two or three of these women present on each day, and to them any man present on the ground, except those already mentioned, may have access.

During the day they sit near to the men watching but taking no part in the preparation of decorations. The natives say that their presence during the preparations and the sexual indulgence, which was a practice of the Alcheringa, prevents anything from going wrong with the performance; it makes it impossible for the head decorations, for example, to become loose and disordered during the performance. At evening the women are painted with red ochre by the men, and then they return to the main camp to summon the women and children to the corrobboree.

In connection with this subject, a curious custom concerned with messengers may be noticed here. In the case of the Urabunna tribe it is usual to send as messengers, when summoning distant groups, a man and a woman, or sometimes two pairs, who are *Piraungaru* to each other. The men carry as evidence of their mission bunches of cockatoo feathers and nose bones. After the men have delivered their message and talked matters over with the strangers, they take the women out a short distance from the camp, where they leave them. If the members of the group which they are visiting decide to comply with their request, all men irrespective of class have access to the women; but, if it be decided not to comply with the request, then the latter are not visited. In much the same way, when a party of men intent on vengeance comes near to the strange camp of which they intend to kill some member, the use of women may be offered to them. If they be accepted, then the quarrel is at an end, as the acceptance of this favour is a sign of friendship. To accept the favour and then not to comply with the desire of the people offering it, would be a gross breach of tribal custom.

So far, then, as the marital relations of the tribes are concerned, we find that whilst there is individual marriage, there are, in actual practice, occasions on which the relations are of a much wider nature. We have, indeed, in this respect three very distinct series of relationships. The first is the normal one, when the woman is the private property of one man, and no one without his consent can have access to her, though he may lend her privately to certain individuals who stand in one given relationship to her. The second is the wider relation in regard to particular men at the time of marriage. The third is the still wider relation which obtains on certain occasions, such as the holding of important corrobborees.

The first of these is purely a private matter, and it is only to this that the term lending of wives can be properly applied, and to it we restrict the term in the following pages. The second and third are what we may call matters of public nature, by which we mean that the individuals concerned have no choice in the matter, and the women cannot be withheld by the men whose individual wives they either are to be, or already are.

In the case of the women who attend the corrobboree, it is supposed to be the duty of every man at different times to send his wife to the ground, and the most striking feature in regard to it is that the first man who has access to her is the very one to whom, under normal conditions, she is most strictly tabu, that is, her *Mura*. This definite way of breaking through the rules of tabu appears to show that the custom has some very definite significance more than can be explained by merely referring it to a feeling of hospitality, and the fact that every man in turn is obliged by public custom to thus relinquish, for the time being, his possession of the woman who has been allotted to him, strengthens the idea. At the same time, as young and old men alike have to do so at some time or other, it is impossible to regard it as a right which is forcibly taken by strong men from weaker ones. It is a custom of ancient date which is sanctioned by public opinion, and to the performance of which neither men nor women concerned offer any opposition.

In connection with this, it may be worth while noting that amongst the Australian natives with whom we have come in contact, the feeling of sexual jealousy is not developed to anything like the extent to which it would appear to be in many other savage tribes. For a man to have unlawful intercourse with any woman arouses a feeling which is due not so much to jealousy as to the fact that the delinquent has infringed a tribal custom. If the intercourse has been with a woman who belongs to the class from which his wife comes, then he is called *atna nylkna* (which, literally translated, is vulva-thief); if with one with whom it is unlawful for him to have intercourse, then he is called *iturka*, the most opprobrious term in the Arunta tongue. In the one case he has merely stolen property, in the other he has offended against tribal law.

Now and again sexual jealousy as between a man and woman will come into play, but as a general rule this is a feeling which is undoubtedly subservient to that of the influence of tribal custom, so far as the latter renders it obligatory for a man to allow other men, at certain times, to have free access to his wife, or so far as it directs him to lend his wife to some other individual as a mark of personal favour to the latter.

Whilst jealousy is not unknown amongst these tribes, the point of importance in respect to the matter under discussion is that it is not strongly enough developed to prevent the occurrence of general intercourse on certain occasions, or the lending of wives at other times; it is, indeed, a factor which need not be taken into serious account in regard to the question of sexual relations amongst the Central Australian tribes. A man in these tribes may be put to death for wrongful intercourse, but at the same time this is no proof of the fact that sexual jealousy exists; it is a serious offence against tribal laws, and its punishment has no relation to the feelings of the individual.

We may now pass on to discuss briefly the customs relating to marriage which have already been enumerated, and in so doing, as we have often to refer to the lending of wives, it must be remembered that we use this term only as applying to the private lending of a woman to some other individual by the man to whom she has been allotted, and do not refer to the custom at corrobborees which has just been dealt with, and which, as it is in reality obligatory and not optional, cannot be regarded as a lending in the same sense in which the term is used in connection with the former custom.

In his well-known work dealing with human marriage, Westermarck[49] has brought together, from various sources, facts relating to similar customs, and, while discussing the hypothesis of promiscuity from an adverse point of view, has endeavoured to explain them as due to various causes. These we may conveniently discuss, examining each briefly in the endeavour to ascertain whether it will or will not serve to explain the marriage customs as we find them in Australian tribes, of which those quoted above may be taken as typical examples. It must be understood that we are here simply dealing with this question so far as the evidence derived from these Australian tribes is concerned.

The first explanation offered is that in certain instances the practice is evidently associated with phallic worship, as, for example, when in the valley of the Ganges, the virgins had to offer themselves up in the temples of Juggernaut. This implies a state of social development very different from, and much more advanced than, anything met with amongst the Australian natives, and the two customs are evidently quite distinct from one another. It is doubtful how far phallic worship can be said to exist amongst the Australian natives.

In other cases where the bride is for a night considered the common property of the guests at a wedding feast, Westermarck suggests that "It may have been a part of the nuptial entertainment—a horrible kind of hospitality no doubt, but quite in accordance with savage ideas, and analogous to another custom which occurs much more frequently—I mean the practice of lending wives." This presupposes, and in fact is co-existent with, what does not take place in Australian tribes, and that is a more or less regular marriage ceremony at which guests assemble, and such an organised proceeding cannot be said to exist amongst the tribes with which we are dealing; moreover, apart from this, which is not perhaps a very serious objection, though it seems to imply a state of development considerably in advance of that of the Australian natives, there still remains what appears to us to be the insuperable difficulty of accounting, on this hypothesis, for the fact that this "hospitality" amongst Australian tribes is only allowed to a limited number of individuals, all of whom must stand in some particular relationship to the woman.

Westermarck further suggests that it is analogous to the custom of lending wives. Now, amongst the Australian natives wives are certainly lent, but only under strict rules; in the Arunta tribe for example no man will lend his wife to any one who does not belong to the particular group with which it is lawful for her to have marital relations—she is in fact, only lent to a man whom she calls *Unawa*, just as she calls her own husband, and though this may undoubtedly be spoken of as an act of hospitality, it may with equal justice be regarded as evidence of the very clear recognition of group relationship, and as evidence also in favour of the former existence of group marriage.

It is quite true, on the other hand, that a native will sometimes offer his wife, as an act of hospitality, to a white man; but this has nothing to do with the lending of wives which has just been dealt with, and the difference between the two acts is of a radical nature. The white man stands outside the laws which govern the native tribe, and therefore to lend him a wife of any designation does not imply the infringement of any custom. This is purely and simply, as Westermarck points out, an act of hospitality, but the very fact that he will only lend his wife, if he does so at all, to another native of a particular designation, seems to at once imply that we are dealing with a custom at the root of which lies something much more than merely an idea of hospitality. The lending of women to men outside the tribe who are not amenable to its laws and customs is one thing, to lend them to men who are members of the tribe is quite another thing, and the respective origins of the customs in these two radically different cases are probably totally distinct—one is no doubt to be explained on the hypothesis of hospitality, the other is not. The hypothesis of hospitality does not, in short, appear to us to be capable of explaining the fact that both at marriage and at certain other times, it is only particular men who are allowed access to particular women.[50]

A third hypothesis suggested to account for certain customs such as the "jus primae noctis," accorded to chiefs and particular individuals, is that "it may be a right taken forcibly by the stronger, or it may be a privilege voluntarily given to the chief man as a mark of esteem; in either case it depends upon his authority."[51] It will be generally admitted that here again no such explanation will account for the customs as met with amongst Australian tribes. In the first place, while the elder men are undoubtedly accorded certain privileges, there is not in any Australian tribe any one individual to whom the term chief can, with strict propriety, be applied, and in the second place the privilege with which we are dealing is by no means enjoyed wholly by the elder men.[52] Unless the leading man in any group stands in a particular relationship to the woman, he has no more right of access to her than the most insignificant man in the group.

A fourth hypothesis is suggested in connection with the right of access granted to men who have assisted the bridegroom in the capture of the woman. "In such cases the 'jus primae noctis' is a reward for a good turn done, or perhaps, as Mr. McLennan suggests, a common war right, exercised by the captors of the woman."[53] There is undoubtedly much to be said in favour of this, but there are objections applying to it as to the second hypothesis dealt with. In the first place, so far as Australia is concerned, it is founded upon such vague statements as that quoted by Brough Smyth upon the authority of Mr. J. M. Davis.[54] Mr. Davis says, "when a young man is entitled to have a *lubra*, he organises a party of his friends, and they make a journey into the territories of some other tribe, and there lie in wait, generally in the evening, by a waterhole, where the *lubras* come for water. Such of the lubras as may be required are then pounced upon, and, if they attempt to make any resistance, are struck down insensible and dragged off. There is also this peculiarity, that in any instance where the abduction has taken place for the benefit of some one individual, each of the members of the party claims, as a right, a privilege which the intended husband has no power to refuse."

Before it is safe, or indeed possible, to draw any conclusion from this, we require to know exactly who the men were, that is in what relationship they stood to the man whom they were assisting. The more detailed is the information acquired in respect to the Australian tribes, the more clearly is it made apparent that on expeditions such as this, when the object in view is the obtaining of a wife, the man only asks the assistance of men who stand in certain definite relationships to himself. It does not at all follow, that, because a man forms a member of a party which captures a woman, he is therefore allowed to have access to her. In the tribes which we have investigated, marriage customs regulate the whole proceedings; the equivalent classes in the tribes are well known and, supposing for example, a party consists of men belonging to two classes, which we will call A and B, and a woman is captured belonging, say, to a third class C, which intermarries with Class A, but not with Class B, then no man in the party, if there be any such present, who belongs to Class B will be allowed, or will attempt, to have access to her. When we have merely such general statements as that quoted above from the report of Mr. Davis, it may look very much as if there did exist such a thing as "a common war-right, exercised by the captors of a woman," but the more detailed our information becomes, the less evidence of any such "common war-right" do we find, and in the Australian tribes generally it may be regarded as very doubtful if any such right really exists. Amongst the tribes with which we are acquainted it certainly does not.

Marriage by capture is again, at the present day, whatever it may have been in the past, by no means the rule in Australian tribes, and too much stress has been laid upon this method. It is only comparatively rarely that a native goes and seizes upon some lubra in a neighbouring tribe; by far the most common method of getting a wife is by means of an arrangement made between brothers or fathers of the respective men and women, whereby a particular woman is assigned to a particular man. Marriage by capture may indeed be regarded as one of the most exceptional methods of obtaining a wife amongst the natives at the present day. We are not of course referring here to customs which may, in many tribes, be explained as indicative of a former existence of the practice; whether, in the remote past, capture was the prevailing method can only be a matter of conjecture, but the customs at marriage in the tribes here dealt with—and it may be pointed out that these occupy a very large area in the centre of the continent, so that we are by no means dealing with an isolated example—do not seem to indicate that they owe their origin to anything like the recognition of the right of captor, as captor.

The fifth hypothesis is that of promiscuity. Certainly at the present day, so far as we can tell, there is some definite system of marriage in all Australian tribes and promiscuity, as a normal feature, does not exist. At the same time none of the hypotheses put forward by Westermarck will serve to explain the curious and very strongly marked features of the marriage customs, the essential points in which are, (1) that men have access to women who are strictly forbidden to them at ordinary times, and (2) that it is only certain definite men standing in—certain particular relationships to the woman who thus have access.

To make use of the same analogy again, it seems that in the evolution of the social organisation and customs of a savage tribe, such features as those which we are now discussing are clearly comparable to the well known rudimentary organs, which are often of great importance in understanding the phylogeny of the animal in which at some time of its development they are present. Such rudimentary structures are emblematic of parts which are perhaps only transient or, at most, imperfectly developed in the animal, but their presence shows that they were, at some past time, more highly developed and functional in ancestral stages.

It is thus perhaps permissible to speak of "rudimentary customs," in just the same way, and with just the same significance attached to them, in which we speak of "rudimentary organs" and we may recognise in them an abbreviated record of a stage passed through in the development of the customs of the tribe amongst which they are found.[55] Such rudimentary customs, like those which are associated with the Maypole for example, point back to a time when they were more highly developed than they are at present, and when the customs were more or less widely different from those now prevailing.

The origin of the marriage customs of the tribes now dealt with cannot possibly, so it seems to us, be explained as due either to a feeling of hospitality, or to the right of captors; nor can they be explained, as in certain cases the "jus primae noctis" can, as a right forcibly taken by the stronger from the weaker. There can be no reasonable doubt but that at one time the marriage arrangements of the Australian tribes were in a more primitive state than they are at the present day, and the customs with which we are dealing can be most simply explained as rudimentary ones serving, possibly in a very abbreviated way, to show the former existence of conditions which are no longer prevalent.

In regard to the marriage customs of the tribes now dealt with, we have the following facts. In the first place we have a group of women who are, what is called *Unawa*, to a group of men and *vice versa*, that is, all of these men and women are reciprocally marriageable. This, it may be observed, is not a matter of assumption but of actual fact. In the Arunta tribe for example a Panunga man will call the Purula whom he actually marries *Unawa*, but he has no name to distinguish her from all the other Purula women whom he does not actually marry, but any one of whom he might lawfully marry.[56] Further than this, while he has no actual right of access to any woman, except his own special *Unawa* woman or women, there are times, as, for example, during special ceremonies, or when he is visiting a distant group, when a woman is lent to him, but that woman must be one who is *Unawa* to him. In other words, we have individual marriage in which a man is limited in his choice to women of a particular group, each one of whom stands to him in the relationship of a possible wife, and with whom it is lawful for him, with the consent of her special *Unawa* man, to have marital relations. However hospitably inclined a man may feel, he will never lend his wife to a man who does not belong to a group of men to each of whom she stands in the relationship of *Unawa* or possible wife. A Panunga man may lend his wife to another Panunga, but for a man of any other class to have marital relations with her would be a gross offence.

In the second place, we have certain customs concerned with marriage which are of what we may call a transient nature. Taking the Kaitish tribe as an example, we find that, when marriage actually takes place, the operation of *Atna-ariltha-kuma* is performed by the elder sister of the woman, and that men of the following relationship have access to her in the order named: *Ipmunna*, that is individuals of the same moiety of the tribe as her own; mothers' brothers' sons; tribal elder and younger brothers; and lastly, men whom she might lawfully marry, but who have no right to her when once she becomes the property of a member of the group to which they belong. By referring to the tables already given, it will be seen that these men, if we take a particular example, say a Panunga woman, are Ungalla, Uknaria, Purula and Panunga. In other words, both men of her own, and of the moiety of the tribe to which she does not belong, have access to her, but only for a very limited time, and the same holds true in the case of all the tribes examined.

It will therefore be seen that (1) for a given time a woman has marital relations with men of both moieties of the tribe, and (2) that she may during her life, when once she has become the special wife of some individual man, have lawfully, but dependent always upon the consent of the latter, marital relations with any of the group of men to each and all of whom she stands in the relationship of *Unawa*.

These are the actual facts with which we have to deal, and the only possible explanation of them appears to us to lie along the following lines. We are here of course only dealing with those tribes in which descent is counted in the male line, the remaining tribe—the Urabunna—in which descent is counted in the female line, will be referred to subsequently. It appears to us that, in the present customs relating to marriage amongst this section of the Australian natives, we have clear evidence of three grades of development. We have (1) the present normal condition of individual marriage with the occasional existence of marital relations between the individual wife and other men of the same group as that to which her husband belongs, and the occasional existence also of still wider marital relations; (2) we have evidence of the existence at a prior time of actual group marriage; and (3) we have evidence of the existence at a still earlier time of still wider marital relations.

The evidence in favour of the hypothesis, that the present marriage system of such a tribe as the Arunta is based upon the former actual existence of group marriage, seems to us to be incontestable. The one most striking point in regard to marriage at the present day is that a man of one group is absolutely confined in his choice of a wife to women of a particular group, and that it is lawful for him to marry any woman of that group. When once he has secured a woman she is his private property, but he may, and often does, lend her to other men, but only if they belong to his own group. Further still, the natives have two distinct words to denote on the one hand surreptitious connection between a man and a woman who is not his own wife, but belongs to the proper group from which his wife comes, and, on the other hand, connection between a man and a woman belonging to forbidden groups. The first is called *Atna-nylkna*, the second is *Iturka*. In the face of the facts which have been brought forward, we see no possible explanation other than that the present system is derived from an earlier one in which the essential feature was actual group marriage.

When we turn to the Urabunna tribe we find the evidence still clearer. Here we have only two classes, *viz.*, Matthurie and Kirarawa. A Matthurie man marries a Kirarawa woman, and *vice versa*. There is no such thing as an individual wife. Every Matthurie man stands in the relationship of *Nupa* to a group of Kirarawa women, and they are, in the same way, *Nupa* to him. Every man has, or at least may have, one or more of these *Nupa* women allotted to him as wives, and to whom he has the first but not the exclusive right of access. To certain *Nupa* women other than his own wives he stands in the relationship of *Piraungaru*, and they to him. These *Piraungaru* are the wives of other men of his own group, just as his own wives are *Piraungaru* to some of the latter men, and we thus find in the Urabunna tribe that a group of women actually have marital relations with a group of men. Westermarck[57] has referred in his work to what he calls "the pretended group-marriages" of the Australians. In the case of the Urabunna there is no pretence of any kind, and exactly the same remark holds true of the neighbouring Dieri tribe.

The matter can be expressed clearly in the form of a diagram used by Mr. Fison in explaining the marriage system of the Dieri tribe:[58]

It must be remembered, of course, that any one woman may be *Piraungaru* to a larger number of men than the two who are represented in the diagram. The relation of *Piraungaru* is established between any woman and men to whom she is *Nupa*—that is, to whom she may be lawfully married by her *Nuthie* or elder brothers. If a group be camped together, and, as a matter of fact groups of individuals who are *Piraungaru* to one another do usually camp together, then in the case of F1, her special *Nupa* man M1 has the first right to her, but if he be absent then M2 and M3 have the right to her; or, if M1 be present, the two have the right to her subject to his consent, which is practically never withheld.

It is difficult to see how this system can be regarded otherwise than as an interesting stage in the transition from group to individual marriage. Each woman has one special individual who has the first right of access to her, but she has also a number of individuals of the same group who have a right to her either, if the first man be present, with his consent or, in his absence, without any restriction whatever.

In this tribe, just as in all the others, connection with women of the wrong group is a most serious offence, punishable by death or very severe treatment.

The evidence in favour of the third grade, that is the existence of wider marital relations than those indicated by the form of group marriage which has just been discussed, is naturally more indefinite and difficult to deal with. Westermarck, after having discussed at length the hypothesis of promiscuity, says:[59] "Having now examined all the groups of social phenomena adduced as evidence for the hypothesis of promiscuity, we have found that, in point of fact, they are no evidence. Not one of the customs alleged as relics of an ancient state of indiscriminate cohabitation of the sexes or 'communal marriage' presupposes the former existence of that state," and further on he says:[60] "It is not, of course, impossible that, among some people, intercourse between the sexes may have been almost promiscuous. But there is not a shred of genuine evidence for the notion that promiscuity ever formed a general stage in the social history of mankind."

It need scarcely be pointed out how totally opposed this conclusion of Mr. Westermarck's is to that arrived at by other workers, and we think there can be little doubt but that Mr. Westermarck is in error with regard to the question of group marriage amongst the Australian natives.

We are here simply concerned with the question as to whether there is any evidence in favour of the supposition that in former times there existed wider marital relations amongst the Australian natives than is indicated in the system of group marriage, the evidence in favour of which has been dealt with. If any were forthcoming, there can be little doubt but that, *a priori*, we should expect to find it in the nature of what we have called a rudimentary custom, such as might be met with at the actual time of marriage, that is, when a woman is handed over to become the possession of one man.

None of the hypotheses brought forward by Westermarck to explain the customs on this occasion can, we think, be considered as at all satisfactory in regard to those of the tribes with which we are dealing. The one striking feature of the marriage customs is that particular men representative of the woman's own moiety, and of the half of the tribe to which she does not belong, have access to her, and always in a particular order, according to which those who, in the present state of the tribe, have lawfully the right to her come last.

These customs, together with the one already dealt with, referring to a general intercourse during the performance of certain corrobborees are, it appears to us, only capable of any satisfactory explanation on the hypothesis that they indicate the temporary recognition of certain general rights which existed in the time prior to that of the form of group marriage of which we have such clear traces yet lingering amongst the tribes. We do not mean that they afford direct evidence of the former existence of actual promiscuity, but they do afford evidence leading in that direction, and they certainly point back to a time when there existed wider marital relations than obtain at the present day—wider, in fact, than those which are shown in the form of group marriage from which the present system is derived. On no other hypothesis yet advanced do the customs connected with marriage, which are so consistent in their general nature and leading features from tribe to tribe, appear to us to be capable of satisfactory explanation.

Chapter IV

The Totems

Every individual is born into some totem—Variations in the significance of the totems in different parts of Australia—Totems of the Urabunna tribe—The child takes the mother's totem—Totems of the Arunta tribe—No relationship of necessity between the totem name of the child and that of the father and mother—Marriage not regulated by totem—Examples of totem names as they exist in particular families—Though differing much from one another in many points, there is a fundamental unity in customs, sufficient to indicate the origin of all Australian tribes from ancestors who practised certain customs which have been developed along different lines in different localities—Ceremonies of the Engwura serving to show the way in which each individual acquires his or her totemic name—The Alcheringa times—The ancestral members of certain totemic groups restricted wholly, or almost so, to members of one moiety of the tribe—The wanderings of certain groups of Alcheringa ancestors, each of whom carried one or more sacred Churinga, with each of which is associated the spirit part of an individual—Where the Churinga are deposited there local totem centres are formed, the native name of which is *Oknanikilla*—Each *Oknanikilla* is associated with one totem, and when a child is born it is one of the spirit individuals resident at a particular spot which goes inside a woman, and therefore its totem is the totem of the spirits associated with that spot—Examples of how a child gets its totemic name—Totem never changes, but the class may—The totems are local in their distribution.

EVERY individual of the tribes with which we are dealing is born into some totem—that is, he or she belongs to a group of persons each one of whom bears the name of, and is especially associated with, some natural object. The latter is usually an animal or plant; but in addition to those of living things, there are also such totem names as wind, sun, water, or cloud—in fact there is scarcely an object, animate or inanimate, to be found in the country occupied by the natives which does not gives its name to some totemic group of individuals.

Much has been written with regard to the totems of the Australian natives since the time when Grey first described them under the name of Kobong, which, it must be remarked, is only of local application in certain parts of the west, the word being entirely unknown over the greater part of the continent. As might have been expected, when we take into account the vast area of land over which the Australian tribes are spread, and the isolation by physical barriers of those occupying the Central area from the tribes living on the east and west, there have arisen, in respect to the totemic system, variations of so important a character that it is by no means possible to describe that which is found in any one tribe or group of tribes and regard it as typical of Australian natives generally. The Arunta, Ilpirra and Luritcha tribes, and there is little doubt but that the same holds true of other tribes to the north, such as the Waagai, Iliaura, Bingongina, Walpari, and Warramunga, differ in important respects from the tribes which either now do, or formerly did, inhabit the east and south-eastern parts of the continent, and to whom nearly all our knowledge of totems in Australia has been confined. Between these central and the southern and south-eastern tribes a sharp line can be drawn, so far as their totemic systems are concerned; indeed it looks very much as if somewhere a little to the north-west of Lake Eyre we had a meeting-place of two sets of tribes, which migrated southwards, following roughly parallel courses, one across the centre of the continent, while the other followed down the course of the main streams on the east, and then turned slightly northward on the west side of Lake Eyre; or, possibly, in their southern wanderings, part of this eastern group spread round the north, and part round the south end of the lake (Fig. 1).

We find, so far as their organisation is concerned, a sharply marked line of difference between the Urabunna tribe, the members of which are spread over the country which lies to the west and north-west of Lake Eyre, and the Arunta tribe, which adjoins their northern boundary. The Urabunna tribe is associated with the migration along the eastern side, while the Arunta is the most southern of the Central tribes.

In the Urabunna and the adjoining Dieri tribe, as well as in those which spread northwards on the east side of Lake Eyre towards the borders of Queensland, and in others who lived along the shores of Spencer Gulf and along the southern coast, we find that descent is counted in the female line. In the Urabunna, for example, we find that all the members of the tribe are divided into two classes, which are called respectively Matthurie and Kirarawa, and each of these again contains a certain number of totems, or, as the natives call them, *Thunthunie*. The same totem name is only to be found in one or other of the two classes, but not in both. Thus, for example, among the Matthurie we find the following totems—Inyarrie (wild duck), Wutnimmera (green cicada), Matla (dingo), Waragutie (emu), Kalathura (wild turkey), Guti (black swan); whilst amongst the Kirarawa are such totems as Kurara (cloud), Wabma (carpet snake), Kapirie (lace lizard), Urantha (pelican), Kutnichilie (water-hen), Wakala (crow).[61]

Now not only must a Matthurie man take as wife a Kirarawa woman, but he must only take one of some particular totem.[62] Thus a wild duck Matthurie man marries a snake Kirarawa woman, a cicada marries a crow, a dingo a water-hen, an emu a rat, a wild turkey a cloud, and a swan a pelican. Every child, male or female, of a wild duck Matthurie man belongs to the class Kirarawa, and to the totem snake to which his mother belonged. Thus in every family the father belongs to one class and totem, while the mother and all the children belong to another. We have already dealt at length with certain aspects of the social organisation of the Urabunna tribe, and enough has now been said to show that it is a typical example of one of the many Australian tribes in which the totem of the child is simply determined by that of the mother.

Passing northwards from the Urabunna into the Arunta tribe, we are brought into contact with a very different organisation, but with one which, in regard to the class names, is typical of tribes which occupy an area extending north and south for some 800 miles, and east and west for perhaps between 200 and 300. We find also essentially the same system in tribes inhabiting other parts of Australia, such as the Turribul, living on the Maryborough river in Queensland.[63] Without entering here into details, which will be fully explained subsequently, we may say that, so far as the class is concerned, descent is counted in the male line. The totem names are, however, at first sight decidedly perplexing. Just as in the Urabunna tribe, every individual has his or her totem name. In the first place, however, no one totem is confined to the members of a particulars class or subclass; in the second place the child's totem will sometimes be found to be the same as that of the father, sometimes the same as that of the mother, and not infrequently it will be different from that of either parent; and in the third place there is no definite relationship between the totem of the father and mother, such as exists in the Urabunna and many other Australian tribes—in fact perhaps in the majority of the latter. You may, for example, examine at first a family in which the father is a witchetty grub and the mother a wild cat, and you may find, supposing there be two children, that they are both witchetty grubs. In the next family examined perhaps both parents will be witchetty grubs, and of two children one may belong to the same totem, and the other may be an emu; another family will show the father to be, say, an emu, the mother a plum-tree, and of their children one may be a witchetty grub, another a lizard, and so on, the totem names being apparently mixed up in the greatest confusion possible.

We give below the actual totem names of five families, selected at random, who are now living in the northern section of the Arunta tribe, and these may be taken as accurately representative of the totem names found in various families throughout the tribe. After making very numerous and as careful inquiries as possible, always directly from the natives concerned, we can say that every family shows the same features as these particular examples do with regard to the totems, the names of the latter varying, of course, from family to family and in different parts of the country, certain totems predominating in some, and others in other parts. You may, for example, find yourself in one district of more or less limited area and find one totem largely represented; travelling out of that district, you may meet but rarely with that particular totem until you come into another and perhaps distant part, where—it may be 40 or 50 miles away—it again becomes the principal one. The reason for, or rather the explanation of, this curious local distribution of totem names, as given by the natives, will be seen presently.

Family 1. Father, little hawk. Wife No. 1, rat; daughter, witchetty grub. Wife No. 2, kangaroo; no children. Wife No. 3, lizard; two daughters, one emu, the other water.

Family 2. Father, eagle-hawk. Wife No. 1, Hakea flower; no children. Wife No. 2, Hakea flower; four sons, who are respectively witchetty grub, emu, eagle-hawk, elonka; two daughters, both witchetty grubs.

Family 3. Father, witchetty grub. Wife No. 1, lizard; two sons, one lizard, the other witchetty grub. Wife No. 2, lizard.

Family 4. Father, emu. Wife, munyeru; two sons, one kangaroo, the other, wild cat; one daughter, lizard.

Family 5. Father, witchetty grub. Wife, witchetty grub; two sons, one, kangaroo, the other, witchetty grub; one daughter, witchetty grub.

Taking these as typical examples of what is found throughout the whole tribe, we can see that while, as already stated, marriages are strictly regulated by class rules, the question of totem has nothing to do with the matter either so far as making it obligatory for a man of one totem to marry a woman of another particular one, or so far as the totem of the children is concerned. The totem name of the child does not of necessity follow either that of the father or that of the mother, but it may correspond to one or both of them. Whether there ever was a time when, in the Arunta and other neighbouring tribes, marriage was regulated by totem it is difficult to say. At the present day it is not, nor can we find any evidence in the full and numerous traditions relating to the doings of their supposed ancestors which affords indications of a time when, as in the Urabunna tribe, a man might only marry a woman of a totem different from his own. In their curious totem regulations, the Arunta and Ilpirra tribes agree, as we know from personal observation, while we have reason to believe that large and important tribes living to the north of them—*viz*. the Kaitish, Warramunga, Waagai, Iliaura, Bingongina and Walpari—are in accord with them on all important points. The difference in this respect between the tribes whose customs and organisation are now described, and those of other tribes which have been dealt with by able and careful investigators, such as Grey, Fison, Howitt, Roth and others, will serve to show that various tribes and groups of tribes, starting doubtless from a common basis, but isolated from one another during long periods of time by physical barriers, have developed along different lines. Except, perhaps, in the extreme north and north-east, Australia has had for long ages no intercourse with outside peoples, and such as it has had has only affected a very small and insignificant coastal fringe of the continent, and even there the influence has been but very slight. What we have to deal with is a great continental area, peopled most probably by men who entered from the north and brought with them certain customs. We are not here concerned with the difficult question of exactly where the ancestors of the present Australian natives came from. The most striking fact in regard to them at the present day is that over the whole continent, so far as is known, we can detect a community of customs and social organisation sufficient to show that all the tribes inhabiting various parts are the offspring of ancestors who, prior to their migrating in various directions across the continent, and thus giving rise to groups separated to a great extent from one another by physical barriers, already practised certain customs and had the germs of an organisation which has been developed along different lines in different localities.

The class and totem systems, variously modified as we now find them in different tribes, can only be adequately accounted for on the hypothesis that, when the ancestors of the present natives reached the country, they spread over it in various directions, separated into local groups, and developed, without the stimulus derived from contact with outside peoples, along various lines, each group retaining features in its customs and organisation such as can only be explained by supposing them all to have had a common ancestry.[64]

However, to return to the totems of the Arunta. It was while watching and questioning closely the natives during the performance of the Engwura ceremony—a description of which will be found in a later chapter—that we were able to find out the way in which the totem names of the individuals originate and to gain an insight into the true nature of their totemic system.

The Engwura ceremony, which forms the last of the initiatory rites through which the Arunta native must pass before he becomes what is called *Urliara*, or a fully developed native, admitted to all the most sacred secrets of the tribe, consisted in reality of a long series of ceremonies, the enacting of which occupied in all more than four months. Those with which we are here concerned were a large number, between sixty and seventy altogether, which were connected with the totems and were performed under the direction of the old men, who instructed the younger men both how to perform them and what they represented.

The native name for these ceremonies is Quabara,[65] and each one is known as a Quabara of a certain totem associated with a particular spot. Thus we have, for example, the Quabara Unjiamba of Ooraminna, which means a ceremony of the Unjiamba or Hakea flower totem of a place called Ooraminna; the Quabara Achilpa of Urapitchera, which means a ceremony of the wild cat (a species of *Dasyurus*) totem of a place called Urapitchera on the Finke River; the Quabara Okira of Idracowra, which means a ceremony of the kangaroo totem of a place called Idracowra on the Finke River, or, to speak more correctly, of a special spot marked by the presence of a great upstanding column of sandstone, called by white men Chamber's pillar, of the native name for which, Idracowra is a corruption; the Quabara Unchichera of Imanda, which means a ceremony of the frog totem of a spot called by the natives Imanda, and by the white men Bad Crossing on the Hugh River. Each ceremony was thus concerned with a special totem, and not only this, but with a special division of a totem belonging to a definite locality, and, further, each ceremony was frequently, but by no means always, in the possession of, and presided over by, an old man of the totem and locality with which it was concerned. It will shortly be seen that the totems are strictly local, but that we have what may be called local centres of any one totem in various districts of the wide area over which the Arunta tribe is scattered. For our present purpose, which is the explanation of the way in which each individual gets his or her totemic name, the following general account will suffice.

The whole past history of the tribe may be said to be bound up with these totemic ceremonies, each of which is concerned with the doings of certain mythical ancestors who are supposed to have lived in the dim past, to which the natives give the name of the "Alcheringa."

In the Alcheringa lived ancestors who, in the native mind, are so intimately associated with the animals or plants the name of which they bear that an Alcheringa man of, say, the kangaroo totem may sometimes be spoken of either as a man-kangaroo or as a kangaroo-man. The identity of the human individual is often sunk in that of the animal or plant from which he is supposed to have originated. It is useless to try and get further back than the Alcheringa; the history of the tribe as known to the natives commences then.

Going back to this far-away time, we find ourselves in the midst of semi-human creatures endowed with powers not possessed by their living descendants and inhabiting the same country which is now inhabited by the tribe, but which was then devoid of many of its most marked features, the origin of which, such as the gaps and gorges in the Macdonnell Ranges, is attributed to these mythical Alcheringa ancestors.

These Alcheringa men and woman are represented in tradition as collected together in companies, each of which consisted of a certain number of individuals belonging to one particular totem. Thus, for example, the ceremonies of the Engwura dealt with four separate groups of Achilpa or wild cat men.

Whilst every now and then we come across traditions, according to which, as in the case of the Achilpa, the totem is common to all classes, we always find that in each totem one moiety[66] of the tribe predominates, and that, according to tradition, many of the groups of ancestral individuals consisted originally of men or women or of both men and women who all belonged to one moiety. Thus in the case of certain Okira or kangaroo groups we find only Kumara and Purula; in certain Udnirringita or witchetty grub groups we find only Bulthara and Panunga; in certain Achilpa or wild cat a predominance of Kumara and Purula, with a smaller number of Bulthara and Panunga.

At the present day no totem is confined to either moiety of the tribe, but in each local centre we always find a great predominance of one moiety, as for example at Alice Springs, the most important centre of the witchetty grubs, where, amongst forty individuals, thirty-five belong to the Bulthara and Panunga, and five only to the other moiety of the tribe.

These traditions with regard to the way in which the Alcheringa ancestors were distributed into companies, the members of which bore the same totem name and belonged, as a general rule, to the same moiety of the tribe, are of considerable importance when we come to consider the conditions which now obtain with regard to totems. It is not without importance to notice that the traditions of the tribe point back to a time when, for the most part, the members of any particular totem were confined to one moiety of the tribe, in face of the fact that at the present day it seems to be a characteristic feature of many tribes—such as the Urabunna, which are in a less highly developed state than the Arunta, Ilpirra and certain other tribes of Central Australia—that the totems are strictly confined to one or other of the two moieties of the tribe, and that they regulate marriage. At the same time it may again be pointed out that the totems in no way regulate marriage in the tribes mentioned, and, further still, we can find no evidence in any of the traditions, numerous and detailed as they are, of a time when marriage in these tribes was ever regulated by the totems.

If now we turn to the traditions and examine those relating to certain totems which may be taken as illustrative of the whole series, we find that they are concerned almost entirely with the way in which what we may call the Alcheringa members of the various totems came to be located in various spots scattered over the country now occupied by the tribe the members of which are regarded as their descendants, or, to speak more precisely, as their reincarnations. We will take as examples the following totems—Achilpa or wild cat, Unjiamba or Hakea flower, Unchichera or frog, and Udnirringita or witchetty grub.[67]

In the Alcheringa there appear to have been four companies of wild cat men and women who, tradition says, appeared first in the southern part of the country. It has been already pointed out that, in the native mind, the ideas of the human and animal nature of these individuals are very closely associated together. Starting from the south out to the east of Charlotte Waters, one of these companies, consisting in this case of Bulthara and Panunga individuals, marched northwards, keeping as they did so considerably to the east of the River Finke. A second and larger party, consisting of Purula and Kumara individuals, came from the south-west and, at a place not far from Henbury on the Finke River, divided into two parties. One of them crossed the Finke and went on northwards to the Macdonnell Ranges, which were traversed a little to the east of Alice Springs, and then passed on northwards. The other half, forming the third party, followed up the Finke for some distance, crossing it at a spot now called Running Waters, after which the Macdonnell Ranges were traversed some twenty or twenty-five miles to the west of Alice Springs, and then the party passed on to the north in the direction of Central Mount Stuart. The fourth party, consisting of Purula and Kumara individuals, started from far away to the south-east, and travelled northwards, crossing the Range at Mount Sonder, and continued its course northwards, so says tradition, until it reached the country of the salt water.

The principal traditions with regard to the Unjiamba or Hakea flower totem refer to the wanderings of certain women. In one account, two women of this totem are described as coming from a place about 35 miles to the north of Alice Springs, where they had a sacred pole or *Nurtunja*.[68] Starting southwards, they travelled first of all underground, and came out at a place called Arapera. Here they spent their time eating Unjiamba. Then leaving here they took their sacred pole or *Nurtunja* to pieces and travelled further on until they came to Ooraminna, in the Macdonnell Ranges, where there is a special water-hole close beside which they sat down and died, and two great stones arose to mark the exact spot where they died. In their journey these two women followed close by the track taken by one of the Achilpa parties, but did not actually come into contact with the latter, which was travelling in the opposite direction.

In addition to these traditions of the wanderings of various companies of men and women belonging to different totems, we meet with others which refer to the origin of special individuals, or groups of individuals, who did not wander about but lived and died where they sprang up. Thus, for example, an Inarlinga or "porcupine" (Echidna) man is supposed to have arisen near to Stuart's waterhole on the Hugh River, while at the Emily Gap, near to Alice Springs, tradition says that certain witchetty grubs became transformed into witchetty men, who formed a strong group here, and who were afterwards joined by others of the same totem, who marched over the country to the Gap.

Each of these Alcheringa ancestors is represented as carrying about with him, or her, one or more of the sacred stones, which are called by the Arunta natives Churinga,[69] and each of these Churinga is intimately associated with the idea of the spirit part of some individual. Either where they originated and stayed, as in the case of certain of the witchetty grub people, or else where, during their wanderings, they camped for a time, there were formed what the natives call *Oknanikilla*, each one of which is in reality a local totem centre. At each of these spots, and they are all well known to the old men, who pass the knowledge on from generation to generation, a certain number of the Alcheringa ancestors went into the ground, each one carrying his Churinga with him. His body died, but some natural feature, such as a rock or tree, arose to mark the spot, while his spirit part remained in the Churinga. At the same time many of the Churinga which they carried with them, and each one of which had associated with it a spirit individual, were placed in the ground, some natural object again marking the spot. The result is that, as we follow their wanderings, we find that the whole country is dotted over with *Oknanikilla*, or local totem centres, at each of which are deposited a number of Churinga, with spirit individuals associated with them. Each *Oknanikilla* is, of course, connected with one totem. In one part we have a definite locality, with its group of wild cat spirit individuals; in another, a group of emu; in another, a group of frog, and so on through the various totems; and it is this idea of spirit individuals associated with Churinga and resident in certain definite spots that lies at the root of the present totemic system of the Arunta tribe.

As we have said, the exact spot at which a Churinga was deposited was always marked by some natural object, such as a tree or rock, and in this the spirit is supposed to especially take up its abode, and it is called the spirit's *Nanja*.[70]

We may take the following as a typical example of how each man and woman gains a totem name. Close to Alice Springs is a large and important witchetty grub totem centre or

Oknanikilla. Here there were deposited in the Alcheringa a large number of Churinga carried by witchetty grub men and women. A large number of prominent rocks and boulders and certain ancient gum-trees along the sides of a picturesque gap in the ranges, are the *Nanja* trees and rocks of these spirits, which, so long as they remain in spirit form, they usually frequent. If a woman conceives a child after having been near to this gap, it is one of these spirit individuals which has entered her body, and therefore, quite irrespective of what the mother's or father's totem may chance to be, that child, when born, must of necessity be of the witchetty grub totem; it is, in fact, nothing else but the reincarnation of one of the witchetty grub people of the Alcheringa. Suppose, for example, to take a particular and actual instance, an emu woman from another locality comes to Alice Springs, and whilst there becomes aware that she has conceived a child, and then returns to her own locality before the child is born, that child, though it may be born in an emu locality, is an Udnirringita or witchetty grub. It must be, the natives say, because it entered the mother at Alice Springs, where there are only witchetty grub spirit individuals. Had it entered her body within the limits of her own emu locality, it would as inevitably have been an emu. To take another example, quite recently the lubra or wife of a witchetty grub man, she belonging to the same totem, conceived a child while on a visit to a neighbouring Quatcha or water locality, which lies away to the east of Alice Springs, that child's totem is water; or, again, an Alice Springs woman, when asked by us as to why her child was a witchetty grub (in this instance belonging to the same totem as both of its parents), told us that one day she was taking a drink of water near to the gap in the Ranges where the spirits dwell when suddenly she heard a child's voice crying out, "*Mia, mia!*"—the native term for relationship which includes that of mother. Not being anxious to have a child, she ran away as fast as she could, but to no purpose; she was fat and well favoured, and such women the spirit children prefer; one of them had gone inside her, and of course it was born a witchetty grub.⁷¹

The natives are quite clear upon this point. The spirit children are supposed to have a strong predilection for fat women, and prefer to choose such for their mothers, even at the risk of being born into the wrong class. We are acquainted with special, but somewhat rare cases, in which a living man is regarded as the reincarnation of an Alcheringa ancestor whose class was not the same as that of his living representative. At Alice Springs there is a man who is an Uknaria belonging to the lizard totem, and is regarded as the reincarnation of a celebrated Purula lizard man of the Alcheringa. The spirit child deliberately, so the natives say, chose to go into a Kumara instead of into a Bulthara woman, and so the man was born Uknaria instead of Purula. Though the class was changed, the totem could not possibly be.

Such examples could be multiplied indefinitely; but these, which may be taken as typical ones, will serve to show that, though at first sight puzzling, yet in reality the totem name follows a very definite system, if once we grant the premises firmly believed in by the Arunta native.

One point of some interest is brought out by this inquiry into the origin of the totem names, and that is that, though the great majority of any one totem belong to one moiety of the tribe, yet there may be, and in fact always are, a certain number of members who belong to the other moiety. Just as in the Alcheringa, all the witchetty grub men were Bulthara and Panunga, so at the present day are the great majority of their descendants who inhabit the local areas in which the mythical ancestors formed witchetty totem centres. So, in the same way, all the Alcheringa emu ancestors were Purula and Kumara, as now are the great majority of their descendants, but, owing to the system according to which totem names are acquired, it is always possible for a man to be, say, a Purula or a Kumara and yet a witchetty, or, on the other hand, a Bulthara or a Panunga, and yet an emu.

Two things are essential—first a child must belong to the totem of the spot at which the mother believes that it was conceived, and, second, it must belong to the moiety of the tribe to which its father belongs. Its totem never changes, but its class may. Once born into a totem, no matter what his class may be, a man, when initiated, may witness and take part in all the sacred ceremonies connected with the totem, but, unless he belong to the predominant moiety, he will never, or only in extremely rare cases, become the head man or Alatunja of any local group of the totem. His only chance of becoming Alatunja is by the death of every member of the group who belongs to the moiety to which the Alcheringa men belonged.

What has gone before will serve to show what we mean by speaking of the totems as being local in their distribution. The whole district occupied by the Arunta, and the same holds true of the Ilpirra and Kaitish tribes, can be mapped out into a large number of areas of various sizes, some of which are actually only a few square yards in extent, while others occupy many square miles, and each of which centres in one or more spots, for which the native name is *Oknanikilla*—a term which may be best rendered by the phrase "local totem centre." Each of these represents a spot where Alcheringa ancestors either originated or where they camped during their wanderings, and where some of them went down into the ground with their Churinga, or where they deposited Churinga. In any case the Churinga remained there, each one associated with a spirit individual, and from these have sprung, and still continue to spring, actual men and women who of necessity bear the totem name of the Churinga from which they come.

We shall, later on, deal in greater detail with the traditions which are concerned with the wanderings of the ancestors of the local totem groups, and also with certain points of importance, such as the various ceremonies connected with the totems and the relationship existing between the individual and his totem. It will be evident from the general account already given that the totemic system of the Arunta and other Central Australian tribes differs in important respects from those of other tribes which have hitherto been described. It is based upon the idea of the reincarnation of Alcheringa ancestors, who were the actual transformations of animals and plants, or of such inanimate objects as clouds or water, fire, wind, sun, moon and stars. To the Australian native there is no difficulty in the assumption that an animal or a plant could be transformed directly into a human being, or that the spirit part which he supposes it to possess, just as he does in his own case, could remain, on the death of the animal, associated with such an object as a Churinga, and at some future time arise in the form of a human being.

The account which the Arunta native gives of the origin of the totemic names of the various members of the tribe is to him a perfectly feasible one. What gave rise in the first instance to the association of particular men with particular animals and plants it does not seem possible to say. The Arunta man accounts for it by creating a series of myths, according to which he is the direct descendant of the animal or plant, and weaves in and around these myths details of the most circumstantial nature.

We shall have to return to the question of the totems after certain of these myths of the Alcheringa have been related; meanwhile it may be said that, though different in certain respects from that of other Australian tribes, yet the totemic system of the Arunta shows us the one essential feature common to all totemic systems, and that is the intimate association between the individual and the material object, the name of which he bears.

Chapter V

The Churinga or Bull Roarers of the Arunta and Other Tribes

General description of Churinga—Mystery attached to their use—Finding of the Churinga when the child is born—The *Nanja* tree or stone—Relationship between an individual and his *Nanja*—The *Ertnatulunga* or sacred storehouse; its sanctity—The earliest rudiment of the idea of a city of refuge—The spirit part placed in the Churinga undergoes reincarnation—The Tundun in the case of the Jeraeil of the Kurnai tribe is associated with a great ancestor—No association between the spirit part of the living man and his Churinga, but between the *Arumburinga*, the spirit double of the man, and the Churinga—The giving of a sacred or Churinga name—Reticence with regard to secret names—The showing of his *Churinga Nanja* to a man—Examination of the Churinga at the *Ertnatulunga*—Ceremony concerned with telling a man his Churinga name—Exact contents of an *Ertnatulunga*—The term "message-stick" misleading as applied to the Churinga—Descriptions of particular Churinga, and explanation of the designs upon them—Resemblance between the initiation rites and Churinga of the Central tribes and those of Central Queensland, described by Mr. Roth—Absence of stone Churinga amongst southern groups—Ownership of the Churinga—Extinction and subsequent resuscitation of a local totemic group—The Churinga taken charge of by another group—Examples of extinction of local totemic groups—The Churinga are under the charge of the Alatunja—Inheritance of Churinga of men and women—Various forms of Churinga—The Churinga of the Kaitish and Waagai tribes—The borrowing and returning of Churinga; ceremonies attendant upon the same.

CHURINGA is the name given by the Arunta natives to certain sacred objects which, on penalty of death or very severe punishment, such as blinding by means of a fire-stick, are never allowed to be seen by women or uninitiated men. The term is applied, as we shall see later, to various objects associated with the totems, but of these the greater number belong to that class of rounded, oval or elongate, flattened stones and slabs of wood of very various sizes, to the smaller ones of which the name of bull-roarer is commonly applied.

The importance and use of these in various ceremonies such as those attendant upon initiation of the young men, was first shown in Australia by Messrs. Howitt and Fison, and since then they have been repeatedly referred to by other writers.

Amongst the aborigines of the Centre, as indeed everywhere else where they are found, considerable mystery is attached to their use—a mystery which has probably had a large part of its origin in the desire of the men to impress the women of the tribe with an idea of the supremacy and superior power of the male sex. From time immemorial myths and superstitions have grown up around them, until now it is difficult to say how far each individual believes in what, if the expression may be allowed, he must know to be more or less of a fraud, but in which he implicitly thinks that the other natives believe.

Whilst living in close intercourse with the natives, spending the days and nights amongst them in their camps while they were preparing for and then enacting their most sacred ceremonies, and talking to them day after day, collectively and individually, we were constantly impressed with the idea, as probably many others have been before, that one blackfellow will often tell you that he can and does do something magical, whilst all the time he is perfectly well aware that he cannot, and yet firmly believes that some other man can really do it. In order that his fellows may not be considered in this respect as superior to himself he is obliged to resort to what is really a fraud, but in course of time he may even come to lose sight of the fact that it is a fraud which he is practising upon himself and his fellows. At all events, and especially in connection with the Churinga, there are amongst the Australian natives beliefs which can have had no origin in fact, but which have gradually grown up until now they are implicitly held. It is necessary to realise this aspect of the native mind in order to understand the influence which some of their oldest and most sacred beliefs and customs have upon their lives.

We may say at once that the Churinga are one and all connected with the totems, and that the word signifies a sacred object, sacred because it is thus associated with the totems and may never be seen except upon very rare occasions, and then only in the distance and indistinctly by women and uninitiated men.

In the last chapter we described the association between men of the Alcheringa and their Churinga. We saw that each spirit individual was closely bound up with his Churinga, which he carried with him as he wandered about his ancestral home, the *Oknanikilla*, or rested on the *Nanja* tree or stone which he is supposed especially to frequent.

The tradition of the natives is that when the spirit child goes inside a woman the Churinga is dropped. When the child is born the mother tells the father the position of the tree or rock near to which she supposes the child to have entered her, and he, together with one or two of the older men, who are close relatives of the man, and of whom the father of the latter is usually one, and also an elder brother of the father, goes to the locality, at once if it be near at hand, or when opportunity offers if it be distant, and searches for the dropped Churinga. The latter is usually, but not always, supposed to be a stone one marked with a device peculiar to the totem of the spirit child and therefore of the newly-born one. Sometimes it is found, sometimes it is not. In the former case, which is stated to occur often, we must suppose that some old man—it is most often the *Arunga* or paternal grandfather who finds it—has provided himself with one for the occasion, which is quite possible, as Churinga belonging to their own totem are not infrequently carried about by the old men, who obtain them from the sacred storehouse in which they are kept. We questioned native after native on this subject—some of them had actually found such stones—but there was no shaking them in the firm belief that such a Churinga was always dropped by the spirit child whether it was found or not. If it cannot be found then they proceed to make a wooden one from the Mulga or other hard wood tree nearest to the *Nanja*, and to carve on it some device or brand peculiar to the totem.

Ever afterwards the *Nanja* tree or stone of the spirit is the *Nanja* of the child, and the Churinga is its *Churinga nanja*.

As might have been expected, there is a definite relationship supposed to exist between an individual and his *Nanja* tree or stone. Whilst the belief is by no means general at the present time, there is at least one definite case known to us in which a blackfellow earnestly requested a white man not to cut down a particular tree because it was his *Nanja* tree, and he feared that if cut down some evil would befall him. Very possibly in times past this feeling was more widely prevalent than it is now. At the present time the special association between a man and his *Nanja* tree lies in the fact that every animal upon that tree is *ekirinja* or tabu to him. If an opossum or a bird be in the tree it is sacred and must not on any account be touched. There is no special ceremony performed by the individual in reference to his *Nanja* tree, but it is one in which he is supposed to have a special interest as having been the home of the spirit whose reincarnation he is.

In each *Oknanikilla* or local totem centre, there is a spot called by the natives the *Ertnatulunga*. This is, in reality, a sacred storehouse, which usually has the form of a small cave or crevice in some unfrequented spot amongst the rough hills and ranges which abound in the area occupied by the tribe. The entrance is carefully blocked up with stones so naturally arranged as not to arouse suspicion of the fact that they conceal from view the most sacred possessions of the tribe. In this, often carefully tied up in bundles, are numbers of the Churinga, and in one or other of these storehouses every member of the tribe, men and women alike, is represented by his or her *Churinga nanja*. When, after the birth of a child, one of the latter is found, or made, it is handed over to the headman of the local totem group within the district occupied by which the child was conceived, and is by him deposited in the *Ertnatulunga*.

The spot at which the child was born and brought up, and at which it will spend probably the greater part of its life, has nothing whatever to do with determining the resting place of the *Churinga nanja*. That goes naturally to the storehouse of the locality from which the spirit child came—that is to the spot where the Churinga was deposited in the Alcheringa. In the case, for example, which has already been quoted, in which a witchetty woman conceived a child in an emu locality, twelve miles to the north of Alice Springs, the latter place being the woman's home, the child was born at the latter and lives there, but the *Churinga nanja* was found at the place of conception and is now deposited in the store-house of that group.

So far as the possession of *Churinga nanja* is concerned, men and women are alike, each possesses one or, as will be seen later, very rarely more than one. Whilst, however, there comes a time when each man is allowed to see and handle his, the women not only may never see them but, except in the case of the very old women, they are unaware of the existence of any such objects. Into the mysteries of the *Ertnatulunga* and its contents no woman dare pry at risk of death. The position of the *Ertnatulunga*—not their exact position, but their locality—is known to the women, who are obliged to go long distances round in order to avoid going anywhere near to them. One of these storehouses was on the side of a deep gap which, for several miles in either direction, is the only way of passing through the ranges which lie to the south of Alice Springs, and, until the advent of the white man, no woman was ever allowed to walk through the gap, but, if she wished to traverse the ranges, she had to climb the steep declivities in order to pass across, and this also at some distance from the gap. Even at the present day, unless in the company of a white man, she carefully avoids the side on which lies the cleft which serves as a store-house for Churinga, and it is only the presence of white men in this locality which has resulted in women being allowed to walk through the gap.

The immediate surroundings of one of these *Ertnatulunga* is a kind of haven of refuge for wild animals; once they come close to one of these they are safe, because any animal—emu or kangaroo or wallaby—which, when pursued, ran by instinct or by chance towards the *Ertnatulunga* was, when once it came close to it, tabu and safe from the spear of the pursuing native. Even the plants in the immediate vicinity of the spot are never touched or interfered with in any way.

The sanctity of the *Ertnatulunga* may be understood when it is remembered that it contains the Churinga, which are associated not only with the living members of the tribe, but also with the dead ones. Indeed, many of the Churinga are those of special men of the Alcheringa, who, as tradition relates, wandered about and descended at these spots into the earth where their Churinga, the very ones which are now within the storehouse, remained associated with their spirit part. Each Churinga is so closely bound up with the spirit individual that it is regarded as its representative in the *Ertnatulunga*, and those of dead men are supposed to be endowed with the attributes of their owner and to actually impart these to the person who, for the time being, may, as when a fight takes place, be fortunate enough to carry it about with him.[72] The Churinga is supposed to endow the possessor with courage and accuracy of aim, and also to deprive his opponent of these qualities. So firm is their belief in this that if two men were fighting and one of them knew that the other carried a Churinga whilst he did not, he would certainly lose heart at once and without doubt be beaten.

The *Ertnatulunga* may be regarded as the early rudiment of a city or house of refuge. Everything in its immediate vicinity is sacred and must on no account be hurt; a man who was being pursued by others would not be touched so long as he remained at this spot. During the Engwura ceremony, when temporary storehouses were made to hold the large number of Churinga which were brought in to the ceremonial ground, and when, as always happens when men from different parts are assembled in large number, there arose any small quarrel, no display of arms was allowed anywhere near to the stores of Churinga. If the men wanted to quarrel they had to go right away from the Churinga stores.

The loss of Churinga is the most serious evil which could befall a group, but, though it might have been expected that stealing them would have been resorted to in times of fighting between different groups, yet this does not seem to take place. This is probably to be accounted for in various ways. In the first place the exact spot, which is under the charge primarily of the headman of the group and of the older men associated with him, is only known to the initiated men of the group, all of whom are equally and deeply interested in keeping the secret. Beyond this any interference by a stranger would surely result sooner or later in the death of the latter. The knowledge also that retaliation of a similar kind would inevitably follow must have acted as a strong deterrent on any individual or group who was at all anxious to interfere with other peoples' Churinga. Whatever the reasons for it may be the fact remains that on the very few occasions on which we could find out that the *Ertnatulunga* had been robbed the aggressors were white men. On each occasion also the natives have attempted to kill the member of the tribe who had shown the spot to the white men, and would certainly have been successful in so doing but for the protection afforded to the guide by the latter. In the case of the removal of the Churinga from one of these *Ertnatulunga*, the men of the group to which they belonged stayed in camp for two weeks weeping and mourning over their loss and plastering themselves over with white pipeclay, the emblem of mourning for the dead.

Whilst, on the one hand, the Churinga seem to be safe from robbers, so far as the natives are concerned, on the other hand, as we shall see shortly, they are occasionally lent as an act of courtesy by one group to another friendly group.

We have already said that the original Churinga—that is those of the Alcheringa, with regard to the origin of which the natives have no tradition—are all, or at least the great majority of them, supposed to have been of stone. What was the origin of these we have been unable to determine; they were present in the Alcheringa, and behind that it is impossible to penetrate. Once we ventured to inquire whether there was no story relating how the Alcheringa men came to have them, but the mirth which the question provoked showed us that to the mind of the Arunta native the idea of the possibility of anything before the Alcheringa was a ridiculous and an incomprehensible one. In this tribe "It was so in the Alcheringa" takes the place of the more usual form of expression: "Our fathers did it, and therefore we do it," which is so constantly the only reply which the ethnological inquirer receives to the question: "Why?"

We have evidently in the Churinga belief a modification of the idea which finds expression in the folklore of so many peoples, and according to which primitive man, regarding his soul as a concrete object, imagines that he can place it in some secure spot apart, if needs be, from his body, and thus, if the latter be in any way destroyed, the spirit part of him still persists unharmed. The further extension of the idea according to which the spirit can undergo reincarnation is, at least so far as Australian tribes are known, a feature peculiar to the Central tribes. At the same time we are not without indications that possibly other tribes, though the system is not so highly developed as in the case of the Arunta, may to a certain extent associate with the bull-roarer the idea of the spirit part of some great ancestor. We are not referring to the fact that, as Mr. Howitt first showed, and as has since been abundantly verified by other workers, the women and children are taught to believe that the voice of the bull-roarer is that of some spirit such as Daramulun, but in Mr. Howitt's paper dealing with the Jeraeil of the Kurnai tribe[73] we meet with the still more suggestive fact that at a certain time during the initiation ceremonies the men who are in charge of the novices say to them, "This afternoon we will take you, and show your grandfather to you." "This," says Mr. Howitt, "is the cryptic phrase used to describe the central mystery, which in reality means the exhibition to the novices of the Tundun, and the revelation to them of ancestral beliefs." The Tundun is the native name amongst the Kurnai for the bull-roarer. In this account we see, first, that the bull-roarer is identified with a man who is regarded as a great ancestor or Weitwin, that is father's father of the Kurnai. He it was who conducted the first ceremony of initiation, and he made the bull-roarer which bears his name and also made another smaller one which represents his wife. It is quite possible that under a somewhat modified form we have in this legend of the Kurnai an expression of the same idea as that which has undergone still further development in the case of the tribes in the centre of the continent.

To return however to the Arunta. We meet in tradition with unmistakable traces of the idea that the Churinga is the dwelling place of the spirit of the Alcheringa ancestors. In one special group of Achilpa men, for example, the latter are reported to have carried about a sacred pole or *Nurtunja* with them during their wanderings. When they came to a camping place and went out hunting the *Nurtunja* was erected, and upon this the men used to hang their Churinga when they went out from camp, and upon their return they took them down again and carried them about. In these Churinga they kept, so says the tradition, their spirit part.

Whilst this is so with regard to the Alcheringa men and women it must be clearly pointed out that at the present day the Arunta native does not regard the Churinga as the abode of his own spirit part, placed in the *Ertnatulunga* for safe keeping. If anything happens to it—if it be stolen—he mourns over it deeply and has a vague idea that some ill may befall him, but he does not imagine that damage to the Churinga of necessity means destruction to himself. In the native mind the value of the Churinga, at the present day, whatever may have been the case in past time, lies in the fact that each one is intimately associated with, and is indeed the representative of, one of the Alcheringa ancestors, with the attributes of whom it is endowed.[74] When the spirit part has gone into a woman and a child has, as a result, been born, then that living child is the reincarnation of that particular spirit individual.

Not only does each member of the tribe have a *Churinga nanja* but, shortly after the birth of the child, the headman of the particular group in whose *Ertnatulunga* the Churinga is deposited consults with the older men of the group and bestows upon him (and the same holds true in the case of a female child) his *Aritna churinga*, or secret name.[75] Every member of the tribe has his or her secret name, which may be either a new one or that of some celebrated man or woman of the Alcheringa whose name has been handed down in the traditions. This secret name is never uttered except upon the most solemn occasions when the Churinga are being examined, and that of any particular individual is only known to the fully initiated men of his own local totem group. To utter such a name in the hearing of women or of men of another group would be a most serious breach of tribal custom, as serious as the most flagrant case of sacrilege amongst white men. When mentioned at all it is only in a whisper, and then after taking the most elaborate precautions[76] lest it should be heard by anyone outside the members of his own group. The native thinks that a stranger knowing his secret name would have special power to work him ill by means of magic.

Before being allowed to see the *Ertnatulunga* the native must have passed through the ceremonies of circumcision and subincision, and have shown himself capable of self-restraint and of being worthy by his general demeanour to be admitted to the secrets of the tribe. If he be what the natives call *irkun oknirra*, that is, light and frivolous and too much given to chattering like a woman, it may be many years before he is admitted to the secrets. When he is thought worthy of the honour, and at a time appointed by the Alatunja of the local group to which he belongs, he is taken, accompanied by the older men, to the *Ertnatulunga*. There he is shown the sacred Churinga which are examined carefully and reverently, one by one, while the old men tell him to whom they now belong or have belonged. While this is going on a low singing of chants referring to the Alcheringa is kept up, and at its close the man is told his Churinga name and cautioned against ever allowing any one, except the men of his own group, to hear it uttered. Then, at least in the witchetty group in which we have witnessed the performance, he is painted on the face and body with a kind of pinkish soapstone and red ochre by the Alatunja and the older men who stand to him in the relationship of *Oknia*, that is actual or tribal father. The pattern with which he is decorated represents the particular device belonging to the totem, and in this instance consisted of long parallel bands copied from the sacred painting which from time immemorial has existed on a smooth rock surface in the Emily gap, the local centre of the witchetty grub totem.

When this has been done the party returns to camp and the painting is allowed to remain on the man's body until in course of time it wears off. The old women are aware that he has been to the *Ertnatulunga*, but even they have no idea of the nature of the ceremony, and to the younger ones it is still more a matter of deep mystery, for no women in the natural condition of the tribe dare go near to the gap in which is the sacred rock painting, and near to which lies the *Ertnatulunga*.

The exact contents of the *Ertnatulunga* vary of course from group to group, important ones containing a large number of Churinga many of which will be stone, but perhaps in the majority of cases the wooden ones will predominate. It does not, of course, follow that even a majority of them will belong to the totem with which the locality is associated; for, owing to, first, the way in which Churinga are inherited, and second, the fact that one group will sometimes lend a certain number to a friendly group, Churinga belonging to various totems will always be found in one *Ertnatulunga*.

We give as a fair example of a small-sized *Ertnatulunga* an account of the contents of a sacred storehouse of the Yarumpa or honey-ant totem at a place called Ilyaba, away to the north-west of Alice Springs. The *Ertnatulunga* itself is a round hole in the side of a rocky hill, which hole was in the Alcheringa an ant nest. What may be called the prize of the collection is the Churinga, though it is only a small wooden one, of a celebrated Alcheringa leader of the Yarumpa people named Ilatirpa, who sent out the wandering bands of Yarumpa from Ilyaba, the great centre of the totem. A long stone Churinga represents a mass of honey which he carried with him and fed upon, and a slender stone Churinga pointed at each end, represents a piece of wood which he used for digging out the honey-ants. These two are the only stone ones in the storehouse which in this respect is rather poor. There are sixty-eight wooden Yarumpa Churinga and several Echunpa or lizard ones, three of which are very old and boomerang-shaped, and have been borrowed from a lizard group living near Hermannsburg on the Finke. In addition to these there are two Achilpa or wild cat Churinga which have been lent to a Yarumpa man by his son-in-law for a time.

We may now describe more in detail the Churinga themselves—that is the Churinga which are associated with the individuals and which, by various writers, have been described as ceremonial sticks and stones, festival plates, message-sticks or magic-sticks. The term message-stick is misleading; it is quite true that one or more of them is carried by certain messengers sent to summon other members of the tribe to ceremonies of various kinds, but there is nothing in common between them and other message-sticks such as are found in other parts of the continent, on which notches and marks of different kinds are cut as an aid to the memory of the messenger, but which without the verbal explanation of the messenger would, in no case, so far as we have reliable evidence, be capable of being deciphered by the recipient of the message. The Churinga carried by an Arunta messenger is, in reality, a badge of office showing the *bona fides* of the bearer, whose person is safe so long as he carries the sacred emblem, and though the showing of the Churinga is regarded in the light of a summons which cannot, except at the risk of a serious quarrel, be neglected, yet it is misleading to apply the same term, message-stick, both to the sacred emblem, and to the stick, the marks, if any, on which are quite arbitrarily drawn by the sender and cannot be deciphered without his assistance. We may remark in passing, that though we have made careful inquiry we have been unable to discover the use of any real message-stick in the Arunta tribe.[77]

The Churinga of the Arunta—that is the particular ones with which we are now concerned—are of two descriptions, stone ones and wooden ones, the latter being sometimes spoken of as *Churinga irula*. The wooden one, just like the stone one, is Churinga—indeed, the term *irula*, which simply means "dressed wood," is seldom used by the natives, and then only as a qualifying term, and never by itself. The stone is no more sacred than the wooden one, and is most highly valued if it be, as many of them are, associated with some special Alcheringa ancestor. At the same time there are often wooden ones of evidently great antiquity, pieced together with sinew of kangaroo or emu to prevent them falling to pieces through decay of the less durable portions, and with holes carefully filled up with porcupine-grass resin, and such as these, though insignificant in appearance, are yet as highly valued as the stone ones. It may be generally said that the value of any particular Churinga, in the eyes of the natives, varies inversely with its value from a decorative point of view; the more obliterated the design, the more it has been patched with resin and bound together with sinew, the more highly is it valued, and the careful way in which many of them have been thus preserved shows the value which is placed upon them by the natives.

Amongst the Churinga in each storehouse are usually a certain number of especially large ones made by Alcheringa men, or by specially celebrated men of olden times who lived since the Alcheringa, for the purpose of being used in the performance of ceremonies connected with the totems. These are spoken of as Churinga, but they differ from the majority in that there is not associated with them the idea of a spirit individual. In addition to these there are also at times other forms of Churinga present in the storehouse which represent such objects, for example, as the eggs of the witchetties, or in some cases a special object such as a *pitchi* which was carried about by an Alcheringa man, or a yam-stick carried by a woman.

In size and shape they differ much. The smallest will be perhaps three or four inches in length, the longest five feet or more. In the Arunta tribe all, with very rare exceptions, are more or less flattened and either oval (rarely roughly circular) in outline, or, most usually, elongate with either end tapering to a more or less rounded point. Five very old wooden Churinga which belonged to two lizard totems differed from all the others of which, in company with the members of the various groups to which they belong, we have seen and examined many hundreds, in having the shape of a curved boomerang.

The stone ones are always flat on either side, the wooden ones may be of the same form or more usually have one side flat, and the other slightly concave, or they may frequently be concavo-convex in transverse section. A certain number of the smaller ones—but this is not usual in those of more than a foot in length—have a hole pierced through them at one end to which is attached a string usually made of human or opossum hair. Those that are bored in this way and are only a few inches in length are used as bull-roarers during certain ceremonies, the sound being produced by whirling them rapidly round with the string kept taut between the hand and the bull-roarer, the latter rotating as it whirls through the air, and tightening the string which vibrates and produces the roaring sound. A certain number of the stone ones are bored like the wooden ones, but such are never used as bull-roarers, nor indeed, at the present day, for any purpose which would require them to be thus bored. At the same time it may be pointed out that we have traditions according to which, in the Alcheringa, the men used to hang up their Churinga on the *Nurtunja*; for this purpose they would require to be bored, and though at the present day there is no need for this, yet that it is sometimes practised is no doubt to be associated with the myths of the Alcheringa.

The stones are usually micaceous in nature, being split off from suitable rock, and then carefully ground down to the desired shape and size. The wooden ones are generally made of Mulga (*Acacia aneura*) for the simple reason first, that this wood is the hardest and most durable known to the natives, and second, that the tree is perhaps the most widely distributed of any species throughout the great Central area and therefore easily obtainable. If, however, Mulga be not obtainable, then it may be made of the pine (*Callitris* sp.) or of some species of Eucalyptus the wood of which (such as that of *E. tesselaris*) the natives have learnt by long experience, is not touched by white ants.

In the great majority of cases the Churinga, wooden ones and stone alike, have patterns incised on their surfaces, the tool used being usually an incisor tooth of an opossum, with which also the hole at one end, if present, is bored. In some cases, though these are quite in a minority, they are perfectly plain and show no markings of any kind, and in others, such as were once present, are now scarcely decipherable, owing to the constant rubbing to which they have been subjected at the hands of generation after generation of natives.

Whenever the Churinga are examined by the old men[78] they are, especially the wooden ones, very carefully rubbed over with the hands. First of all dry red ochre is powdered on to them, and then rubbed in with the palm of the hand, the grease of which doubtless assists in preserving the wood to a certain extent. The stone ones are, some of them, rubbed with red ochre, but others with charcoal, which is never used in the case of the wooden ones.

We now come to deal with the patterns on the Churinga all of which have a definite meaning attached to them, though to decipher each individual one, it is essential to gain the information from a man of the totem to which it belongs. Other natives may volunteer information, but as the same device will mean one thing to a native of one totem and quite another thing to a man who belongs to another totem, and as a man's knowledge is strictly confined to the designs of his own totem, it is quite unsafe to ask, say, an emu man to describe to you the markings on a wild cat Churinga, or *vice versâ*.

The whole design consists, with few exceptions, of a conventional arrangement of circular, semi-circular, spiral, curved and straight lines together often with dots. The most frequent design met with is that of a series of concentric circles or a close set spiral, the sets of circles or the spirals varying in number from two or three to as many as twenty, or even more; and these, when present, usually indicate the most important object which it is intended to represent in the whole design. In one Churinga each will represent a tree, on another a frog, on another a kangaroo and so on, so that it will easily be realised that to obtain a true interpretation of any one Churinga, it is absolutely essential to obtain the information from some one to whom it is personally known, and such an one can only be an old man of the particular local totemic group to which it belongs; it is only the old men who continually see and examine the Churinga of the group, which are very rarely indeed seen by any one who does not belong to the latter. Time after time, when the *Ertnatulunga* is visited, the Churinga are rubbed over and carefully explained by the old men to the younger ones, who in course of time come to know all about them that the old men can impart, and so the knowledge of whom the Churinga have belonged to, and what the design on each one means, is handed on from generation to generation.

We will now explain the meaning of the designs on a few of the Churinga, as these will serve to illustrate and to give some general idea of them. The descriptions now given were obtained from the special individual in charge of whom the Churinga was, which is described in each instance.

Figure A. represents the *Churinga nanja* of a dead man of the frog totem. On either side of the Churinga, which is a wooden one 39 cm. in length, are three large series of concentric circles (*a*), which represent three large and celebrated gum-trees which grow by the side of the Hugh River at Imanda, the centre of the particular group of the frog totem to which the owner of the totem belonged; the straight lines (*b*) passing out from them on one side of the Churinga represent their large roots, and the two series of curved lines at one end (*c*) their smaller roots. These trees are intimately associated with the frog totem, as out of them frogs are supposed to come, which is doubtless an allusion to the fact that in the cavities of old gum-trees one species of frog is often found, and can be always heard croaking before the advent of rain. The smaller series of concentric circles on the same side of the Churinga (*d*) represent smaller gum-trees, the lines attached to them being their roots, and the dotted lines (*e*) along the edge are the tracks of the frogs as they hop about in the sand of the river bed. On the opposite side of the Churinga the large series of double concentric circles represent small frogs which have come out of the trees, and the lines connecting them are their limbs. This device of small concentric circles united by lines is a very common one on frog Churinga.

Figure B. represents the *Churinga nanja* of the celebrated Ilatirpa of the Yarumpa or honey-ant totem, and is in the storehouse at Ilyaba. The series of circles (*a*) with a hole bored in the middle of them represent the eye. The circles (*b*) represent the intestines, (*c*) the painting on the stomach, and (*d*) the posterior part of the man. On the reverse side the circles (*g*) represent the intestines of the Alatirpa, a little bird which is regarded as the mate of the Yarumpa.

Figure C. represents the Churinga of an Achilpa or wild cat man. The three series of circles (*a*) represent Unjiamba or Hakea trees, while the circles of spots (*b*) represent the tracks of the men dancing round them. The lines (*d*) represent the Wanpa sticks, which are beaten together to keep time to the dancing; and the dots (*e*) represent again the tracks of dancing men. This Churinga is in the store-house at Imanda, and was used during the Engwura ceremony.

Figure D. represents the Churinga of an Udnirringita or witchetty grub man, and is in the Emily Gap store-house. The curved lines (*a*) represent a large grub, (*b*) represents a lot of grubs in a hole which is scooped out in the ground, and (*c*) represents a man sitting down and squeezing the dirt out of the animals preparatory to cooking them. On the reverse side, (*d*) represents a grub, (*e*) the eggs of various sizes, and (*f*) marks on the body of the grub.

Figure E. represents one side of the *Churinga nanja* of the elder of the two women who accompanied the Ulpmirka men of the Ukakia or plum-tree totem (*Santalum sp.*) in the Alcheringa, and were taken away to the north by a celebrated individual called Kukaitcha. The three series of concentric circles (*a*) represent frogs, the two outer rows of dots represent the tracks of the women. The lines across the Churinga (*b*) represent bark of gum-trees, and the curved lines at one end (*c*) represent an old woman collecting frogs.

Figure F. represents one side of the *Churinga nanja* of the younger of the same two women. Here again the concentric circles (*a*) represent frogs, the semi-circles (*b*) represent women sitting down opposite to each other, while the dots between them (*c*) are the holes which they make in scratching the frogs out of the sand. The three dotted lines at the end (*d*) bored through represent the vulva.

Figure G. represents the *Churinga nanja* of an Echunpa or lizard man (the large lizard, *Varanus giganteus*), and is remarkable as being one of the only five Churinga of this shape which we have seen amongst a very great number. On one side the greater part is occupied by four roughly parallel, sinuous lines which represent the long tail of the animal; the semi-circular lines are the indications of ribs, and the dotted lines at one end are the tracks. On the other side, (*a*) represents the shoulder of the animal; (*b*) the spotted black marks across the chest; (*c*) the large ribs—those, as the natives say, with much fat on them; (*d*) the smaller ribs, and (*e*) the spotted marks along the under surface of the animal. This Churinga was evidently a very old one; it was slightly broken at one end, and by constantly repeated rubbing the design was indistinct in parts.

The workmanship of the Churinga varies to a considerable extent in its quality on some the lines are clearly cut, and, considering the hardness of the material and the crudity of the tool used, the result is surprisingly good so far as the regularity of the design is concerned; but in all cases the design is a purely conventional one, and never attempts to indicate in form the specific object which it is supposed to represent, or rather to indicate. The most important feature is almost always indicated by a series of concentric circles or by spiral lines, while tracks of men and animals seem to be represented by dots arranged in circular or straight lines. Individual men and women appear to be uniformly represented by semi-circular lines, and may be said, speaking generally, to be regarded as subordinate to the animal or plant indicated in the design by complete circles or spirals, though, as will be noted, the latter is not by any means of necessity the totem of the individual to whom the Churinga belongs. When dealing later on with the decorative art of the natives we shall refer further to these designs; meanwhile it may be pointed out here that the concentric circles appear to have been derived from what was originally a spiral, and not *vice versa*. Whence the Central natives derived a style of decoration of their sacred objects which is so entirely different from that of the tribes living both on the east coast and to the west of them, it is difficult to understand. One thing is certain, and that is that wherever they derived it from they have had it for long ages, as it is associated with their oldest traditions. The entirely different scheme of ornamentation found amongst the tribes of the eastern and south-eastern coasts, of the centre and of the west, points to the fact that these three large groups, each of which consists of many tribes, must have diverged from one another at an early date, and that each one has since pursued its own path of development practically uninfluenced by the others. In connection with this it may be noted that, though as yet but little is known concerning the West Australian natives, the initiation rites of the Eastern coastal tribes, whilst they agree in all important points amongst themselves, are markedly different from those of the Central tribes, including amongst these those of the internal parts of Queensland and New South Wales, in regard to certain of which we have recently had most valuable information published in the monograph by Mr. W. E. Roth, dealing in great detail with the northwest-central Queensland aborigines. The physical conditions of the continent have also been such as to shut off for probably long ages the Central tribes from those of either the eastern and south-eastern coastal districts, or those of the west.

At the same time, though the initiation rites of the tribes described by Mr. Roth are closely similar to those of the Central tribes, and though certain of the bull-roarers figured by him are identical in form and ornamentation with those of the latter, and are, as he describes, used in connection with initiation ceremonies and as love charms, and may not be seen by women, yet there does not appear to be the significance attached to them in the tribes studied by Mr. Roth that there is in the Central tribes.

Various local groups differ to a great extent in the number of the Churinga in their possession, and amongst some, especially in the southern part of the tribe, stone ones may be absent, and only wooden ones present. Why this is so we cannot say; the natives themselves simply say that originally all totem groups had stones ones, and that those which have not got them now have lost them; but if this be so, it is not easy to understand why, as is actually the case, it is only in the south that we meet with groups without any stone Churinga. A group without any of the stone ones is certainly regarded as inferior to a group which does possess them; and possibly this absence of them in the south may point back to a time when they were stolen.

We now come to deal with the question of ownership of the Churinga. It will be seen from a consideration of the way in which each individual acquires his own totem name, that it is not at all improbable that every now and again a particular local group of some totem may become extinct. If no child happens for some length of time to be conceived in some particular totem locality—and some of these are very limited in extent—then there may come a time when that particular group has no men or women representing it.

Every local group is regarded as owning collectively the locality in which lies its *Ertnatulunga*. The boundaries of this locality are well known, and if it happens that all the individuals associated with it die, then a neighbouring group will go in and possess the land. It is not, however, any neighbouring group which may do this, but it must be one the members of which are what is called *Nakrakia* to the extinct group—that is, they belong to the same moiety of the tribe as the latter. For example, supposing the extinct group consisted mainly of Purula and Kumara men, then the new occupiers must be of the same sub-classes, and not Bulthara and Panunga.

It is also clear that a group temporarily extinct may be resuscitated at any time, for the Churinga of the Alcheringa and their associated spirit individuals still inhabit the spot, so that no one knows when one of these may enter a woman, and the once extinct group spring into human existence again.

When any group becomes thus extinct, the Churinga are either taken care of by the new comers, or they may be handed over to some other local group of the same totem. Two instances which came under our notice will illustrate what actually takes place. In the first, all the members of a wild dog group, consisting mainly of Kumara and Purula men, died out; a contiguous group of the same sub-classes, but of a different totem, took possession of the land, but carefully sent the Churinga from the *Ertnatulunga* to a distant group of wild dogs.[79] In the second case, all the men of a lizard totem, situated some twelve miles to the north-east of Alice Springs, died out. They belonged to the Bulthara and Panunga moiety, and accordingly their locality was taken possession of by a neighbouring group of Bulthara and Panunga, who belonged to the Unchalka totem (a little grub), and in this instance these men also took care of the Churinga, leaving them undisturbed in the *Ertnatulunga*, the old men periodically examining them and rubbing them over with red ochre, so as to keep them in good state, just as if they were their own. After some time a child was conceived in the old lizard locality, and thus the local totemic group was again brought to life, and the child—a boy—having reached mature age, was given charge of the Churinga which belonged to his totemic ancestors. The ceremony of handing over the Churinga which we witnessed took place during the Engwura and is described in connection with this.

Whilst the Churinga are always under the immediate charge of the Alatunja, or head man of the local totem group, various individuals are regarded as having a special proprietary right in certain Churinga. Every one, in the first instance, has his own *Churinga nanja*, but in addition to this he most probably has others which have come to him by right of inheritance, the line of descent which they follow being strictly defined. Supposing a man dies, if he has a son of mature age, the latter—the eldest son, if there be more than one—is given charge of the dead man's Churinga. If he has no son of mature age, they are handed over to a younger brother, never to an elder one, and the former will take care of them until such time as the son is old enough to be entrusted with the duty of periodically rubbing and polishing them. It must be understood that they are always under the control of the Alatunja, without whose consent they cannot be touched even by the man who has, under his direction, special charge of them. If there be no son, then the younger brother retains charge of them, and in course of time they descend to his son or younger brother, and so on from generation to generation.

In the case of a woman's Churinga they do not descend to her son, but to a younger brother, if she has one. It never descends to an elder brother, and if she have no younger brother-in-blood, then the men who stand in the relationship of *Oknia* (blood and tribal fathers) and *Arunga* (blood and tribal grandfathers) decide upon some man younger than herself, standing to her in the relationship of *Witia*—that is blood or tribal younger brother—and to him the charge of the Churinga is given.

It will be seen that in the descent of the Churinga of men and women they always remain in the custody of a man belonging to the moiety of the tribe to which the individual belonged. If a woman's Churinga went to her son, then, as descent is counted in the paternal line, they would pass into the possession of a man belonging to the moiety to which she did not belong.

The question of totem does not enter into consideration in regard to the descent of the Churinga, and the fact that this is so accounts for what was at first a matter of considerable perplexity to us. Whilst the Churinga during the Engwura were, as frequently happened, brought on to the ceremonial ground to be examined and rubbed over with red ochre, a man would show us perhaps as many as twenty belonging to various totems, and in which it was evident that he had a special proprietary right. He would speak of them as belonging to him, though the great majority were Churinga of totems other than his own, and it was only after inquiry into a number of special cases that we came to understand how the Churinga of dead men and women were inherited by particular individuals. A man, for example, would tell us that such and such Churinga in the store lying in front of us had belonged to his *Oknia*, and that when the latter died then they came to him. Now a man calls his actual father *Oknia*, and also his father's brothers, and a man may inherit, as we have already seen, Churinga which belonged to his own father and to the elder brothers of the latter. As we found frequently, you cannot tell, without further inquiry, whether a particular Churinga belonged to a man's actual father or to an elder brother of his father.

A man may thus inherit (1) the Churinga which belonged to his own father—that is, not only his father's *Churinga nanja*, but any which have descended to him by right of inheritance; (2) the Churinga which belonged to an elder brother who has died, leaving no son to inherit them; and (3) the *Churinga nanja* of an elder (but not of a younger) sister. Not only does he inherit these Churinga, but at the same time, and along with them, he also inherits certain sacred ceremonies which belonged to the Alcheringa individuals who are represented by the Churinga—a matter to which we shall have to again refer when we are dealing with the Quabara or ceremonies concerned with the totems.

In addition to these which have already been dealt with, and all of which belong—so far as their shape is concerned—to the type of object popularly called a bull-roarer, there are other objects which are equally called Churinga, but both the external form as well as the significance of which renders them quite distinct from the former. The one point in which all the various articles agree, to which the name of Churinga is applied, is this—they are all in some way associated with individual men, women, plants, or animals of the Alcheringa, and at the present day are strictly tabu to women. Thus, for example, at Undiara, the great centre of the Okira (kangaroo) totem, there lies buried beneath the ground a slab of stone, triangular in section and about three feet in length, which represents part of the tail of a celebrated kangaroo which was killed there in the Alcheringa, and has ever since remained in the form of this stone, which is Churinga, and only to be seen by initiated men during the performance of certain totemic ceremonies. Again, in the witchetty grub totem each man has associated with himself, in addition to the usual Churinga, a few small rounded stones called *Churinga unchima*. Each of these is usually about an inch in diameter, and represents one of the eggs with which the bodies of the Alcheringa individuals were filled. Large numbers of these were deposited at various camping places of the Alcheringa witchetty ancestors, the greater number being left at the central camp in the Emily Gorge near to the present site of Alice Springs. The spirit individual carries a certain number of these about with him as well as his usual Churinga, and deposits them around the base of his *Nanja* tree, where they may be found after the birth of the child to which he gives rise. Usually the older witchetty men carry a small number of these about with them, and when a man is dying a few of them are always placed under his head, being brought from the *Ertnatulunga* for this special purpose, if he does not happen to have any in his possession, and after death they are buried with him. Of the origin and meaning of this particular custom the natives have no idea, and this was the only occasion on which we could discover that anything of a sacred nature was buried with the men. This of course applies to men of the witchetty grub totem, but it is quite possible that in other totems there may be somewhat similar objects present, though we have not been able to learn of the existence of any amongst the representatives of a large number of totems with whom we have come into contact.

Stones which are evidently Churinga are met with amongst other Central Australian tribes. In the Ilpirra and Luritcha we can say from personal knowledge that their use and meaning is precisely similar to that already described amongst the Arunta. In the case of the Kaitish and Warramunga tribes, which are located further to the north, the Churinga are distinct in shape from those of the Arunta. Each consists of a flat, micaceous slab, which in outline is characteristically pear-shaped, with always a small lump of resin affixed to the narrow end. The stone may either be quite plain, or ornamented with designs similar to those of the Arunta Churinga, or, again, in the Kaitish tribe it may be decorated with a design painted on with charcoal and pipe-clay, the stone itself having been previously coloured red with ochre. Those in our possession are enclosed in a covering of emu feathers, both to preserve them from getting chipped and to prevent their being seen by the women (Fig. 21).

Amongst the Waagai, both flat and somewhat spherical shaped stones are known, the latter looking much like one of the *Churinga unchima* of the witchetty men. The flattened stone (Fig. 22) has, unlike the Churinga of the Arunta or Ilpirra, its edge marked with very definite serrations; the incised design consists of concentric circles, while at one end a hole is bored, to which a strand of hair string is attached.

There can be little doubt but that the same essential idea underlies the Churinga in all these tribes. We have traced through them all the same system of social organisation, with descent counted in the paternal line, together with corresponding terms of relationship, and, judging by the nature of their Churinga,[80] it seems highly probable that the same, or at least essentially the same, totemic system exists amongst the Waagai, Kaitish and Warramunga as we know to exist among the Arunta, Luritcha and Ilpirra tribes.

In the Urabunna tribe the equivalent of the sacred stick of the Arunta is called Chimbaliri, and has the form of a plain piece of wood with each end rounded, so that it has the general form of a wooden Churinga. It differs from the latter in being very distinctly concavo-convex in section, in having no incised pattern, and in not being red-ochred. The one figured (Fig. 20) measures 67 cm. in length and 9 cm. in width. After the initiation ceremony a Chimbaliri is given to the youth to carry about until the wound is healed.

We have previously stated that one group will occasionally lend Churinga to a neighbouring and friendly group as a very special mark of good-will. It is somewhat difficult to find out the idea which is present in the native mind with respect to the lending and borrowing of Churinga beyond the fact that it is universally regarded as a most desirable thing to have possession of as large a number as possible, because with them the spiritual part of their former possessors is associated. So far as we can find out, they are not borrowed or lent for any very definite purpose, but only because, on the one hand, a particular group is anxious to have in its possession for a time a large number, with the general idea that it will in some vague and undefined way bring them good fortune, and, on the other hand, the second group is willing to lend them, and thus show a kindness which at the same time reflects a certain amount of dignity upon itself owing to the very fact that it has a large number to lend. Beyond this there is the important item from the point of view of the lenders that the borrowing group is always supposed to make presents to the former on the occasion of returning the Churinga.

It is not necessary for the two groups concerned to belong to the same totem—they may or they may not.

The following is an account of what actually took place, when, two or three years ago, an Erlia, or emu totem, group, living in the Strangway Range, lent some of its Churinga to another Erlia group which lives about twelve miles to the east of Alice Springs. These Churinga have only recently been returned, and the ceremonies enacted at both the borrowing and returning will serve to show what takes place on these occasions, though in various parts of the tribe and in the case of different totems there are, of course, differences in detail.

The Alatunja or headman of the group which is anxious to borrow the Churinga sends a properly accredited messenger to the Alatunja of the group from which it is desired to borrow them. This messenger, who is called *Inwurra*, carries with him as his credentials a few Churinga, perhaps three or four, and they are usually stone ones. When he reaches the country of the strange group, he remains at some little distance from the main camp, the fact of his acting as a messenger being known at once from his behaviour. After some little time, during which he is left entirely to himself, as is usual on the approach of a stranger to a camp, the Alatunja and some of the older men go out to the spot at which he has remained seated since his approach. He then, in a whisper, asks the Alatunja to take care of the few Churinga which he has brought with him and to keep them safe for the group which he represents. Nothing whatever is said on either side as to the real object of his visit, but what this is is at once known from the fact of his asking the Alatunja to take care of his Churinga. If the Alatunja in whose hands, after consultation with the older men, the matter lies, does not feel disposed to lend Churinga, he politely declines to keep the *Inwurra's* offering, and the messenger at once returns to his own group, carrying his Churinga with him. In this particular case the Alatunja accepted the Churinga, thereby implying that he was willing to lend a larger number in return, though no words to that effect passed on either side, and the messenger at once went back and reported the success of his mission. As soon as he had returned, the Alatunja of the borrowing group organised a deputation, which, headed by himself, went across to the Strangway Range group of emu men.

When the party came within a distance of about half a mile of the main camp, a halt was ordered by the Alatunja, and a messenger was sent on to announce the advent of the party. Presently the Alatunja of the local group and some of the older men, as usual, came out to the halting-place and sat down in perfect silence. After a short time they embraced the visitors; and during the next two or three hours the embracing was repeated at intervals, conversation with regard to the Churinga being carried on in whispers. As a general rule there are upon these deputations one or two of the more recently initiated men who are being gradually inducted into such ceremonies, but are not, as yet, allowed to see everything which takes place. For example, though they come with the others, they will not be shown the stone Churinga, at least not close to, as this is the first important mission with which they have been associated.

As usual on such occasions, the deputation had arrived about mid-day. Until sunset the men remained at the meeting-place, and then, when it had grown dark, they were conducted by their hosts to the ordinary corrobboree ground, where a performance was given in their honour. On such occasions it is esteemed a polite attention to guests to perform a part of an *Altherta* or ordinary corrobboree, belonging to the district from which the visitors come, and in which one or two of the latter are usually asked to take part.

When the dancing was over the visitors were conducted to the camp of the single men, where the night was spent. The performance lasted several days, while the visitors remained as guests in the camp. At its termination, and when all the women had been sent away from the corrobboree ground, the local Alatunja, accompanied by some of the older men, went to the *Ertnatulunga*, or sacred store-house, and, choosing out the Churinga to be lent, returned with them to the ground where the visitors had remained. During the night the Churinga were carefully inspected, greased, rubbed with red ochre, and stacked in an elaborately decorated shield. At daylight they were solemnly handed over to the visiting Alatunja, the lender saying in low tones, "Keep the Churinga safely, they are of the Alcheringa; we lend them to you freely, gladly; do not be in a hurry to return them." While he was saying this, the older men murmured approvingly; the young men present who had only recently been initiated had been sent some little distance away. Then the leader of the deputation replied, speaking in low tones, and supported by the fervent "*Auatta, auatta*" ("Yes, yes") of his colleagues on the deputation. He said, "We will watch over them with care, and return them to you after some time; the emu Churinga are good, the emu men are strong and good." After a further conversation in whispers, during which the virtues of the Churinga were dilated upon, the deputation departed, waving spears and shouting loudly, "*Uwai! Uwai! Uwai!*"—an exclamation used to denote fear or danger, or to frighten women and children, who, when they hear it, will quickly make off out of the way.

The return journey was made by the least frequented path, so as to avoid as far as possible any chance of meeting women. On arrival in camp, the Churinga were carefully examined by the old men, and then hidden away amongst their own in the *Ertnatulunga*. There then followed a corrobboree, in which those who took part introduced a Strangway Range performance.

After rather more than two years had elapsed, the Churinga were returned. It is usual for this to take place within the area occupied by the lending group, but on this particular occasion it was arranged that the ceremony should take place at a spot on the Todd River, just within the district of the borrowing group.

To this spot accordingly came the Alatunja of the Strangway Range group, attended by his men. While camped here and awaiting the coming of the party returning the Churinga, various ceremonies concerned with the emu totem were performed at night-time, in the centre of a large space which had been specially cleared for the purpose.

On the day on which the deputation was to come in, the men assembled here, all painted with charcoal and birds' down in front, and with designs on their backs copied from the *Churinga Ilkinia*, or designs peculiar to the totem. About half an hour before the main deputation reached the spot, a single messenger arrived and, approaching the Alatunja with an air of great deference, told him that the *Inwurra* bearing the sacred Churinga were close at hand. Two shields were placed on the ground in front of the Alatunja, who sat down in the native fashion, with his legs bent up under him, so that his knees projected towards the shields. All the other men with him, between forty and fifty in number, sat down, forming a solid square, the front row of which was occupied by the elder men, with the Alatunja in the middle. A little to the right of him was a shield, on which had been placed a flat cake called *ekulla* made from crushed grass seeds, and on the top of this were placed a number of freshly-made *Imitnya*, or fur string head bands. A few yards distant, on either side of the square, a man was stationed, sitting on the ground, and each of these men alternately struck the ground heavily with a hard flat piece of wood, while those within the square, led by the Alatunja, sang with great gusto, the sidesmen continuing to beat time upon the ground, until, at length, the *Inwurra* emerged into the pathway which had previously been prepared for them to traverse by clearing away the stones, bushes, and tussocks of grass.

As soon as they came in sight of the waiting men they at once halted, shouting loudly, "*Uwai, Uwai!*" and brandishing their weapons, the man who carried the bundle of Churinga being well in front of the column. The men of the waiting group at once stopped singing, and shouted excitedly, "*Erlia! Erlia!*"— the native name of their totem, the emu. After a short halt, the *Inwurra* party came on at a trot, with the curious high knee action always adopted by the natives when engaged in performing ceremonies. Spears and boomerangs were waved about, amid shouts of "*Uwai! Uwai!*" and answering cries of "*Erlia, Erlia!*" The leading old man, who carried the Churinga, imitated, as he came along, the action and characteristic zig-zag course of a running emu, the bundle of Churinga, which was held at an angle above his head, giving him, indeed, somewhat the appearance of the animal.

At this time, those who were seated in the square began to sing, except only the old Alatunja, whose head was bent low down, as if he were too much overcome with emotion to take any part in the singing.

When the strangers had reached the waiting group, the Churinga were placed on one of the shields, the singing ceased, and the new-comers sat down so that they formed a second square immediately facing the other one. The old men occupied the front row, with the Alatunja in the centre of it.

After a short pause, the leader of the *Inwurra* bent over and whispered in the ear of the Alatunja, every one meanwhile assuming a strikingly grave demeanour, as if something of the greatest importance were taking place. Then all, except the two leaders, joined in a short chant and when it was over, the leader of the *Inwurra* and other old men of his party took up the bundle of Churinga and deposited it on the lap of the Alatunja, who took it up, rubbed it several times against his stomach and thighs, and then against those of the older men who were sitting beside him. The object of this rubbing is, so the natives say, to untie their bowels, which become tightened and tied up in knots as a result of the emotion felt when they once more see their Churinga. The latter were then placed on the lap of the leader of the *Inwurra*, and then the Alatunja sitting immediately opposite to him, as well as the old men on each side of him, leaned across and rubbed their foreheads against the stomachs of the front row of the *Inwurra* party. This was done to show that they were friends, and were not angry with the visitors because they had kept the Churinga for such a long time.

The leader of the *Inwurra* party now began to unwind the *Imitnya*, which were quite newly made of opossum fur, and in which the Churinga were swathed, forming altogether a torpedo-shaped bundle about four feet in length. Every now and then they paused and repeated the rubbing of the stomachs with their foreheads, until, finally, when the *Imitnya* and a number of *Uliara*, or human hair girdles, lying under them, had all been removed, the Churinga were displayed. Then, one by one, they were handed over to the Alatunja, who carefully examined each one, and rubbed it over his stomach and thighs, and over those of the men of his group, and then placed it on one of the shields in front of him.

This performance occupied a considerable time, and it was conducted with great solemnity. Then the leader of the *Inwurra* addressed the Alatunja and his men, saying in effect, "We return your great Churinga, which have made us glad. We bring you a present of these *Imitnya* and *Uliara*, and we are sorry that we could not bring more, but the *Anthinna* (opossum) is scarce and hair does not grow quickly." This was somewhat modest, as there must have been, at the least, fifty large new *Imitnya* or opossum fur-string bands, besides a great number of *Uliara*.

The Alatunja replied, "It is good, yes, we are glad you kept our Churinga so well; they are all here. We accept your present and offer you these *Imitnya* in return; we are sorry we cannot give you more." Then he handed the *Imitnya*, about fifteen in number, which were placed on one of the shields, to the leader of the *Inwurra*, and taking up the *ekulla* or cake of grass seed, he divided it into two with a Churinga, and, giving one half each to the leader and another old man of the latter's party, said, "Eat, feed your men with our *ekulla*."

After the old men of the local party had spent a long time in carefully examining the Churinga, the ceremony came to an end, and the Alatunja told the old men, in whispers, that he was about to perform the ceremony of *Intichiuma* of the emu totem. This is not, however, of necessity performed when the Churinga are returned, and is described in the chapter dealing with the *Intichiuma* ceremonies of various totems.

Chapter VI

Intichiuma Ceremonies

Object of the ceremonies—No absolute restriction with regard to eating the totem—Eating of totem obligatory on certain occasions—Restriction with regard to eating of the wild cat—The disease *Erkincha*—Individuals who may attend the ceremonies—Time of holding of the ceremonies—*Intichiuma* of the Udnirringita or Witchetty grubs—Ceremony of eating and distributing the Udnirringita after the Intichiuma—*Intichiuma* of the Erlia or Emu—*Intichiuma* of the Unjiamba or Hakea—*Intichiuma* of the Ilpirla or Manna—*Intichiuma* of the Yarumpa or Honey-ant—*Intichiuma* of the Quatcha or Water—Undiara—Description of the spot—Cave containing the *Nanja* stone of a Kangaroo animal—Different position held by women at the present day in comparison with that held in the past—Traditions concerned with Undiara—History of Ungutnika and his boils—Ungutnika pursued by the wild dogs—Reconstitutes himself, but is finally killed and his tail buried near to Undiara—The Kangaroo and the Okira men—An Arunga or Euro man changes himself into a Kangaroo man and pursues the Kangaroo—Arrival at Undiara and killing of the Kangaroo; the ceremonial stone arising to mark the place where its body was deposited in the cave—*Intichiuma* of the Okira totem—Relationship between the individual and his totem—An Arunga man making a Churinga of his totem to assist a Plum Tree man in catching Arunga—Ceremonies concerned with eating the totem after *Intichiuma*—Traditions referring to the eating of the totemic animal or plant.

THE name *Intichiuma* is applied to certain sacred ceremonies associated with the totems, and the object of which is to secure the increase of the animal or plant which gives its name to the totem. These ceremonies are perhaps the most important of any, and it does not seem possible to discover when and how they arose. The natives have no tradition which deals with their origin.

In connection with them we may note an interesting feature with regard to the relationship existing between an individual of the Arunta and other tribes in the centre of the continent and his totemic animal or plant. We find amongst these tribes no restriction according to which a man is forbidden to eat his totem, as is stated to be the case amongst certain other Australian tribes. On the other hand, though he may only under ordinary circumstances eat very sparingly of it, there are certain special occasions on which he is, we may say, obliged by custom to eat a small portion of it or otherwise the supply would fail. These occasions are those on which the *Intichiuma* ceremonies now to be described are performed. Further still, the lead in the ceremony must be taken by the Alatunja, and when we asked the Alatunja of the witchetty grub totem why he ate his totem, which is always regarded by the native as just the same as himself, the reply was that unless he did eat a little, he would not be able to perform properly the ceremony of *Intichiuma*.

There is however one notable exception to the restrictions upon eating, and this is concerned with the Achilpa or wild cat[81] totem. Only a very little of this is allowed to be eaten, and that only by the old people; but in this case the restriction is not confined to the members of the totem, but is of universal application, applying to every member of the tribe. There is no similar restriction applying to any other animal or plant, but, in the case of Achilpa, there are reasons given for not eating it which serve to show that for some cause or other this particular animal has associations with the tribe as a whole which do not exist in respect of any other. In the first place, it is supposed that any one, save an old man or woman, eating Achilpa would be afflicted with a special disease called *Erkincha*; and in the second, it is believed that if any man who had killed another at any time of his life were to eat this particular animal, then his spirit part or *Yenka*[82] would leave his body and he would soon be killed by some enemy, so that to a man who has ever killed another—and there are very few men who do not lay claim to this distinction—the Achilpa is tabu or forbidden for life, no matter what be his age. There are amongst the traditions dealing with the Achilpa of the Alcheringa, very explicit references to the *Erkincha* disease, though why this should be especially associated with the Achilpa people it is difficult to say, and the natives have no explanation to offer.[83]

We may now describe the ceremonies of *Intichiuma* as they are performed in the case of certain of the totems. Each totem has its own ceremony and no two of them are alike; but though they differ to a very great extent so far as the actual performance is concerned, the important point is that one and all have for their sole object the purpose of increasing the number of the animal or plant after which the totem is called; and thus, taking the tribe as a whole, the object of these ceremonies is that of increasing the total food supply. To this question we shall have to return, as in connection with it there are certain points of very considerable interest.

Every local totemic group has its own *Intichiuma* ceremony, and each one is held at a time decided upon by the Alatunja under whose direction it is carried out. Any man who is a member of the totem can attend irrespective of the class to which he belongs, though, as we have already pointed out, the great majority of the members of any local group belong to one moiety of the tribe. In some cases men who are in the camp at the time when the ceremony is to be performed, and who belong to the right moiety of the tribe, are invited by the Alatunja to be present; but this is rather an exceptional thing, and under no circumstances are men who belong neither to the totem nor to the right moiety allowed to be present.

In connection with the times at which the ceremonies are held, it may be said that while the exact time is fixed by the Alatunja in each case, yet the matter is largely dependent on the nature of the season. The *Intichiuma* are closely associated with the breeding of the animals and the flowering of the plants with which each totem is respectively identified, and as the object of the ceremony is to increase the number of the totemic animal or plant, it is most naturally held at a certain season. In Central Australia the seasons are limited, so far as the breeding of animals and the flowering of plants is concerned, to two—a dry one of uncertain and often great length, and a rainy one of short duration and often of irregular occurrence. The latter is followed by an increase in animal life and an exuberance of plant growth which, almost suddenly, transforms what may have been a sterile waste into a land rich in various forms of animals, none of which have been seen for it may be many months before, and gay with the blossoms of endless flowering plants.

In the case of many of the totems it is just when there is promise of the approach of a good season that it is customary to hold the ceremony. While this is so, it sometimes happens that the members of a totem, such as, for example, the rain or water totem, will hold their *Intichiuma* when there has been a long drought and water is badly wanted; if rain follows within a reasonable time, then of course it is due to the influence of the *Intichiuma*; if it does not, then the non-success is at once attributed to the evil and counter influence of some, usually, distant group of men. With the meaning of the ceremonies we shall deal later on; meanwhile it may be said here that their performance is not associated in the native mind with the idea of appealing to the assistance of any supernatural being.

INTICHIUMA OF THE UDNIRRINGITA OR WITCHETTY GRUB TOTEM

When the ceremony is to be performed at Alice Springs the men assemble in the main camp, and then those who are about to take part in the proceedings leave the camp quietly, slinking away to a meeting place not far off, the women and men who do not belong to the totem not being supposed to know that they are gone. A few, perhaps two or three, of the older men of the totem stay in camp, and next morning they ask the men who do not belong to the totem to return early from their hunting. Every man has left all his weapons in the camp, for all must go quite unarmed and without any decoration of any kind; even the hair girdle, the one constant article of clothing worn by the men, must be left in camp. They all walk in single file except the Alatunja, who sometimes takes the lead and at others walks by the side of the column to see that the line is kept. On no account must any of the men, except the very old ones, eat any kind of food until the whole ceremony is over; anything which may be caught in the way of game has to be handed over to the old men. The procession usually starts late in the afternoon, so that it is dusk by the time that a special camping ground near to the Emily Gap is reached, and here they lie down for the night.

At daylight the party begins to pluck twigs from the gum trees at the mouth of the Gap, and every man carries a twig in each hand except the Alatunja, who carries nothing save a small *pitchi* or wooden trough, which is called *Apmara*.[84] Walking again in single file they follow—led by the Alatunja—the path traversed by the celebrated Intwailiuka, the great leader of the Witchetty grubs in the Alcheringa, until they come to what is called the *Ilthura oknira*, which is placed high up on the western wall of the Gap. In this, which is a shallow cave, a large block of quartzite lies, and around it are some small rounded stones. The large mass represents the *Maegwa*, that is, the adult animal. The Alatunja begins singing and taps the stone with his *Apmara*, while all the other men tap it with their twigs, chanting songs as they do so, the burden of which is an invitation to the animal to lay eggs. When this has gone on for a short time they tap the smaller stones, which are *Churinga unchima*, that is, they represent the eggs of the *Maegwa*. The Alatunja then takes up one of the smaller stones and strikes each man in the stomach with it, saying, "*Unga murna oknirra ulquinna*" ("You have eaten much food"). When this has been done the stone is dropped and the Alatunja strikes the stomach of each man with his forehead, an operation which is called *atnitta ulpilima*. Leaving the *Ilthura* the men descend from the range to the bed of the creek in the Gap, and stop under the rock called *Alknalinta*, that is, the decorated eyes, where, in the Alcheringa, Intwailiuka used to cook, pulverise and eat the grub. The Alatunja strikes the rock with his *Apmara*, and each man does the same with his twigs, while the older men again chant invitations to the animal to come from all directions and lay eggs. At the base of the rock, buried deeply in the sand, there is supposed to be a very large *Maegwa* stone.

It was at this spot that Intwailiuka used to stand while he threw up the face of the rock numbers of *Churinga unchima*, which rolled down again to his feet; accordingly the Alatunja does the same with some of the Churinga which have been brought from the store-house close by. While he is doing this the other members of the party run up and down the face of the rocky ledge, singing all the time. The stones roll down into the bed of the creek and are carefully gathered together and replaced in the store.

The men now fall once more into single file and march in silence to the nearest *Ilthura*, which is about a mile and a half away from the Gap in the direction of Alice Springs. The Alatunja goes into the hole, which is four or five feet deep, and scoops out with his *Apmara* any dirt which may have accumulated in it, singing as he does so a low monotonous chant about the *Uchaqua*. Soon he lays bare two stones which have been carefully covered up in the base of the hole; the larger one is called *Churinga uchaqua*, and represents the chrysalis stage from which emerges the adult animal; the smaller is one of the *Churinga unchima* or egg. When they are exposed to view, songs referring to the *Uchaqua* are sung, and the stones are solemnly handled and cleaned with the palm of the hand. One by one the men now go into the *Ilthura*, and the Alatunja, lifting up the *Churinga uchaqua*, strikes the stomach of each man with it, saying again, "You have eaten much food." Finally, dropping the stone, he butts (this is the only word expressive of the action) at each man in the abdomen with his forehead.

There are altogether some ten of these *Ilthura*, in each one of which is a *Churinga uchaqua*, and each *Ilthura* is visited in turn by the party and the same ceremony is repeated.

When the round of the *Ilthura* has been made and the same ceremony enacted at each one, then a start is made for the home camp. When within a mile or so of the latter they stop and decorate themselves with material which has been purposely brought to the spot. Hair string is tied round their heads, and *Chilara* or forehead bands are put on, beneath which twigs of the *Udnirringa*[85] bush are fixed so that they hang downwards. Nose bones are thrust through the nasal septum, and rat tails and topknots of cockatoo feathers are worn in the hair. The Alatunja is but little decorated; he has only the *Chilara* across his forehead, and the *Lalkira* or nose bone. Under his arm he carries the *Apmara*, and in his hand a twig of the *Udnirringa* bush. While the men walk along they keep their twigs in constant motion, much as if they were brushing off flies. The totem *Ilkinia* or sacred design is painted on the body of each man with red ochre and pipe clay, and the latter is also used to paint the face, except for the median line of red. When the decorations are complete a start is again made, all walking in single file, the Alatunja at the head with his *Apmara* under his arm. Every now and then they stop and the old Alatunja, placing his hand above his eyes, as if to shade the latter, strikes an attitude as he peers away into the distance. He is supposed to be looking out for the women who were left in camp. The old man, who had been left in charge at the camp during the absence of the party, is also on the look-out for the return of the latter. While the men have been away he has built, away from the main camp, a long, narrow wurley, which is called *Umbana*, and is intended to represent the chrysalis case from which the *Maegwa* or fully-developed insect emerges. Near to this spot all those who have not been taking part in the ceremony assemble, standing behind the *Umbana*. Those men who belong to the other moiety of the tribe—that is, to the Purula and the Kumara—are about forty or fifty yards away, sitting down in perfect silence; and the same distance further back the Panunga and Bulthara women are standing, with the Purula and Kumara women sitting down amongst them. The first-named women are painted with the totem *Ilkinia* of red and white lines; the second are painted with lines of white faintly tinged with red. When the old man at length sees the party approaching he steps out and sings—

"Ilkna pung kwai, Yaalan ni nai, Yu mulk la, Naan tai yaa lai."

The Alatunja, as the party comes slowly along, stops every now and then to peer at the women. Finally all reach the *Umbana* and enter it. When all are inside they begin to sing of the animal in its various stages, and of the *Alknalinta* stone and the great *Maegwa* at it base. As soon as the performers enter the wurley, the Purula and Kumara men and women lie face downwards, and in this position they must remain until they receive permission to arise. They are not allowed to stir under any pretext whatever. The singing continues for some time; then the Alatunja in a squatting position shuffles out of the *Umbana*, gliding slowly along over the space in front, which has been cleared for a distance of some yards. He is followed by all the men, who sing of the emerging of the *Maegwa* from its case, the *Umbana*. Slowly they shuffle out and back again until all are once more in the wurley, when the singing ceases and food and water are brought to them by the old man who had remained in camp and built the *Umbana*. This, it must be remembered, is the first food or drink which they have partaken of since they originally left the camp, as, except in the case of the very old men, it is peremptory that the ceremony be carried out without any eating or drinking on the part of the participants. When it is dusk they leave the wurley, and go round to the side away from that on which the Purula and Kumara men are lying, so that, to a certain extent, they are hidden from their view. A large fire is lighted, and round this they sit, singing of the witchetty grub. This is kept up till some little time before daybreak, and during all that time the women of the right moiety must stand peering about into the darkness to see if the women of the other moiety, over whom they are supposed to keep watch, continue to lie down. They also peer about, watching the *Intichiuma* party just as the women did in the Alcheringa. Suddenly the singing ceases, and the fire is quickly put out by the Alatunja. This is the signal for the release of the Purula and Kumara men and women, who jump to their feet, and these men and all the women of whatever class they may be, at once run away to the main camp. The *Intichiuma* party remains at the wurley until daylight, when the men go near to the *Ungunja*,[86] make a fire and strip themselves of all their ornaments, throwing away their *Udnirringa* twigs. When all the *Uliara, Imitnya, Lalkira* and cockatoo feathers are removed, the Alatunja says, "Our *Intichiuma* is finished, the *Mulyanuka* must have these things or else our *Intichiuma* would not be successful, and some harm would come to us." They all say, "Yes, yes, certainly;" and the Alatunja calls to the *Mulyanuka (i.e.* men of the other moiety of the tribe), who are at the *Ungunja*, that is the men's camp, to come up, and the things are divided amongst them, after which the old man, who before brought them food, goes to the various camps and collects a considerable quantity of vegetable food which is given to him by the women. This is brought back and cooked and eaten by the fire, where they still remain. During the afternoon the old man again visits the camp, and brings back with him some red ochre and the fur string which belongs to the various members of the party, and, just before sundown, the old men rub red ochre over their bodies, and over those of the younger men, thus obliterating the *Ilkinia* and the painting on the face. The men then put on their arm strings, &c., and return to their respective camps, and with this the main part of the ceremony is brought to a close. When all is over, the *Apmara* or *pitchi* of the Alatunja is held in great regard, and the Panunga and Bulthara women enjoy the privilege, each in turn, of carrying it about.

INTICHIUMA OF THE ERLIA OR EMU TOTEM

The *Intichiuma* of the Erlia or emu group of Strangway Range, differs very considerably from the ceremony which has just been described, and it must be remembered that there are considerable differences in detail between the *Intichiuma* ceremonies of even the different local groups of the same totem.

We have already described the returning of the emu Churinga to the Strangway Range men by the members of another group to which they had been lent, and the following ceremony was performed upon this occasion. As is always the case, the decision to hold the *Intichiuma* was arrived at by the Alatunja. He and a few other men, amongst whom were his two sons, first of all cleared a small level plot of ground, sweeping aside all stones, tussocks of grass and small bushes, so as to make it as smooth as possible. Then several of the men, the Alatunja and his two sons amongst them, each opened a vein in their arms, and allowed the blood to stream out until the surface of a patch of ground, occupying a space of about three square yards, was saturated with it. The blood was allowed to dry, and in this way a hard and fairly impermeable surface was prepared, on which it was possible to paint a design. This is the only occasion on which we have known of any such method being adopted. With white pipe clay, red and yellow ochre, and powdered charcoal mixed with grease, the sacred design of the emu totem was then outlined on the ground. In this particular case, when the design was for the special occasion drawn on the ground, it was called an *Ilpintira*, which is simply one of the *Ilkinia* or totemic designs drawn under these conditions. The drawing was done by the Alatunja, his blood brothers, and two sons. It is supposed to represent certain parts of the emu; two large patches of yellow indicated lumps of fat, of which the natives are very fond, but the greater part represented, by means of circles and circular patches, the eggs in various stages of development, some before and some after laying. Small circular yellow patches represented the small eggs in the ovary; a black patch surrounded by a black circle was a fully-formed egg ready to be laid; while two larger concentric circles meant an egg which has been laid and incubated, so that a chicken has been formed. In addition to these marks, various sinuous lines, drawn in black, red, and yellow, indicate parts of the intestines, the excrement being represented by black dots. Everywhere over the surface, in and amongst the various drawings, white spots indicated the feathers of the bird, the whole device being enclosed by a thin line of pale pink down. It will be noticed that this design differs in important respects from others associated with the sacred objects of the totem. The latter, such as the designs on the Churinga, have no definite relationship, and no attempt at any resemblance to the objects which they are supposed to indicate, but in this drawing, though it is to a certain extent conventionalised, still we can see very clearly that an attempt is made to actually represent the objects. The large yellow patches representing fat, the small yellow circles the eggs in the ovary, and the patches with enclosing circles, eggs with shells, serve to show that the original designer had a definite idea of making the drawing, conventional though it be to a large extent, indicative of the objects which it is supposed to represent.

During the day, and in fact throughout the whole ceremony, the Alatunja was treated with the greatest deference; no one spoke to him except in a whisper, and he it was who regulated the whole proceedings, even down to the minutest detail.

The drawing, or *Churinga ilpintira*, was completed before the arrival of the messengers bearing the borrowed Churinga, and, when done, it was carefully concealed from view with branches. After the Churinga had been returned with the formalities already detailed, the Alatunja informed the visitors of his intention to perform *Intichiuma*, and, rising from the ground, he led the way, carrying the Churinga, to the spot close by where the *Ilpintira* was concealed. He removed the boughs, and, placing the Churinga on one side, squatted down, all the rest of the men following his example. In the intervals of a monotonous chant, which lasted for half an hour, he explained the different parts of the drawing, which was then again covered up and the men returned to the original meeting place, where, for the rest of the night, they chanted, sitting round the Churinga.

During the night three large wooden Churinga, each about four feet in length, were decorated with series of concentric circles of red and yellow ochre and of white pipe clay, and tipped with bunches of emu feathers and the red-barred tail feathers of the black cockatoo. The Alatunja selected three of the older men to act the part of *Inniakwa*, who are supposed to represent ancestors of the emu totem of considerable antiquity, but not so far back as the Alcheringa. At the same time a number of the younger men were chosen to act the part of *Illiura*, who are the descendants of the *Inniakwa*, and they were painted on their chests with designs belonging to the totem, in charcoal and white down.

At daylight the decorated Churinga were fixed on the heads of the *Inniakwa*, and, while three or four of the *Illiura* were despatched to the women's camp, the rest of the men assembled at, and sang round, the drawing. Just at sunrise the party left the camping ground and went to an open space, which had been previously selected for the purpose, on the opposite side of a ridge of low scrub-covered hills. The *Illiura* had meanwhile driven the women and children out from their camp, and shortly after the arrival of the main party of men the former came running towards the ceremonial ground and took up a position at one end. The *Inniakwa* stood in the centre some distance away from, but still clearly seen by, the women and children, and without moving their feet imitated the aimless gazing about of the emu, each man holding a bunch of twigs in his hands, the Churinga on the head with its tuft of feathers being intended to represent the long neck and small head of the bird. The women watched intently, for this is one of the very few occasions on which they are allowed to see, even at a distance, a sacred ceremony. Then, with a curious gliding movement, the performers moved in the direction of the women, who thereupon uttered cries of alarm. Once more the three men stood quietly, moving only their heads, and then again ran for a few yards. Upon this the women turned and fled towards their camp, while the audience of men moved their arms as if with the one to urge the women to run away and with the other to call back the *Inniakwa* to the centre of the ground.

When the women and children were out of sight the *Inniakwa*, accompanied by the other men, ran over the low hill back to the camping ground, where the Churinga were taken from the heads of the *Inniakwa* and placed upright in the ground. About midday the Churinga, which had been brought back by the visiting group and had been placed on a small platform, were taken down and brought to the centre of the ceremonial ground, where they were again examined and rubbed with red ochre by the Alatunja and the older men to the accompaniment of continuous chanting on the part of the other men who sat around. When this was over all gathered together at the *Ilpintira*, the meaning of which was again explained by the Alatunja. Singing continued at intervals during the day, and just before dusk three newly appointed *Inniakwa* were decorated, the *Illiura* again drove the women and children from their camp to the ceremonial ground, and the performance of the early morning was repeated.

On the second day precisely the same programme was gone through, after which the men returned to their camping place, the three Churinga were divested of their decorations, the *Ilpintira* was very carefully obliterated by the Alatunja and his sons, and the ceremony came to an end. The strange natives then went back to their country, and the returned Churinga were taken by the Alatunja and the old men of his group and placed in the sacred store-house.

INTICHIUMA OF THE UNJIAMBA OR HAKEA FLOWER TOTEM

At a place called Ilyaba the ceremony is performed by men of the Bulthara and Panunga classes, and the exact spot at which it takes place is a shallow, oval-shaped pit, by the side of which grows an ancient Hakea tree. In the centre of the depression is a small projecting and much worn block of stone, which is supposed to represent a mass of Unjiamba or Hakea flowers, the tree being the *Nanja* tree of an Alcheringa woman whose reincarnation is now alive.

Before the ceremony commences the pit is carefully swept clean by an old Unjiamba man, who then strokes the stone all over with his hands. When this has been done the men sit around the stone and a considerable time is spent in singing chants, the burden of which is a reiterated invitation to the Unjiamba tree to flower much, and to the blossoms to be full of honey. Then the old leader asks one of the young men to open a vein in his arm, which he does, and allows the blood to sprinkle freely over the stone, while the other men continue the singing. The blood flows until the stone is completely covered, the flowing of blood being supposed to represent the preparation of *Abmoara*, that is, the drink which is made by steeping the flower in water, this being a very favourite beverage of the natives. As soon as the stone is covered with blood the ceremony is complete.

The stone is regarded as a Churinga, and the spot is *ekirinja*, or forbidden to the women, children and uninitiated men.

INTICHIUMA OF THE ILPIRLA OR MANNA TOTEM

Ilpirla is a form of "manna," very similar to the well-known sugar-manna of gum trees but peculiar to the mulga tree (*Acacia aneura*).

About five or six miles to the west of Ilyaba there is a great boulder of grey-coloured gneissic rock, curiously marked with black and white seams, at which the men of the Ilpirla totem perform the ceremony of *Intichiuma*. On the top of the boulder, which stands about five feet above the ground, there is a similar stone weighing about twenty pounds, together with smaller ones, all of which represent masses of *Ilpirla*. The large boulder, on which the others lie, has the same significance, and is supposed to have been deposited there in the Alcheringa by a man of the Ilpirla totem, who has at the present time no living representative.

When *Intichiuma* is performed, a clear space is first of all swept round the base of the stone, and after this the Alatunja digs down into the earth at the base of the boulder, and discloses to view a Churinga which has been buried there ever since the Alcheringa, and is supposed to represent a mass of *Ilpirla*. Then he climbs on to the top of the boulder and rubs it with the Churinga, after which he takes the smaller stones and with these rubs the same spot, while the other men sitting around sing loudly, "*Inka parunta, nartnapurtnai, urangatcha chuntie, urungatcha chuntie.*" The meaning of these words is an invitation to the dust produced by the rubbing of the stones to go out and produce a plentiful supply of *Ilpirla* on the mulga trees. Then with twigs of the mulga he sweeps away the dust which has gathered on the surface of the stone, the idea being to cause it to settle upon the mulga trees and so produce *Ilpirla*. When the Alatunja has done this, several of the old men in turn mount the boulder and the same ceremony is repeated. Finally, the Churinga is buried at the base in its old position, and with this the ceremony closes.

INTICHIUMA OF THE YARUMPA[87] OR HONEY-ANT TOTEM

In this ceremony, as performed at Ilyaba, the majority of men are Panunga and Bulthara, only a few Kumara and Purula belonging to the totem.

At early morning on the appointed day the men assemble at the men's camp, where they decorate their foreheads, arms and noses with twigs of the *Udnirringa* bush and smear their bodies all over with dry red ochre. Then they march in single file, the Alatunja at the head, to a spot about fifty yards from, and opposite to, the *Erlukwirra* or women's camp, where the women and children stand silently. Here the Alatunja, turning his back upon the women, places his hand as if he were shading his eyes and gazes away in the direction of the *Intichiuma* ground, each man as he does so kneeling behind him so as to form a straight line between the women and the *Intichiuma* ground. In this position they remain for some time, while the Alatunja chants in subdued tones. After this has been done, all stand up, and the Alatunja goes to the rear of the column and gives the signal to start. In perfect silence and with measured step, as if something of the greatest importance were about to take place, the men walk in single file, taking a direct course to the ground. Every few yards the Alatunja, who is in the rear, goes out first to one side and then to the other, to see that the men keep a straight line.

After having traversed perhaps half a mile one man is sent by the Alatunja to the *Ertnatulunga* to bring a special stone Churinga, which is required during the ceremony.

The *Intichiuma* ground is situated in a depression in a rocky range, at a considerable elevation above the surrounding plains, and all over the depression are blocks of stone standing up on end and leaning in all directions, each of which is associated with a honey-ant man of the Alcheringa. The messenger sent to the *Ertnatulunga* arrives at the ground as the party approaches; he has to go a long way round, and must run the whole way.

All the men then group themselves round a pit-like depression in the rocks which is surrounded with a horseshoe-shaped wall of stone, open at the western end. On the east side is an ancient *mulga* tree, which is the abode of the spirit of an Alcheringa man, whose duty it was to guard the sacred ground. In the centre of the pit is a stone, which projects for about eighteen inches above the ground, and is the *Nanja* of an Alcheringa man who originated here and performed *Intichiuma*.

On the arrival of the party the Alatunja at once goes down into the pit, and some time is spent in clearing out the débris, while the other men stand round in perfect silence. After a time he beckons to some of the older men to come down and assist him, and then they all begin to sing while the sacred stone, which represents an Alcheringa man called Erkiaka, is disclosed to view and taken out of the earth, together with a smaller smooth round pebble, which represents a mass of honey collected by the ants and carried about by the man.

When the stone has been taken out it is rubbed over reverently with their hands by the old men, and then rubbed over with the smaller stone, after which it is replaced in the ground. This done, the big stone Churinga from the

Ertnatulunga, which represents a mass of honey carried about by a celebrated *Oknirabata*[88] of the Alcheringa, named Ilatirpa, is brought up. This Ilatirpa was the leader of the Yarumpa and sent out the wandering parties who started from this spot. In the *Ertnatulunga* is a long, thin, stone Churinga, pointed at each end and evidently very old, the markings being nearly effaced, which represents the piece of wood which was carried by Ilatirpa for the purpose of digging up the ants on which he fed. This and the large Churinga are the only stone ones in this particular *Ertnatulunga*.[89]

The old Alatunja takes up the Churinga, and calling the men up one by one, each of them walks into the pit, and lies down, partly supported on the knees of two or three of the older men. In this position the Alatunja, keeping up all the time a low chant, first of all strikes each man's stomach sharply two or three times with the Churinga, and then moves it about with a kind of kneading action, while another old man butts at the stomach with his forehead. When all have passed through this performance the singing ceases, the Churinga is handed back to the man who brought it, with instructions to take it back to the *Ertnatulunga*, and the column forms again and marches back, taking a different course, which, however, just as on the first occasion, leads them past the women's camp, where again the women and children are standing in silence.

On the way home a halt is made at a spot in the Ilyaba creek, where in the Alcheringa, as now, the final act of the ceremony was performed. On the banks of the creek are a number of *mulga* trees, each of which is associated with, in fact is the *Nanja* tree of, an Alcheringa man, who stood watching the performance as it was being conducted in the bed of the creek. In the same way the stones standing out from the banks have each of them their association with an Alcheringa man. On arrival at this spot all the men sit down, and about an hour is spent in singing of the Yarumpa men, of their marchings in the Alcheringa, of the honey, of the ant nests, of the great man Ilatirpa, and of those Yarumpa men who, in the Alcheringa, changed into the little birds now called *Alpirtaka*, which at the present day are the mates of the honey-ant people, to whom they point out where the ant nests can be found. After some time the decoration of the Alatunja commences, while he leads the singing, which now has reference to the men on the banks, who are supposed, in spirit form, to be watching the performance from their *Nanja* trees. The decorations on the body of the performer are intended to represent the chambers in the ant nests, and those on the arms and neck the passages leading to the inner parts of the nests where the honey-ants are found. The performer squats on the ground, and for some time the other men run round and round him in the usual way, while he occupies himself with brushing the ground between his legs with little twigs, pausing every now and then to quiver. When this is over the decorations are removed, and the party starts back for the men's camp, passing as described, the women's camp on the way.

INTICHIUMA OF THE QUATCHA OR WATER TOTEM

In connection with the making of rain there are certain ceremonies, some of which are not of the nature of sacred Quabara, and take the form of ordinary dancing festivals which any member of the tribe, men and women alike, irrespective of class or totem, are permitted to see; but there is in addition to these a special and sacred ceremony, only shared in by the initiated men of the totem, and this is the *Intichiuma*.

As in the case of the kangaroo totem the majority of the members of the water totem belong to the Purula and Kumara. To them the secret of rain-making was imparted in the Alcheringa by an individual named Irtchwoanga, who also settled upon the exact places at which the ceremony should be performed. One of the most important of the water totem groups is a local subdivision of the Arunta people, inhabiting a district of about fifty miles to the east of Alice Springs, this part being known as *Kartwia quatcha*, or the "rain country."[90] The Alatunja of this group at the present time is a celebrated rain-maker, and the ceremony which is described below is the one which is performed by him. The office of Alatunja, or as it is called in these eastern groups "Chantchwa," descended to him from his father, who died recently, and the fact that he is now the head man, and not his elder brother, illustrates an interesting point in regard to the inheritance of the office of Alatunja in the Arunta tribe. The office has, in fact, descended to him, and not to his elder brother, for the simple reason that he was born a water man, while the woman who is the mother of both of them conceived the elder one in an opossum locality. The latter man is therefore the reincarnation of an Alcheringa opossum individual, and so it is of course impossible for him to be the head of a water group. If the old Alatunja had had no son of the right totem then the office would have descended to one of his blood brothers—always provided of course that he were of the right totem—and failing such a one, to some tribal brother or son of the water totem as determined upon by the elder men, or, more probably still, by the old Alatunja before his death. As soon as the Chantchwa has decided to hold the ceremony he sends out messengers, called *Inwurra*, to the surrounding groups, to inform them of his intention, and to call the members of the totem together. In addition to the latter other men are invited to come, though they will not be allowed to take any part in the actual *Intichiuma* ceremony. Each messenger carries in this instance a human hair girdle, a bunch of black cockatoo tail feathers and a hollow nose bone stopped at one end with a plug made of the resin obtained from the porcupine-grass, and ornamented at the other with a small bunch of owl feathers. These objects are the property of the Chantchwa, and to refuse to attend to the request of a messenger thus accredited would be considered a grave discourtesy, and the person committing such an offence would be spoken of as *irquantha*, that is churlish.

When all are assembled, those who are to take part in the ceremony, that is the men of the totem, march into camp, painted with red and yellow ochre and pipeclay, and wearing bunches of eagle-hawk feathers on the crown and sides of the head. At a signal from the Chantchwa all sit down in a line, and with arms folded across their breasts sing the following words for some time:—"*Ulgaranti alkwarai lathrik alkwaranti ulgaraa-a.*" Suddenly, at another signal from the Chantchwa, all jump to their feet and silently march out of the camp. They walk in single file, and camp for the night at a spot some miles away. At daybreak they scatter in all directions in search of game, which is cooked and eaten, but on no account must any water be drunk, or the ceremony would fail. When they have eaten they again paint themselves, this time broad white bands of bird's down being fixed on as usual with human blood, so that they encircle the stomach, legs, arms, and forehead. Some of the older Purula and Kumara men have meanwhile been building a special bough wurley or hut, which is called *nalyilta* at a spot not far distant from the main camp, where all the women and those men who are not taking part in the ceremony have remained behind. The floor of the hut is strewn with a thick layer of gum leaves to make it as soft as possible, as a considerable time has to be spent lying down here. When the decorating is complete, the men march back, silently and in single file, to where the wurley has been built; this always takes place about sunset, and on reaching the hut the young men go in first and lie face downwards at the inner end, where they have to remain until the ceremony is over. Meanwhile, outside the wurley, some of the older men are engaged in decorating the Chantchwa. Hair girdles covered with white down are placed all over the head, while the cheeks and forehead are covered with pipeclay and two broad bands of white down pass across the face, one over the eyebrows and the other over the nose. The front of the body has a broad band of pipeclay outlined with white down, rings of which adorn the arms. When fully decorated the Chantchwa takes up a position close to the opening into the wurley, from which extends, for thirty yards, a shallow trench. The old men, who sit around him, now begin to sing, and continue to do so for some time, the following words:—

"Illunga ilartwina unalla
Illunga kau-wu lungalla
Partini yert artnuri elt artnuri
Yerra alt nartnura alla
Partinia yarraa alt nartnurai
Yerra alla partinia atnartnurai
Yokaa wau wai."

When the singing comes to an end the Chantchwa comes out of the wurley and walks slowly twice up and down the trench, while he quivers his body and legs in the most extra-ordinary way—far more than is customary in other ceremonies in many of which a quivering movement is a characteristic feature. While this performance is taking place the young men arise and join the old men in singing—

"Purlaarau kurlaa
Rumpaa arri
Umpaakunla karla
Rumpaa arri
Paakur tai,"

the Chantchwa's movements appearing to accord with the singing. When he re-enters the wurley the young men at once lie down again—in fact they are always in this position while the Chantchwa is in the wurley. The same performance is repeated at intervals during the night, the singing continuing with but little intermission, until, just at daybreak, the

Chantchwa executes a final quiver, which lasts longer than usual, and at the end of which he appears to be thoroughly exhausted, the physical strain of the performance having been, as can be well imagined, of a severe nature. He then declares the ceremony to be at an end, and at once the young men jump to their feet and rush out of the wurley, screaming in imitation of the spur-winged plover. The cry is heard in the main camp, and is taken up with weird effect by the men and women who have remained there. The decorations of the Chantchwa are removed, and then all march, led by him, to a spot just within sight of the main camp, where an old Purula or Kumara woman has cleared a large space and then covered it with gum-tree leaves. Here they lie down for a short time and then go to the main camp, where food and water await them. The whole performance may last forty-eight hours, and on the next night one of the ordinary rain dances, as they are popularly called by white men, is held, in which all the men take part, either as performers or as audience. The women do not perform, but may look on and assist in singing and beating time to the dancing of the men.

UNDIARA

About fifteen miles to the east of Henbury, on the Finke River, is a spot called by the natives Undiara.[91] Here, at the base of a steep quartzite ridge, which runs east and west, and forms part of what is now called Chandler's Range, there lies under the shelter of a gum tree a small water-hole, which has ever since the far away times of the Alcheringa been associated with the members of the Okira or kangaroo totem. From the side of the water-hole the rocks rise perpendicularly for some fifty feet, and over them, in the short rainy seasons, the water falls from a pool on a rock ledge, behind which again rises the bare summit of the ridge. This pool arose to mark the spot where the Engwura fires burned in the Alcheringa, and the ledge is called by the natives the *Mirra Engwura*, or Engwura camp of the

Alcheringa. In dry seasons there is no water. From the rocks a small gum creek meanders away, but is soon lost in the dry sandy country stretching out to the south.

Immediately on the eastern side of the water-hole is a shallow cave, about twenty feet in height and thirty in length, where the rocks have weathered in such a way as to leave a ledge of rock about ten feet high, running along the length of the cave, the top of which can be gained by a partly natural, partly artificial series of rough steps lying at the end next to the pool. Tradition says that on this ledge the Alcheringa men cooked and eat their kangaroo food.

A short distance away from the eastern side of the cave is a curious rocky ridge, with a very sharply marked vertical slit, which indicates the spot where an Alcheringa Kumara man named Abmilirka performed the rite of *Ariltha* upon himself.

The ledge arose, so says tradition, in the first instance to mark the spot where the body of a great kangaroo was deposited in the Alcheringa. It was, in fact, the *Nanja* stone of this kangaroo inhabited by its spirit part; and tradition says further that to this stone came great numbers of other kangaroo animals, who went into the earth, leaving their spirits in the same way in the rocky ledge. To this tradition we shall have to refer at a later time, when discussing the nature of the *Intichiuma* ceremonies; meanwhile the interesting point may be drawn attention to, that, just as the Alcheringa individual has his *Nanja* tree or stone, so in certain cases such as this the Alcheringa animal is possessed of one. In this instance, for example, the natives are very clear upon the subject that the tradition deals with an animal and not with an Alcheringa man—in fact, one of the latter was in pursuit of and killed the former, dragging the body into Undiara.

Another tradition relates how one night a group of kangaroo Alcheringa men had arranged a number of *Nurtunjas* or sacred poles close by the water-hole, with a specially large one in the centre and smaller ones all round it. While they slept two Alcheringa women of the Unjiamba totem came down from the north, and very quietly, without waking the men, took away the large *Nurtunja*, and, clambering up a slit, which is still to be seen in the perpendicular face of the rock above the pool, made their way to the north again to a place called Arapera, where they kept the *Nurtunja*, which figures prominently in certain ceremonies connected with that spot.

This tradition, like very many others dealing with the Alcheringa times, may be, with little doubt, regarded as indicative of the fact that at some past time the women were possessed of greater privileges than they enjoy at the present day. There is a great gap between the Alcheringa and recent times, and a very noticeable feature is the change which has in some way been brought about with regard to the position of women. The contrast in this respect may be well seen from a comparison of the former tradition with one which relates to a time which the natives say was very long ago, but since the Alcheringa. At this time the women were not allowed to go anywhere near to Undiara, where the sacred Churinga of the group were stored. One day, however, a woman, being very thirsty, ventured in to the water-hole to drink and saw the sacred pool and the ceremonial stone. She was detected in the act, and after a great deal of what the natives call "growling" at her, it was decided to punish her by making her for the time being common property to all the men—a punishment which is not infrequently inflicted after the committal of some serious offence, as an alternative to that of being put to death. In consequence of this men of all classes had intercourse with her, and when this was over she was returned to her proper *Unawa* man.

After, however, the woman had seen the place, the peculiar sacredness of the spot was lost, the Churinga were removed to another place, and the women were allowed to see the water-hole, except of course when the ceremony of *Intichiuma* was being performed. As a matter of fact, though a woman would not actually be put to death if she came near, the old feeling is still so strong that the women do not often venture near to the spot unless compelled to do so by thirst.

We may now give a short account of one or two traditions which are concerned with Undiara and the kangaroo totem, as they serve to illustrate certain points of interest in connection with the totems and totemic animals generally.

THE HISTORY OF UNGUTNIKA OF UNDIARA

At the present day there is living an aged man of the Okira or kangaroo totem, named Ungutnika. He is the reincarnation of a celebrated kangaroo of the Alcheringa, who sprang into existence at Undiara, close to the big gum tree which overhangs the water pool. Ungutnika was sorely afflicted with boils, called *Tukira*, which appeared first in the form of hard lumps. He bore with them for a long time, and then, being angry, pulled them out and placed them on the ground alongside of where he sat.[92] They became changed into stones, and have remained there ever since. He was not as yet fully grown, and was an *Okira kurka*, or a little kangaroo, and after a short time he set out to go to a place called Okirilpa. After he had travelled about three miles, he came to an open plain, upon which he saw a mob of *Ukgnulia*, or wild dogs, who had come from Okirilpa, and were then lying down close to their mother, who was very large. He hopped about looking at the wild dogs, and presently they saw and chased him, and, though he hopped away as fast as he could, they caught him on a plain called Chulina, and, tearing him open, eat first his liver, and then, removing the skin, they threw it on one side and stripped all the meat from off the bones. When they had done this they again lay down.

Ungutnika was not however completely destroyed, for the skin and bones remained, and, in front of the dogs, the skin came and covered the bones, and he stood up again and ran away, followed by the dogs, who caught him this time at Ulima, a hill a little to the north of a spot now called the Bad Crossing on the Hugh River. Ulima means the liver, and is so called because on this occasion the dogs did not eat the liver, but threw it on one side, and the hill, which is a dark-looking one, arose to mark the spot. The same performance was once more gone through, and again Ungutnika ran away, this time as far as Pulpunja, which is the name given to a peculiar sound made in imitation of little bats, and at this spot Ungutnika turned round and, jeering derisively at the dogs, made the noise. He was at once caught, cut open, and again reconstituted himself, much to the wonder of his pursuers. After this he ran straight towards Undiara, followed by the dogs, and when he reached a spot close to the water-hole they caught and eat him, and, cutting off his tail, buried it at the place where it still remains in the form of a stone, which is called the *Churinga okira pura*, or Kangaroo tail Churinga, which is always shown and carefully rubbed at the *Intichiuma* ceremony. The Churinga which he carried with him was associated with his spirit part, and the latter has since entered into a woman and been born in human form.

THE KANGAROO AND THE KANGAROO MEN

A Kumara man named Ulpunta, whose last descendant was a celebrated medicine man, who died during the course of the Engwura ceremony described in this work, started from Okruncha, carrying only spears and other weapons and no *Nurtunja*. He was in pursuit of a large kangaroo, which carried a small *Nurtunja*, and followed it till he came close to Chuntilla, but being unable to catch it, gave up the chase and turned back, a stone arising to mark the spot. He ever afterwards stayed at Okruncha. The kangaroo went on and camped at Chuntilla, and a stone marks the spot where it stood up and looked over the country. Here it was seen by a Bulthara man of the Arunga or euro totem, who at once changed himself into an Okira or kangaroo man and gave chase to the kangaroo, as he wanted to kill and eat it. For a long way he followed the kangaroo, the two camping apart from each other at various places. At Thungalula or Pine Tree Gap, in the Macdonnell Range, the kangaroo made a large *Nurtunja* and carried it away to Ilpartunga, not far from Owen's Springs, a small sand-hill arising where the animal lay down, and a *mulga* tree where the man camped. Travelling south along the Hugh River, they came to Alligera, where the kangaroo planted his *Nurtunja*, a large gum tree now marking the spot. Hearing a noise, he raised himself up on his hind legs and saw a kangaroo running about. A stone twenty-five feet high now represents him standing on his hind legs. After this he scratched out a hole for the purpose of getting water, and this hole has remained to the present day. Travelling south, he came to the Doctor's Stones, and here erected the *Nurtunja* for the last time, as he was too tired to carry it any further, so it was left standing and became changed into a fine gum tree, which is now called *Apera Nurtunja*, or the *Nurtunja* tree.

Still following down the Hugh River, the kangaroo reached Ulpmura utterly worn out, and lay down. In a little time a number of kangaroo men from Undiara came up and saw the Bulthara man, who had also arrived. The Undiara men, using gesture language, said to the Bulthara man, "Have you got big spears?" And he replied, "No, only little ones; have you got big spears?" And they replied, "No, only little ones." Then the Bulthara man said, "Put down your spears on the ground;" and they replied, "Yes, put yours down too." Then the spears were thrown down, and all the men advanced upon the kangaroo, the Bulthara man keeping in his hand a shield and his Churinga. The kangaroo was very strong and tossed them all about; then they all jumped upon him, and the Bulthara man, getting underneath, was trampled to death.

The kangaroo also appeared to be dead. They buried the Bulthara man with his shield and Churinga, and then took the body of the kangaroo into Undiara. The animal was not then really dead, but soon died, and was placed in the cave but not eaten. The rock ledge in the cave arose where the body was put, and when the animal was dead its spirit part went into this, which thus became the animal's *Nanja*. Shortly afterwards the men died, and their spirit parts went into the water pool close by. Tradition says that great numbers of kangaroo animals came at a later time to the cave, and there went down into the ground, their spirits also going into the stone.

INTICHIUMA OF THE OKIRA OR KANGAROO TOTEM

In the Alcheringa the Okira or kangaroo men of Undiara belonged almost, but not quite, entirely to the Purula and Kumara moiety of the tribe; and at the present day the same holds true, but to a somewhat less extent, for, as in the case of all totems, there is a certain admixture of the members of both moieties. The head man, or Alatunja, is a Purula, and under his direction the ceremony of *Intichiuma* is performed at intervals, though being now an old man, he sometimes deputes the performance to his eldest son, who will succeed to the position on the death of the old man.

When the ceremony is to be performed a camp is made at a spot a little to the west of the cave and out of sight of the water-hole, which is placed in a slight dip in the range from which the small gum creek leads. Early in the morning of the day on which the ceremony is to take place, one of the younger men is sent on ahead to a special spot which lies about a hundred yards to the west of the water-hole. The object of this is to make certain that no women or uninitiated men, or men other than members of the totem, are in the neighbourhood. The main body of men comes up skirting closely the base of the range, and halts at the place where the young man is stationed. Here there lies hidden underground a block of soft grey sandstone, about three feet in length and one foot in greatest diameter, its shape in transverse section being triangular. The apex of the stone lies about a foot below the surface, and as the men gather round the spot, the position of which is precisely known,[93] the leader clears away the sandy soil and brings the sacred stone into view. Its sides, worn smooth by constant rubbing, are covered over with smaller stones, amongst which is a special flattened one with which the rubbing is done. The Alatunja takes this stone in his hands, and in the presence of all the men, who stand round in perfect silence, rubs over the exposed surface. When this has been done the stone may be lifted up so as to be seen better. It is the *Churinga okira pura*, that is, the tail of the Alcheringa kangaroo, which was driven in by the wild dogs from Okirilpa, and deposited by them, as already described, in the ground at this spot. Certain large blocks of sandstone, which have evidently tumbled down from the hillside and lay close by—the largest of them being fully eight feet in height—are said to represent the dead bodies of the wild dogs.

After the stone has been rubbed by the Alatunja and then examined by all present, it is covered up and the party moves onward, still skirting the base of the hill, so that the cave and ceremonial stone are not seen until they are close at hand. A halt is made at the water-hole on the side away from the cave, where the men drink, and then come round and sit right in front of, and at the base of the ceremonial stone. On the left hand, looking towards the stone, sit the Panunga and Bulthara men, and on the right the Purula and Kumara. Then the head man, who is at the present day a Purula, and a man to whom he is *Gammona*, and who is therefore Bulthara, go out from the rest, who remain seated, and climb up the hillside just to the east of the stone. Here at a height of about twenty feet above the level of the plain, are two special blocks of stone projecting immediately above one another from the hill-side. One is supposed to represent an "old man" kangaroo and the other a female. The former is rubbed with a stone by the Purula man and the latter by the Bulthara man. This over, the two men descend and rejoin the main party, which is the signal for the decoration of the rock-ledge to begin. Red ochre and powdered and calcined gypsum are used, and with these alternate vertical lines are painted on the face of the rock, each about a foot in width, the painting of the left side being done by the Panunga and Bulthara men, and that of the right by the Purula and Kumara.

The red stripes are supposed to represent the red fur of the kangaroo (*Macropus rufus*), while the white ones represent the bones.

When the painting is done, a certain number of young men, perhaps two or three Panunga and Bulthara and five or six Purula and Kumara, go on to the top of the ledge. The former sit down at the left and the latter at the right side, and then they open veins in their arms and allow the blood to spurtle out over the edge of the ceremonial stone on the top of which they are seated. While this is taking place, the men below sit still watching the performers and singing chants referring to the increase of the numbers of the kangaroos which the ceremony is supposed to ensure.

When the blood-letting is over, the old men go back to the camp and remain there, while the rest of the day is spent by the young men out on the rocks and plains in search of game, which is brought in and presented to the old men. This may extend over several days, and at night-time sacred Quabara are performed in camp.

RELATIONSHIP BETWEEN THE INDIVIDUAL AND THE TOTEM

There are certain points of considerable interest with regard to the totems which may be briefly referred to now, in which certainly the Arunta and Ilpirra and, in all probability, others of the Central tribes agree together and differ, so far as is yet known, from other Australian tribes. The first point is the important one, to which we have had occasion to make frequent reference, as it is, we may say, the fundamental feature of the totemic system of these tribes, namely, that each individual is the direct reincarnation of an Alcheringa ancestor, or of the spirit part of some Alcheringa animal (as in the case of Ungutnika of the kangaroo totem), which carried a Churinga, and the spirit associated with which became, so to speak, humanised, and subsequently entered a woman and was born in human form.

The second point is concerned with the relationship which at the present day is supposed to exist between the individual and his totem. A man will only eat very sparingly of his totem, and even if he does eat a little of it, which is allowable to him, he is careful, in the case, for example, of an emu man, not to eat the best part, such as the fat.[94] The totem of any man is regarded, just as it is elsewhere, as the same thing as himself; as a native once said to us when we were discussing the matter with him, "that one," pointing to his photograph which we had taken, "is just the same as me; so is a kangaroo" (his totem). That they claim a special connection with, almost in certain respects a right to, their totemic animal or plant may be seen from the fact that, for example, in the witchetty grub totem, while the members of the latter do not eat it, or, at least, only sparingly themselves, the members of the local group who do not belong to the totem must not eat it out of camp like ordinary food, but must bring it into camp and cook it there, else the men of the totem would be angry and the supply of grubs would fail. We may, in fact say, that each totemic group is supposed to have a direct control over the numbers of the animal or plant the name of which it bears, and further that, in theory at least, they have the first right to the animal or plant. That this is so, and that it is well recognised, will be seen from the following facts.

The first is concerned with a curious, but suggestive use of a Churinga. In the possession of a man of the Akakia or plum tree totem, we found a stone Churinga, roughly circular in shape and about 8 cm. in diameter, wrapped up carefully in fur string, so as not to be seen by women as he carried it about with him. It was a Churinga, which had been specially made for him by a man who was *Ikuntera* or father-in-law to him. The man belonged to the euro totem, and the Churinga in question was marked with a design belonging to the same, a series of concentric circles in the middle of each side representing the intestines of the animal, while two groups of semi-circles indicated, one of them a male, and the other a female euro. The Churinga had been sung over or charmed by the euro man and then given by him to the plum tree man for the purpose of assisting the latter to hunt the animal.

The second is a series of equally suggestive ceremonies, which are connected with the close of the *Intichiuma* performance in various local totem groups.

After the performance of *Intichiuma*, the grub is, amongst the Witchetty grubs, tabu to the members of the totem, by whom it must, on no account, be eaten until it is abundant and fully grown; any infringement of this rule is supposed to result in an undoing of the effect of the ceremony, and the grub supply would, as a consequence, be very small. The men of the Purula and Kumara classes, and those of the Panunga and Bulthara, who are not members of the totem, and did not take part in the ceremony, may eat it at any time, but it must always be brought into camp to be cooked. It must, on no account be eaten like other food, out in the bush, or the men of the totem would be angry and the grub would vanish. When, after *Intichiuma*, the grub becomes plentiful and fully grown, the witchetty grub men, women and children go out daily and collect large supplies, which they bring into camp and cook, so that it becomes dry and brittle, and then they store it away in *pitchis* and pieces of bark. At the same time, those who do not belong to the totem, are out collecting. The supply of grubs only lasts a very short time—the animals appearing after rain—and when they grow less plentiful the store of cooked material is taken to the *Ungunja*, or men's camp, where, acting as usual under instructions from the Alatunja, all the men assemble. Those who do not belong to the totem, place their stores before the men who do, and the Alatunja then takes one *pitchi*, and with the help of other men of the totem, grinds up the contents between stones. Then he and the same men all take and eat a little, and when this has been done, he hands back what remains to the other people. Then he takes one *pitchi* from his own store and after grinding up the contents, he and the men of the totem once more eat a little, and then pass the bulk of what remains over to those who do not belong to the totem.

After this ceremony the Witchetty grub men and women eat very sparingly of the grub. They are not absolutely forbidden to eat it, but must only do so to a small extent for, if they were to eat too much, then the power of successfully performing the *Intichiuma* would depart from them, and there would be very few grubs. On the other hand it is equally important for them, and especially for the Alatunja, to eat a little of the totemic animal as to eat none would have the same effect as eating too freely.

In the case of the kangaroo totem of Undiara, after the men have allowed the blood to pour out of their arms over the stone ledge they descend, and after rubbing themselves all over with red ochre return to the main camp, which is always placed at some distance from the rock so as to prevent the women and children from being able to see anything of what is going on. All of the younger men then go out hunting kangaroo which, when caught, they bring in to the older men who have stayed in camp. It is taken to the *Ungunja*, or men's camp, and there the old men of the totem, the Alatunja being in the middle of them, eat a little and then anoint the bodies of those who took part in the ceremony with fat from the kangaroo, after which the meat is distributed to all the men assembled. The men of the totem then paint their bodies with the totem design or *Ilkinia* in imitation of the painting on the rock at Undiara, and that night is spent in singing about the doings of the Alcheringa kangaroo people and animals. On the next morning the young men again go out hunting and bring in more kangaroo to the old men, and the ceremony of the previous day is repeated. The night is spent in singing, and the proceedings terminate with the performance of a number of sacred Quabara connected with Undiara, the great centre of the totem. After this the animal is eaten very sparingly by the kangaroo men, and there are certain parts, such as the tail, which are regarded as the choice bits, which a kangaroo man, or of course woman, must on no account touch.

In the Irriakura totem (the Irriakura is the bulb of a Cyperaceous plant) the members of the totem do not, after *Intichiuma*, eat the totem for some time. Those who do not belong to the totem bring a quantity in to the *Ungunja*, where it is handed over to the Alatunja and other men of the totem, who rub some of the tubers between their hands, thus getting rid of the husks, and then, putting the tubers in their mouths, blow them out again in all directions. After this the Irriakura people may eat sparingly.

In the Idnimita totem (the Idnimita is the grub of a large longicorn beetle) the grub must not, after *Intichiuma*, be eaten by the members of the totem until it becomes plentiful, after which those men who do not belong to the totem collect it and bring it into the *Ungunja*, where the store is placed before the Alatunja and men of the totem, who then eat some of the smaller ones and hand back the remainder to the men who do not belong to the totem. After this the men of the totem may eat sparingly of the grub.

In the Bandicoot totem the animal is not eaten, after *Intichiuma*, until it is plentiful. When it is, those who do not belong to the totem go out in search of one which, when caught, is brought into the *Ungunja*, and there they put some of the fat from the animal into the mouths of the bandicoot men, and also rub it over their own bodies. After this the bandicoot men may eat a little of the animal.

It will be seen from what has now been described that at the present day the totemic animal or plant, as the case may be, is almost, but not quite, tabu or, as the Arunta people call it, *ekirinja* to the members of the totem. At the same time, though a man will tell you that his totem is the same thing as himself, he does not mean to imply by that what Grey says with regard to the totems of the natives whom he studied, and who always killed with reluctance an animal belonging to their totem under the belief "that some one individual of the species is their nearest friend, to kill whom would be a great crime, and to be carefully avoided."[95]

The members of each totem claim to have the power of increasing the number of the animal or plant, and in this respect the tradition connected with Undiara, the great centre of the kangaroo totem, just as the Emily gap is the great centre of the Witchetty grub totem, is of especial interest. In the Alcheringa, as we have already described, a special kangaroo was killed by kangaroo men and its body brought to Undiara and deposited in the cave close by the water hole. The rocky ledge arose to mark the spot, and into this entered its spirit part and also the spirit parts of many other kangaroo animals (not men) who came subsequently and, as the natives say, went down into the earth here. The rock is in fact the *Nanja* stone of the kangaroo animals, and to them this particular rock has just the same relationship as the water hole close by has to the men. The one is full of spirit kangaroo animals just as the other is full of spirit men and women. The purpose of the *Intichiuma* ceremony at the present day, so say the natives, is by means of pouring out the blood of kangaroo men upon the rock, to drive out in all directions the spirits of the kangaroo animals and so to increase the number of the animals. The spirit kangaroo enters the kangaroo animal in just the same way in which the spirit kangaroo man enters the kangaroo woman.

In this tradition we have probably the clue to the general meaning of the series of *Intichiuma* ceremonies, the object of each of which is to increase the number of the totemic animal or plant. Further still, attention may be drawn to the fact that the object of increasing the number of the totem is, in all cases, such as that of the Hakea or the Irriakura or plum tree amongst plants, or the kangaroo, euro, lizard, snake and so forth amongst animals, in which the totemic animal or plant is an article of food, that of increasing the food supply. That the totemic animal or plant is not regarded exactly as a close relative, whom it would be wrong to kill or to assist anyone else to kill, is very evident; on the contrary, the members of one totem not only, as it were, give their permission to those who are not of the totem to kill and eat the totemic animal or plant, but further, as shown clearly in the case of the euro man who made and charmed a special Churinga with the express object of assisting a plum tree man to catch euro, they will actually help in the destruction of their totem.

The question of the killing and eating of the totem which this opens up, quite apart from the ceremonial eating of a small portion of the same, after the performance of *Intichiuma*, is, so far as these tribes are concerned, one of considerable difficulty to deal with. We may first of all draw attention to certain points in the traditions which bear upon the question. These traditions or myths, whichever they be called, cannot be regarded as having been invented simply to account for certain customs now practised, for the simple reason that they reveal to us a state of organisation and a series of customs quite different from, and in important respects at variance with, the organisation and customs of the present time. In connection with the eating of the totem, for example, though we find very circumstantial references to this, there is no attempt to explain how the present tabu arose, but we find, on the contrary, that, in the far away times to which the traditions are supposed to refer, there simply was no such tabu. Under these circumstances we are probably justified in regarding the traditions in question as actually indicative of a time when customs in this and in other respects were very different from those in force at the present day.

So far as the eating of the totem is concerned the following incidents, amongst others, are of importance. A euro man named Algura-wartna was in pursuit of a euro which carried fire in its body. After following it up for some time the man killed it and, taking the fire out of its body, cooked therewith some euro which he carried with him. After that he cooked and eat the one which he had killed.

In a Quabara relating to an *Oruncha*[96] man, the decoration on the head referred to an Idnimita (grub of beetle) man who was killed by this *Oruncha*. The man was carrying with him Idnimita grubs, which were specially represented in the decorations, and on which he was feeding. In a Chankuna (small edible berry) ceremony a Chankuna man was represented as eating the berries which he plucked from his beard.

At a spot called Erathippa a plum tree woman was out

finding plums to eat when a man came and stole her *Nurtunja* which she had left in camp.

An Irpunga (fish) man was seen by certain wild cat men during their wanderings, fishing in a small pool to catch the fish on which he fed.

An opossum man was robbed by another man of the moon which he carried about with him at night time so as to help him to catch opossums.

During the wanderings of a party of wild cat men they are reported to have come to a certain spot where they met some men who were what is called *Ulpmerka* of the plum tree totem. The wild cat men went into the earth and arose as plum tree men, and after that went on eating plums. A bandicoot woman started out with a Hakea woman. After some time, she, the bandicoot woman, made *Quabara undattha*, that is performed a sacred ceremony, and painted the Hakea woman with down used during the ceremony, thus changing her into a bandicoot woman, after which, says the tradition, the latter went on feeding upon bandicoot. An Arunga or euro man started out in pursuit of a kangaroo which he was anxious to kill and eat but, to enable himself to do this, he first of all changed himself into a kangaroo man.

These and other statements of a similar nature are so precise (they are, as it were, often dragged into the tradition apropos of nothing), and are yet so entirely different from the present customs of the tribe, that they can only be understood on the hypothesis that they refer to a former time in which the relationship of the human beings to their totemic animals or plants was of a different nature from that which now obtains.

At some earlier time it would appear as if the members of a totem had the right to feed upon the totemic animal or plant as if this were indeed a functional necessity, though at the same time it must be remembered that in the same traditions from which the above extracts have been made for the purpose of drawing attention to this feature, there are also plenty of references to men and women eating animals and plants other than their own totem.[97] The idea of a kangaroo man freely eating a kangaroo or a bandicoot woman feeding on bandicoots is so totally opposed to the present custom of the tribe that we are obliged to regard these traditions as referring to a past time when customs in respect of the totems were different from what they are now.

In his *Vocabulary of the Dialects of South-Western Australia*,[98] Sir George Grey, when giving the meaning of certain of the native names for totems, says, in regard to the Ballaroke, a small opossum, "Some natives say that the Ballaroke family derived their name from having in former times subsisted principally on this little animal"; and again of the Nag-karm totem, he says, "From subsisting principally in former times on this fish, the Nagarnook family are said to have obtained their name." In regard further to five totemic groups, which bear the names of birds, he says, that they, that is the members of the respective totems, are said to be the birds transformed into men. The curious agreement between this and what we have just described as occurring in the Arunta tribe is of considerable interest. In the latter, the belief in the origin of the members of any totem from the animal or plant whose name they bear is universal and is regarded as a satisfactory reason for the totemic name. It may be that in the traditions dealing with the eating of the totem, we have nothing more than another attempt to explain the origin of the totem name. Judging, however, from the curious traditions of the Arunta tribe, taken in conjunction with the ceremonies of *Intichiuma*, this does not seem to be so probable as that they point back to a past time when the restrictions with regard to the eating were very different from those now in force. It is quite possible that the curious ceremony in which the members of any local group bring in to the men's camp stores of the totemic animal or plant and place them before the members of the totem, thus clearly recognising that it is these men who have the first right of eating it, as well as the remarkable custom according to which one man will actually assist another to catch and kill his—*i.e.*, the former's—totemic animal, may be surviving relics of a custom according to which, in past times, the members of a totem not only theoretically had, but actually practised, the right of eating their totem.

It may perhaps be that this eating of the totem shows that for some reason, as Mr. Frazer[99] has suggested in the case of certain other tribes in which the totem is eaten, the respect for the totem has lessened in comparison with what it once was; but, in face of the solemn ceremony of *Intichiuma* and of the explicit traditions to which reference has been made, it is difficult to believe that this can be so. The two traditions, in one of which a bandicoot woman is stated to have changed her companion, a Hakea woman, into a bandicoot woman, who after that went on feeding on bandicoot, while in the other a euro man is described as changing himself into a kangaroo man for the purpose of being able to pursue, kill and eat a kangaroo, are perhaps sufficient to show, taken in conjunction with the *Intichiuma* ceremonies, that, in the Arunta and Ilpirra tribes, a man is most intimately associated with his totem, but in a way quite unlike that which is usually associated with the idea of a totem. At the same time, though the relationship is different in certain respects from that which exists in other tribes, yet it will be clearly seen that what have been described as the totems agree in fundamental points with the definition given by Mr. Frazer,[100] *viz.*, "A totem is a class of material objects which a savage regards with superstitious respect, believing that there exists between him and every member of the class an intimate and altogether special relation;" and further still we can see, to use Mr. Frazer's terms, the existence of both a social and a religious aspect. The former is not so strongly developed as it is in many other Australian tribes, amongst whom not only does the totem regulate marriage, but the members of the totem are bound to mutually assist one another. In the Arunta tribe the most striking feature from a social point of view is the strongly local character, though at the same time it must be remembered that any initiated member of a particular totem, whatever local group he belongs to, may take part in the totemic ceremonies. The religious aspect is most clearly seen in connection with the ceremonies of *Intichiuma* and the subsequent solemn eating of the totem, though here again the relationship between the man and his totem cannot be described as one "of mutual respect and protection."[101] It seems as if, in the case of the Central Australian tribes, the totemic system has undergone a somewhat curious development; at all events, it differs in certain respects from that of all other Australian tribes with which we are as yet acquainted.

Chapter VII

Initiation Ceremonies

All Australian natives, with rare exceptions, have to pass through some initiation ceremony before being admitted to the secrets of the tribe—Enumeration of ceremonies amongst the Arunta and Ilpirra tribes—Absence of the knocking out of teeth as an initiation rite—Ceremonies amongst natives of Finke River—First ceremony—Throwing the boy up in the air—The second ceremony—Circumcision or *Lartna*—The *Apulla* ground—Women dancing—Decorating of the boy—Appointment of officials to conduct various parts of the ceremony—Boy receives title of *Wurtja*—Handing the firestick to the boy—Seclusion in the bush—Performance of certain sacred ceremonies—Ceremony of *Okoara*—The *Waninga*, its construction and meaning—Woman running off with the *Wurtja*—Appointing an official to paint a totemic design on the novice's back—Painting of the boy—Bringing in of the *Arachitta* poles—Two women rub the design off the boy's back—The women stripping the *Arachitta* poles while the men dance—Setting fire to the brakes—The women retire—*Arachitta* poles placed on the *Wurtja*—Performance of the actual ceremony—Presentation to the novice of the men who had acted as officials—Giving Churinga to the novice and sending him into the bush—Restrictions to be observed by certain relatives of the boy while he is out in the bush—Ceremony of head-biting—Ceremony of subincision or *Ariltha kuma*—The *Nurtunja*, its construction and meaning—Burning the blood after *Ariltha*—Men submitting to a second operation of *Ariltha*—Recovery from subincision—Taking the *Ertwa-kurka* to the women—Elder sisters cutting off hair from the *Ertwa-kurka*—Throwing a boomerang in the direction of the mother's camp in the Alcheringa—Putting the *Ertwa-kurka* on the fire—Various grades passed through during initiation—Ceremony of circumcision in the northern part of the tribe—Meaning of subincision—Nothing to do with preventing procreation—Customs in the Southern Arunta—Initiation of women.

EVERY Australian native, so far as is known, has in the normal condition of the tribe to pass through certain ceremonies of initiation before he is admitted to the secrets of the tribe, and is regarded as a fully developed member of it. These ceremonies vary both in their nature and number to a very large extent in different tribes. Those of the eastern and south-eastern coastal districts are entirely different from those of the central tribes, amongst whom they are more elaborate and spread over a long series of years, the first taking place at about the age of ten or twelve, whilst the final and most impressive one is not passed through until probably the native has reached the age of at least twenty-five, or it may be thirty. In the Arunta and Ilpirra tribes the ceremonies are four in number:—

1. Painting and throwing the boy up in the air.
2. Circumcision or *Lartna*.
3. Subincision or *Ariltha*.
4. The *Engwura* or fire ceremony.

The times at which these take place and the details of the ceremonies vary to a certain extent in various parts of the tribes, which, it must be remembered, occupy an area of country stretching from Charlotte Waters in the south to at least 100 miles north of Alice Springs, that is over an area measuring 300 miles north and south by at least 100 miles east and west, and comprising in the south a wide extent of upland, stony plains and sand hills, and in the north a succession of ranges running east and west, and reaching an elevation of 5,000 feet.

One of the most noticeable features of the ceremonies, from a negative point of view, is the absence of the knocking out of teeth as a general custom associated with the initiatory rites. Amongst many tribes of the eastern coastal district this forms a prominent feature, but amongst the Central Australian natives, whilst it may be performed, it has nothing to do with initiation, and is, in fact, practised by men as well as women, the rite having no sacred significance of any kind; and yet, as we shall see later, there is not only evidence which shows that it has once been a ceremony of greater importance than it is at the present day, but also that there are certain details which are curiously similar to those concerned with the ceremony in parts where it forms the most important initiation rite.

In the case of particular local groups amongst the Arunta, as, for example, the natives now living in the district to the north and north-east of Alice Springs, it is much more widely practised than elsewhere; but, speaking generally, the knocking out of teeth is amongst the Arunta and other central tribes a matter partly of individual and partly of local taste and fashion.[102] The custom is probably to be regarded as one which was at some distant time prevalent amongst the common ancestors of the central and eastern coastal tribes, but which has undergone changes as the tribes became separated from one another and developed, so far as their customs are concerned, along different lines. In some it has retained its old significance, or may have even acquired still greater importance as an initiatory rite, but in others, as, for example, all those inhabiting the central area, it has lost its old meaning, its place has been taken by other rites, and now it is merely what we may call a rudimentary custom.

To a certain extent, as we have said, the details of the various initiation ceremonies differ in different parts of the tribe. We will first of all describe them as carried out in the groups living on the Finke River, and will then point out variations in the ceremonies as they are enacted, first in the northern, and secondly in the southern parts.

THE FIRST CEREMONY—THROWING THE BOY UP IN THE AIR

The first ceremony takes place when a boy is between ten and twelve years of age. The men, and in this instance the women also, assemble at a central spot near to the main camp, and the boys who have reached the right age—the number varying from ceremony to ceremony—are taken one by one and tossed in the air several times by the men, who catch them as they fall, while the women dance round and round the group, swinging their arms and shouting loudly, "*pau, pau, pau-a-a*," the last cry being very prolonged.[103] This over the boys are painted on their chests and backs, as shown in the illustration, with simple designs consisting of straight or curved bands outlined by lines of red or yellow ochre. These have not of necessity any reference to the totem of the boys. They are painted by men who stand to the boys in the relation of *Umbirna*, that is, brother of a woman whom the boy may marry. In some cases, at all events, they are copied from old rock paintings, certain of which are associated with particular totems, but the boy will not of necessity be decorated with a design of his own totem. Certain of these particular designs are described in connection with the sacred drawings. If the boy has what is called an *Unjipinna*[104] man, then it is the latter who will draw the design upon him at the close of the ceremony of throwing up.

In all the ceremonies of initiation the youth or man has certain designs painted on his body, and in no case have they of necessity any reference to his own totem, though they are emblematic of some totem with which usually the man who does the painting is associated. These designs come under the general term of *Ilkinia*, the name applied to the designs, as a whole, which are emblematic of the totems; and so long as the boy, youth or man has one or other of these painted on him, it does not signify which. It must be remembered that the man who does the painting is usually the person who decides upon the nature of the design, and it may also be noted that in the performance of sacred ceremonies men are constantly decorated with designs of totems other than their own.

In the case of this, the first of the initiatory ceremonies, the painting of each boy is done as stated by men who stand to him in the relationship of *Umbirna*, that is, a man who is the brother of a woman of the class from which his, *i.e.* the boy's, wife must come. The design is called *Enchichichika*, and while they are being painted the boys are told that the ceremony through which they have just passed will promote their growth to manhood, and they are also told by tribal fathers and elder brothers that in future they must not play with the women and girls, nor must they camp with them as they have hitherto done, but henceforth they must go to the camp of the men, which is known as the *Ungunja*. Up to this time they have been accustomed to go out with the women as they searched for vegetable food and the smaller animals such as lizards and rats; now they begin to accompany the men in their search for larger game, and begin also to look forward to the time when they will become fully initiated and admitted to all the secrets of the tribe, which are as yet kept hidden from them.

The ceremony of throwing up is called *Alkirakiwuma* (from *alkira* the sky, and *iwuma* to throw), and very shortly after this sometimes even before it, the boy has his nasal septum bored through, usually by his father or paternal grandfather, and begins to wear the nose bone. This boring is practised by men and women alike, and the operation is attended by a short but interesting special ceremony, which is elsewhere described. Amongst the women the nose boring is usually done by the husband immediately after marriage, and it may be remarked in passing that in both sexes the constant wearing of the nose bone emphasises the flattening out of the lobes of the nose.

A good many years may elapse between the throwing up ceremony and the performance of the two much more important ceremonies of circumcision or *Lartna*, and that of subincision or *Ariltha*. Speaking generally, it may be said that circumcision may take place at any age after the boy has arrived at puberty.

Before the time at which the boy is thrown up in the air he is spoken of as an *Ambaquerka*, which is the term applied to a child generally, of whichever sex it may be. After the throwing up, and until the ceremony of circumcision, he is called *Ulpmerka*.

THE SECOND CEREMONY—CIRCUMCISION OR LARTNA

When it has been decided by the boy's elder male relatives (usually his elder brothers) that he has arrived at the proper age, preparations are made unknown to him, for the carrying out of the ceremony. These consist first of all in the gathering together of a large supply of food material for the ceremonies are attended with the performance of what are usually spoken of as corrobborees, which last over several days. If a stranger belonging to any other group happens to be present in camp when the operation is being performed he will take part in the proceedings, but in the Arunta tribe there is usually no sending out of messengers to other groups to bring them in to the performance, as there is in the coastal tribes; nor is it usual to operate upon more than one, or at most two, novices at the same time; each boy is initiated when he is supposed to have reached the proper age, and the ceremony is controlled by the men of his own local group, who may ask any one to take part or not in it just as they feel disposed.

In the following account we will describe what took place during an actual ceremony, which was conducted recently by a group of natives associated with a spot called Undiara,[105] one of the most important centres of the kangaroo totem situated near to the Finke River. It must always be remembered that the details of these initiation ceremonies vary to a certain extent according to the locality in which they are performed; thus at Undiara the men of the kangaroo totem directed the proceedings, and therefore sacred ceremonies concerned with this particular totem were much in evidence; had Undiara been an emu locality then emu ceremonies would have predominated. Bearing this in mind, the ceremony now to be described may be regarded as typical of the rite of circumcision as carried out by the natives living along the Finke River, who are often spoken of as Larapinta blacks to distinguish them from other groups, Larapinta being the native name of the river.

The boy was seized early in the evening at the *Ungunja*, or men's camp, by three young men, who were respectively *Okilia*, *Umbirna* and *Unkulla* to him. As soon as they laid hands on him they shouted loudly, "*Utchai, utchai*," while being frightened, he struggled, trying to get free from them. He was at once carried off bodily to the ceremonial ground which had been carefully prepared at some distance from and out of sight of the main camp, so that the women, when at the latter, could not see anything of what was taking place at the former, which is called the *Apulla*. The nature of this can be seen from the accompanying plan. A path about five feet wide is cleared of grass and shrubs, and the surface soil is heaped up on either side, so as to form a low, narrow bank of the same length as the path, which is some forty or fifty feet in length, and always made so as to run east and west. At a distance of about forty feet from the eastern end was a brake of boughs at which the men were assembled. The women were grouped at the spot marked C.

Once on the ground, and in the presence of all the men and women, the boy made no further resistance, but apparently resigned himself to his fate. He was taken to the men and sat down amongst them, while the women, who had been awaiting his arrival, at once began to dance, carrying shields in their hands. The reason assigned for this is that in the Alcheringa certain women called *Unthippa*[106] carried along with them as they travelled over the country a number of young boys who were just being initiated. As they travelled along, dancing the whole way, they also carried shields: and therefore it is that, at the present day, the initiation ceremony must commence with an imitation of the *Unthippa* dance of the Alcheringa.[107] Except in connection with this ceremony women may never carry shields, which are exclusively the property of the men, just as much as a digging-stick is the peculiar property of a woman. While the women were dancing the men sang of the marching of the *Unthippa* women across the country. After the boy had watched and listened for some time, an *Unkulla*[108] man came up and twined round and round his hair strands of fur string, until it looked as if his head were enclosed in a tight-fitting skull cap. Then a man who was *Gammona* to him came up and fastened round his waist a large *Uliara*, that is, the human hair girdle worn by the men, the girdle being provided by an *Oknia* of the boy. The two first-named men were respectively the brother of the boy's mother and the son of this man, the *Oknia* being a tribal brother of the boy's father who was dead, as also was the actual mother. After this a council of the *Oknia* and *Okilia*[109] of the novice was held, and three men, who were respectively *Mura*, *Gammona* and *Chimmia*, were told off to take the boy away and paint him. These men are afterwards called *Wulya*, or *Uwilia*, by the boy. They first of all went away and built a second brake of bushes at the western end of the *Apulla*, at a distance of about forty feet from the end of the cleared path, so that in position the second brake corresponded to the first one at the opposite end. This was henceforth to be the brake behind which the boy had to remain except when brought on to the ground to witness performances. When this had been made the three men returned and led the boy through the dancing women to his brake, where, with great deliberation, they rubbed him all over with grease, and then decorated his body with pinkish-white clay and bird's down.

During all the proceedings every detail, such as the appointing of the various officials, was determined upon by a council of men consisting of the *Oknia* (tribal fathers) and

Okilia (blood and tribal elder brothers) of the novice, and of this council the elder *Oknia* was head man.

After painting him, the *Uwilia* told the boy that he was now no longer an *Ulpmerka* but a *Wurtja*, that during the proceedings about to follow he must render implicit obedience, and on no account must he ever tell any woman or boy anything of what he was about to see. Should he ever reveal any of the secrets, then he and his nearest relations would surely die. He must not speak unless spoken to, and even then his words must be as few as possible, and spoken in a low tone. He was further told to remain crouched down behind his brake when left there, and that on no account must he make the slightest attempt to see what the men at their brake were doing. Should he try to see what was going on at the *Apulla*, except when taken there and told to watch, some great calamity would happen to him—*Twanyikira*, the great spirit whose voice was heard when the bull-roarers spoke, would carry him away. When these instructions had been given to him by the *Uwilia* they went away, and he was then visited by his *Okilia*, who repeated precisely the same instructions, and after this the *Wurtja* was left for an hour or two to his own reflections. Meanwhile a man had been appointed to act as *Urinthantima*, whose duty will be seen shortly, and until daylight dawned the dancing and singing went on with astonishing vigour. Then one of the *Okilia* went and brought back the *Wurtja*, passing with him as before through the middle of the dancing women, who opened out to allow them to pass through, and placed him sitting on the lap of the *Urinthantima* man.

The oldest *Mia* woman of the boy (his actual *Mia* or mother being dead) had brought with her from her own camp a fire-stick, which she had been careful to keep alight all night. At daylight she lit a fire by means of this, and then took two long sticks with which she had provided herself, and, lighting them at the fire, went and sat down, holding them in her hands, immediately behind the *Urinthantima* man. The *Uwinna*, that is the sisters of the boy's father, went and also sat down along with her. Then, as the men began to sing a special fire song, she handed one of the fire-sticks to the woman who was the *Mura tualcha* of the boy, that is the woman whose eldest daughter, born or unborn, has been assigned to the *Wurtja* as his future wife, so that she is potentially his mother-in-law. While the singing went on this woman approached the boy, and, after tying round his neck bands of fur string, she handed to him the fire-stick,[110] telling him as she did so to always hold fast to his own fire—in other words not to interfere with women assigned to other men. After this, at a signal from an old *Okilia*, the *Wurtja* got up and ran away, followed by a number of shouting boys, who after a short time returned, and, along with the women, left the *Apulla* ground and ran back to the main camp. The old *Mia* took her fire-stick with her, and in camp guarded it with great care, fixing it at an angle into the ground so as to catch the wind and ensure its being kept alight. The *Wurtja* had, whilst in his camp, to guard his fire-stick in just the same way, and was cautioned that if he lost it, or allowed it to go out, both he and his *Mia* would be killed by *Kurdaitcha*. On the day on which he was taken back to the camp, they both threw away their fire-sticks.

When the *Wurtja* left the *Apulla*, he was accompanied by some *Okilia* and *Unkulla* men who remained out in the bush with him for three days. During this time nothing of any special nature happened to him beyond the fact that he might not speak unless he was first spoken to, which seldom took place, and that he might not eat freely, though as yet he was not bound by the restrictions with regard to food which he would shortly have to obey. The main object of this partial seclusion is to impress him with the fact that he is about to enter the ranks of the men, and to mark the break between his old life and the new one; he has no precise knowledge of what is in store for him, and the sense that something out of the ordinary is about to happen to him—something moreover which is of a more or less mysterious nature—helps to impress him strongly with a feeling of the deep importance of compliance with tribal rules, and further still with a strong sense of the superiority of the older men who know, and are familiar with, all the mysterious rites, some of which he is about to learn the meaning of for the first time.

On the fourth day the *Wurtja* was brought back, and at once placed behind his brake, which is called *Atnumbanta*, and from which he might not move without the permission of one of the *Okilia* who had been told off to guard him, and whose father was the *Oknia* who acted as the head man of the council. On the night of the fourth day the men sang of the marchings of the men of the Ullakuppera (little hawk) totem in the Alcheringa, and of their operations with their famous *Lialira* or stone knives. It was these men who, according to tradition, first introduced the use of a stone knife at circumcision, the operation having been previously conducted by means of a fire-stick.[111] At times they broke into the *Lartna* song:

"Irri yulta yulta rai
Ul katchera ul katchar-rai,"

which is always sung in loud fierce tones. About midnight two *Okilia* went to the *Wurtja's* brake, and having put a bandage round his eyes led him to the men who sat as usual on the side of their brake facing towards the *Apulla*. Here he was placed lying face downwards, until two men who were going to perform a ceremony were in position between the *Apulla* lines. The Quabara, which they were about to perform, was one of a certain number which are only performed at a time such as this, though in all important respects these Quabara are identical with those performed during various ceremonies concerned with the totems. When the boy was told by his *Okilia* and *Oknia* to sit up and look he saw, lying in front of him, and on his side, a decorated man whom the *Okilia* and *Oknia*, both of them speaking at once, told him represented a wild dog. At the other end of the *Apulla* a decorated man stood, with legs wide apart, holding up twigs of Eucalyptus in each hand, and having his head ornamented with a small *Waninga*,[112] which is a sacred object emblematic of some totemic animal, in this particular case a kangaroo. This man moved his head from side to side, as if looking for something, and every now and then uttered a sound similar to that made by a kangaroo, which animal he was supposed to represent. Suddenly the dog looked up, saw the kangaroo, began barking, and, running along on all fours, passed between the man's legs and lay down behind the man, who kept watching him over his shoulder. Then the dog ran again between the kangaroo-man's legs, but this time he was caught and well shaken, and a pretence was made of dashing his head against the ground, whereupon he howled as if in pain. These movements were repeated several times, and finally the dog was supposed to be killed by the kangaroo. After a short pause the dog ran along on all fours to where the *Wurtja* sat and laid himself on top of the boy, then the old kangaroo hopped along and got on top of both of them, so that the *Wurtja* had to bear the weight of the two men for about two minutes. When the performers got up, the *Wurtja*, still lying down, was told by the old men that the Quabara represented an incident which took place in the Alcheringa, when a wild dogman attacked a kangaroo-man, and was killed by the latter. The article which the kangaroo wore on its head was a *Waninga*, which was a sacred object, and must never be mentioned in the hearing of women and children; it belonged to the kangaroo totem, and was indeed the representative of a kangaroo. When all had been explained to him, he was led back to his brake, and the men continued singing at intervals all night long.

The Quabara, which are performed at these initiation ceremonies, vary according to the locality in which they are being performed, and the men who are taking the leading part in them. If, for example, the old man who is presiding belongs to the emu totem, then the Quabara will at all events to a certain, and probably a large extent, deal with incidents concerned with ancestral emu men. In the particular ceremony upon which this account is based, the old man presiding belonged to the kangaroo totem, and therefore Quabara belonging especially to this totem were much in evidence. The totem of the novice has no influence whatever on the nature of the particular Quabara performed. Each old man who presides over, or takes the leading part in, a ceremony such as this has possession of a certain number of Quabara, and naturally those performed are chosen from this series as they are the ones which he has the right to perform. It is necessary also to remember that ceremonial objects, such as the *Waninga*, which figure largely in some districts, are unknown in others where their place is taken by entirely different objects. Thus, for example, in the northern part of the Arunta and in the Ilpirra tribe, a sacred pole called a *Nurtunja* is used, and in these parts this has precisely the significance of the *Waninga*, which is never met with in the northern districts, just as the *Nurtunja* is never met with in the south.

On the fifth day, in the afternoon, another performance in which two kangaroos and one dog figured was given. The kangaroos wore, as before, small *Waninga* in their hair, and this time carried between their teeth, and also in their hair, bunches of wooden shavings soaked in blood, which were supposed to represent wounds received from the bites of the dogs. The performance was essentially similar to that of the previous day, and the antics of the dog as he ran round and looked up, barking at the kangaroo or howled lustily as his head was bumped against the ground brought smiles to every face except that of the *Wurtja*. Finally the dog ran along and got on top of the *Wurtja*, and then the two kangaroos followed, so that this time the boy had three men on top of him. When all was over he was once more instructed, cautioned, and taken back to his brake.

On the sixth day the *Wurtja* was taken out hunting by *Okilia* and *Umbirna* men, and the night was spent in singing with little intermission songs which referred to the wanderings of certain of the Alcheringa ancestors, to which the *Wurtja*, sitting quietly at the men's brake, listened.

It must be remembered that it is now for the first time that the *Wurtja* hears anything of these traditions and sees the ceremonies performed, in which the ancestors of the tribe are represented as they were, and acting as they did during life. In various accounts of initiation ceremonies of the Australian tribes, as, for example, in the earliest one ever published—the one written by Collins in 1804—we meet with descriptions of performances in which different animals are represented, but except in the case of the Arunta tribe, no indication of the meaning and signification of these performances has been forthcoming beyond the fact that they are associated with the totems. In the Arunta and Ilpirra tribes they are not only intimately associated with the totemic system, but have a very definite meaning. Whether they have a similar significance in other tribes we have as yet no definite evidence to show, but it is at all events worthy of note that whilst the actual initiation rite varies from tribe to tribe, consisting in some in the knocking out of teeth, and in others in circumcision, &c., in all, or nearly all, an important part of the ceremony consists in showing to the novices certain dances, the important and common feature of which is that they represent the actions of special totemic animals. In the Arunta tribe, however, they have a very definite meaning. At the first glance it looks much as if all that they were intended to represent were the behaviour of certain animals, but in reality they have a much deeper meaning, for each performer represents an ancestral individual who lived in the Alcheringa. He was a member of a group of individuals, all of whom, just like himself, were the direct descendants or transformations of the animals, the names of which they bore. It is as a reincarnation of the never-dying spirit part of one of these semi-animal ancestors that every member of the tribe is born, and, therefore, when born he, or she, bears of necessity the name of the animal or plant of which the Alcheringa ancestor was a transformation or descendant.

The nature of these performances may be gathered from one which was performed on the next—the seventh day. As usual in all these ceremonies, the body of the performer was decorated with ochre, and lines of birds' down, which were supposed to be arranged in just the same way as they had been on the body of the Alcheringa man. From his waist was suspended a ball of fur string, which was supposed to represent the scrotum of the kangaroo, and when all was ready the performer came hopping leisurely out from behind the men's brake, where he had been decorated, lying down every now and then on his side to rest as a kangaroo does. The boy had, as usual, been brought blindfolded on to the ground, and at first was made to lie flat down. When the performer hopped out he was told to get up and watch. For about ten minutes the performer went through the characteristic movements of the animal, acting the part very cleverly, while the men sitting round the *Wurtja* sang of the wanderings of the kangaroo in the Alcheringa. Then after a final and very leisurely hop round the *Apulla* ground the man came and lay down on top of the *Wurtja*, who was then instructed in the tradition to which the performance refers. He was told that in the Alcheringa a party of kangaroo men started from a place called Ultainta, away out to the east of what is now called Charlotte Waters, and that after wandering about they came to a spot called Karinga (in the Edith Range about thirty miles south-west of Alice Springs), where one of the party who was named Unburtcha died; that is, his body died, but the spirit part of him was in a sacred Churinga, which he carried and did not die, but remained behind along with the Churinga when the party travelled on. This spirit, the old men told him, went, at a later time, into a woman, and was born again as a Purula man, whose name was, of course, Unburtcha, and who was a kangaroo man just as his ancestor was. He was told that the old men know all about these matters, and decide who has come to life again in the form of a man or woman. Sometimes the spirit child which goes into a woman is associated with one of the sacred Churinga, numbers of which every Alcheringa individual carried about with him or her (for in those days the women were allowed to carry them just as the men were), and then, in this case, the child has no definite name, but of course it belongs to the same totem as did the individual who had carried the Churinga about in the Alcheringa; that is, if it were a kangaroo man or woman, so of course must the child be, and then the old men determine what shall be its secret or sacred name.

It is in this way that the boy during the initiation ceremonies is instructed, for the first time, in any of the sacred matters referring to the totems, and it is by means of the performances which are concerned with certain animals, or rather, apparently with the animals, but in reality with Alcheringa individuals who were the direct transformations of such animals, that the traditions dealing with this subject, which is of the greatest importance in the eyes of the natives, are firmly impressed upon the mind of the novice, to whom everything which he sees and hears is new and surrounded with an air of mystery.

After the performance was over, the *Wurtja* was led back to his brake, and then a council was held for the purpose of selecting a man to perform the operation, and another man to act as assistant. Both these men are called *Atwia atwia* and in addition to them, another man was selected, whose duty it was to hold up the shield upon which the boy was seated during the operation, this man being known by the name of

Elucha. The conversation was carried on in whispers, the men when speaking, placing their mouths close to each other's ears. While this consultation was in progress, the other men sitting close to the brake sang in fierce loud tones, the *Lartna* song—"*Irriyulta yulta rai*," &c.

After discussing matters for some time, it was decided that an old man who was *Mura* to the boy, was to perform the ceremony, and that a man who was *Gammona* to the former, was to act as assistant, while another old man who was *Ikuntera*, that is possible father-in-law, was to act as shield-bearer or *Elucha*. It must be remembered that, in addition to the honour attaching to these offices, there are certain emoluments, for, when the operation is all over, the boy has to provide each of these men with an offering of food. As soon as this decision had been arrived at, the singing stopped, and the three *Okilia* went and sat in a line at the end of the *Apulla* path, looking very grave, as if the business now to be performed were of the deepest importance. Each one of them then got up in turn, and bringing one of the appointed officials, each of whom made a pretence of reluctance, placed him in front of the line occupied by himself and his brother *Okilia*, so that now there were two rows of men facing each other. The old *Mura* man sat in the middle of his row, and facing him was the eldest of the *Okilia*. The latter then smoothed with his hand the surface of the ground between the two lines, and then, picking up a spear-thrower by the end to which the point was attached, he thrust his beard into his mouth, as did also the *Mura* man, and for a short time both glared fiercely at one another. Then without taking his eyes off the *Mura* man, he scooped up with the chisel end of the weapon a little soil, and, gliding along on his knees, emptied it into the hands of the former. Then he embraced him, rubbed their bodies together, and finally rubbed his forehead against the stomach of the *Mura* man. When this was over, he repeated the whole performance with the two other officials, and then the three old men were embraced in turn by the other *Okilia*, who, however, did not present them with dirt.

The meaning of the ceremony is simply, so they say, to imply that the youth is intrusted to them for the purpose of being initiated, with as little hesitation as the dirt is placed in their hands.

This little ceremony is called *Okoara*, and was conducted with much solemnity. When it was over, the men who had taken part in it joined the others, and once more the *Lartna* song was sung with much fierceness. Singing was kept up all night long with only short intervals of rest. Early in the evening, the *Wurtja* was brought from his brake, and spent the night amongst the men, listening to, but taking no part in, the singing.

The morning of the eighth day was spent in preparing for a ceremony concerned with the Illuta (a rat) totem. The particular rat-man or man-rat—for, as already said, the identity of the human individual is sunk in that of the object with which he is associated, and from which he is supposed to have originated—to whom this ceremony referred, is supposed to have travelled from a place called Pulkira, west of the Finke River to Walyirra, where he died, and where his spirit remained associated as usual with the Churinga. In connection with this ceremony a large *Waninga* was used, which was made as follows. A long spear was taken, and close to each end a bar of wood about two feet in length was fixed at right angles to the length of the spear. Then strands of hair string were tied on so that they ran from cross bar to cross bar parallel to the central spear, and at each end the strands passed off, slantwise, to the latter. In some *Waningas* there may be three cross bars, in which case the top one is much smaller than the other two, and an extra series of strands of string pass from the outer part of the second cross bar to the top one, as shown in the figure (Fig. 39). The string is not all of one kind, but, in the one figured for example, the strands nearest to the central spear were of black human hair, then followed a band consisting of about eight strands of red-ochred opossum fur string, then a band of grey bandicoot fur string and again, on the margin, another band of opossum fur. The whole *Waninga* had white birds' down sprinkled over it and made to adhere to the string, as usual, by means of human blood. This object is the most elaborate and certainly the most artistic of all those which are used in connection with the various ceremonies.

In this particular ceremony the whole *Waninga* represented the body of a rat, the main part was supposed to be the trunk of the animal, the point end, the tail, and the handle end, the head, so that when in use the latter was carried downwards. The cross bars represented the limbs. The *Waninga* was carried by an *Okilia* while another man walked behind to steady it. Two other men were decorated to represent two *Kutta kutta* or little night hawks. When all was ready the *Wurtja* was brought blindfolded as usual from his brake to the *Apulla* ground, where he remained with his head covered up until the performers had got into position in front of him. They approached from the south side, making a circuit and walking with their backs turned towards the *Apulla* until they got opposite to, and about thirty yards from, the *Wurtja*, when the bandage was at once taken from his eyes. The two little hawk men with legs wide apart and hands grasping the ends of a stick which was held across the shoulders, came along down the *Apulla* lines towards the audience, sliding and quivering as they did so. Then they quickly returned, and were followed by the *Waninga* carriers who ran down the lines, stooping and bending the *Waninga* towards the *Wurtja*, but without touching him. Stopping every now and then, they stood erect and quivered or stood still. This was done several times, and then finally all four men came into the *Apulla* lines at the same time, the two little hawk men being at first in front; the latter then retired to the sides, and the *Waninga* carriers came on quivering. Then a man who was *Ikuntera* to the boy stepped out, and taking the *Waninga*[113] set it up in the *Apulla* path, and the *Wurtja* was told by *Oknia* and *Okilia* men to go out and embrace it, which he did for some minutes, while the men who had carried it stood by, and the others, gathered together at the brake, sang of the *Waninga*, and of the wanderings of the rat men in the Alcheringa. Once more the usual instructions and warnings were given to the *Wurtja*, and he was made to lie down with his head covered while another ceremony of a simple nature was prepared. The men around him occupied the time in singing about a party of Alcheringa individuals who started to walk from a place called Ayaiya. After the singing had gone on for about an hour, the *Wurtja* was told to look up, and, when he did so, he saw a number of men lying about the *Apulla* ground who at once began to hop about and to imitate the sound made by kangaroos. One old man in particular was noticeable from the way in which he mimicked the movements of an old and disabled animal. After hopping in and about the *Apulla* ground for some minutes, they bunched up together at the western end of the ground and then suddenly, rising with a loud shout of "*Pau pau pau*," ran away to a small gully out of sight of the *Wurtja*, who was told that these represented a party of Alcheringa men starting off from Ayaiya. After this, and while further preparations were being made, the *Wurtja* remained with the audience, but had his head covered. The tradition dealing with this special group of kangaroos relates that the party split into two, a larger and a smaller one, and that the larger one travelled on ahead of the smaller one. When preparing for the ceremony, the bodies were first of all rubbed over with red ochre, then two young men opened veins, first in one arm and then in the other, and allowed the blood to flow out in a stream over the heads and bodies of those who were about to take part in the ceremony. These men, who were ten in number, were then ornamented with little patches of down, but, unlike the usual plan of ornamentation, there was no regular pattern made, the reason for this being that the Alcheringa men had not used any regular pattern.

Each man carried on his head, and also between his teeth, a small mass of wooden shavings saturated with blood.

When all was ready they went, with the exception of three who stayed behind, on to the *Apulla* ground, walking in single file and carrying twigs of Eucalyptus in their hands. When they reached the ground a young man, who led the column and represented a young and frolicsome kangaroo which, according to tradition, accompanied the marchers, lay down sideways across the entrance to the path, with his back towards the *Wurtja*. The other men stood in the path with their legs wide apart, one behind the other, shifting their heads from side to side and making the twigs quiver. Then the *Wurtja* was told to sit up and the performers at once greeted his appearance with imitations of the sounds made by kangaroos; then the young kangaroo called *Kulla Kulla*, began frisking about and pretending to rush at the other performers, and, finally, darted between the legs of each man and emerged at the western end of the column, where he lay down quietly a few minutes. After he had gone through this performance four times, he was caught up as he came through the legs of the man nearest to the *Wurtja*. The two front men then picked him up and carried him bodily, standing astride of him, and laid him on his back on top of the *Wurtja*, upon whom all of the performers then threw themselves, so that the unfortunate novice had actually to bear the weight of the whole mass of men. As a result of this the *Wurtja* himself did not appear to be any the worse for what must have been a somewhat trying experience, but one of the two men who had carried the *Kulla Kulla* fainted as soon as the men extricated themselves. The stoical calmness of the *Wurtja* was most marked throughout the whole ceremony. After this first act in the performance, the men who had taken part in it seated themselves amongst the audience, and the remaining three men came on to the ground and went through the same performance, one of them personating a young kangaroo, who was carried up to and laid on the *Wurtja*, the other two men lying on the top of him. For this lying down on the top of the *Wurtja* there is a special term used—*wultha-chelpima*. After the usual explanations and cautions the *Wurtja* was led back to his brake.

On the morning of the ninth day the *Wurtja* was carefully greased all over by the *Okilia*, who was especially in charge of him, and he remained crouching or lying down at his brake until noon, when he was brought blindfolded to the ground. Then the kangaroo performance of the previous day was again enacted, the performance including the lying down upon the *Wurtja*.

In addition, however, to the decorations of the previous day, four of the old men wore on their heads a half circle made of grass stalks, bound round with fur string and decorated with white down called *Atnuta*. Each of these represented a dead kangaroo, which was carried on the head by the Alcheringa kangaroo ancestor as he marched across the country. In connection with this myth it is of interest to note that at the present day when a kangaroo or wallaby is killed the limbs are always dislocated at the joints, which makes them hang more limply and so renders them more easy to carry. In this condition the body is spoken of as *Atnuta* and the act of dislocating is called *ullakakulla*. After the performance the *Atnuta* were taken off the heads and handed round, while each man squatting on the ground kept the object pressed round his stomach for a few minutes, the *Wurtja* doing this also.

After this two more kangaroo ceremonies were performed, the second of which was of some importance. The principal performer carried a *Waninga*, which was really a double one, the top part representing a separate small one attached to the large one. The large *Waninga* represented an old man kangaroo and the small one his son. Two men, as usual, carried the *Waninga*, the front one supporting it on his back while the other man helped to keep it upright as they advanced and retreated along the *Apulla* path, stopping every now and then to quiver and to bend the *Waninga* over towards the *Wurtja*. The *Ikuntera* man then stood up, and taking the *Waninga* from the performers, fixed it upright in the path, and the boy was once more told to go up and embrace it. The showing of the *Waninga* to the *Wurtja* is called *amba-keli-irrima*, which means the child sees and knows. The embracing of the *Waninga* is called *eliaqua erkuma*. After the performance the *Wurtja* was once more instructed and cautioned not to reveal anything to women and children, and then made to lie down, while in loud fierce tones the men sang the *Lartna* song, "*irri yulta yulta rai*," &c., striking the ground with their shields as they did so. Then the *Wurtja* was taken back to his brake, where he remained till about nine o'clock at night, when he was brought to the *Apulla*, and there his head was decorated with stalks of cane grass, while at the same time the other men decorated themselves in the same way, inserting, in addition, stalks beneath their arm bands.

When this had been done the brake of boughs at which the men assembled was built higher and the men all crouched behind it. Then, at a signal from the old *Oknia*, the women once more approached from the main camp, shouting as they did so, "*pai! pai! pai!*" and took possession of the *Apulla* ground upon which they danced for some minutes. Then they went and stood on one side, which was the signal for the men to come out and stand on the *Apulla*. Then once more the women came up and joined the men, while the latter danced round, and the women, shouting "*pai! pai! pai!*" plucked the grass stalks from their heads. The men all danced with their faces turned towards the east as in the stripping dance at a later time, one or more women standing behind each man.

Then the *Mura* woman, who had previously given the fire-stick to the novice, after having stripped the *Wurtja* as he danced along with the other men, suddenly stopped, and, placing her head through his legs from behind, hoisted him on to her shoulders, and ran off with him followed by all the other women to a spot behind, and in a line with, the *Apulla*, from which it was distant about fifty yards. Here she placed him sitting on the ground, she herself sitting behind, clasping him in her arms, while some *Mia* and *Uwinna* women sat close behind her. The rest of the women continued to dance in front of the *Wurtja* shouting "*pai! pai! pai!*" and making a movement of invitation by slightly lifting the hands up and down with the arms bent at the elbows, while moving the fingers as if to beckon the *Wurtja* to them. This characteristic movement is adopted by the women during the course of various ceremonies, and is always associated with the idea of inviting the men to come to them. At the *Apulla* the men sat down and sang the fire song:—

"Atnylinga etunja illa althara wuntama,"

over and over again. *Atnylinga* is the red flower of a species of Eremophila, which, in the Alcheringa, was made red by much burning; *etunja* is a twig of Eucalyptus; *althara* means blazing up; and *illa wuntama* is the term applied to a fire which is rushing along, like one which has been lit on a windy day amongst the porcupine-grass on the sand hills. This special song is always sung on the night preceding the preparation of the *Arachitta* poles, the twigs used for swathing which are always put through a blazing fire.

The singing continued for about half an hour, after which the *Urinthantima* man, as well as another *Mura* man and the *Okilia* in charge of the novice, ran towards the women holding shields before their faces. The first-named seized the *Wurtja*, and, assisted by the other two, took him back to the *Apulla*, where he was told to lie down and his face was covered while the singing of the fire-song continued at intervals all night long. As soon as the *Wurtja* was taken from them the women ran away to the main camp.

At daybreak the *Urinthantima* man rubbed the *Wurtja* all over with dry red ochre and then wound fur string round his head, so as to completely hide his hair from sight, while the other men sang—

"Purta purta airpinta airpintina,"

the song sung while preparing the *Arachitta* poles. *Purta* is to arrange the leaves, to settle them in their right places; *airpinta airpintina* means round and round again. While this was being done the women came up to the *Apulla* and danced between the lines, backwards and forwards, in front of the *Wurtja*, making with their hands the movement of invitation and shouting "*pai! pai! pai!*" Suddenly the *Urinthantima* man hoisted the *Wurtja* up on to his shoulders and ran off with him followed by a number of the younger men, upon which the women at once ran back to their camp and the singing ceased. When out of sight of the *Apulla* the *Wurtja* was put down and the men proceeded to a spot about half a mile distant, where they made big fires and cut down a number of slender saplings which were to be used for *Arachitta* poles. The branches were then scorched in the flames while the men sang the fire-song "*Atnylinga etunja*," &c. When sufficient material was prepared they sat down and began to tie twigs on to the poles, the *Wurtja* assisting by breaking off twigs and handing them around; but he did not prepare a pole himself, and during the proceedings was never once spoken to. While at work the men sang "*purta purta airpinta airpintina*," and it was afternoon before the poles, about thirty in number and each about ten feet in length, were ready. Then a start was made for the *Apulla* ground, the poles being carried to a spot about two hundred yards from the *Apulla*, where they were stacked. Here, assisted by the boy's *Okilia*, the *Urinthantima* man tied twigs of Eremophila on to the *Wurtja's* body and head and then signalled to the men at the *Apulla* that they were ready, whereupon they moved away from the ground and shouted to the women who were waiting at some little distance out of sight. The women at once ran up and took possession of the *Apulla*, carrying shields and shouting "*pai! pai! pai!*" On the ground they stood with their backs to the men's brake and their faces towards the west, from which direction the *Wurtja's* party was coming. As the latter approached the women began dancing up and down the lines, making the movement of invitation and all the time holding their shields against their breasts. The party, led by the *Urinthantima* man, approached at a run, with the *Wurtja* concealed in the centre. Each man carried several pieces of bark which, as they came close at hand, were thrown at the women while the men shouted loudly "*whirra*," and the women shielded their faces. At close quarters a final volley of pieces of bark was the signal to the women to go, which they did, running away pell mell, their pace accelerated by the vehement shouting of the men who were standing about in all directions away from the *Apulla*, to which they returned as soon as the women had gone. The bushes were taken off the *Wurtja* by the *Urinthantima* and *Okilia*, and he was told to remain in a crouching position.

The *Apulla* ground was now carefully cleaned, and the *Wurtja's* brake removed to within a few yards of the western end of the path, after which a council, in which *Oknia*, *Okilia* and *Gammona* took part, was held, the object being to appoint another official known as *Wulya*, whose duty was that of painting a design on the back of the *Wurtja*. The choice of the design is left entirely to the *Wulya*, but it must be one of the *Ilkinia*, that is, the series of designs emblematic of the totems, and he is expected also to choose one belonging to a totem group of his own locality. During this conference two *Okilia* had been sitting opposite to one another, and as soon as the choice had been made, one of them smoothed over the ground between them, and then the other, who in this instance belonged to the same locality as the *Wurtja*, crossed over and sat down between the legs of the first man. Then a man, *Gammona* too, and of the same locality as the *Wurtja*, stepped out and brought back the old man who was *Ipmunna* to the *Wurtja*, and upon whom the choice had fallen. He came with well-simulated reluctance, as if he felt himself overpowered with the honour thus conferred upon him, and sat down in front of the two *Okilia* in the space vacated by the man who had crossed over. When he was seated, the front one of the two *Okilia* took up a boomerang, and with much deliberation drew the flat side three times steadily along the ground, thus making a smooth little trench, out of which he scooped a little soil, and then, shuffling along on his knees, emptied it into the hands of the *Ipmunna* man. Then he embraced him and rubbed his head against the old man's stomach. Then the other *Okilia*, the *Gammona* and the *Oknia*, in the order named, embraced the old man. The latter belonged to a northern locality, and in choosing him a well-recognised compliment had been paid both to himself and to his local group, as the *Wurtja* belonged to a southern group of the tribe. A somewhat unusual occurrence now took place. The old *Atwia atwia* man, who had been appointed to perform the actual operation of circumcision, came up and held a whispered conversation with the newly appointed *Wulya*, the gist of which was that he was an old man, that his eyesight was failing, and that he desired the consent of the council who determined these matters to depute his duties to his son. This necessitated a long whispered consultation, not that there was any serious objection to the proposal; indeed the old man is regarded as so great a man in the tribe, being recognised as an *oknirabata*, that no one would dream of opposing his wish in a matter such as this, but simply because anything like hasty action, in connection with an affair of mysterious import like one of the initiation ceremonies, would be completely out of keeping with the feelings of the natives. It was decided to grant the request, and the son was then called up, and after another whispered conversation the council broke up. When this was over, all the men began to decorate themselves with various patterns, which had no special significance; the two *Atwia atwia* were prominently painted on the face, and their cheeks were blackened with charcoal, so that they were easily distinguishable from the others. The *Wurtja* remained crouching at his brake for some little time, after which the newly appointed *Wulya*, together with the two men of the same name who had done the first painting, came up to him and began to paint on his back a design of the Okranina or carpet snake totem of a place called Tharlinga, away to the north in the Hanns range, that is, in the locality of the man who did the painting, but it must be remembered that there was no obligation upon the man to paint a design of either his own or the boy's totem. As a matter of fact, the totem of the *Wurtja* was a grass seed and that of the painter a crow. The design, which occupied the greater part of the boy's back, was done in white pipe-clay, and before commencing to draw it, the newly appointed *Wulya* rubbed the boy over with grease while he explained to his two companions the nature of the design which he intended to paint. All three men took part in the drawing, which consisted of a few concentric circles in the centre, with corkscrew-like lines around. The circles represented the snake's hole in the ground, and the other lines were supposed to be snakes playing round the hole. While the painting proceeded, and it was done with great deliberation, occupying more than an hour, the old *Ipmunna* man sang in a low monotonous voice about the snakes of Tharlinga. When at length it was finished an *Okilia* of the *Wurtja's* locality came up and placed in his hair two bunches of owl feathers, and then, going away again, he brought the two *Atwia atwia* to inspect the drawing.

At this stage the men who had previously made the *Arachitta* poles ran away from the *Apulla*, shouting, "*Pai! pai! pai!*" and brought the poles back with them from where they had been deposited. When within about fifty yards of the *Wurtja* they separated into two parties, one crossed in front of him from left to right, and the other from right to left, and the poles were deposited about twenty yards to either side of him; what was the meaning of this cannot be said, the native explanation as usual being that it was thus done in the Alcheringa. Possibly it may be associated in some way with the division of the tribe into two moieties, but there was no evidence of this so far as the actual constitution of the two parties was concerned, that is, members of one moiety did not go to one side and members of the other to the other.

Just before dusk two *Okilias* went out and stood, one on the eastern end of each of the raised banks, with their arms in a somewhat curious attitude, the palm of the hand being turned so that it faced backwards and the elbow bent, so that the hand lay in the arm-pit. The *Urinthantima* man went and sat down in the place usually occupied by the *Wurtja* when he was watching a ceremony, while the other men seated around him sang, "*Elunja apirra arara*"—"Hark to the lizards in the tree." At a signal from an old *Mura* man, the women, who were waiting out of sight, came and stood in two groups, one to the left and one to the right of the *Apulla*. It may be mentioned that here again the separation had no reference to the classes, though there are certain occasions during some of the ceremonies connected with initiation when this separation does take place. As soon as the women arrived the two *Okilias* came down from the bank, ran to the *Wurtja's* brake and quickly tore down the bushes which hid him from view, so that he was seen crouching down. The *Okilias* then knelt down, one on either side of him, and the three at once ran quickly, on all fours, to the *Apulla*, where the *Wurtja* lay down on top of the *Urinthantima*, who was himself lying down on his back. In this position the two remained for about ten minutes. While this was taking place a woman who was *Mia* to the *Wurtja* came and sat down behind one of the *Oknia*, while two others sat behind two other *Oknia*. At the same time the men who had brought in the *Arachitta* poles, and were about to wear them attached to their legs, were busily engaged, with the assistance of other men and some of the women, in fastening them on. At the end of the ten minutes the *Urinthantima* man wriggled out from underneath the boy, who remained lying face downwards on the ground. The old *Ipmunna* stood close by, explaining the design on the back of the *Wurtja*, and after a time called up two old women, who, like himself, were *Ipmunna*[114] to the boy, to come up and rub out the design. They came forwards with apparent reluctance, though in reality highly honoured by being thus chosen, and, stooping down, effaced the drawing by rubbing it over with their foreheads.

The men with the *Arachitta* poles were now ready to come on to the *Apulla*, and there, with the poles attached to their ankles, they ran up and down between the banks, dancing and singing, while the women, shouting, followed them all about, stripping the leaves as they did so from off the poles. It was now dark, but piling the two brakes, which had served their purpose and would not be used again, on top of one another, the whole mass was set on fire,[115] and the flames lighted up a scene of the weirdest description possible, on which the *Wurtja* looked in silence apparently quite unmoved. Suddenly the old *Mura* man gave out a great roar, the dancing ceased, and, followed by menacing shouts from the men, the women made haste back to their own camp, while from all sides the sound of bull-roarers was heard. At this signal the *Wurtja* was laid down on his back, and some of the *Oknia* and *Okilia* men, taking up a number of the *Arachitta* poles, stacked them on top of him, lifting them up and down as if beating time with them on his body, while they all sang wildly:—

"Ingwa alkirna alkirni li
Urtnanthi alkirli impara."

Ingwa means night or darkness; *alkirna*, twilight; *alkirni li*, a great clear light; *urtnanthi*, a lot of trees growing close together; *alkirli*, like the sky; *impara*, rising red like the sun.

All was now excitement; the fire was giving out a brilliant light, and the two *Atwia atwia* men took up a position at the western end of the *Apulla* path. With their beards thrust into their mouths, their legs widely extended and their arms stretched forwards, the two men stood perfectly still, the actual operator in front and his assistant pressing close up behind him, so that their bodies were in contact with each other. The front man held in his extended right hand the small flint knife with which the operation was to be conducted, and, as soon as they were in position, the *Ikuntera* man, who was to act as shield bearer, came down the lines, carrying the shield on his head and at the same time snapping the thumb and first finger of each hand. Then, facing the fire, he knelt down on one knee just a little in front of the operator, holding his shield above his head. During the whole time the bull-roarers were sounding all round so loudly that they could easily be heard by the women and children in their camp, and by them it is supposed that the roaring is the voice of the great spirit *Twanyirika*, who has come to take the boy away.[116]

The *Arachitta* poles were then quickly removed from the top of the *Wurtja*, and he was at once lifted up by *Okilia* and *Oknia* men, who ran, carrying him feet foremost, and placed him on the shield. Then in deep, loud tones the *Lartna* song was sung, indeed almost thundered out, by the men:—

"Irri yulta yulta rai
Ul katchera ul katch ar-arai
Irri yulta yulta rai
Ul katchera ul katch ai."

The assisting *Atwia atwia* at once grasped the foreskin, pulled it out as far as possible and the operator cut it off, and immediately, along with all the men who had acted in any official capacity during the whole course of the proceedings, retired out of the lighted area, while the boy, in a more or less dazed condition, was supported by his *Oknia* and *Okilia*, who said to him, "You have done well, you have not cried out." Then he was led back to where the old brake had stood and received the congratulations of the men, and at the same time the blood from the wound was allowed to flow into a shield, which was given to him by a young *Oknia*, to whom afterwards he will have, in return, to present an offering of food.

While he was still bleeding an *Okilia* brought up some of the bull-roarers and, pressing them on the wound, told him that it was these and not *Twanyirika* which made the sound, that they were sacred Churinga and must never be shown or even mentioned to the women. To this the boy listened in silence. After a time, when the bleeding had diminished, he was led to the eastern end of the *Apulla*, where he stood between two *Okilia* looking towards the west, while two other *Okilia*, each taking an *Arachitta* pole, mounted the bank and holding their poles over the path shouted loudly, moving them up and down as they did so, "*Arara, arara, arara*," which is the signal for the officials, who had been standing on one side in the shade, to come on to the *Apulla* ground once more. This they did, one at a time, in the following order, though there did not appear to be any rule with regard to precedence, as one man would urge another to go up:—*Wulya*, who superintended the first painting; *Urinthantima*; *Wulya*, *Wulya*, these two had assisted at the first painting; *Atwia atwia*, the actual operator; *Atwia atwia*, the assistant; *Wulya*, of the final painting; *Wulya*, the assistant of the last man; *Elucha*. As each man came up the *Okilia* shouted, "This is *Wulya* (and so on through the list), do not mention his name," and then each of them embraced the boy in turn, pressing their bodies together.[117] As each man came up and the presentation was made, the same ceremony was gone through, and in turn every one of those who had taken any special part was named by the *Okilia*, whose cry, "*Arara, arara, arara,*" rang out sharply in the darkness, for the fire had now burnt down. When the presentations were over the oldest *Okiüa* produced a bundle of Churinga (wooden ones for stone ones are never used on this occasion), saying as he did so, "Here is *Twanyirika*, of which you have heard so much, they are Churinga, and will help to heal you quickly; guard them well and do not lose them, or you and your *Mia, Ungaraitcha* and *Quitia* (that is, blood and tribal mothers and sisters) will be killed; do not let them out of your sight, do not let your *Mia, Ungaraitcha* and *Quitia* see you, obey your *Okilia*, who will go with you, do not eat forbidden food." These commands were spoken sternly, as if to impress them forcibly upon the novice, who stood silent with bent head.

In the particular ceremony here described, as soon as these instructions had been given, a man who had been dispatched for the purpose brought on to the ground two young *Arakurta* who had been operated upon five or six weeks before. Acting on instructions from their guardian, they at once knelt down in front of and with their backs to the newly-made *Arakurta*, and he, being told what to do by his *Okilia*, took a Churinga from his bundle, and, holding it in both hands, scraped their backs with the sacred implement. This is called *Untungalirrima*, and places all three *Arakurta* on equal terms and makes them friends. The two kneeling *Arakurta* were then told to go away quickly to their own camp, which they did. This does not, of course, frequently take place, but only when two operations have followed closely on one another.

For some time the boy, who has now reached the stage of *Arakurta*, the term *Wurtja* applying to him only during the relatively short interval between the time when he is painted and that at which the operation of circumcision is performed, remained standing over a fire, the smoke from which is supposed to be efficacious in healing his wounds. Finally he was taken away by a single *Okilia* man, in whose charge he was to remain until his wounds were healed and the operation of *Ariltha* was performed. On this occasion he joined the other two *Arakurta* in their camp.

Whilst there is no fixed rule on the subject, the man who takes charge of the *Arakurta* is preferably one to whom the boy's sister has been promised, failing such an one he may be an *Oknia*, *Okilia* or a *Mura* man.

There are certain restrictions and customs which must be observed by the more immediate relations of the boy which may be here noticed, as they will serve to show still more clearly the importance attached to the initiation ceremonies in the eyes of the natives. From the time at which the boy receives the fire-stick brought by his *Mia*, until his complete recovery from the operation of sub-incision, the *Mia* must have no intercourse with the father of the boy. Any breach of this rule would result in the boy growing up into *Ertwa akurna*, a bad man, or *Atna-arpinta*, that is, too much given to sexual pleasures, while strict observance will ensure his growing up *Ertwa mura*, or a good man (using the terms good and bad in the native sense).

After the presentation of the fire-stick and until *Lartna* has been performed, the *Mura tualcha* woman (that is, the future mother-in-law of the boy) is tabu to the actual *Mia*, or, if she be dead, to the *Mia* who hands to her the fire-stick. When *Lartna* has been performed, the *Mura tualcha* woman goes to the camp of the *Mia*, and, approaching her from behind, rubs her all over with red ochre; then the *Mia* hands to her a *pitchi* full of seed, and in this way the tabu is removed.

While the *Arakurta* is out in the bush the *Mia* may not eat opossum, or the large lace lizard, or carpet snake, or any fat, as otherwise she would retard her son's recovery. Every day she greases her digging-sticks and never allows them out of her sight; at night time she sleeps with them close to her head. No one is allowed to touch them. Every day also she rubs her body all over with grease, as in some way this is supposed to help her son's recovery.

After the operation of *Lartna*, the foreskin, amongst the Finke River groups of natives, is handed over to the eldest *Okilia* of the boy who is present, and he also takes charge of the shield in the haft of which the blood from the wound was collected. The piece of skin he greases and then gives to a boy who is the younger brother of the *Arakurta*, and tells him to swallow it, the idea at the present day being that it will strengthen him and cause him to grow tall and strong. The shield is taken by the *Okilia* to his camp, where he hands it over to his *Unawa*, or wife, and she then rubs the blood over the breasts and foreheads of women who are *Mia alkulla*, that is, elder sisters of the boy's actual *Mia* and *Ungaraitcha*, or elder sisters of the boy.

These women must not on any account touch the blood themselves, and after rubbing it on, the woman adds a coat of red ochre. The actual *Mia* is never allowed to see the blood.

Amongst some groups of Western Arunta the foreskin is presented to a sister of the *Arakurta*, who dries it up, smears it with red ochre, and wears it suspended from her neck.

THE CEREMONY OF HEAD BITING

While the *Arakurta* is out in the bush the men go and visit him occasionally, and on these occasions he has to undergo a painful rite called *Koperta kakuma*, or head biting. He is placed, lying face downwards, while men of all classes sit round, singing about the biting of the head of the *Arakurta* and urging the biters to bite deeply. The men who are to do the biting and who may be of any class and are usually from two to five in number, are chosen, on each occasion on which the operation is performed, by the oldest *Okilia* of the *Arakurta*. Their duty is to bite the scalp as hard as they can, until blood flows freely, the patient often howling with pain. Each man may content himself with one bite or he may bite two or even three times. The object of this really painful operation is, so they say, to make the hair grow strongly, and at times the chin may be bitten as well as the scalp.

THE CEREMONY OF SUB-INCISION OR ARILTHA

As a general rule there is an interval of about five or six weeks between the ceremony of *Lartna* and that of *Ariltha*, but at times it may be even longer, and it depends simply upon the length of time occupied by the recovery of the boy from the effects of the first operation.

The operation of *Ariltha* is regarded as of at least equal importance with that of circumcision, and, unlike the latter, the women are completely excluded and not allowed to take any part.

The particular ceremony now to be described took place when the operation was performed upon the two *Arakurta* to whom reference was made in the account of the *Lartna* ceremony. One of them belonged to the Purula and the other to the Kumura class. As a general rule the operation is only performed on one *Arakurta* at a time, but this is a matter of no importance and simply depends upon whether or not more than one boy has recently undergone the earlier ceremony of *Lartna* and is ready for this second one. We have never heard of the operation being performed upon more than two at the same time and even this is not of very common occurrence.

When the ceremony was to take place the men assembled at the camp of the *Arakurta*, out in the bush, where they had been living away from every one else since the last operation had been performed on them. They were under the charge of an *Okilia*, and when the men had assembled the two *Arakurta*, who were not informed of what was about to happen, though very probably they were perfectly well aware, when all the men assembled, that something further was in store for them, were told to lie flat down on the ground. Then their heads were covered over and all the young men of the same two sub-classes as the *Arakurta* were made to lie down beside them, though they had of course all of them passed through the ceremony before, as none but initiated men are allowed to be present on an occasion such as this. The older Kumara and Purula and all the Bulthara and Panunga men gathered together and for hours sang of the Achilpa men belonging to the group which marched north by way of Henbury on the Finke River. During the night there was performed first a Quabara belonging to the Achilpa (wild cat) totem, and at the close of the performance the two *Arakurta* joined in the dance round the performers. When it was over they were told who the individuals were with whom the Quabara was concerned, they were also told that they must not speak of it to women and children, and then it was explained to them that certain Quabara belonged to particular groups of men who alone had the right to perform them. Later on during the night another Quabara was performed, this time concerned with the emu totem. Then once more they were made to lie down, while the old men went away to a brake of boughs which had been built at a distance of about fifty yards from the spot at which the boys lay down under the charge of their guardian. The rest of the night was spent in singing over and over again a short chant concerning the bandicoot totem and the *Nurtunja*. The reason for this was that the *Oknia* and *Okilia* of the two *Arakurta*, who formed again a kind of council to direct the proceedings, had requested an old bandicoot man to perform a sacred ceremony in which a *Nurtunja* was used, as it was essential in this part of the tribe to have one of these in connection with the ceremony of *Ariltha*. The old bandicoot man was a Panunga and belonged to the Ilpirra tribe away to the north of the Arunta. The *Nurtunja*, to which we shall have occasion to refer frequently, figures largely in many of the sacred ceremonies and varies very much in form. The one used in the present instance was made out of a long spear around which grass stalks were laid and the whole was then ensheathed with human hair string. It was then ornamented with alternate rings of red and white bird's down, while a large tuft of eagle-hawk feathers was fixed into the upper end. Very often on these occasions, but not on the particular one now dealt with, a few Churinga are hung on to the *Nurtunja*. Two men, one of them *Oknia* of the Purula boy and the other *Okilia* of the Kumara, were decorated by the old bandicoot man to perform the ceremony, and just at daybreak the *Arakurta* were led from their camp and the performance began. The Quabara was concerned with an Alcheringa man who lived at a place called Yerapinthinga and the man who personated him carried the *Nurtunja* on his back, while he moved backwards and forwards, towards and away from another man who personated an Alcheringa woman, whom the bandicoot man was supposed to be attempting to catch and who warded him off with bushes held in the hand. After a short time the audience, including the two *Arakurta*, ran in and danced in front of and under the *Nurtunja* which was bent over them by the performer, while the dancers held up their hands as if to catch it, shouting loudly all the time "*Wah! Wah!*" After this had gone on for some time, the man personating the woman suddenly jumped round on the ground where he had remained seated all the time and turned his back on the *Nurtunja*, which was the sign for the dancing to cease. The *Nurtunja* was taken off the performer's back by the old bandicoot man to whom it belonged and then, after scooping out a hole in the ground, he fixed it upright. As soon as this was done the two *Arakurta* were told by *Oknia* and *Okilia* men to go up to and embrace the *Nurtunja*, and while they were doing this they were told that they were about to undergo the rite of *Ariltha* and that the embracing of the *Nurtunja*, which lasted ten minutes, would prevent the operation from being painful and that they need not be afraid.

The oldest *Okilia* man now said "Who will be *Tapunga?*" Two men volunteered, one man a Panunga and the other a Purula. The former at once lay on his stomach on the ground and the latter on the top of him, and when this kind of living table was ready the Kumara *Arakurta* was led from the *Nurtunja*, close to which the men had lain down, and then placed lying at full length on his back on top of the *Tapunga*. As soon as ever he was in position another man sat astride of his body, grasped the penis and put the urethra on the stretch. The operator who is called *Pininga* and is chosen by the *Oknia* and *Okilia*, then approached and quickly, with a stone knife, laid open the urethra from below. The man was an *Ikuntera* of the *Arakurta*. As soon as this was done, the boy was lifted off and immediately the Purula *Arakurta* was placed in position on the same *Tapunga* and the same man again performed this operation. When all was over, the two, who had now passed beyond the *Arakurta* stage and were *Ertwa-kurka* or initiated men, were led to one side while they squatted over shields into which the blood was allowed to drain. After this, *Okilia* men came up to them and tied the pubic tassels on, telling them that they were now *Ertwa-kurka* and that they had no more operations to fear and that they were admitted to the ranks of the men.

After the operation of *Ariltha* has been performed, the newly made *Ertwa-kurka* sits down as described on a shield into the haft of which the blood is allowed to flow and from which it is emptied into the centre of a fire which is made for the purpose. If much pain be caused by the wound he will return to the ash heap and scooping out a little hole in the centre, will place therein some glowing pieces of charcoal and upon these he will urinate, thus causing steam to arise which is said to give great relief to the pain. Until the young man's wound has healed he is supposed to lie only upon his back for otherwise the organ would grow crooked.[118]

Until the *Arakurta* has undergone and quite recovered from the ceremony of sub-incision, he is forbidden to eat the flesh of opossum, snake, echidna and all lizards. Should he eat any of these his recovery would be retarded and his wounds would become much inflamed. In addition to these there exists in the case of each individual the restriction with regard to the eating of his totem, and to every one not only at this, but at all times, there exists the general restriction with regard to the eating of the wild cat.

At the moment when the *Arakurta* is seized for the purpose of having the rite of *Ariltha* performed upon him the men set up a loud shout of "*Pirr-rr*"—loud enough to be heard by the women in their camp. The latter at once assemble at the *Erlukwirra*, that is the women's camp, and the *Mia* of the boy cuts the *Unchalkulkna* woman across the stomach and shoulders, and then makes similar cuts upon women who are the boy's *Mura* and elder and younger sisters, as well as upon those who are her own elder sisters. While making the cuts she imitates the sound made by the *Ariltha* party. These cuts, which generally leave behind them a definite series of cicatrices, are called *urpma* and are often represented by definite lines on the Churinga. It very often happens that, as soon as the operation has been performed on an *Arakurta*, one or more of the younger men present, who have been operated on before, stand up and voluntarily undergo a second operation. In such cases the men do not consider that the incision has been carried far enough. Standing out on the clear space close by the *Nurtunja*, with legs wide apart and hands behind his back, the man shouts out "*Mura Ariltha atnartinja yinga aritchika pitchi*";—"*Mura* mine come and cut my

Ariltha down to the root." Then one *Mura* man comes and pinions him from behind, while another comes up in front and seizing the penis first of all cuts out an oval shaped piece of skin which he throws away and then extends the slit to the root. Most men at some time or other undergo the second operation and some come forward a third time, though a man is often as old as thirty or thirty-five before he submits to this second operation which is called *ariltha erlitha atnartinja*.

The *Ertwa-kurka* carry the Churinga about with them just as the *Arakurta* did until they have completely recovered. When the man in charge of them announces that they are recovered from the effects of the operation, the men all assemble out in the bush, and the *Oknia* and *Okilia* appoint a man to act as what is called *Irkoa-artha*. It is his duty to remove all the decorations from the body of the *Ertwa-kurka*, after which the latter is told to lie down on his face while the men sing a chant, which is supposed to have the effect of promoting the growth of his hair, and he is told that he must not speak for some time to the *Irkoa-artha* and then not until he has made a present of food, which is called *Chaurilia*, to the individual in question.

Then the men, accompanied by the *Ertwa-kurka*, assemble at some little distance from the main camp and begin to sing in loud tones:

"Chuk-ur-rokerai yaa li chaakaa-a
Yaama kank waa
Inkwurkna inkwurkna atnai
Inkwurkna inkwurkna atnai."

The women, hearing the singing, assemble near to the main camp and begin to dance as they did at the *Apulla*. The song of the men ceases as soon as they approach the women, and at a distance of about fifty yards they halt and shout "*tirra, tirra, tirra,*" a sound which much resembles that made by whirling bull-roarers and which is at once taken up by the women. The young *Ertwa-kurka*, who is now completely undecorated, steps out from the group of men, runs up close to the women, who continue dancing, and then suddenly wheels round and runs off into the bush, where he is followed by a number of the men who camp with him for the night, during which, without the performance of any special ceremony, singing is kept up until daybreak. Before it is light the *Ertwa-kurka* is dressed up by *Okilia* and *Umbirna* men with all the ornaments such as forehead band, arm strings, tail tips, etc., which are worn by a native beau. He is also provided with a shield and spear-thrower, and just about daylight the party starts for the main camp, the young man walking in the centre by the side of the *Irkoa-artha* man, while all shout loudly "*tirra, tirra, tirra.*" When within about fifty yards of the women, who are dancing and shouting as before, the men halt, and the *Irkoa-artha* leads the *Ertwa-kurka* on but only accompanies him for a few yards, after which he goes on alone, carrying his shield in front, so as to hide his face. When he comes close up to the women one or two *Ungaraitcha*, that is blood and tribal elder sisters, who are in the lead carrying *pitchis* (all the other women carry tufts of rat-tails in their hands), throw the *pitchis* at his shield and then press their hands on his shoulders from behind, and also rub their faces on his back, after which they cut off some locks of his hair, which they afterwards use to make up into hair string ornaments for themselves. This ceremony is called *anainthalilima*, and after it is over the *Ertwa-kurka* is free to go into the presence of the various officials who have taken part in any of the ceremonies, though he must not speak to or of them until some months have past, nor must he speak loudly in their presence.

At daylight on the morning of the next day the men provide themselves with fire-sticks and, surrounding the young man, conduct him to the women, who are again waiting to receive him. He is fully decorated and carries a shield and boomerang and some twigs of Eremophila. When the party is within a short distance of the women the men throw down their firesticks and halt, and the young man steps out from the centre of the group and throws his boomerang high up in the direction of the spot at which his mother was supposed to have lived in the Alcheringa. This throwing of the boomerang in the direction of the mother's Alcheringa camp, that is, of course, the spot at which the Alcheringa individual of whom his mother is supposed to be the reincarnation, lived, occurs during the performance of other ceremonies, such, for example, as those which accompany the knocking out of teeth in eastern groups of the Arunta and also in the Ilpirra tribe. It may in all likelihood be regarded as intended to symbolize the idea that the young man is entering upon manhood and thus is passing out of the control of the women and into the ranks of the men. The fact that he is using the boomerang is indicative of this, and his throwing it towards his mother's camp is an intimation to her of the fact that he is passing away from her control; at the same time there remains the curious feature, the exact significance of which it is difficult to see, that it is thrown towards the Alcheringa camp rather than towards the mother herself.

After the throwing of the boomerang, the *Ertwa-kurka* is led forward by the *Irkoa-artha* man, holding, as before, his shield before his face, and is placed squatting on a fire which has been prepared by the women, and which is now covered by green leaves. Behind this the women stand making the movement of invitation already described and shouting "*tirra, tirra, tirra.*" The women place their hands on his shoulders and gently press him down. After remaining on the fire for a short time he is taken off by the *Irkoa-artha* and handed over to a few young boys who have not yet been initiated, and who are told to camp with him but on no account to speak to him. After three days, during which he speaks to no one, men who are his *Okilia* come out from the men's camp and invite him to join them, after which he becomes a permanent member of the camp. Before, however, he may speak to any of the officials who took any part in the various ceremonies he must go out into the bush and procure game as an offering to each one of them, this gift being known as *Chaurilia*.

At the presentation of *Chaurilia* the man to whom it is given always performs some sacred ceremony, after which the mouth of the *Ertwa-kurka* and those of all present are touched with some sacred object which has been used during the ceremony, such as a *Nurtunja*, and in this way the ban of silence is removed. When these ceremonies have been passed through the native is regarded as an initiated member of the tribe and may take part in all the sacred ceremonies of his group, though it is not until he has passed through the Engwurra that he becomes what is called *Urliara* or a fully-developed man.

The following names, which may be called status names, indicating the different grades of initiation, are applied to the boy, youth and man at the times indicated:—

    1.   *Ambaquerka*, up to the time of throwing up.
    2.   *Ulpmerka*, after the throwing-up ceremony and until that of circumcision.
    3.   *Wurtja*, after the first ceremony of painting in connection with circumcision.
    4.   *Arakurta*, after circumcision and before sub-incision is performed.
    5.   *Ertwa-kurka*, after sub-incision and until he has passed through the Engwura.
    6.   *Urliara*, after the Engwura has been passed through.

In the northern part of the tribe the ceremonies agree in all essential points with those which have been described in the case of the natives living along the Finke river. There are however, certain differences in detail which may be mentioned. Early on the day on which the ceremony of *Lartna* or circumcision is to commence, the *Ulpmerka* is taken away from the camp on some pretext, while the men and women spend the day in preparing the collected food supplies, such as the seeds of acacia or *munyeru*. Every now and then they break out into the monotonous chant of a corrobboree, to which the women, but not the men, dance, while a feeling of suppressed excitement throughout the camp indicates that some ceremony of more than ordinary importance is about to take place. At sundown the boy is brought into camp, and, unconscious of what is in store for him, spends the evening as usual at the men's camp, lying down to sleep there. Towards the middle of the night, when all is quiet, an elder brother of the boy, after seeing that the latter is sound asleep, wakens the other members of the camp, and all together, men and women, they go to the spot close at hand which has previously been selected. The women stand quietly on one side while the men, with as little noise as possible, clear the grass and rubbish away, and thus prepare the *Apulla* ground. Then all, except three brothers of the boy and two young women, sit down around the *Apulla*, while the five selected ones go to the camp to awaken and bring the boy. The two women go in advance, each of them carrying an *Alparra*, which is a scooped-out piece of wood such as the women use to carry food and water in, and, creeping quietly up to the *Ulpmerka*, suddenly strike him sharply with their *Alparras*, crying out loudly at the same time, "*Utchai! Utchai!*" The boy, naturally dazed and startled, springs to his feet, when the three men take hold of him, and tell him that the time has come when he must no longer remain an *Ulpmerka*, but must be made into a man—an *Ertwa-kurka*. So soon as the cry of "*Utchai*" is heard the men begin to sing and the women to dance.

The subsequent proceedings, including the painting by *Uwilia* men and the handing of the fire-stick by an *Unchalkulkna* woman, though there may be more than one of these, are much the same as those already described. On the day on which the actual operation is to be performed there is, however, a slight variation in the procedure. After being ornamented with twigs of Eucalyptus, two rows of spears are fixed upright, one row on either side of the *Apulla* path. They form a kind of grove, with the path running between them. About midday, when all is ready, some of the men leave the camp to go and bring the boy in. When the signal of their return with the boy, who is hidden out of sight of the women, is given, then the latter at once go in between the line of spears, and, while some of the older men sing, perform the *Unthippa* dance, and then, standing by the poles, strip these of their leaves. As the men with the boy approach they all throw pieces of bark at the women, a signal to them to disperse and go to their camp, out of sight of the *Apulla*. The boy is placed at one end of the path behind a brake of boughs, of which, in this instance, only one and not two, as described before, is made. At night the women are brought back, and sit on either side of the path at the base of the stripped spears. Two *Okilia* go to where the boy is as yet hidden from the women, throw on one side the boughs, and then, accompanied by the *Ulpmerka*, hop down the path until they have traversed half its length, when they diverge, one to the right and one to the left, while the boy goes on until he collides with a man who has been purposely placed so that he shall do this. This man is here called *Tapunga*, and at once he rolls over on to his back, and the boy lies on the top of him. Silence is now maintained by all. In this position the painting is rubbed off the *Ulpmerka's* back. Then the *Arachitta* poles are brought in, and as the men dance the women strip the poles, which are tied on to the legs as described. The men remain calm, but the women grow wilder and wilder, singing:—

"Atnintu rappira ka perka-a-a
Ok nar inta
Yur a puncha kwi
Yur a puncha kwi."

Whilst this is in progress the boy gets off the man's back and sits up watching the dance, which suddenly ceases when the sound of a bull-roarer is heard. At once the women run off, and very shortly after the operation is performed. In this district the man who holds the shield is termed the *Urinthantima*, and he must belong to the moiety of the tribe to which the boy does not. The operation is almost always performed by a man who is *Ikuntera* to the boy, and who is assisted by one, or it may be two men, who are called *Killarina*, and who must also belong to the other moiety of the tribe. When all is over the boy is given a bundle of Churinga and sent out in charge of a man as previously described, until he has recovered, and is ready for the further operation.

The rite of sub-incision, which may be said to be characteristic of the great group of tribes occupying the interior parts of Queensland,[119] New South Wales, and South Australia, right away to the far north, and at all events a very large part of West Australia,[120] has frequently been alluded to by Curr and other writers under the name of the "terrible rite"—a term which, as Dr. Stirling suggested, may well be discarded. It consists, as is well known, in sub-incision of the penis, so that the penile urethra is laid open from the meatus right back to the junction with the scrotum. It is certainly a most extraordinary practice, and one which it might be thought would be frequently attended with serious results; but none such apparently ever follow, though in their native condition the operation is performed merely with a sharp chipped piece of flint or a small knife made of a hard flaked quartzite. The Arunta natives have no idea as to the origin of the practice, and it seems almost useless to speculate upon it. Mr. Roth has suggested that the mutilation of the women, which takes place, so far as is known, in all those tribes where sub-incision is practised by the men, was indirectly the origin of the latter, "that, on the principle of a form of mimicry, the analogous sign was inflicted on the male to denote corresponding fitness on his part." This still leaves unexplained the mutilation of the women, and it would seem to be almost simpler to imagine that this was a consequence of the mutilation of the men. In the Arunta tribe tradition ascribes the origin of the custom to the members of the wild cat totem and points clearly to the fact that it was introduced by the members of some powerful group at a time subsequent to the introduction of the rite of circumcision.

One thing is clear, and that is that at the present day, and as far back as their traditions go, the Arunta natives at least have no idea of its having been instituted with the idea of its preventing or even checking procreation. In the first place it does not do this. Every man without exception throughout the Central area, in all tribes in which the rite is practised, is sub-incised. Under the normal conditions he must be before he is allowed to take a wife, and infringement of this rule would simply mean death to him if found out. Though it is true that the number of children rarely exceeds four or perhaps five in a family, and, as a general rule, is less still, perhaps two or three, yet the cause of this is not sub-incision. It is infanticide which is resorted to for the purpose of keeping down the number of a family. And here we may say that the number is kept down, not with any idea at all of regulating the food supply, so far as the adults are concerned, but simply from the point of view that, if the mother is suckling one child, she cannot properly provide food for another, quite apart from the question of the trouble of carrying two children about. An Australian native never looks far enough ahead to consider what will be the effect on the food supply in future years if he allows a particular child to live; what affects him is simply the question of how it will interfere with the work of his wife so far as their own camp is concerned; while from the woman's side the question is, can she provide food enough for the new-born infant and for the next youngest?

The Arunta native does not hesitate to kill a child—always directly it is born—if there be an older one still in need of nourishment from the mother, and suckling is continued up to the age often of three years or even older. With an easy solution, which moreover he does not hesitate to practise, of the difficulty arising from the birth of too many children, it is scarcely conceivable that the men should deliberately pass through a most painful ordeal with the idea of achieving a result which can be obtained otherwise without pain or trouble to themselves, and when also they know perfectly well that the desired result is not obtained by the performance of the operation. Added to this we have amongst the Arunta, Luritcha, and Ilpirra tribes, and probably also amongst others such as the Warramunga, the idea firmly held that the child is not the direct result of intercourse, that it may come without this, which merely, as it were, prepares the mother for the reception and birth also of an already-formed spirit child who inhabits one of the local totem centres. Time after time we have questioned them on this point, and always received the reply that the child was not the direct result of intercourse; so that in these tribes, equally with those dealt with by Mr. Roth, the practice of sub-incision cannot be attributed to the desire to check procreation by this means.

In the south of the Arunta tribe the ceremonies again are somewhat different from these, both in the west and in the east. At Charlotte Waters, for example, the following is an account, in outline, of what takes place.

When the time arrives for a boy to be initiated, his *Okilia* talks to men who are *Umbirna* to the boy and arranges with two of them to carry out the first part of the proceedings. Towards evening the two *Umbirna* go to the boy, who has no idea of what has been arranged, and one of them takes hold of him while the other comes up from behind, carrying a special small white stone called *aperta irrkurra*, which he puts under the armpit of the boy. Then taking hold of him, one by each arm, they take him along with them to the camp of his mother and father. Here, by previous arrangement, the different members of the camp are assembled. All the men sit in a roughly semi-circular group, and together with them are women who stand in the relationship of *Mia* and *Uwinna* to the boy. The latter, with an *Umbirna* man on either side of him, is then told to lie down in front of the group, and behind him again are gathered together the women who are *Ungaraitcha, Itia, Unawa* and *Unkulla* to him. These women commence to dance to the singing of the men, and when this has gone on for some little time they retire behind the group of men, and then the boy is allowed to go to sleep, watched over during the night by the two *Umbirna* who are called *Ukarkinja*. The latter wake him early and, after tying up his hair with whitened string, decorate it with tufts of eagle-hawk feathers. When this has been done the boy is called *Au-aritcha*. This over, the boy's *Ungaraitcha* and *Itia* bring him food in the shape of *munyeru* or grass seed, of which he eats some and gives the rest to his two *Umbirna*. Then, if she be present, the *Mura* woman whose daughter has been allotted as wife to the boy, or, in her absence, the *Umbirna* men, paint him all over with red ochre. After this, the further ceremonies may either be carried out on the spot or else the boy may be taken away to a different local group, where the first part of the ceremonies will then be performed. There does not appear to be any rule in regard to this. In the event of the boy being taken away, he goes under the charge of the same two *Umbirna* men, wearing, as he walks, his hair-string, and carrying the stone under his arm. On approaching the strange camp the men call out "*Pau! Pau!*" sharply and loudly, while at the same time each of them swings backwards one of the boy's arms. The strangers recognise what is happening, and the men get up, leave the camp near to which the visitors have halted, and while the women lie down in camp they come out to meet the three. The hair-string and stone are then taken away from the boy, who is thrown up in the air by the strangers, who catch and strike him as he falls. This throwing up is called *Au-aritcha iwuma*. When this is over the stone is given back to the boy, but the hair-string is given to the strangers. The boy himself has to go some little distance away and may not be spoken to by the women, though the men go near and speak to him freely.

Preparations are then made for the return to the home camp, all the men and women coming, while the boy, with his two *Umbirna*, walks behind. At some little distance from the spot at which the men have, during the boy's absence, made the camp at which the operation of *Lartna* will be performed, a halt is made, and here the boy and the two *Umbirna* stay behind for the purpose of painting his body with white pipe clay, tying up his hair and putting on the waist band which he now wears for the first time. The strangers, marching on, announce their approach by the usual sharp cry "*Pau! Pau!*" The resident old men and women are sitting down at the camp, but the young men have to go away, to some little distance, so as not to be seen as yet by the boy. At first the strangers sit down in the customary way at a short distance from the camp, which they do not enter until, at a later time, they are invited to do so by the older men. When the *Au-aritcha* and the *Umbirna* come up they take a position in front of the strangers and between them and the resident group. After a short pause the boy's *Ungaraitcha* come out and give him food, and then, together with his two guardians, he returns to the bush, which is the signal for the younger men to come from their hiding place and join the strange group, the members of which come into camp usually about dusk.

In the evening the same women dance as on the previous occasion, the dance being called *Ilchilcha-intum wuthaperrima*. The dance is repeated during the course of the following evening, and during the two days whilst the boy is out of the camp there takes place both a lending and an interchange of women, the usual class restrictions being, however, observed.

Two men belonging to the resident group will, for example, determine without saying anything previously to two visiting men to lend their wives each to one of the latter. During the dance these two men will get up from the group of men watching the dance, and each one taking a fire-stick will give it to his wife, who is amongst the dancers. The woman knows what this means and retires to some distance. Then the two men return to the main group, and each going behind the man to whom he desires to show attention, either in return for some past act of kindness or in anticipation of favours to come, lifts him up by his elbows and informs him of his intention. The exchange, or lending, is merely a temporary one, and in this instance only takes place between those who are *Unawa* to each other.

When the two days are over the boy is brought back and the women are sent away from the camp where the dancing has taken place and where the operation of *Lartna* will shortly be performed. As in the case of the south-western or the Larapinta groups already referred to, various ceremonies are performed in which a *Waninga* is used, and this the boy is made to embrace before the operation is performed. When this is about to take place, the boy is told to lie down on the ground while an *Okilia* puts his hand over the former's eyes, and a man who is *Unkulla* to the boy goes away to some little distance. While this takes place, a few, perhaps half a dozen, men lie down on the ground so as to form a kind of table, and when the *Okilia* lifts his hand from his eyes the boy sees the *Unkulla* man approaching at a run. This man places him on the top of the prostrate men, whom the boy afterwards calls *iruntuwura*, and at once the operation is performed by an *Ikuntera* man whom the boy calls *urtwi-urtwia*. The *Okilia* stand by shouting *"arakwirra, arundertna"*—"You be quiet, do not cry."

As always, the blood is collected in a shield and is handed over to the *Okilia*, who thereupon makes a hole in the ground and buries in this the blood and the foreskin; then small stones are put on top of the latter, and the hole is filled with sand, on the surface of which a short piece of stick, perhaps six inches long, is laid down horizontally. This stick is called *Ultha*, and neither the boy who has been operated upon nor yet any woman, may go near to it.

When the operation of *Lartna* is over, the boy is called *Atnurrinia*. As soon as he has recovered, the operation of *Ariltha* is performed in much the same manner as already described, except that in this southern district no *Nurtunja* is made. The men who lie down on the ground are called *Atrapurntum*; the *Unkulla* man who sits on the boy's chest is called *Ikwarta*, and the *Ikuntera* man who performs the ceremony is called *Pininya*. It is usual during the ceremony for the *Unkulla* man to take off his hair girdle and to lay it down close beside the boy with the object of preventing too great a flow of blood.

After the operation of *Ariltha* the novice is called *Allallumba*. When it is over he is taken out into the bush by an *Okilia* who may be accompanied by a *Gammona* man, and after recovery his body is painted white, the hair-string girdle and the pubic tassel are put on, he is brought up to the men's camp and then taken on to where, close to the *Erlukwirra*, the women are waiting. The throwing of a boomerang, the meeting between the boy and his *Ungaraitcha*, when the latter hit him on the back, and the smoking of the novice are carried out in essentially the same way as already described. When all this is over, the novice returns with the men to their camp, and during the night a ceremony concerned with the owl totem is always performed; why this is so we have not been able to discover. For some time the newly initiated man may not speak to any of the men or women who have taken part as officials in any of the ceremonies, but, as previously described, the ban of silence is ultimately removed after he has presented to each one separately an offering of food.

In regard to the initiation ceremonies of women, it is clear that, as was first shown by Roth, there are certain ceremonies which are evidently the equivalents of the initiation ceremonies concerned with the men. Such ceremonies occur, though not to such an extent as described by Mr. Roth, in the Central tribes. The first one takes place when the girl's breasts are rubbed with fat and red ochre, and the second, when the operation of opening the vagina is performed. This is clearly regarded as the equivalent of sub-incision in the male, the name of the latter ceremony being *pura ariltha kuma*, while in the case of the woman it is called *atna ariltha kuma*. There is no special name given to a female after any initiation rite. Up to the first menstrual period she is called *quiai*, the ordinary name for a girl, just as *wiai* is the ordinary name for a boy; after that she is called *wunpa*, a name which she retains until the breasts hang pendent, after which she is called *arakutja*, the ordinary term for a grown woman. The first ceremony may perhaps be regarded as the equivalent of the throwing up and painting of the boys, there being amongst the women no equivalents of the *Lartna* (circumcision) or Engwura ceremonies of the men.

We have described the ceremonies attendant on what may be called the initiation of women, the first in connection with other ceremonies peculiar to women,[121] the second in the chapter dealing with the social organisation, as it has important bearings upon this, and may be most conveniently dealt with in connection therewith.

Chapter VIII

Initiation Ceremonies (Continued) the Engwura Ceremony

Five phases of the Engwura—Summoning the members of the tribe to the Engwura—Plan of the ground on which the ceremonies were held—Division of the tribe into two moieties—Disposal of the Churinga in two corresponding groups—General remarks on the ownership and names of the ceremonies—Control of the Engwura—First phase—Performance of two ordinary corrobborees—Passing on of corrobborees from one group to another—Building of the *Parra* on the Engwura ground—Separation of the younger men from the women—Second phase—Performance of sacred ceremonies—Description of the last eight days of the second phase—The making of a *Nurtunja*—Examination of Churinga—"Singing" the ground—Various ceremonies—Handing over of Churinga which had been taken care of by a neighbouring group during the temporary extinction of the group to which they belonged—The making and meaning of a *Waninga*—Making the younger men *abmoara* to certain of the older ones—The younger men are now called *Illpongwurra*.

THE Engwura, or, as it is called in some parts of the tribe, Urumpilla, is in reality a long series of ceremonies concerned with the totems, and terminating in what may be best described as ordeals by fire, which form the last of the initiatory ceremonies. After the native has passed through these he becomes what is called *Urliara*, that is, a perfectly developed member of the tribe. We cannot fully translate the meaning of either term, but each of them is formed, in part, of the word *ura*, which means fire. The natives themselves say that the ceremony has the effect of strengthening all who pass through it. It imparts courage and wisdom, makes the men more kindly natured and less apt to quarrel; in short, it makes them *ertwa murra oknirra*, words which respectively mean "man, good, great or very," the word good being, of course, used with the meaning attached to it by the native.

Evidently the main objects of it are, firstly, to bring the young men under the control of the old men, whose commands they have to obey implicitly; secondly, to teach them habits of self-restraint and hardihood; and thirdly, to show to the younger men who have arrived at mature age, the sacred secrets of the tribe which are concerned with the Churinga and the totems with which they are associated.

The Engwura may be performed in various places, but, as it is a ceremony at which men and women gather together from all parts of the tribe, and sometimes also from other tribes, a central position is preferred if it be intended to carry it out on a large scale. It is, indeed, a time when the old men from all parts of the tribe come together and discuss matters. Councils of the elder men are held day by day, by which we do not mean that there is anything of a strictly formal nature, but that constantly groups of the elder men may be seen discussing matters of tribal interest; all the old traditions of the tribe are repeated and discussed, and it is by means of meetings such as this, that a knowledge of the unwritten history of the tribe and of its leading members is passed on from generation to generation. Not only this, but while the main effect is undoubtedly to preserve custom, yet, on the other hand, changes introduced in one part of the tribe (and, despite the great conservatism of the native such changes do take place) can by means of these gatherings, become generally adopted in much less time than would be the case if they had to slowly filter through, as it were, from one locality to another.

Some idea of the importance of the ceremony may be gathered from the fact that the one which we witnessed commenced in the middle of September, and continued till the middle of the succeeding January, during which time there was a constant succession of ceremonies, not a day passing without one, while there were sometimes as many as five or six within the twenty-four hours. They were held at various hours, always one or more during the daylight, and not infrequently one or two during the night, a favourite time being just before sunrise.

Whilst the whole series of ceremonies followed one another without a break, yet there were five clearly marked phases, each of which was characterised by certain important features peculiar to it, and these phases we will describe in succession. They may be briefly outlined as follows:—

Phase 1. Sending out the messengers. Assembling of the tribe. Performance of introductory corrobborees. Building of the *Parra* on the Engwura ground, and the commencement of the sacred ceremonies. The characteristic feature of this phase is the holding of ordinary dancing corrobborees at night-time, in which the women take part. When once these are over, which takes place between two and three weeks from the start, the women take no further share until close to the end of the ceremonies.

Phase 2. The men are separated from the women and live on the Engwura ground, where sacred ceremonies are performed day and night. This extends over, perhaps, six weeks, and lasts until the men who are being initiated are made *abmoara* to certain elder men who take charge of them. After this they are called *Illpongwurra*.

Phase 3. The sacred ceremonies are continued, the *Illpongwurra* being distinguished by wearing twigs of a special shrub, and may not speak to their *abmoara* men. This phase lasts until a special ceremony connected, in this instance, with the frog totem is performed, to witness which the young men are brought on to the Engwura ground to the accompaniment of the sound of bull-roarers, which, after this, are much used. This phase extends over about eight days.

Phase 4. The *Illpongwurra* are taken out of camp in the morning and brought in at night-time by old men who carry bull-roarers. This is the most important phase, and during its continuance the fire ceremonies are passed through. It extends over two weeks or more, and after the final ceremony of this phase the initiated men rank as *Urliara*.

Phase 5. The newly-made *Urliara* are kept out in the bush. Corrobborees, in which women take part, are held at night-time, and at intervals sacred ceremonies are performed in connection with the removal of the ban of silence between those who are *abmoara* to one another. This phase lasts an indefinite length of time, but after its commencement the camp breaks up and the different members begin to return to their respective localities.

When it has been decided by any particular group to hold an Engwura,—and the initiation rests with the Alatunja, the latter, after consultation with the older men, sends out messengers to other groups. Each of these carries with him one or two *Churinga irula*, that is, wooden Churinga, carefully concealed from view in a casing of emu feathers. The Engwura messenger is called *Ilchinkinja*, a term derived from the two words *ilcha*, a hand, and *ilkinja*, to raise or lift up, so that it may perhaps be best rendered by the phrase "the beckoning hand." In the normal condition of the tribe no native dare disobey the summons thus received under penalty of most serious ill to himself, which would be certain to ensue should he neglect to follow the Churinga. Sometimes the one set of messengers passes through from group to group, sometimes each Alatunja, to whom the Churinga comes, provides fresh men, and so, in course of time, after having travelled many hundreds of miles, the Churinga at last returns to the original sender.

When a messenger reaches any group he shows the Churinga as an emblem of his *bona fides* to the Alatunja and elder men, and then delivers his verbal message, saying when and where the tribe will assemble. Amongst the Arunta and Ilpirra there is no such thing as a message stick in the true sense of the term, that is, there is no such thing as a stick cut with notches or other marks for the purpose of reminding the bearer of the message, such as is frequently met with amongst other Australian tribes.

Gradually the various local groups begin to arrive at the chosen spot, the group inhabiting which has meanwhile been gathering in stores of food such as grass seed, or *munyeru*. A spot is chosen for the Engwura ground which is more or less secluded, and so placed that the women and children who are in the main camp cannot see what is taking place on it. The plan on the following page shows the arrangement of the camp during the Engwura. In the particular instance now described the ground was a level stretch bounded on the east by the river Todd, with its belt of low scrub and gum trees, and on the west by a rough quartzite range. At the base of the range ran a small creek, in the bed of which—for there was, as usual in Central Australia, no water in either river or creek—the performers were decorated without any risk of their being seen by any one who had no right to do so.

The natives who assembled came from all parts of the tribe, some travelling a distance of two hundred miles to be present, and a few of them came from the Ilpirra tribe, which lies immediately to the north of the Arunta, and in which a ceremony similar to the Engwura is held.

As the various contingents reached Alice Springs, each one comprising men, women and children, camps were formed on the eastern side of the creek, the position of any camp indicating roughly the locality of its owner. Thus the southern men camped to the south and the northern men to the north, and, as is always the case, Bulthara and Panunga men on the one hand, and Kumara and Purula men on the other hand, camped close together. A very noticeable feature also was the disposal of the Churinga. Those belonging to the Panunga and Bulthara men were all placed together on a small platform which was built in a *mulga* tree on the hill-side at the south-west end of the camp, where they were under the immediate charge of the Alatunja of the Alice Springs group, who is himself a Bulthara man. Those belonging to the Purula and Kumara men were under the charge of a Purula man, and were placed on a small platform at the northern end of the ground. To this storing place of the Churinga during the Engwura the name of *thanunda* is given.

This division of the tribe into two moieties, which stands out so clearly on the occasion of a ceremony such as the Engwura, points to the fact of the original division of the tribe into two halves, each of which has again divided into two; as a matter of fact the division has gone on to a greater extent, with the result that in the northern section of the tribe we find eight divisions, four corresponding to each of the original moieties.

We were hoping that on the occasion of the Engwura, when the two moieties were so markedly distinct from one another, it might be possible to discover the original names applied to them prior to their division, but this was not the case, nor were we able to discover any meaning attached to the present names of the divisions.

For the purpose of making things clear we may briefly refer again to the constitution of the tribe. The whole area over which it extends is divided up into a large number of localities, each of which is owned and inhabited by a local group of individuals, and each such locality is identified with some particular totem which gives its name to the members of the local group. The term used by the native, which is here translated by the word totem, is *Oknanikilla*. If you ask a man what is his *Oknanikilla* he will reply Erlia (emu), Unchichera (frog), Achilpa (wild-cat), &c., as the case may be.

Special men of the Alcheringa are associated with special localities in which they became changed into spirit individuals, each associated with a Churinga, and with each locality are associated also certain ceremonies which in the Alcheringa were performed by these individuals, and have been handed down from that time to the present. Each local group has also, as already described, its own *Ertnatulunga*, or sacred storehouse, in which the Churinga are kept. The men assembled at the Engwura represented various local totem groups, and they—that is, the older men of each group—had brought with them numbers of the Churinga from the storehouses.

Each totem has its own ceremonies, and each of the latter may be regarded as the property of some special individual who has received it by right of inheritance from its previous owner, such as a father or elder brother, or he may have, in the case of the men who are supposed to possess the faculty of seeing and holding intercourse with the *Iruntarinia* or spirits, received it as a gift directly from the latter, who have at some time, so he tells his fellows, performed it for his benefit and then presented it to him. This means either that he has had a dream during which he has seen a ceremony acted, which is quite as real a thing to him as actually seeing it when awake, or that being of a more original and ingenious turn of mind than his fellows—as the men skilled in magic certainly are—he has invented it for himself and has then told the others, who implicitly believe in his supernatural powers, that the spirits have presented it to him.[122]

Each ceremony, further, is not only connected with some totem, but with a particular local group of the totem, and its name indicates the fact. Thus we have the Quabara Unjiamba of Ooraminna,[123] which is a performance connected with the Unjiamba or Hakea flower totem of a place called Ooraminna, the Quabara Ulpmerka of Quiurnpa, which is a ceremony concerned with certain *Ulpmerka*, or uncircumcised men of the plum tree totem of a place called Quiurnpa, and so on.

Naturally the ceremonies performed at any Engwura depend upon the men who are present—that is, if at one Engwura special totems are better represented than others, then the ceremonies connected with them will preponderate. There does not appear to be anything like a special series which must of necessity be performed, and the whole programme is arranged, so to speak, by the leading man, whose decision is final, but who frequently consults with certain of the other older men. He invites the owners of different ceremonies to perform them, but without his sanction and initiation nothing is done. Very often the performance is limited to one or perhaps two men, but in others a larger number may take part, the largest number which we saw being eleven. The man to whom the performance belongs may either take part in it himself, or, not infrequently, he may invite some one else to perform it, this being looked upon as a distinct compliment. The performer, or performers, need not of necessity belong to the totem with which the ceremony is concerned, nor need they of necessity belong to the same moiety of the tribe to which the owner does. In some cases while preparations are being made for the ceremony only the members of one moiety will be present, but very often there is no such restriction as this. In many instances those who are present during the preparation are the men who belong to the district with which the ceremony is associated. Frequently we noticed, for example, that the men from a southern locality would be associated in preparing for a ceremony connected with a southern locality, and, in the same way, men from the north would be present during the preparations for a ceremony concerned with a northern locality.

Not infrequently two performances would be prepared simultaneously, and when this was so one of them would be a ceremony concerned with Panunga and Bulthara men and the other with Purula and Kumara men. Under these circumstances one group would consist of the one moiety and the other of the other moiety, and they would be separated by some little distance and so placed in the bed of the creek that they could not see one another.

Speaking generally, it may be said that every man who was a member of the special totem with which any given ceremony was concerned would have the right of being present during the preparation, but no one else would come near except by special invitation of the individual to whom it belonged, and he could invite any one belonging to any class or totem to be present or to take part in the performance. The mixture of men of all groups is to be associated with the fact that the Engwura is an occasion on which members of all divisions of the tribe and of all totems are gathered together, and one of the main objects of which is the handing on to the younger men of the knowledge carefully treasured up by the older men of the past history of the tribe so far as it is concerned with the totems and the Churinga.

On this occasion everything was under the immediate control of one special old man, who was a perfect repository of tribal lore. Without apparently any trouble or the slightest hitch he governed the whole camp, comprising more than a hundred full-grown natives, who were taking part in the ceremony. Whilst the final decision on all points lay in his hands, there was what we used to call the "cabinet," consisting of this old man and three of the elders, who often met together to discuss matters. Frequently the leader would get up from the men amongst whom he was sitting, and apparently without a word being spoken or any sign made, the other three would rise and follow him one after the other, walking away to a secluded spot in the bed of the creek. Here they would gravely discuss matters concerned with the ceremonies to be performed, and then the leader would give his orders and everything would work with perfect regularity and smoothness. The effect on the younger men was naturally to heighten their respect for the old men and to bring them under the control of the latter. With the advent of the white man on the scene and the consequent breaking down of old customs, such a beneficial control exercised by the elder over the younger men rapidly becomes lost, and the native as rapidly degenerates. On the one hand the younger men do not take the interest in the tribal customs which their fathers did before them, and on the other the old men will not reveal tribal secrets to the young men unless they show themselves worthy of receiving such knowledge.

After these few general remarks we may pass on to describe more in detail certain of the ceremonies which will serve to illustrate the long series.

The first phase of the proceedings was opened by the Alice Springs natives performing the *Atnimokita* corrobboree, which occupied ten evenings. As a mark of respect and courtesy it was decided by the Alatunja of the group, after, as usual, consultation with the older men, that this corrobboree should be handed over in a short time to the man who took the leading part in the Engwura and who belonged to a more southern group. When once this handing over has taken place, it will never again be performed at Alice Springs.[124] As soon as the *Atnimokita* performance was concluded, another called the *Illyonpa* was commenced, and this also occupied ten nights. Two days after it had begun the old leader of the Engwura went down to the ground which had been chosen— the corrobborees mentioned taking place at a separate spot visited by men and women alike—and digging up the loose, sandy soil he made a low mound called the *Parra*, measuring about thirty feet in length, two feet in width and one foot in height. It was ornamented with a row of small gum tree boughs, which were fixed one after the other along the length of the mound, and is said to represent a tract of country, but, despite long inquiry, we have not been able to find out what is the exact meaning of the word *Parra*. All that the men could tell us was that it had always been made so during the Engwura—their fathers had made it and therefore they did—and that it was always made to run north and south, because in the Alcheringa the wild cat people marched in that direction. On the level flat to the western side of this *Parra* the sacred ceremonies forthwith began to be performed.

When the *Illyonpa* corrobboree had come to an end, no more ordinary dancing festivals were held until the close of the whole proceedings some three months later. From this time onwards, and until the last act of the Engwura is performed, the younger men who are passing through the ceremony must separate themselves completely from the women, and are entirely under the control of the older men. They must obey the latter implicitly. Their days are spent either in hunting, so as to secure food, the greater part of which is supposed to be brought in to the older men who remain in camp, or in watching the ceremonies, or in taking part in them under the guidance of the old men, and their nights are spent on, or close to, the Engwura ground.

With the opening of the second phase, the performance of the sacred ceremonies concerned with the totems began in earnest, and as descriptive of this, we may relate what took place during the last eight days of the five weeks which it occupied.

About ten o'clock on the morning of the first day it was decided to perform a ceremony called the Quabara Unjiamba of Ooraminna. This is concerned with certain women of the Unjiamba or Hakea totem, who in the Alcheringa came down from the north and marched southwards as far as a spot called Ooraminna, about twenty-five miles to the south of Alice Springs. The head man of the local group is the owner of this ceremony, and together with six Purula men and one Panunga man, he repaired to the bed of the small creek, where they all sat down under the shade of a small gum tree. The other men remained in various places round about the Engwura ground, but no one came near to the place where the preparations were being made.

On occasions such as this every man carries about with him a small wallet, which contains the few odds and ends needed for decoration in the performance of the various ceremonies. The wallet consists of a piece of the skin of some animal, such as one of the smaller marsupials, with the fur left on, or else some flat strips of a flexible bark tied round with fur string are used. In one of these wallets will be found a tuft or two of eagle-hawk and emu feathers, bunches of the tail feathers of the black cockatoo, some porcupine-grass resin, pieces of red and yellow ochre and white pipe-clay, an odd flint or two, balls of human hair and opossum fur string, a tuft or two of the tail tips of the rabbit-kangaroo, and not least, a dried crop of the eagle-hawk filled with down.

The men squat on the ground, and their wallets are leisurely opened out. There is no such thing as haste amongst the Australian natives. On this occasion the owner of the Quabara had asked his younger brother to perform the principal part in the ceremony. He was a Purula man of the Hakea totem, and he had also invited another man who was a Panunga of the Achilpa or wild cat totem, to assist in the performance. The reason why the latter man was asked, though he belonged neither to the same moiety nor totem as those to which the owner of the ceremony did, was simply that his daughter had been assigned as wife to the owner's son, and therefore it was desired to pay him some compliment. After some preliminary conversation, carried on in whispers, which had reference to the ceremony, the performers being instructed in their parts, and also in what the performance represented, a long spear was laid on the ground. One or two of the men went out and gathered a number of long grass stalks in which the spear was swathed, except about a foot at the lower end which was left uncovered. Then each man present took off his hair waist-girdle and these were wound round and round until spear and grass stalks were completely enclosed, and a long pole, about six inches in diameter and about eight feet in length, was formed. Then to the top of it was fixed a bunch of eagle-hawk and emu feathers. When this had been done one of the men by means of a sharp bit of flint—a splinter of glass, if obtainable, is preferred—cut open a vein in his arm, which he had previously bound tightly round with hair string in the region of the biceps. The blood spurted out in a thin stream and was caught in the hollow of a shield, until about half a pint had been drawn, when the string was unwound from the arm and a finger held on the slight wound until the bleeding ceased. Then the down was opened out and some of it was mixed with red ochre which had been ground to powder on a flat stone. Four of the Purula men then began to decorate the pole with alternate rings of red and white down. Each of them took a short twig, bound a little fur string round one end, dipped the brush thus made into the blood, and then smeared this on over the place where the down was to be fixed on. The blood on congealing formed an excellent adhesive material. All the time that this was taking place, the men sang a monotonous chant, the words of which were merely a constant repetition of some such simple refrain as, "Paint it around with rings and rings," "the *Nurtunja* of the Alcheringa," "paint the *Nurtunja* with rings." Every now and again they burst out into loud singing, starting on a high note and gradually descending, the singing dying away as the notes got lower and lower, producing the effect of music dying away in the distance. Whilst some of the men were busy with the *Nurtunja*, the Panunga man taking no part in the work beyond joining in the singing, another Purula man was occupied in fixing lines of down across six Churinga, which had been brought out of the Purula and Kumara store for the purpose of being used in the ceremony. Each of them had a small hole bored at one end, and by means of a strand of human hair string passed through this it was attached to the pole from which, when erect, the six hung pendant. Of the Churinga the two uppermost ones were supposed to have actually belonged to the two Hakea women who in the Alcheringa walked down to Ooraminna. Of the remaining four, two belonged to women and one to a man of the same totem, and the remaining one was that of a man of the Achilpa totem.

The decorated pole which is made in this way is called a *Nurtunja*, and in one form or another it figures largely in the sacred ceremonies, especially in the case of those which are associated with northern localities. Its significance will be referred to subsequently.

As soon as the *Nurtunja* was ready, the bodies of the performers were decorated with designs drawn in ochre and bird's down, and then, when all was ready, the *Nurtunja* was carried by the Purula man to the ceremonial ground, and there, by the side of the *Parra*, the two men knelt down, the hinder one of the two holding the *Nurtunja* upright with both hands behind his back. It is curious to watch the way in which every man who is engaged in performing one of these ceremonies walks; the moment he is painted up he adopts a kind of stage walk with a remarkable high knee action, the foot being always lifted at least twelve inches above the ground, and the knee bent so as to approach, and, indeed, often to touch the stomach, as the body is bent forward at each step.

The Purula man who had been assisting in the decoration now called out to the other men who had not been present to come up. This calling out always takes the form of shouting "*pau-au-au*" at the top of the voice, while the hand with the palm turned to the face, and the fingers loosely opened out is rapidly moved backwards and forwards on the wrist just in front of the mouth, giving a very peculiar vibratory effect to the voice. At this summons all the men on the ground came up at a run, shouting as they approached, "*wh'a! wha! wh'r-rr!*" After dancing in front of the two performers for perhaps half a minute, the latter got up and moved with very high knee action, the *Nurtunja* being slowly bent down over the heads of the men who were in front. Then the dancers circled round the performers, shouting loudly "*wha! wha!*" while the latter moved around with them. This running round the performers is called *Wahkutnima*. Then once more the performers resumed their position in front of the other men, over whose heads the *Nurtunja* was again bent down, and then two or three of the men laid their hands on the shoulders of the performers, and the ceremony came to an end. The *Nurtunja* was laid on one side, and the performers, taking each a little bit of down from it, pressed this in turn against the stomach of each of the older men who were present. The idea of placing hands upon the performers is that thereby their movements are stopped, whilst the meaning of the down being pressed against the stomachs of the older men is that they become so agitated with emotion by witnessing the sacred ceremony that their inward parts, that is, their bowels, which are regarded as the seat of the emotions, get tied up in knots, which are loosened by this application of a part of the sacred *Nurtunja*. In some ceremonies the *Nurtunja* itself is pressed against the stomachs of the older men, the process receiving the special name of *tunpulilima*.

The whole performance only lasted about five minutes, while the preparation for it had occupied more than three hours. As soon as it was over the performers sat on the ground; the down was removed from their bodies and preserved for future use and the *Nurtunja* was dismantled, the hair string being carefully unwound and returned to its respective owners.

The ceremony refers to two Alcheringa women of the Unjiamba or Hakea totem. As they travelled they kept close to the tracks of one party of Achilpa or wild cat men, but do not appear to have ever seen or come in contact with the men, who were travelling in the opposite direction. It is a remarkable fact that in some way or other the Achilpa and Unjiamba totems seem to be connected together, but what the exact connection is we have been unable to discover. The Unjiamba women referred to followed as they travelled close by, but not actually along, the track of one of the main Achilpa parties, and the two groups walked in opposite directions. Again, very many of the Achilpa ceremonies refer to the men eating Unjiamba, a feature which is not met with in the ceremonies of any other totem, and it will further be noticed that in the ceremony just described, out of six Churinga attached to the Nurtunja, no fewer than five belonged to Unjiamba individuals.

When the ceremony was over there was a rest for an hour or two, and then, early in the afternoon, two lots of Churinga were brought in from the Panunga and Bulthara store to be examined. Men of all groups—about fifteen in number—gathered together in the bed of the creek, with the Churinga in the middle of the group. The first lot belonged to the Achilpa of Ooraminna, the second to the Irritcha, or eaglehawk men of a place called Undoolya, out to the east of Alice Springs. During the examination certain of the younger men were present, and in this instance the Churinga, which were bound up in parcels tied tightly round with human hair string, were unpacked by the sons of the Alatunjas of the two localities to which they respectively belonged. While this was taking place the men sang as usual, pausing every now and then while some old man leant over to whisper in the ear of some one opposite to him. No loud talking was allowed, and every one looked as solemn as possible. The Churinga having been at last unpacked—for in these ceremonies everything is done with the utmost and, to the onlooker, often exasperating deliberation—they were taken up one by one by the Alatunja, in whose charge they were, and after a careful examination of each he pressed them in turn against the stomach of some one or other of the old men present. The man thus honoured held the Churinga, gazing down upon it, while a whispered conversation was kept up with regard to each one and its former possessor. Amongst them was one which was the *Churinga nanja* of one of the wives of the Alatunja of the Alice Springs group, and this was handed over to the woman's son for him to carefully examine.

When the examination was complete they were all carefully wrapped up and taken back to the store, and then preparations were made for another ceremony. Previous to this, however, at a signal from the head man, all the Purula and Kumara men had left the ground with the exception of two old ones, who were the *Gammona* of the head man and who were especially invited by him to stay and watch.

The Quabara to be performed was one associated with the *Ulpmerka* of Quiurnpa, the latter being a group of men belonging to the Akakia or plum tree totem; the men are called *Ulpmerka* because in the Alcheringa they were, as will be explained in another chapter, left uncircumcised—that is, they remained *Ulpmerka*, or boys. The materials having been opened out, singing began, the burden being a constant repetition of the words "the sand hills are good." This Quabara was in the possession of the Alatunja of Alice Springs, and he invited a man to perform it who was a tribal son to himself, belonging to the Panunga division and to the Irriakura totem. First of all the Alatunja's eldest son went over to where the man sat and rubbed his forehead against the latter's stomach, then embraced him round the neck and ended by rubbing his stomach against that of the man in question. Then a Bulthara man came up, that is a tribal father, and the same process of embracing was repeated. The meaning of this was that the young man had expressed a sense of his unfitness to undertake the duty, but when he had once been embraced in this way by men who were especially associated with the ceremony it was impossible for him to refuse any longer. As soon as this was over the Alatunja of Alice Springs at once went over to where he sat and began to decorate his head. Twigs of a species of Cassia were fixed on to the top of his head enclosing his hair, which was gathered into a bunch so as to form, with the twigs, a long rounded structure about two and a half feet in length, projecting upwards and slightly backwards on the top of his head. The twigs were bound round and round with hair string. The Alatunja of the Undoolya group, who was the father of the performer, bled himself, the blood being taken on this occasion, as it very often was, from the subincised urethra, which was probed with a sharp pointed piece of wood. As the decorations proceeded—that is, while the head-dress was being covered with a design in white and red down, the men sitting around sang of the hair top-knot of Kukaitcha, the latter being a celebrated man of the Alcheringa associated with the plum tree totem, the top-knot having reference to the manner in which the hair is worn previous to the boys passing through the ceremony of circumcision.

"Yai yai Kukai
Ul lal arai
Yai yai Kukai
Yai yai Acheri
Malarai."

Time after time some such simple refrain was repeated while the down was fixed on to the performer's head-dress and body. When all was ready the performer, preceded by an old man, walked in a crouching attitude along the creek bed until he came opposite to the *Parra*, when he ran straight across and squatted in front of and close beside it.

It was just sunset as he came on to the ground, and at the same moment the arrival of a fresh contingent of natives from the south was announced. They had come into camp on the other side of the river and had, according to strict etiquette, sat down there for some little time apart from the other men. By way of welcome a party of the natives with spears, shields and boomerangs ran across to where they sat and, with the usual high stepping action, danced round and round them, brandishing spears and boomerangs and shouting loudly; suddenly they turned, crossed the river and came, still running, up the bank, threw their weapons on one side amongst the bushes and, without stopping, came on and circled round and round the performer, shouting *"wah! wah!"* After a short time two Purula men went and sat down, one in front of and one behind the performer; then a third came and, as he bent forward over the front one, the three placed their hands on the shoulders of the performer and he ceased the quivering and wriggling movements which he had been executing, while the men danced round him. The performer then got up and embraced the older men one after the other, this being done to assuage their feelings of emotion.

The evening was spent, as it usually was, singing on the ground close to the *Parra*. During all the first six weeks a considerable length of time was always occupied during the night in what was called "singing the ground." The young men who were passing through the Engwura for the first time stood up forming two or three lines close behind one another, like lines of men in a regiment of soldiers, and, led by one or two of the older men, either moved in a long line parallel to the *Parra* mound, shouting *"wha! wha!"* alternating this at intervals with a specially loud *"whrr-rr-rr,"* when with one accord they bent forwards and, as it were, hurled the sound at the *Parra*, or else they would sometimes rush closely round and round the mound in a single line, shouting in just the same way. The noise was deafening, and the loud *"wha,"* and still more penetrating cry of *"whrr-rr-rr,"* could be heard a mile or two away echoing amongst the bare and rocky ranges surrounding the Engwura ground. When this singing was over—that was about midnight—they all lay down around their camp fires, and for a few hours there was a welcome silence. Usually at night there were a few of the men awake preparing, by the light of scattered fires, for ceremonies which often took place in the dead of the night or else just before the day broke.

The morning of the second day was entirely occupied with the examination of Churinga. Early in the afternoon the Quabara Iruntarinia Irritcha was performed. This will serve as a good example of what is called an Iruntarinia ceremony, that is, one which is supposed to have been imparted to a special individual by the *Iruntarinia* or spirits. The favoured person to whom this particular one had been shown was a celebrated medicine man, or *Railtchawa*, the son of the Alatunja of an Irritcha or eagle-hawk locality, but who was himself an Udnirringita or witchetty grub man. The *Iruntarinia* can present Quabara to whomsoever they choose to honour in this way, quite regardless of the recipient's totem. The latter may retain possession of the ceremony himself or he may pass it on, as a gift, to some other man, but in that case the individual must be of the totem with which the ceremony is concerned. Naturally the possession of such a ceremony is a mark of distinction, and it also gives the possessor a peculiar advantage over others, not only because he is so favoured by the spirits, but because he has something in his possession which enables him to confer a favour on some other man to whom he may decide to hand on the Quabara. On this occasion the recipient had handed on the ceremony to his own father, who was the head of the eagle-hawk group, and from whom, in course of time, it will descend to an eagle-hawk son.

Two men were invited to perform, both of them being sons of the Alatunja, and they were respectively of the eagle-hawk and emu totems. Only Panunga and Bulthara men were present during the preparations. The hair of each man was bunched up and, together with a conical crown of Cassia twigs, was bound round and round with hair string. Then blood, drawn in the usual way, was smeared over the front part of the head-dress and across the body in the form of a broad band round the waist and a band over each shoulder, the two uniting back and front. Each band was about six inches broad, and had the form when the decoration was complete of a solid mass of pink down, edged with a line of white. Into the hair-girdle behind was fixed a large bunch of the black feathers of the eagle-hawk, and into the top of each man's head-dress were fixed three Churinga, decorated with close rows of down coloured alternately red and white, each Churinga being about three feet in length and decorated at its end with a tuft of eagle-hawk feathers. In his mouth one man carried a small cylindrical mass, about eight inches in length and two in diameter, made of grass surrounded with hair string and covered with lines of down.

When the decoration was complete they came into the open and each of them sat down on his haunches on the convex side of a shield, so that they faced one another at a distance of about eight feet. Each man had his arms extended and carried a little bunch of eucalyptus twigs in his hands. They were supposed to represent two eagle-hawks quarrelling over a piece of flesh which was represented by the downy mass in one man's mouth. At first they remained squatting on their shields, moving their arms up and down, and still continuing this action which was supposed to represent the flapping of wings, they jumped off the shields and with their bodies bent up and arms extended and flapping, began circling round each other as if each were afraid of coming to close quarters. Then they stopped and moved a step or two at a time, first to one side and then to the other, until finally, they came to close quarters and began fighting with their heads for the possession of the piece of meat. This went on for some time and then two men stepped out from amongst the audience and took away the Churinga, which were a great weight and must have caused a considerable strain on the head, especially in the great heat of the afternoon sun, for it must be remembered that it was now well on into the summer. Then once more they began going round and round each other flapping wings, jumping up and falling back just like fighting birds, until finally they again came to close quarters, and the attacking man at length seized with his teeth the piece of meat and wrenched it out of the other man's mouth. The acting in this ceremony was especially good, the actions and movements of the birds being admirably represented, and the whole scene with the decorated men in front and the group of interested natives in the background was by no means devoid of picturesqueness.

Later on in the afternoon there was performed the Quabara Unjiamba of Ooraminna. In this ceremony, we again find, as in the one already described, the close connection between the Unjiamba and Achilpa totems. The two men who performed, and neither of whom belonged to the totems, were decorated each with a broad band round the waist, and one passing over each shoulder and joining, back and front, in the middle line. The area occupied by these bands was first of all rubbed with grease and then with powdered wad, an ore of manganese which gives, when used in this way, a peculiar pearl-gray tint, which harmonises well with the chocolate-coloured skin and stands out in strong contrast to the edging of white down which everywhere margins the bands. Over each ear was suspended a tuft of the tail tips of the rabbit-bandicoot. One of the two men carried a large Churinga on his head, fixed into the usual helmet made of twigs bound round with string. During the preparation the natives sang chants concerning the *Kauaua* (a sacred pole about which there will be more said subsequently) and referring also to the carrying round of the *Nurtunja*.

Both of the performers represented Achilpa men and they sat down immediately facing one another near to the *Parra*, the man carrying the Churinga having a shield in front of him, and in his hands a few twigs supposed to represent the flowering Hakea—that is the Unjiamba. These he pretended to steep in water so as to make the decoction of Hakea flower which is a favourite drink of the natives, and which the man sitting opposite to him pretended to suck up with a little mop made of a twig with fur string tied round it. While they did this the other men ran round and round them shouting "*wha! wha!*" Suddenly, the man who had been drinking sprang round so as to place his back just in front of the other man, who then put the shield behind his back with his arms holding it there, and the two for a few moments swayed from side to side slightly raising themselves from their squatting position as they did so. Those who were running round dropped out one by one until only three were left and they then put their hands on the performers' shoulders and the performance was at an end. The same ceremony was enacted about eleven o'clock at night, and then after the usual "singing" of the ceremonial ground the day's work came to a close.

On the morning of the third day the Quabara Achilpa of Urapitchera was performed. This was a ceremony concerned with a group of wild cat men who in the Alcheringa walked across from south to north of the eastern side of the country now occupied by the Arunta tribe; whilst doing so they camped for a time at a spot called Urapitchera on the Finke River. The ceremony is now in the possession of the Alatunja of the Imanda group of men of the emu totem and he received it from his father who was a wild cat man. At the request of the owner it was performed by an old Purula man who was the head of the Elkintera, or large white bat totem, at a spot close to Imanda which itself lies on the Hugh River. In this performance two *Nurtunjas*, each of them about ten feet in length, were prepared. Unlike most of the *Nurtunjas* there was no central support such as a spear, but the whole structure was made of a very large number of flexible grass stalks bound round with hair string and decorated with the usual rings of red and white down, so that each of them was somewhat flexible. The performer was decorated with lines and bands of down passing from his head along either shoulder and then down the body as far as the knees. On the *Parra* ground the *Nurtunjas* were arranged so that one end of each was under the man's waist-girdle, while the other, ornamented with a bunch of eagle-hawk feathers, rested on the ground, the two diverging from each other. Then the other men were called up and began running round and shouting and then all passed under the *Nurtunjas* which the performer lifted up for the purpose, the men with their hands and shoulders helping to support them, for they had been carried in that way in the Alcheringa. Finally, the old Purula man to whom the ceremony belongs came up and embraced the old performer, who was in fact about the oldest man upon the ground and almost blind, but as full of energy as the youngest man present.

In the afternoon of the same day a remarkable ceremony was performed which had no special relationship to the Engwura inasmuch as, though owned by the head man of a particular totem—the Ullakuppera or little hawk—it had no reference to either his or any other totem, but was a performance representing the doings of certain *Kurdaitcha* men. The description of it is therefore given in connection with that of the *Kurdaitcha* custom to which it more properly belongs. We could not find out why it was given during the Engwura at all, but it was evidently a favourite one with the natives, by most of whom it seemed to be well-known, and the opportunity was taken, while a large number were gathered together, to show it to those who had not previously seen it. It was repeated at a later date and was the only ceremony which was performed which had no special significance as regards the Engwura.

Early on the morning of the fourth day a very special examination of Churinga took place. Some years ago there was a small group of Echunpa or large lizard men who lived about twelve miles to the west of Alice Springs. Gradually the group became extinct until finally no man was left to inherit and take care of the sacred storehouse containing the Churinga belonging to the group. Under these circumstances, the extinct group having consisted mainly of Panunga and Bulthara men, a contiguous group which was *nakrakia* with the extinct one, that is consisted mainly of the same moiety of the tribe, entered into possession. The totem of this group was Unchalka, or little grub, and its head man, as no other lizard men lived anywhere near, took charge of the storehouse and of its contents. Some years later it chanced that the wife of a man of the Alice Springs group conceived a child in the old lizard locality and so, in the person of her son, the local Echunpa group was resuscitated. The lizard man had now arrived at maturity and advantage was taken of the Engwura to hand over to him, in the presence of representatives of the tribe, the Churinga of his ancestors.

On the evening before, the head man of the Unchalka had sent out special messengers to bring in the Churinga, and about nine o'clock in the morning they brought them into camp and handed them over to their custodian, who at once took them down into the creek where a number of the older men were gathered together as well as some of the younger ones, amongst whom was the man to whom they were to be handed over. First of all, the Alatunja of the Unchalka totem and those of the two important witchetty-grub groups, the one at Undoolya and the other at Alice Springs, knelt over towards one another and held a lengthy whispered conversation which was now and again shared in by other older men in the group, the most solemn silence being, as usual, observed by all the rest. The purport of this conversation was the holding of an Echunpa or lizard ceremony as soon as the present business had been carried through, so far, that is, as it was to be carried that day. When this matter, and the performers, had been decided upon, the old Unchalka man retired to the edge of the group. Then the Churinga were laid on shields and small boughs cut from the gum tree under which they sat; there were about sixty of them all together, and as soon as they were all unpacked, the man to whom they were being handed over was called up and took his seat along with the older men next to the Churinga. A long conversation, again carried on in whispers and with much solemnity, then ensued between the recipient and the two old men who told the former what the Churinga meant and whom they had belonged to. When this was over the new possessor rubbed his hands over the forehead of the Alatunja of the Undoolya group, who was a very old man, and then embraced him and having done this went down on his knees and rubbed the old man's stomach with his forehead. It may be noted here that the deference paid to the old men during these ceremonies of examining the Churinga is most marked; no young man thinks of speaking unless he be first addressed by one of the elder men and then he listens solemnly to all that the latter tells him. During the whole time the presence of the Churinga seems to produce a reverent silence as if the natives really believed that the spirits of the dead men to whom they have belonged in times past were present, and no one, while they are being examined, ever speaks in tones louder than a whisper.

The old man just referred to was especially looked up to as an *Oknirabata* or great instructor, a term which is only applied, as in this case, to men who are not only old but are learned in all the customs and traditions of the tribe, and whose influence is well seen at ceremonies such as the Engwura where the greatest deference is paid to them. A man may be old, very old indeed, but yet never attain to the rank of *Oknirabata*.

When the young man had rubbed the stomach of the *Oknirabata*, the latter went over to where the Alatunja of the Unchalka sat and did the same to him in acknowledgment of the fact that he had safely kept the Churinga. The reason for this action on the part of the *Oknirabata* lay in the fact that he was the oldest *Oknia* or father of the young man. Then he went to an old Okira or kangaroo man and did the same. The territory of this man's group lay close to that of the Unchalka men, but not being *nakrakia* with the extinct lizard men he and his people could not go in and inherit the land. Still the local relationship, which enters in a vaguely defined but unmistakable way into the customs concerned with the totems, found on this occasion its expression in this act of courtesy paid to the head of a neighbouring group by the father on behalf on his son. The natives said that this was done to keep the old kangaroo man from being jealous and unfriendly. As the handing over of the Churinga was a matter of great importance it could not be properly carried through at one sitting and so, after a long time had been spent in their examination, the completion of the ceremony was postponed to another day.

The preparation for the lizard ceremony then began. The old *Oknirabata* was to perform it, and after his head had been encased in a strong helmet, the whole of this, as well as his face and the upper part of his body and arms, were covered with a dense mass of white down, two half rings of which also adorned the front of each thigh. A large bunch of eagle hawk feathers was fastened behind into his waistband, and on his head he carried no fewer than seven large Churinga belonging to the totem, two of them being remarkable from the fact that they were curved in shape like a boomerang. These were the only ones of this shape on the Engwura ground, and they were evidently very old ones,[125] as the original pattern with which they had been ornamented was almost entirely obliterated by the innumerable rubbings to which they had been subjected in course of time. When decorated the performer went at first some distance along the creek bed so as to be out of sight of the other men, who assembled not far from the *Parra* at a spot where they spread out a small patch of gum boughs. Standing behind this they waited for a few minutes, after which the lizard was seen in the distance throwing up clouds of dust as he came up from his hiding place in the creek and approached the ground. He came on slowly in a zig-zag course, stooping down and assuming a variety of attitudes, always of course with the high knee action. The younger man, to whom the Churinga were being handed over, now appointed two men to go and meet him. This they did about thirty or forty yards away from the group, after which the performer pretended every now and then to turn back, whereupon the two men circled round him holding their arms up as if to prevent him from going away while they cried out *"chrr-chrr,"* and did their best to encourage him to come on to where the group of men stood waiting. Gradually he came on, and, when close to, the men forming the audience went to the boughs and spread them out as if inviting him to sit down, which he did after a short time, and then shouting *"wha! wha!"* they circled round him in the usual way. The two men who went to meet him represent little birds called *Thippa-thippa*, which tradition says are the descendants of Alcheringa men who came and watched and ran round and round some lizard men who were travelling along towards Simpson's Gap. The *Thippa-thippa* changed into birds of the same name, who ever afterwards became the mates of the lizard people. The night was spent as usual singing on the ground.

On the morning of the fifth day we were introduced to a new form of ceremony. As might have been expected amongst a tribe occupying such an extent of territory as does the

Arunta, there are certain features in regard to the ceremonies which vary in different parts. Not only do the Arunta extend in a north and south direction for more than three hundred miles, but at their southern limit they are in contact with tribes whose customs vary much from their own and in which the social organisation is radically different. Where two such tribes come into contact with one another each has a certain influence upon the other, and thus we find that the southern Arunta have gained certain things from their southern neighbours which are not found in the north, and *vice versa*. We have already pointed out that the *Nurtunja* in one form or another plays an important part in the sacred ceremonies. When we come to the southern Arunta its place is taken to a large extent by what is called the *Waninga*. This is a structure which varies much in size and form, but consists essentially of a framework of sticks which in its simplest form has the shape of a cross, and to which are fixed lines of string. We will describe first the ceremony as performed at the Engwura, and will then add a few general remarks on the subject of the *Waninga*. On this occasion it was used in connection with the Quabara Quatcha of Idracowra, that is a rain ceremony associated with what is called by white men Chambers Pillar, not far from the Finke River. Idracowra is a corruption of the native words *iturka wura*, the native name for the pillar.

Two men, one a Purula the other a Bulthara, both of them belonging to the emu totem, were decorated for the ceremony with white bands of down, two on each side of the body. On the top of their heads each wore a bunch of parings of gum tree wood smeared with human blood. The front man had a freshly cut gum stick about two and a half feet in length with the green bark still on, and, like the parings, smeared with blood. This he carried across his shoulders, one hand holding it at either end. His back was adorned with a bunch of eagle-hawk feathers fixed in to his waist girdle. The other man, who walked immediately behind him, carried the

Waninga, which he grasped with both hands at the back of his neck. The strain on his arms must have been very great, as it was carried in an upright position. With particularly high knee action, and with their bodies quivering, they came up out of the bed of the creek while the audience sat on the ground by the side of the *Parra*, the front row of men, who belonged to the southern district from which the *Waninga* came, beating the ground with boomerangs. The performers advanced slowly for about thirty or forty yards, stopping every now and then, until finally they came close to the seated men. Then a Kumara man got up and took the *Waninga* away, and placed it carefully on one side. The performers then simply walked up to the group, sat down, and were pressed upon the shoulders in the usual way.

In this instance the *Waninga* was made out of a long desert-oak spear ten feet in length; at right angles to its length were fixed two sticks about three feet in length, each of them at a distance of two and a half feet from one end of the spear. Between the two, and running parallel to the length of the spear, were strung tightly, and very close together, lines of human hair-string. Each line took a turn round the transverse stick at either end, and then passed off in a slanting direction to the central spear round which it was passed, and then ran back again to the transverse bar; from here it was carried back along the length of the structure, between the two bars, close by the side of the first line, and so on, time after time, until the whole space between the two bars was filled in with closely-set parallel bands of string. At either end the strands passing off to the central spear formed a triangular-shaped structure. A certain number of lines forming a band an inch and a half in width, and running all round, about the same distance, within the margin, were made of opossum fur string whitened with pipeclay, the same width of string on each side of it being red-ochred, while the remainder was left in its normal black colour. Tufts of the red-barred tail feathers of the black cockatoo were attached to the upper end of the spear and to each end of the transverse bars, and finally a number of bands of white down were attached in roughly parallel lines across the length of the lines of string, little masses of the same material covering the bases and tips of the feathers. The whole structure took several hours to prepare, and showed no little ingenuity and a considerable amount of artistic capacity on the part of its makers.

The various parts of the *Waninga* have their different meanings, but it must be remembered that the same structure will mean one thing when it is used in connection with one totem and quite a different thing when used in connection with another. This particular *Waninga* was emblematic of the Quatcha, or water totem. The red string represented thunder, the white band lightning, and the ordinary uncoloured string was the rain falling. The white patches and bands of down naturally represented clouds, while the red of the feathers and the blood smeared on the parings of wood worn on the men's heads represented the masses of dirty brown froth which often float on the top of flood waters.

This was the only occasion on which, during the Engwura, the *Waninga* was used, the reason being that in perhaps the greater part of the tribe, and certainly in the northern half, the *Nurtunja* is most largely employed in totemic ceremonies with, it must be remembered, precisely the same significance as the *Waninga*, that is, in each instance the *Waninga*, or the *Nurtunja*, as the case may be, is emblematic of the particular totem with which the ceremony being performed is associated. As we pass right into the south the *Nurtunja* completely disappears and the *Waninga* takes its place. At Charlotte Waters, for example, or Crown Point on the lower part of the Finke River, no *Nurtunja* is ever used; when the rite of circumcision is practised a *Waninga* is made, and after it has been used in the performance of a sacred ceremony it is fixed up in the ground and the novice embraces it.[126] Occasionally a kind of compound one is made in which a small one is attached to the top of a larger one, in much the same way in which a small *Nurtunja* is sometimes attached to the top of a larger one.

The use of the *Waninga* extends far south, right down, in fact, to the sea coast at Port Lincoln, and it evidently passes out westwards, but how far it is impossible to say. At Charlotte Waters various totems use it, such as the Irrunpa or lizard (the equivalent of the Echunpa of the north), Okira or kangaroo, Arunga or euro, and Quatcha or water. The Irrunpa *Waninga* is similar in structure to that of the Quatcha, but the parts have an entirely different significance; the projecting end represents the head, the triangular part following this the neck, the top transverse bar the fore limbs, the main part the body, the lower bar the legs, and the bottom end of the spear the tail. Exactly as in the case of the different marks on the Churinga, so in the *Waninga* the different parts represent entirely different objects according to the totem with which the particular one is associated.

In connection with this ceremony and the use of the *Waninga,* we learned the following particulars with regard to the wanderings of certain Okira, or kangaroo men, in the Alcheringa, which we insert here to give some idea of the nature of the instruction with respect to the doings of their ancestors in the Alcheringa, which is given by the old men to the younger ones during the performance of the Engwura. Somewhere out from the far west there came two kangaroo men who carried with them a large *Waninga*. They stayed for some time, first of all at a spot close to Idracowra, at a waterhole called Umbera-wartna, and there they formed an *Oknanikilla*, that is they deposited some of the Churinga which they carried in the ground, and so left behind spirit individuals of the kangaroo totem; then they walked on down the Finke River to a place called Urpunna, where they erected their *Waninga* and formed another *Oknanikilla*. Then, carrying the *Waninga*, they went underground and crossed beneath the

Lilla Creek which enters the Finke from the west, and on the southern side they met a mob of kangaroos and euros who came to look at them. Travelling on they came out of the ground at a group of hills called by the natives Amanda, and probably identical with what is now called Mount Watt, one of a group of silurian sandstone hills which rise out of the level plains and sand hills about forty-five miles to the southwest of the junction of the Finke and Lilla. Here they rested for some time and formed an *Oknanikilla*. Then they turned south-east, and travelling underground crossed beneath the Wichinga (now called the Hamilton) creek, and then on under the Alberga, until once more they emerged at Marpinna, where they formed an *Oknanikilla*, and where also they opened veins in their arms and allowed the blood to stream out over the ground, and so made a great level clay plain which has remained to the present time. Then, after going still further south and passing out of what is now the country of the Arunta, they turned to the west and made a big circuit through the sand hill country now occupied by a part of the Luritcha tribe, until finally, turning north, they came to the George Gill Range, and crossed this so as to reach a spot now called Tempe Downs, where they formed an *Oknanikilla*. Then following this to its junction with the Palmer they went a little way up the latter, and, together with their *Waninga*, they ceased from wandering, and went down into a well-known water-hole called Illara, where they stayed, forming an important *Oknanikilla* of the kangaroo totem. The importance of the traditions relating to the wanderings of the Alcheringa ancestors has already been pointed out in connection with the discussion of the totems. It must be remembered that it is during the Engwura ceremony especially that a knowledge of these matters is imparted by the elder to the younger men, on whose memory the traditions are firmly fixed by means, to a large extent, of the ceremonies, each one of which is associated with some special spot and some special individual or group.

On the sixth day the ceremonies opened with one relating to *Ulpmerka* men who belonged to the Inguitchika (a grass seed) totem of a place called Imiunga, on the Jay River. This particular ceremony belonged to a Purula man, who invited a Bulthara man, assisted by a Panunga, to perform it; the former belonged to the witchetty-grub and the latter to the emu totem. The Bulthara man was son of an Inguitchika woman, the other performer being the son of a woman of the Illonka (little yam) totem, the locality of which adjoined that of the former. The man to whom the ceremony belonged was *Witia*, or younger brother, of the Inguitchika woman, and has charge of her *Churinga nanja*.

For the performance two sticks were taken, each about four feet long; when swathed in grass stalks and bound round with hair-string, each of them was about nine inches in diameter. The ends were ornamented with bunches of white and pink cockatoo feathers and eagle hawk. The two were bound together tightly in the form of a cross, and each was further ornamented with rings of down. The whole structure formed a *Nurtunja*. During the performance the two men squatted down close to one another, each carrying in his hand a small twig of gum tree, the *Nurtunja* being fixed on to the head of the hinder of the two men, who simply swayed their bodies about from side to side while the other men ran round and round them, except two old men who squatted down to one side singing about the walking about of the *Ulpmerka* men in the Alcheringa.

During the evening of this the sixth day, the men seated by the side of the *Parra* began to sing about the *Kulchia* or fur armlets being bound around the arms of the young men who were passing through the Engwura, and also began singing about the *Kauaua*, or sacred pole, which was to be erected later on.

On the seventh day an important Quabara of the *Ulpmerka* of Quiurnpa was performed. In this there were seven performers, three of whom represented boys who wore top-knots on their heads—the usual style of doing a boy's hair. Two others, who represented an individual called Kukaitcha, the leader of the *Ulpmerka*, wore decorated Churinga fastened as usual into a head-dress, which was made of twigs bound round with hair-string. One represented an *Ulpmerka* man, and wore a large tuft of eagle hawk-feathers on his head, while the last man had an enormous head-dress two feet six inches in height, made in the usual way and decorated with broad bands of down. Through this was stuck a bent stick about four feet in length, carrying at each end a tuft of feathers, while from the head-dress were suspended four *Ulpmerka* Churinga, two of them belonging to women and two to men.

Each of the performers was profusely decorated with bands of yellow ochre, charcoal or wad, edged with down. The preparation for the performance took between two and three hours, and was under the superintendence of the Alatunja of Alice Springs, in whose charge at present are all the Churinga belonging to this group of *Ulpmerka* men of the plum tree totem. They will some day be handed over to the only living representative of the totem, who is at present too young to receive them.

During the preparations the men sang of putting twigs on to the head of Kukaitcha, of the *Paukutta*, or top-knots of the boys, and of the walking of the *Ulpmerka* in the Alcheringa. The man with the special head-dress was supposed to represent a great Alcheringa Kukaitcha, and the head-dress itself was a form of *Nurtunja*, which in this case represents a plum tree, the stick which passed through it representing the branches. When all was ready the performers divided into three sets. One of the Kukaitchas went to a spot at the north-east end of the ground; the man with the *Nurtunja* was led by the Alatunja up to the *Parra*, beside which he squatted, while the other five went to the north-west end of the ground. Of the latter the three representing boys sat down in a line, two facing one way and one the other. At the end of the line, where the first mentioned sat, stood one of the Kukaitchas with two Churinga in his hands which he kept beating together, the idea being that he was teaching the boys to sing. At the other end stood the *Ulpmerka* man pretending to knock plums off a tree, which the boy in front of him picked up and ate. When all the performers were ready in their allotted places, the other men, who had meanwhile remained out of sight in the bed of the creek, were called up on to the ground. They were supposed to represent a mob of *Ulpmerka* men, and coming at a run on to the ground they went first of all to the solitary Kukaitcha man and danced, shouting, around him; then suddenly, accompanied by him, they ran across to where the five men were arranged, acting as already described. After the usual dancing, shouting, and laying-on of hands, the whole party ran across to where the great Kukaitcha sat, and all joined in a dance round him while he swayed about from side to side. The usual embracing of the old men by the performers brought the ceremony to an end.

There is a curious tradition of the natives which is concerned with this special group of *Ulpmerka* men, with which we were acquainted before the Engwura took place, and with part of which this ceremony is concerned. About fifteen miles to the S.S.E. of Alice Springs is a plum tree totem locality. In the Alcheringa the totem included a number of men who were designated *Ulpmerka* of the plum tree totem for the simple reason, as explained elsewhere, that they had not been circumcised. In the same way it may be remarked that we meet with *Ulpmerka* men of other totems such as the grass seed. The plum tree *Ulpmerka* men had, so says tradition, only two women amongst them, who both belonged to the bandicoot totem, and had joined the *Ulmerka* party after wandering alone for some time over the country. At first they were considerably alarmed at the *Ulpmerka* men, but the latter made a large *Nurtunja*, and after the women had been shown this, then, for some reason, they were no longer afraid. The younger woman was then gorgeously decorated with down, a small, bluntly conical *Nurtunja* was placed on her head, and the men then danced round her shouting, *"wah! wah!"* Then she was taken and laid down by the side of the large *Nurtunja*, which was fixed upright in the ground, and the operation of *atna ariltha-kuma*, the equivalent ceremony to that of *pura ariltha-kuma* as practised upon the men, was performed by means of a large stone knife, after which all the men had access to her. The two women were then taken to the camp of the Kukaitcha, who was the headman of the local *Ulpmerka* men, and who claimed the women as his own, but allowed the others to have access occasionally to the woman who had been operated upon as just described. After a time a special messenger or *Inwurra*, who was also named Kukaitcha, came down from the north—from the country, as the natives say, of the *Quatcha alia*—that is the salt water. He called the men to him and told them that they were to leave their own country and follow him. Then he took the two women away from the local Kukaitcha, and a start was made for the north. After travelling as far as a place now called Wigley Springs, four miles to the north of Alice Springs, the *Nurtunja* which they carried with them was erected, and the elder of the two women was operated upon. All the men as before had access to her; and the party remained at this spot for some little time. Then they went on towards what is now Bond Springs, close to which they camped, and here one man, a Kumara, was left behind. His name was Kukaitcha, and at the present day his reincarnation is living at Alice Springs. and his *Nanja* stone is a small block which arose to mark the spot where his Alcheringa ancestor went down into the earth, leaving behind him his spirit part in his Churinga. From this spot they went on to the Burt Plain close to, and camped at, Allan Waters, after which they went up into the sky and continued in a northerly course for some twenty-five miles, camping at

Umbaltna-nirrima, and here it is related that the *Ulpmerka* played with pieces of bark just as boys do now. Travelling on, they again performed *ariltha-kuma* on the younger woman, to whom, by permission of Kukaitcha, all had access. The women always travelled along with Kukaitcha, at a little distance to the side of the main party. At Ulathirka one man, named Apallana, had intercourse without permission with the younger woman, and accordingly he was killed, but, though thus killed, his spirit part remained in his Churinga. At the same spot a Purula man was left behind, and his descendant is now living, but as yet he is only a young boy not initiated. Halting at various places, they travelled northwards until at length they came to the country of the salt water, where they remained ever afterwards.

The ceremony, which has been described as it was performed during the Engwura, represents the *Ulpmerka* men of the south being collected together round the Kukaitcha from the north prior to their accompanying him. First of all there were two performances in which the *Ulpmerka* men were shown dancing round their own Kukaitcha, who was the head of the local group, and then all of them went and joined together afterwards in dancing round the Kukaitcha from the north, signifying, as it were, that they regarded him as the greater man and as their leader.

In the afternoon the Quabara Interpitna of a place called Uratinga on the Finke River, between Henbury and Idracowra, was performed. The Interpitna is a fish totem, the particular form being known locally as the bony bream (*Chatoessus horni*), which is plentiful in the water holes, such as the one at the spot known to white men as the Main camp, with which the totem is associated. The possessor, and also in this case the performer, of the Quabara was an old Panunga man of the Obma or snake totem, who had inherited it from his father. His hair was done up as usual, and the whole front of the head-dress, as well as his face, was covered with a mass

of white down, above which stood out in strong contrast a
large bunch of black eagle-hawk feathers. His body was
decorated with bands of charcoal, edged with white down.
Squatting on the ground, he moved his body and extended
his arms from his sides, opening and closing them as he
leaned forwards, so as to imitate a fish swelling itself out and
opening and closing its gills. Then he moved along, imitating
by means of twigs in his hands the action of a man driving
before him, with boughs, the fish in a small waterhole, just as
the natives do. Four men, all from the same southern locality
as himself, but of different totems, squatted down to one side
of him singing, while one of them beat time with a stick on
the ground. Suddenly one of the latter jumped across and sat
down in front of him, gradually approaching nearer and
nearer, until he came close enough to put his hands on the
old man's shoulders.

Late on at night just before midnight another Quabara of the
Ulpmerka of Quiurnpa was performed, representing three
men eating plums.

On the eighth day a Quabara of the Irriakura totem of a place
called Oknirchumpatana, on what is now called Soda Creek,
was performed. The Irriakura is a favourite food of the
natives, and is the name given to the bulbs of *Cyperus rotundus*.
One man only was decorated, but the design was a very
quaint and striking one. A ring of grass stalks bound firmly
together with human hair-string, and measuring about two
feet in diameter, was made and covered with white down. On
the shoulders, stomach, and arms of the performer were
drawn broad bands of a light pearl colour, made by rubbing
on some wad; each band was edged with white down. The
hair was done into a head-dress, all the front of which, as well
as the man's face, was covered with down. Then, when he
had been thus ornamented, the ring was put over his head
and, rested slanting forwards and downwards, on his
shoulders. A large number—not less than a hundred—little

bunches of the red-barred tail feathers of the black cockatoo had been prepared, half of them tipped with red and half with white down, and these were stuck into the ring so as to radiate outwards all round it, while numbers of others were stuck into his head-dress and beard. The dark chocolate colour of the skin, the black and red feathers, the gray bands on the body and the white and pink down, together with the light yellow sand on which the man sat, formed a striking mixture of colours which was by no means unpleasing, and the whole decoration was extremely quaint. The man seated himself in front of a dozen bunches of cockatoo tail feathers, decorated with down, just like those on his person, and arranged in a straight line in the sand. Then, moving slightly from side to side, he scooped at intervals, and one after another, the bunches up with both hands, pausing every now and then to look around him and to put himself into the most ridiculous attitudes, as if he heard something which frightened him, but could not tell what or where it was. The tufts of feathers represented the growing Irriakura, which he was supposed to be gathering. The other men sat to one side watching the performance and singing about Unatunpika, the name of the man whom the ceremony represented, and which was also in this instance the Churinga name of the performer. With the uprooting of the last of the tufts, the ceremony came to an end, and then the ring called *Ilyappa* was taken off and put in turn on the heads of the other Irriakura men who were present, and also on those of other of the older men. The tradition connected with this performance is as follows. In the Alcheringa, Unatunpika sat down eating Irriakura at the other side of Oknirchumpatana, when suddenly he heard the *Irripitchas,* that is the ringnecked parrots, who were the mates of the Irriakura men, cry out to warn him that a mob of strange men were coming up. He dropped his Irriakura and came across to Oknirchumpatana. The mob, which also consisted of Irriakura men, left two individuals there, whose reincarnations are now living in the form of two individuals, called respectively Irrturinia and

Irriakura. Then they went on to the other side of the Jay River, to a place called Unbanjun, where they formed the *Oknanikilla,* from which sprung, amongst others, some of whom are women, an individual now living at Alice Springs, called Tukerurnia.

After midnight there was performed the Quabara Akakia (plum-tree), of a place called Iliakilia in the Waterhouse Range. This was acted by four men, who were respectively Purula and honey-ant totem; Purula and "native pheasant"; Purula and white bat; Bulthara and *illonka*.[127] First of all one man came up to where the audience was sitting by the *Parra*. He pretended to knock plums down and to eat them, and after a short time he sat down amongst the audience. Then two others came up, one of whom remained standing, while he knocked down imaginary plums, which were eaten by the other man, who seated himself on the ground. This over, both of the men went and joined the audience, and the fourth man came and went through the same pretence of knocking down and eating plums. The interesting point in connection with this and many other very similar ceremonies lies in the fact that the Alcheringa ancestors are so frequently represented as freely eating the animal or plant, from which they derive their totemic name.[128] At the present time the conditions with regard to this point are markedly different from those which evidently obtained in times past.

During the evening close by the *Parra* a dense group was formed with the older men standing in the centre, and the younger ones on the outside. In this way, as closely packed as possible, they sang together for some two hours, the group as a whole swaying backwards and forwards without ceasing. Then towards midnight they all sat down, and in this position, still closely packed together, they continued singing till between one and two o'clock, when the old men decorated the heads of the younger men with twigs and leaves of an Eremophila shrub. This material, which is worn from now till the end of the ceremonies, is called *wetta*. The old men who did the decorating were *Urliara*, who had already been through the Engwura, and to each one of these, four or five young men had been allotted by the presiding old man. There were no restrictions as to the relationship of the men; for example, a Panunga man could take charge of men of any class, but, until the end of the ceremonies, the young men who had been decorated became *ab-moara* to the man who had charge of them, and he to them. They might not either speak to, or in the presence of, the old man without his permission.

From this time on right to the very end of the ceremonies the young men were called collectively by the name *Illpongwurra*, which means not smeared with grease or colour; and with this the second phase of the Engwura came to an end.

Chapter IX

Initiation Ceremonies (Continued) the Engwura Ceremony (Concluded)

Third phase: Changes occurring in customs—The ceremonies refer to times when customs in regard to such matters as marriage restrictions, cannibalism, etc., were different from those of the present day—The Engwura may serve both to maintain customs and also as a means of introducing changes—Further examination of Churinga—*Oruncha,* or "devil-devil" men—Arunta have no conception of a permanently malevolent spirit—Final handing over of Churinga—Rubbing of Churinga to promote growth of beard—The *Erathipa* stone and tradition—Tradition concerning wild cat men changing into plum tree men eating plums—Performance of a special ceremony concerned with the frog totem—Association of particular objects, such as *Nurtunjas* and Churinga, with particular animals and plants—Fourth phase: *Illpongwurra* sent out into the bush—They have to bring in food for the old men—Fire-throwing in the women's camp at morning and night when the *Illpongwurra* go out and return—Ceremony representing the cooking of a man—The last fire-throwing in the women's camp—Cutting down the tree to form the *Kauaua*—Throwing firesticks over the women in their camp at night—The *Ambilyerikirra* ceremony—Taking the *Ambilyerikirra* to the women's camp—Possible explanation of these ceremonies—Decoration and erection of the *Kauaua*—Putting the *Illpongwurra* on the fire out in the bush—Painting the backs of the *Illpongwurra*—Visit to the women's camp and the placing of the *Illpongwurra* on fires—Return to the Engwura ground—The newly-made *Urliara* remain out in the bush—Fifth phase: Women's dance—Ceremonies concerned with removal of the ban of silence between men who are *ab-moara* to each other—Ceremonies of *aralkalilima* and *anainthalilima.*

APART from the fact that the young men had now received a definite name, and that each one had been made *ab-moara* to some older man under whose charge he was, the details of the third phase were closely similar to those described as characteristic of the second. The same examination of Churinga was carried on, and ceremonies of the same nature as the preceding ones were enacted day after day and night after night. The sustained interest was very remarkable when it is taken into account that mentally the Australian native is merely a child, who acts, as a general rule, on the spur of the moment. On this occasion they were gathered together to perform a series of ceremonies handed down from the Alcheringa, which had to be performed in precisely the same way in which they had been in the Alcheringa. Everything was ruled by precedent; to change even the decoration of a performer would have been an unheard-of thing; the reply, "it was so in the Alcheringa," was considered as perfectly satisfactory by way of explanation. At the same time despite the natural conservatism of the native mind, changes have come over the tribe since the times when their ancestors lived, to whom the ceremonies now being dealt with refer. For example, not a few of them deal with the existence of cannibalism, and though this may not yet have been wholly discarded, still it is not practised amongst the Arunta except to a very slight extent, whereas, if there be anything in the traditions, it must, in the Alcheringa, have been largely practised. Then again, the marriage customs are very different from those with which we are brought into contact in the ceremonies concerned with these Alcheringa people. We have already had occasion in another place to deal with this question, meanwhile it may be said here that the Engwura, from this point of view, appears to serve two distinct purposes, or rather it always serves one, and might serve a second. In the first place its main result is undoubtedly to preserve unchanged certain customs, and to hand on a knowledge of past history, or rather tradition, from generation to generation, but in the second place, and to a much lesser extent, it may serve as the vehicle for the introduction of changes.

The third phase was ushered in by the examination of a large number of Churinga which were brought in from the witchetty grub storehouse in the Heavitree gap, which cuts through the Macdonnell Ranges, and forms a passage from north to south, for the Todd River. They were under the charge of the Alatunja, who specially invited his *Gammona, Umbirna* and *Ikuntera*, to come up and take part in the proceedings. The Churinga, wrapped up in bundles, round which large quantities of human hair-string were tied, were laid on shields in the bed of the creek, and the men sat round them, those of the Panunga and Bulthara divisions occupying the inner circle, and the Purula and Kumara men the outer circle. This arrangement was due to the fact that the witchetty grub totem is mainly composed of men belonging to the Panunga and Bulthara moiety.

The Churinga having been solemnly spread out, the Alatunja of the local totem took one up, and, having ground up and placed on it some red ochre, the old Alatunja of the Undoolya locality leaned over and pressed down on the Churinga the hand of the son of the first-named; then he rubbed the young man's hand up and down upon it while he whispered to him, telling him to whom the Churinga had belonged, who the dead man was, and what the marks on the Churinga meant. Then it was passed on to a Purula who was the young man's *Umbirna*, and who was seated on the outside of the group. This over, a second Churinga was treated in just the same way. Special attention was paid to the *Churinga nanja* of one of the brothers of the local Alatunja who had died a few years ago. It was first of all passed on to a younger brother of the Alatunja who slightly rubbed it. Then it was pressed against the stomach of another younger brother, who kept it in this position for a minute or two while he and others literally shed tears over it, amidst perfect silence on the part of all the others present. Then two other *Churinga nanja* of dead men were examined, rubbed over with red ochre, and their meaning explained in whispers by a Bulthara man to a Purula, who was his son-in-law. After an hour had been thus passed, a particular Churinga belonging to an *Oruncha* or "devil-man" was shown, and on the production of this there was, for the first and only time, general though subdued laughter. These *Oruncha* of the Alcheringa are always the source of a certain amount of mirth, whether it be during the examination of their Churinga or on the occasion of the performance of ceremonies concerned with them. The particular individual whose Churinga was now examined has given his name, Chauritchi, to a rocky hill close to Alice Springs where he is reported to have gone into the earth and where his spirit still lives. Though they laugh at him when they are gathered together in daylight, at night-time things are very different, and no native would venture across this hill after dusk. It will be noticed that there is something very different in the case of these *Oruncha* individuals from what obtains in the case of other people of the Alcheringa. The most striking point is that whereas, like every one else, they had their Churinga and spirit part associated with it, yet they never formed any *Oknanikilla;* each one still inhabits the same spot in spirit form where, in the Alcheringa, he went down into the earth, but he never undergoes reincarnation. He is regarded as a more or less mischievous creature, a kind of Bogey-man who, if met with when out alone in the dark, will carry off his victim into the earth. Partly, no doubt, the idea is a creation of men of old to act as a wholesome check upon women who might be prone, without the fear of some such mysterious and invisible creature, to wander away under cover of the darkness from their domestic hearth, and it does undoubtedly act as a strong deterrent to any wandering about at night by men and women alike. There are times when the *Oruncha* will take a man down into the ground and transform him into a medicine man. On the whole the *Oruncha* may be regarded as a mischievous spirit who will in some way harm those whom he comes across in places where they should not be, that is where they know they are likely to meet him if they venture alone after dark, rather than as a distinctly malevolent spirit whose object is at all times to injure them. Of such a permanent malevolent spirit, the Arunta do not appear to have formed a conception; in fact the place of such an individual is largely supplied by their beliefs with regard to the Kurdaitcha and various forms of magic.

Some few days later the ceremony of handing over the lizard Churinga to their new owner, the initial stage in connection with which has already been described, was completed. After the Alatunja, who had previously had charge of them, had brought them into camp, they were placed in the store of the Panunga and Bulthara men at one end of the Engwura ground. Together with a large number of others, perhaps as many as two hundred in all, they were again brought down into the bed of the creek where the old men were assembled, only three of the younger men being allowed to be present. The others were sent out of camp. After the usual whisperings, handing round of the Churinga and rubbing of them with red ochre, they were placed on a shield and handed over to their new possessor. Then all the old men in turn came and pressed their foreheads against the young man's stomach, he for some time trying, or pretending to try, to prevent the very old *Oknirabata*—the Alatunja of the Undoolya group—from doing so. This ceremony is a somewhat striking one, and is evidently a form of recognition of the new position held by the young man, who with the presentation of the Churinga became the recognised head of the local group of lizard people.

There was amongst the Churinga one curious one which was also remarkable as being the only stone one present at the Engwura, the reason of which is to be associated with the fact that they are brought mainly with the object of using them during the ceremonies, and for this purpose stone ones are not suitable. This special one was elongate-oval in shape and about six inches in length. From end to end ran a band of black charcoal, an inch in width, the part on either side of this being coloured red with ochre. The Churinga was that of a Jerboa-rat totem, the rat in question having especially long whiskers which were represented by the black band, and it is supposed that the rubbing of this Churinga on the chin of a young man is very beneficial in promoting the growth of hair on the part touched. In connection with this, it may be noted that the length and fullness of the beard is a striking feature in the members of the Arunta and other tribes of Central Australia.

Though the Churinga are now in the keeping of the lizard man he is not supposed to have absolute possession of them until he has, at some future date, made a present of a considerable quantity of hair-string to the Alatunja of the Unchalka or little grub group who took charge of, and preserved them from harm upon the temporary extinction of the old lizard group.

As already said, the days and nights during the third phase were spent very much in the same manner as they were during the second, so that we will only describe here, without reference to the order in which they occurred, as this was a matter of no importance, the more important and typical of the ceremonies.

Two ceremonies were concerned with the *Oruncha* or, as the natives call them, the *Orunchertwa,* the word *ertwa* meaning man. The first of these was the Quabara Oruncha of Kulparra, a place now called the Deep Well about fifty miles to the south of Alice Springs. The ceremony belongs to a Purula man, and the two performers were respectively a Purula man of the "native pheasant"[129] totem, and a Kumara man of the kangaroo totem. Each man wore, fixed into his head-dress, four Churinga, while his body was decorated with bands of charcoal edged as usual with white down, a bunch of eagle-hawk feathers being fixed into his waist-band in the middle of his back. When decorated they were led on to the *Parra* ground with the usual high knee action. Then old men, from the neighbourhood of the locality to which the ceremony belongs, sat down and began beating boomerangs on the ground while the two performers ran backwards and forwards on all fours, sometimes chasing one another, sometimes turning round face to face and pretending to growl and to frighten one another. After acting in a way which much amused the audience for about five minutes, the two *Oruncha* came and laid themselves down in front of the old men, whom, after getting up again, they embraced.

The second of the ceremonies was the Quabara Oruncha of Chauritchi, the latter being the native name for Alice Springs. This ceremony belongs to the local Alatunja, and the most remarkable feature connected with it was the enormous head-dress formed of twigs of Cassia bush bound round with yards and yards of human hair-string so as to form a solid mass two feet six inches in diameter, the whole structure weighing at least thirty pounds. It was, as usual in the case of all the head-dresses, built up on the performer's head, and, as can be imagined, the strain upon the muscles of his neck must have been severe, for though the actual performance only lasted a few minutes the preparation for it occupied two hours. The front of the head-dress and the face were covered with a mass of white down; a band of blue-grey wad[130] ornamented his shoulders and chest, and in the middle was joined to another which ran round above the waist, each having an edging of white down. From the front of the head-dress projected two sticks, each of which was nearly a yard in length, and was covered with rings of down. In the noonday heat of midsummer, with the sun shining straight down so that you sat, or stood, on your own shadow, the remarkable and weighty head-dress must have been particularly trying to wear. The performer sat down on a heap of small gum tree boughs and began swaying about from side to side and brushing flies off with little twigs. At the same time he kept constantly peering about as if he were on the look-out for some one; every now and then he would crouch down amongst the boughs as if to gather himself together into as small a space as possible; when he did so, the back view was a somewhat comical one, consisting mainly of a glimpse of a large bunch of eagle hawk feathers, and beyond this the great disc-shaped head-dress. The idea was that he was in search of men with the object of catching and eating them. When caught, his custom was to carry them on his head until they were wanted for consumption, and the massive head-dress was supposed to represent a man whom he had killed and was thus carrying about with him.

The two sticks in the front projecting like two horns are somewhat suggestive. They are simply pointing sticks—called in this instance *inwunina*—which the *Oruncha* uses for the purpose of pointing at and killing his prey, and the thought suggested itself that possibly the two traditional horns of the devil, as he is pictured amongst more highly civilised peoples, may, sometimes at all events, owe their origin to an early belief in the efficacy of pointing sticks like those at present actually used amongst various races of savage people, such as the Australian natives.

This particular *Oruncha* went in the Alcheringa down into the hill close to Alice Springs, which is still spoken of as the *Mirra oruncha*, that is the *Oruncha's* camp, and he is supposed at times to come out and seize upon men and women who are wandering about after dusk. Every now and again he will take some man down into the earth, and then, after a time, the man is found in a dazed condition, but transformed by the *Oruncha* into a medicine man.

In connection with the Quabara Iruntarinia Unjiamba of a place called Apera-na-unkumna, a somewhat remarkable *Nurtunja* was used. This was a ceremony which had been imparted to a Purula man by the *Iruntarinia* of the locality named. It was now being presented by its owner to another man of the totem with which it was concerned; and, as this was the first time on which it had been performed in this locality, etiquette prescribed that only men of the Purula and

Kumara moiety should be present during the preparation, all others remaining at some distance from the creek. The *Nurtunja* consisted of a long spear, grass stalks, and hair-string bound together in the usual way, but in addition, from near to the upper end, there hung down a shorter pole about five feet long. Each part was decorated with elongate lines of pink and white down instead of the customary circles which are so characteristic of the usual large *Nurtunja*. The large pole indicated a Hakea tree, and the small one a young tree, and it was supposed to be identical in form with a double *Nurtunja* which two Alcheringa Unjiamba men carried about with them in their wanderings.

Another ceremony associated with a remarkable tradition was the Quabara Ambaquerka of Erathipa. This was in the possession of the Alatunja of Alice Springs, and at his request was performed by a Panunga man. The performer is supposed to be a woman with a newly-born child, the latter being represented by an oval mass of twigs and grass stalks encased in hair-string and down, about two feet in length by one foot in diameter. The whole was covered with close-set bands of white down, two black spots being left to indicate the eyes. The performer held the supposed child in his hands while he sat down swaying about and quivering, the other men dancing and singing as they ran round him. When it was over the oval mass was pressed against the stomach of the Alatunja, who then took and pressed it against that of the old Purula man who presided over the Engwura.

The tradition with which this is associated is as follows: In the locality of a plum-tree totem about fifteen miles S.S.E. of Alice Springs, is a special rounded stone which projects from the ground amidst mulga scrub for about a height of three feet. This stone is called *Erathipa*. In the Alcheringa a man named Inta-tir-kaka, who belonged to the plum-tree totem and was not an *Ulpmerka*, came from a place called Kulla-ratha, a fine waterhole out to the north of Mount Heuglin, in the western Macdonnells, and, crossing a depression in the latter range close to Mount Gillen, he proceeded to Uk-ang-wulla, which means the hollow or hole, and lies close to Quiurnpa, where he found a *Nurtunja* erected but could not see any people to whom it belonged, so he proceeded to appropriate it; but, when he tried to pull it up out of the ground, all that he could do was to slightly loosen it; seeing that he could not secure it whole he broke it off at the butt and down it tumbled with a loud crash. The *Nurtunja* was the property of a plum-tree woman, named Unkara, who, with her little baby boy, was out hunting for the plums on which they fed. She had originated at this spot and had lived alone here, having nothing to do with the plum-tree *Ulpmerka* men who lived not far away. When she heard the crash she came quickly back to her camp, and there she saw what had taken place and was greatly grieved; as the natives say, her bowels yearned after her *Nurtunja*. She put her baby boy into the hollow where the *Nurtunja* was broken off, just below the surface, and, leaving with him a large number of Churinga, went in pursuit of the thief. The boy went into the ground, taking with him the store of Churinga, and the *Erathipa* stone arose to mark the spot, and forms the centre of an *Oknanikilla* of the plum-tree totem, the stone being, of course, the home of all the many spirit individuals, one of whom was associated with each of the Churinga.

The women went straight up into the sky and, following the course taken by Intatirkaka, she alighted at a place called Oki-ipirta where he had camped, from here she walked on towards the north-west, and then again went up into the sky and did not descend until she reached Kulla-ratha, from which place the man had come originally, and to which he had returned. Here she found a large number of plum-tree people, but could not see her *Nurtunja* because the thief had placed it right in the middle of a big group of *Nurtunjas* which belonged to the party. In grief at not being able to recover it she sat down and died.

However, to return to the *Erathipa* stone. There is on one side of it a round hole through which the spirit children are supposed to be on the look-out for women who may chance to pass near, and it is firmly believed that visiting the stone will result in conception. If a young woman has to pass near to the stone and does not wish to have a child she will carefully disguise her youth, distorting her face and walking with the aid of a stick. She will bend herself double like a very old woman, the tones of whose voice she will imitate, saying, "Don't come to me, I am an old woman." Above the small round hole a black line is painted with charcoal, and this is always renewed by any man who happens to visit the spot. It is called *Iknula,* and a black line such as this, and called by the same name, is always painted above the eye of a newly-born child, as it is supposed to prevent sickness. Not only may the women become pregnant by visiting the stone, but it is believed that by performing a very simple ceremony, a malicious man may cause women and even children who are at a distance to become so. All that has to be done is for the man to go to the stone by himself, clear a space of ground around it, and then, while rubbing it with his hands, to mutter the words "*Arakutja wunka oknirra unta munja aritchika,*" which means, literally translated, "Plenty of young women, you look and go quickly." If, again, a man wishes to punish his wife for supposed unfaithfulness, he may go to the stone and, rubbing it, mutter the words "*Arakutja tana yingalla iwupiwuma ertwa airpinna alimila munja ichakirakitcha,*" which means, "That woman of mine has thrown me aside and gone with another man, go quickly and hang on tightly;" meaning that the child is to remain a long time in the woman, and so cause her death. Or again, if a man and his wife both wish for a child, the man ties his hairgirdle round the stone, rubs it, and mutters, "*Arakutja thingunawa unta koanilla arapirima,*" which means, "The woman my wife you (think) not good, look."

The word *Erathipa* means a child, though it is seldom used in this sense, the word *Ambaquerka* being most often employed.

Similar *Erathipa* stones are found at other spots. There is one near to Hermannsburg on the Finke River, another at the west end of the Waterhouse Range, and another near to Running Waters on the Finke.

Another ceremony called the Quabara Anthinna of Arimurla was associated with a curious and rather complicated tradition. Anthinna is the opossum totem, and Arimurla is a place now called Winnecke's depot, by reason of its having been used as such during early days; it is in reality merely a gorge leading through the rocky ranges which form the eastern continuation of the Macdonnells. The ceremony refers to two Purula women of the opossum totem. They both originated at and never left Arimurla. Each of the performers had a curious T-shaped *Nurtunja* on his head. From the cross-bars of each there were suspended Churinga which had once belonged to the two women.

When the ceremony, which consisted of the usual swaying to and fro on the part of the performers, and of the running round and round of the other men, was concluded, we were told the following. In the Alcheringa a party of wild cat people who, unlike the other wild cat parties, consisted for the main part of Pulthara and Panunga, started from near Wilyunpa out to the east of Charlotte Waters. They journeyed on to the north, halting and forming *Oknanikilla* at various places. After a time they came close to Arimurla, but passed by without seeing the two Purula opossum women who were sitting down there. Going on they met a man who had come down from the salt water country far away to the north; he was of the same totem as themselves, but lived alone and was called *atnabitta,* a contemptuous name applied to a man who is given to interfering with women. Him they killed, and to the present day a stone in Paddy's creek at a spot called Achilpa Itulka represents the slain man. Having done this, they walked on, eating Hakea and driving mosquitoes before them, and, when they could not get water, drinking their own blood. At a place called Irri-mi-wurra they all died, but sprang up again as *Ulpmerka*, that is uncircumcised boys, and after that they went on eating plums. Reference to this will again be made when dealing with the question of the eating of the totem. In this, as in not a few of the traditions, we see that the eating of the totemic animal or plant seems to be a special feature, and one to which attention is particularly drawn.

After eight days had been spent in the performance of ceremonies, it was evident that an important change in the proceedings was about to take place. Under the direction of the leader of the Engwura the small gum boughs, which had hitherto decorated the top of the *Parra*, were removed, and the mound was left bare. All the young men were ordered away from the ground, and spent the greater part of the day in the bed of the river under the charge of the Alatunja of Alice Springs. Meanwhile, close by the *Parra*, a group of elder men who were already *Urliara* were assembled. All classes were represented, and the next five hours were spent in preparations for an important ceremony called the Quabara Unchichera of Imanda. At Imanda, which is known to white men as the Bad Crossing on the Hugh River, is an important Unchichera or frog totem centre, and during the Engwura a large number of ceremonies connected with this were enacted as the leader came from this locality, and, though not himself belonging to the frog totem, he had inherited a large number of ceremonies concerned with this and the wild cat totem from his father. He performed the ceremony himself. On his head was a large somewhat flat helmet made in the usual way, and completely covered with concentric circles of alternate pink and white down. These represented the roots of a special gum tree at Imanda. The whole of his back and chest as far down as the waist was a complete mass of white spots, each of which was encircled by white down; they were of various sizes, and indicated frogs of different ages; on the inner side of each thigh were white lines representing the legs of fully-grown frogs. On his head he wore a large frog

Churinga, five feet in length, decorated with bands of down and tipped with a bunch of owl feathers. All around the base of this were arranged tufts of black eagle-hawk feathers, each fastened on to a stick, so that they radiated from the head-dress. About twenty strings, each of them two feet in length and made of opossum fur-string, had been covered with pink and white down, and ornamented at one end with tufts of the black and white tail tips of the rabbit-kangaroo. These were suspended all round from the head so as almost completely to hide the face, which was itself enveloped in a mass of down. The Churinga represented a celebrated tree at Imanda, and the pendant strings its small roots. When all was ready a shallow pit about a yard in diameter was scooped out in the sand, and in this the performer squatted with a short stick in his hands. Except for the presence of the latter, it was difficult to tell that the elaborate decoration concealed from view a man.

When he was seated in the pit, he sent out three old men who were *Urliara* across the river. Two of them carried small Churinga attached to the end of hair-string. The man who did not carry one went behind the spot where the young men were gathered together, while the other two went one to each side. Then the sound of the bull-roarer was heard, as the Churinga were whirled round and round, and, amidst much shouting and excitement, the young men were driven in a body across the river and up the opposite bank on to the Engwura ground. Running through the scrub which bordered the river, they suddenly came in sight of the performer, who was slightly swaying his body from side to side and digging the earth up with the stick in his hands. For a moment, when first he came in view, the young men halted and lifted up their hands as if in astonishment, and then driven up by the three *Urliara* men they ran up to and circled round and round the performer shouting, "*wha! wha!*" at the top of their voices. The old men stood to one side, and the two with the Churinga went round and round the young men as if to drive them in as close as possible. This went on for about three minutes, when one of the younger men, who was a Purula and the son of a dead man of the frog totem of Imanda, laid his hands on the shoulders of the performer, who then ceased moving, and the ceremony was over. After a short pause the decorated man got up, and first of all embraced the young man who had stopped him, and then went round and did the same to various old Bulthara and Panunga men, and touched with a piece of white down the navel of the old Purula man of the white bat totem, whose locality lay close to that with which the ceremony was associated[131] Then he sat down and called the young Purula man up to assist him in removing the decorations.

After each ceremony the down is carefully removed from the body, though naturally a not inconsiderable portion adheres so firmly that it must be rubbed off, and so each performance means the loss of a certain amount. As soon also as ever a Churinga or a *Nurtunja* has once been used, the decorations are taken off. No *Nurtunja* is used more than once; even if two ceremonies follow close upon one another, each of them requiring one, a fresh one is made for each. The reason of this is that any particular *Nurtunja* represents and is symbolic of one particular object with which the ceremony is concerned, it may be a gum-tree, a Hakea, an emu or a frog, and, when once that particular *Nurtunja* has been used in a ceremony, it is henceforth symbolic of one, and only one thing, though, so far as its appearance and structure are concerned, it may be precisely similar to a *Nurtunja*, which means something totally different. Suppose, for example, that, as on the last occasion, a large Churinga or a *Nurtunja* represents a gum-tree, then in the mind of the native it becomes so closely associated with that object that it could not possibly mean anything else; and if a precisely similar Churinga or *Nurtunja* were wanted an hour afterwards to represent, say an emu, then a new one must be made.

The reason for the showing of the performance just described, was that on the previous day the young Purula man already referred to had gone out into the bush and had brought in a present of game in the form of euro, as an offering to the older man who had charge of the Unchichera ceremonies of Imanda. This gift of food is called *chauarilia*, and when bringing it in he had told the old man that there was food waiting for him along the creek. This remark was perfectly understood as a request, though this must not be made in any more direct way, that he should be shown some ceremony connected with his dead father's totem. With this the third phase of the Engwura came to an end.

The fourth phase was a very well-marked one, as with it were ushered in the series of fire ordeals which are especially associated with the Engwura. The young men had already had by no means an easy time of it, but during the next fortnight they were supposed to be under still stricter discipline, and to have to submit themselves to considerable discomfort in order to prove themselves worthy of graduating as *Urliara*.

Just at sunrise the *Illpongwurra* were collected together close to the *Parra*. The leader of the Engwura had meanwhile appointed three elder men, who were already *Urliara*, to look after them during the day. About a dozen of the older men had provided themselves with small Churinga, and with a great amount of shouting, and amidst the strange weird roar and screech of the bull-roarers, no two of which sounded alike, the *Illpongwurra* were driven in a body away from the camp. Each man amongst them carried his shield, spear, and boomerang, for it was their duty now to go out into the bush all day hunting game for the benefit of the old men who stayed in camp performing ceremonies. The idea was to test still further the endurance of the young men and their obedience to their elders. Out in the bush they are not supposed to eat any of the game which they catch, but must bring it all in to the old men who may, or may not, give them a share of it when they return to camp. Whether this rule is rigidly adhered to on the part of the younger men may perhaps be doubted, the temptation offered by the sight of a fat little wallaby must be very strong to a full-grown young man who has not been having too much to eat for some three or four weeks past, and though old men go out in charge, it can be scarcely possible to keep a strict watch over all of the *Illpongwurra*.

Avoiding on this, the first morning of the new departure in the ceremonies, the women's camp, which lay out of sight of the Engwura ground on the other side of the river, the *Illpongwurra* were taken out through a defile amongst the ranges on the west side of the camp. As the day wore on it became evident that there was unusual excitement and stir in the women's camp. One of the older ones had been informed that the *Illpongwurra* would return in the evening, and that they must be ready to receive them. She had been through this part of the ceremony before, and knew what had to be done, but the great majority of the women required instructing. About five o'clock in the evening all the women and children gathered together on the flat stretch of ground on the east side of the river. The Panunga and Bulthara separated themselves from the Purula and Kumara. Each party collected grass and sticks with which to make a fire, the two being separated by a distance of about one hundred yards. A man was posted on the top of a hill overlooking the Engwura ground on the west, and just before sunset he gave the signal that the *Illpongwurra* were approaching. They stopped for a short time before coming into camp, at a spot at which they deposited the game secured, and where also they decorated themselves with fresh twigs and leaves of the Eremophila bush. These were placed under the head-bands, so that they drooped down over the forehead, under the arm-bands, and through the nasal septum. Then, forming a dense square, they came out from the defile amongst the ranges. Several of the *Urliara* who were carrying Churinga met them, some going to either side, and some going to the rear of the square. Then commenced the swinging of the bull-roarers. The women on the tip-toe of excitement lighted their fires, close to which were supplies of long grass stalks and dry boughs. The *Illpongwurra* were driven forwards into the bed of the river, pausing every now and then as if reluctant to come any further on. Climbing up the eastern bank, they halted about twenty yards from the first group of women, holding their shields and boughs of Eremophila over their heads, swaying to and fro and shouting loudly "*whrr! whrr!*" The Panunga and Bulthara women to whom they came first stood in a body behind their fire, each woman, with her arms bent at the elbow and the open hand with the palm uppermost, moved up and down on the wrist as if inviting the men to come on, while she called out "*kutta, kutta, kutta,*" keeping all the while one leg stiff, while she bent the other and gently swayed her body. This is a very characteristic attitude and movement of the women during the performance of certain ceremonies in which they take a part. After a final pause the *Illpongwurra* came close up to the women, the foremost amongst whom then seized the dry grass and boughs, and setting fire to them, threw them on to the heads of the men, who had to shield themselves, as best they could, with their boughs. The men with the bull-roarers were meanwhile running round the *Illpongwurra* and the women, whirling them as rapidly as possible; and after this had gone on for a short time, the *Illpongwurra* suddenly turned and went to the second group of women, followed, as they did so, by those of the first, and here the same performance was again gone through. Suddenly once more the men wheeled round and, followed by both parties of women who were now throwing fire more vigorously than ever, they ran in a body towards the river. On the edge of the bank the women stopped, turned round and ran back, shouting as they did so, to their camp. The *Illpongwurra* crossed the river bed and then ran on to the Engwura ground where, sitting beside the *Parra*, was a man decorated for the performance of an Unjiamba ceremony.

Still holding their shields, boomerangs, and boughs of Eremophila, they ran round and round him shouting *"wha! wha!"* Then came a moment's pause, after which all the men commenced to run round the *Parra* itself, halting in a body, when they came to the north end to shout *"wha! wha! whrr!"* more loudly than before. When this had been done several times they stopped, and then each man laid down his shield and boomerangs and placed his boughs of Eremophila so that they all formed a line on the east side of and parallel to the *Parra*, at a distance of two yards from this. When this was done the *Illpongwurra* came and first of all sat down in a row, so that they just touched the opposite side of the *Parra* to that on which the boughs were placed. In less than a minute's time they all lay down, in perfect silence, upon their backs, quite close to one another, with each man's head resting on the *Parra*.[132] All save one or two old men moved away, and these few stayed to watch the *Illpongwurra*. For some time not a sound was to be heard. None of them might speak or move without the consent of the old men in whose charge they were. By means of gesture language one or two of them asked for permission to go to the river and drink at a small soakage which had been made in the sand. In a short time they returned, and then it was after dark before they were allowed to rise. The sudden change from the wild dance round the performer and the *Parra*, accompanied by the loud shouting of the men whose bodies were half hidden by thick clouds of dust, which the strong light of the setting sun illuminated, was most striking.

About nine o'clock the men got up and began the usual singing, running sideways along by the *Parra*, shouting loudly as they did so. Shortly before midnight a curious ceremony was performed, which was associated with certain *Oruncha* men of Imanda. There were four performers, and the ceremony was divided into two parts. Three men were engaged in the first and more important scene. A long hole, just big enough to hold a man's body, but not deep enough to conceal it, was scooped out. In this, at full length, one of the men lay while a second knelt down over his legs and the third knelt at the head end. These two were supposed to be *Oruncha* men, engaged in baking the man in the earth oven, and each of them with two boomerangs imitated the action of basting him and of raking the embers up over his body, whilst he himself imitated admirably the hissing and spluttering noise of cooking meat. After a few minutes the three got up and joined the audience, and then out of the darkness—for the fire beside the *Parra* served only to light up the ceremonial ground—came a decorated man who was supposed to represent an Alcheringa man of the frog totem. He moved about from spot to spot, sniffing as if he detected the smell of cooking, but could not detect where it came from. After a minute or two he joined the audience and the performance stopped.

There was not much rest to be had that night; the *Illpongwurra* lay down again while the older men close to them kept up an incessant singing, and at two o'clock all were called up to witness the performance of a ceremony of the wild cat totem, in which three men took part, who were supposed to be performing an ordinary dancing festival or *altherta* in the Alcheringa. Just at daybreak another ceremony was ready, which was again connected with the frog totem of Imanda. It was performed by one of the oldest men present, the old white bat man, and he was decorated to represent a particular tree at Imanda, which suddenly appeared full-grown on the spot, where an Alcheringa man of the frog totem went into the ground; it became the *Nanja* tree of the spirit part of him which remained behind associated with his Churinga.

It was now getting daylight. The leader decided upon three *Urliara*, who were to accompany and take charge of the *Illpongwurra* during the day, and just after the sun rose they were once more driven out of the Engwura ground amidst the whirling of bull-roarers. The old men spent the day in camp preparing two or three ceremonies, but reserving a somewhat elaborate one for the benefit of the *Illpongwurra*, who were driven in at dusk by way of the women's camp, where the fire-throwing was repeated. Once more the ceremony of first sitting and then lying down by the *Parra* was enacted; in fact this was carried out every evening during the next two weeks.

At midnight the *Illpongwurra* were aroused to witness a ceremony of the white bat totem. Eleven men—the greatest number which we have seen taking part in any one of these sacred ceremonies—were decorated. Ten of them stood in a row facing and parallel to the *Parra*, and they were all connected together by a rope of human hair-string, which was decorated with pink and white down, and was passed through the hair waist-girdle of each man. Four of them had Churinga on their heads, and were supposed to represent special gum trees near to Imanda, the long rope being the roots of the trees; the other six were supposed to be bats resting in the trees. The eleventh man was free from the rope and his decoration differed from that of the rest, who were ornamented with white pipe-clay and red and white down, while he had a long band of charcoal on each side of his body, outlined with red down. He began dancing up and down in front of the others, holding his body in a stooping position, and making all the while a shrill whistling noise, like that made by a small bat as it flies backwards and forwards. In his hands he carried twigs which he rubbed together. The ten men meanwhile moved in line, first to the right and then to the left, and with the other man dancing in front of them the whole formed a curious scene in the flickering light of the camp fire. At a signal from the leader of the Engwura two men went out from the audience, each carrying a long spear which was held behind the line of performers so as to touch the back of each man—the signal for them to stop. Each performer in turn touched with a piece of down first the stomach of the leader, and then that of the old white bat man to whom the ceremony belonged.

During the next day ceremonies were held as usual, but there was no fire-throwing. At sunrise on the following morning the *Illpongwurra* were driven out of camp to the sound of bull-roarers, by way of the women's camp, where they again had fire thrown over them, and in the evening the same ceremony was repeated when, just at sunset, they were brought in to camp over the ranges on the eastern side.

The following day saw a slight change in the programme. The *Illpongwurra* were taken out to the west, not going near to the women's camp. During the day news was brought in of the death of a very old and very celebrated *Railtchawa*, or medicine man, who lived far away out to the west. We were assured that his death was due to the evil magic of a native who lived at a place called Owen Springs on the Hugh River—an instance of the fact that the native is quite unable to realise death from any natural cause, as the old man in question had died simply from senile decay. The sounds of wailing came all day long from the camp of the women, who struck each other blows with their waddies and cut themselves with knives.

During the day the old men performed ceremonies concerned with a group of wild cat people who, in the Alcheringa, marched out from the south of what is now Oodnadatta, and then turned northwards and followed a track which led them across the west part of the present Arunta country and through certain spots such as Illamurta in the James Range. At sunset the *Illpongwurra* came in from the west and found two ceremonies prepared, one belonging to the Bulthara and Panunga men, to which they went first. After dancing round the performer, who represented one of the *Ulpmerka* of the plum-tree totem sitting at the foot of a *Nurtunja*, they came to the second, which belonged to the

Purula and Kumara. This ceremony was associated with the frog totem of Imanda, and was performed by two men, both of whom had Churinga on their heads, and had their bodies decorated with patches and lines of down representing frogs and roots of trees. First the *Illpongwurra* danced round them and then rushed off to the *Parra*, round and round which they ran, raising clouds of dust through which they could be dimly seen. After a short pause and led by the two frog performers, who had removed the Churinga from their heads and carried each two boomerangs which they kept striking together, they ran across the river to the women's camp, where the fire-throwing was performed in the usual way, after which the *Illpongwurra* came back to camp and lay down beside the *Parra*.

When it was dark the men were arranged in a double line close to the *Parra*, and then, with their bodies bent almost double, their arms extended in front, and their hands clasped together, they moved, first in one direction and then in the other, parallel to the length of the mound, stamping on the ground as they did so and shouting *"wha! wha! whrr!"* at the top of their voices. This peculiar dance is one which is especially performed by the members of the Ilpirra tribe during the course of the Engwura, and as one or two Ilpirra men had come down to take part in this Engwura, it was danced on this occasion. Just before midnight a wild cat ceremony was performed, and it was not until early in the morning that the dancing and singing ceased, and the *Illpongwurra* were allowed to take a little rest.

While the *Illpongwurra* were out in the bush during the next day they had to undergo the first of another form of fire ordeal, an account of which will be given subsequently in connection with its second performance. In camp the old men performed a ceremony called the *Ingwurninga inkinja*, which is associated with the emu totem of a spot close to Imanda. The Quabara belongs to the Alatunja of the locality, and he requested two men, one a Panunga of the snake, and the other a Bulthara of the wild cat totem, to perform. Each man was decorated with the usual head-dress, the front of which, as well as their face and beard, was covered with white down, while on each side of the body and extending down to the knee, was a line of circular patches of charcoal edged with white down. These patches were supposed to represent the skulls of slain and eaten men. The two performers were called *ulthana*, that is, the spirits of dead men, and in this instance they were supposed to have arisen from the bones of two men who had been eaten. They came up from the creek and remained at first crouching behind and hidden by a small bush from the sight of the old men who gathered by the *Parra*. Then they got up and came on, each of them bending forwards and supporting himself by a stick in either hand, as if they were decrepit old men who could hardly walk. For some time they prowled about looking first to one side and then to the other, as if they were in search of something; and, following an irregular course, came towards the *Parra*, where the old men were seated beating the ground with boomerangs.

At sunset the *Illpongwurra* once more came in by way of the women's camp where the fire-throwing took place, and then, on the Engwura ground, they stood in a long line beside the *Parra* watching the performance of an emu ceremony, which consisted in a man decorated with a tall head-dress tipped with a bunch of emu feathers and having his body decorated with a large number of parallel lines of white down walking backwards and forwards in the aimless way of an emu.

That night was at last a quiet one, as every one seemed to be getting somewhat exhausted. The next morning a fish ceremony was performed, and at sunset when the *Illpongwurra* came in—this time direct on to the Engwura ground—a ceremony called the Quabara Ungamillia of Ulkni-wukulla was prepared. Ungamillia is the evening star and Ulkni-wukulla is the name of a spot close to a gap in the

Macdonnell Range, about fifteen miles to the west of Alice Springs. A Kumara woman of that totem is supposed to have originated and to have lived there during the Alcheringa. The natives say, "she had a *Nurtunja* and lived alone." The woman's name was Auadaua, and there is now living near to Bond Springs a woman who is the reincarnation of that particular individual.

The Alice Springs natives have a legend with regard to the evening star, according to which it goes down every evening into a big white stone at Ulkni-wukulla, where Auadaua sat in the Alcheringa. The stone lies in the middle of a tract of country, which, just except this spot, belongs to the large lizard people. If a woman imagines that a child enters her when she is at that stone, then it is one of the spirit individuals who belonged to one or other of the Churinga which Auadaua carried with her and left behind when she went into the earth, where the stone now stands; and therefore the child must belong to the evening star totem; if, however, she thinks it entered her in the bed of the creek close by, then it belongs to the lizard totem.

Late at night an emu ceremony was performed, and the whole evening was occupied until midnight in singing by the *Parra*, the old men as before sitting in the midst of a large circle of young men, all being huddled close together. On occasions such as this the singing is always a monotonous repetition of a few phrases such as "the sand hills are good," "the Achilpa walked in the Alcheringa to Therierita," "Bind the *Nurtunja* round with rings and rings," and so on; and it is wonderful to see for how many hours they will continue, without apparently their spirits flagging or their voices becoming husky.

The next day, as the thermometer registered 114° in the shade, it was too hot for even the old men to venture on a performance until late in the afternoon, but as a fitting close to a warm day the *Illpongwurra* were brought in by way of the women's camp, and on this occasion some of the men as well as the women took a share in the fire-throwing, scorching more than usual some of the less fortunate men who did not efficiently shield themselves with boughs. On the Engwura ground an Unjiamba ceremony was performed when the *Illpongwurra* came across the river.

During the next two days various ceremonies of the kangaroo, wild cat and bandicoot totems were performed, the most important being a kangaroo one concerned with Undiara near to the Finke river at Henbury. The *Nurtunja* for this was made of twenty long spears lashed together and reached a height of eighteen feet (Fig. 81). To it were attached fourteen Churinga, and the ceremony was performed just at daylight. At night-time the singing was mainly concerned with the putting up of the *Kauaua* or sacred pole, the erection of which marked the close approach of the termination of the Engwura.

In connection with one of the wild cat ceremonies a somewhat curious performance took place. The *Nurtunja* used represented one which in the Alcheringa had belonged to wild cat men, who had at first stayed for some time close to Imanda, and at a later time had carried it away with them when they travelled northwards to a place called Arapera, with which the ceremony now performed was associated. It was made by men of the northern groups belonging to the Bulthara and Panunga moiety, and, whilst it was being made, no southern men were present. When it was completed, but some time before the performance of the ceremony for use in which it had been made, the northern men called up the southern men and showed them the *Nurtunja*. One special man who belonged to the wild cat group near to Imanda, from which the Alcheringa *Nurtunja* had been originally taken, was first of all embraced by one or two of the northern men, and then led up to the *Nurtunja*, upon which his hands were pressed. Then the leader of the Engwura, who also belonged to Imanda, was similarly embraced, and his hands placed on the *Nurtunja*, the idea being, so the natives said, to assuage the grief of these men, which was caused by the sight of a *Nurtunja* which had passed away from their country to the north and so into the possession of another group of wild cat people.

The ceremonies now became more and more interesting, though the exact meaning and significance of some of them it is impossible to state. The leader of the Engwura remained in camp preparing, with the aid of the men of his locality, a special sacred object which consisted of two large wooden Churinga, each three feet in length. They were bound together with human hair-string so as to be completely concealed from view, and then the upper three quarters were surrounded with rings of white down, put on with great care, and so closely side by side, that when complete the appearance of rings was quite lost. The top was ornamented with a tuft of owl feathers. When it was made, it was carefully hidden in the bed of the creek, so that none of the *Illpongwurra* could see it. This object is called the *Ambilyerikirra*.

Whilst this was being made, three of the older men, who had been especially associated with the leader throughout the ceremonies, had gone out of camp across the hills to the west, and had cut down a young gum tree, the trunk of which was about nine inches in diameter and some twenty feet in height. This was to serve as the *Kauaua*, and it had to be cut down with care, as it was not allowed to touch the ground until it was brought on to the Engwura ground. The branches were lopped off and it was stripped of its bark, and then, while the *Illpongwurra* were away in the bush, it was carried into camp and placed out of sight in the bed of the creek.

As usual the *Illpongwurra* returned at sunset, coming in from the west without, on this occasion, going to the women's camp, as the last fire-throwing ceremony by the women had been held. At the northern end of the ground an *Ulpmerka* ceremony was held, and then they came on to the *Parra* in front of which sat the leader of the Engwura, supported on one side by a Bulthara, and on the other by a Kumara man; these two were to assist him during the night. Perfect silence was maintained while the men placed their branches of Eremophila on the long heap which had been gradually accumulating, and then came and lay down with their heads upon the *Parra*, the ground in front of which had been dug up by the older men during the day, so as to make it softer to lie upon.

Until shortly before nine o'clock perfect silence was maintained by the *Illpongwurra*, and even the old men only spoke in low whispers, and then very rarely, as they moved quietly about, the three men seated in front of the *Illpongwurra* remaining motionless and silent. Then a number of small fires were made, and bundles of sticks, each one about two feet long, were arranged in radiating groups with one end in the fire. There would be from four to eight of these radiating bundles in each of the fires. When the leader, who remained seated, gave the signal, the old men told the *Illpongwurra* to get up. This they did, while a few of the older men went across the river to where the women and children were gathered together, and stood amongst them, holding sticks and boughs over their heads, and telling the women to do the same, and to protect themselves as best they could. Then at a signal from one of the old men on the Engwura ground, each of the *Illpongwurra* took a bundle of fire-sticks, and in a body they went towards the river. On the bank they broke up and rushed pell-mell across the bed and on up the opposite bank, dividing, as they ran across the level stretch between the river and the women's camp, into three parties, one going to each side of the women and one to the front of them. When they were twenty yards away from where the women stood, and still running on, all, at a given signal, hurled their fire-sticks in rapid succession over the heads of the women and children; hundreds of them whizzed like rockets through the darkness; the loud shouting of the men, the screaming of the women and children, and the howling of scores of dogs produced a scene of indescribable confusion. Suddenly all once more became dark, the men turned back, and, running as rapidly as they could, crossed the river and reached the *Parra*, where they again laid themselves down, and once more there was perfect silence in the camp. They were not again allowed to move under any pretext. While they were away the leader, who had remained on the Engwura ground, had taken the *Ambilyerikirra* in his hands, and with his arms linked in those of his supporters, he lifted the former up and down without any cessation, save for a few seconds at a time, during the whole night. When the *Illpongwurra* returned from their fire-throwing, he was hidden from their view by a group of old men who sat down in front of him, so that they did not actually see him until morning.

All night long the *Illpongwurra* lay silent. One old man who had been told off to watch them, walked backwards and forwards along the line, now and then joining in the singing which, after a short time, was started by the old men, but in which the *Illpongwurra* took no part, or halting in his walk to whisper instructions or information about the Alcheringa to one or other of the young men. There was very little rest to be had, the monotonous rising and falling of the *Ambilyerikirra* went on without ceasing, as also did the singing of the old men, the aged white bat being particularly prominent. Shortly after five o'clock the *Illpongwurra*, who had been instructed by the old men keeping watch over them what they had to do, were roused. Then, for the first time since nine o'clock on the previous evening—that was after a stretch of eight hours' duration—the leader and the two men supporting him ceased from lifting the *Ambilyerikirra* up and down. There was little wonder that they looked tired and haggard, but even yet their work was not quite done. Getting up, they moved to the north end of the *Parra*, the two sidesmen still retaining hold of the leader's arms. The *Illpongwurra* went to the line of *wetta* and, having taken boughs of this, arranged themselves so as to form a solid square behind the leaders. Most of the older men remained on the Engwura ground, from which one of them, the watcher over the *Illpongwurra*, shouted instructions across to the women. The main party, headed by the three men bearing the *Ambilyerikirra*, and accompanied by a few of the older men, moved in the form of a solid square out from the Engwura ground, over the river and up the opposite bank to where the women stood grouped together. All stood beckoning to the men to come on in the way already described, and at the same time they called quietly "*kutta, kutta, kutta.*" The party approached slowly and in perfect silence, and when within five yards of the front rank of the women, the men who carried the *Ambilyerikirra* threw themselves headlong on the ground, hiding the sacred object from view. No sooner had they done this than the *Illpongwurra* threw themselves on the top, so that only the heads of the three men could be seen projecting beyond the pile of bodies. Then, after remaining thus for two minutes, the *Illpongwurra* got up and formed into a square facing away from the women, after which the three leaders rapidly jumped up, turned their backs on the women, and were hustled through the square which they then led back to the Engwura ground, and with this the *Ambilyerikirra* ceremony came to an end.

As will be noticed, there are three leading incidents; the first is the throwing of fire-sticks over the women, the second the lying down of the *Illpongwurra* all night without moving, while the *Ambilyerikirra*, incessantly rising and falling, is held upright before them; the third is the carrying across of the sacred Churinga to the women's camp.

All that the natives can say in explanation of this is that the rushing across to the women's camp represents an attack by a party of wild cat men, who are *Illpongwurra* and not yet made *Urliara*, upon another party, and that the lying down quietly in front of the *Ambilyerikirra* represents the "taming" of the wild *Illpongwurra* under the influence of the sacred Churinga. They also say that if from any cause the strength of the men who are lifting up and down the Churinga should fail, then the *Illpongwurra* will die. They have no idea as to what is the meaning of the third incident—the carrying over of the Churinga to the women's camp.

Whilst any explanation must at best be a mere conjecture, it is perhaps worth while suggesting that the whole ceremony may be commemorative of a reformatory movement which must at one time have taken place in the tribe in regard to the question of cannibalism. Traces of this still linger on, but only traces, and two or three of the ceremonies which had been performed during the few days immediately preceding that of the *Ambilyerikirra* seem to show that at a much earlier time it was practised to a much greater extent. The natives say that the idea of attacking another party, as represented in the first incident, is connected with eating the men who were killed. This, taken in conjunction with the fact that the second incident indicates a taming of the wild men whose natures are thereby made less fierce, may perhaps point back to a time when some powerful man, or group of men, introduced a reformation in regard to the habit of cannibalism. The *Ambilyerikirra* is a ceremony of the Unchichera or frog totem, the Imanda centre of which is one of the most important in the tribe, as close by are also local centres of the Achilpa or wild cat the Elkintera or white bat, and the Unchipera or little bat totems. Engwuras were held in the Alcheringa, and one tradition relates how, while the frog people, aided by the white bats and the little bats, were holding one at Imanda, the Achilpa gathered there also and took part in it, and were made *Urliara* by the Unchichera men, after which they started on their travels to the north.

One important feature of the Engwura is that it is supposed to make the men who pass through it more kindly natured, and perhaps we have in the few traditions bearing upon the point sufficient evidence to warrant the conjecture that the Unchichera men whom we know to have formed an influential totem introduced the reformatory movement in the matter of cannibalism. If so it will explain the fact of the *Ambilyerikirra* ceremony being associated with the Unchichera totem, and we can see why the wild *Illpongwurra* who rush with fire-sticks over to attack the women should be represented as Achilpa men who have not been made into *Urliara*.

The third incident, though the natives can give no explanation of it, may possibly be capable of being explained somewhat as follows. It takes place after the taming of the wild *Illpongwurra*, who are, it will be noticed, led across, following the old men and the sacred Churinga by means of which their natures are supposed to have been changed. Instead of on this occasion attacking the strange party, they fall down in front of them as if to show that their fierce nature has been changed. The showing of the *Ambilyerikirra* to the women is very difficult to understand, but in this instance it may be pointed out that they are supposed to represent the members of a strange camp, men and women included, not merely women, and, further, that they represent individuals of the Alcheringa, living at a time when women not only saw but carried about with them Churinga and *Nurtunjas*. At the Engwura, when the men are living together separated from the women, if there is to be a strange party for the *Illpongwurra* to attack, it must be composed of the women, to whom the whole affair is a matter of the deepest mystery, which is probably not a little heightened by the small part which, every now and then, they are allowed to take in it. They do not actually see the Churinga, though doubtless the older ones amongst them are quite aware of the nature of the *Ambilyerikirra*, but that it is a most unusual occurrence is emphasised by the fact that the moment the men come close to the women they fall flat down so as completely to hide from view the sacred object, and when they arise they rapidly turn round and are immediately surrounded by the other men.

At the fire-throwing in the women's camp it will have been noticed that the men who carry the Churinga actually go close up to the women and children, but the Churinga are kept in such rapid and continual movement that there is no chance of their being actually seen; still there remains the fact that on these two occasions women are present when Churinga are used, whereas there is no doubt whatever that the most severe punishment follows even the accidental seeing of one of them by a woman under any other circumstance. We could get no explanation whatever from the natives in regard to the matter, except the inevitable one that it had always been so in the Alcheringa; and it can only be added that, as a matter of fact, what little the women do see simply serves to add to their mystification.

It was still early morning when the *Illpongwurra* returned to the Engwura ground from the women's camp, and, just after sunrise, they were sent out with instructions to remain away for two days. In camp everything was quiet, as the night had been an exhausting one, and no one, except perhaps one or two of the younger ones, had had any sleep. During the day about thirty short sticks made out of gum-tree wood were prepared. Each was about an inch in diameter and from six to nine inches in length. They were carefully rubbed with red ochre, and then later on in the day the leader hid them in the loose soil forming the *Parra* mound. These sticks are called *Unchichera irrunpa*, they may not be seen by women, and are supposed to represent young frogs. When it became dark the older men assembled by the *Parra* from which the sticks were taken, as if they were frogs hiding in the ground, as most of the Central Australian species do, and then, accompanied by the continuous clunk, clunk of the sticks, the one held in the right hand being allowed to fall upon the one in the left, the men sang for two or three hours.

On the next day, while the *Illpongwurra* were all far away out in the bush, the sacred pole, or *Kauaua*, was first of all ornamented and then erected in the middle of the ceremonial ground. It had been lying all night in the bed of the creek, where the preparations for ceremonies were made, and in the morning the men who had brought it in began to decorate it. First of all one of these men, a Kumara, bled himself, opening for the purpose a vein in his arm. From this he allowed blood to flow until there was enough to fill five times over the haft of a shield. This was quite the equivalent of five half pints, and, as if that were not enough, he ended by walking slowly once up and down by the side of the pole, allowing the blood to spurtle over it in the form of a thin stream. He did not seem to be any the worse for the loss of so much blood; in fact, during the whole Engwura, an astonishing quantity was used, and the natives appeared to think nothing whatever about it, no one objecting for a moment to open a vein in his arm or, just as frequently, to obtain it from the subincised urethra, these being the two parts from which the blood is obtained. The blood in the shields was then smeared with a small brush, made of a stick and opossum fur-string wound round one end, on to the pole, until the latter was reddened all over, and, being upwards of twenty feet in length, it took, as may be imagined, a considerable amount. Then to the top was affixed a large bunch of eagle-hawk feathers; white *Chilara* or head-bands were tied round under this; then *Alpita* tail tips were suspended in two bunches, one on either side, and just below the *Chilara* a long nose bone was attached,—in fact the decoration was just that of a human head. Then a few Churinga, which might be of any totem, were strung on near to the top, and the pole thus decorated was brought on to the ground.[133] A hole was dug two feet deep by means of a pointed digging stick, and in this it was firmly implanted at a distance of about six yards from the *Parra* and opposite to the middle of the mound.

In the early part of the afternoon of this day the *Illpongwurra* had to submit themselves for the second time to an ordeal by fire. A secluded spot amongst the ranges some two miles away from Alice Springs was selected, and here, while the young men rested by the side of a water-hole in the bed of the Todd, the *Urliara*, who were in charge of them, went to the chosen spot and made a large fire of logs and branches about three yards in diameter. Then the young men, of whom forty were present, were called up, and putting green bushes on the fire they were made to lie down full length upon the smoking boughs, which prevented them from coming into contact with the red-hot embers beneath. The heat and smoke were stifling, but none of them were allowed to get up until they received the permission of the Urliara. After they had all been on once, each one remaining for about four or five minutes on the fire, the old men came to the conclusion that they must repeat the process, and so making up the fire again, they were once more put on in the midst of dense clouds of smoke, one of the older men lifting up the green boughs at one side with a long pole so as to allow of the access of air and ensure the smouldering of the leaves and green wood. There was no doubt as to the trying nature of the ordeal, as, apart from the smoke, the heat was so great that, after kneeling down on it to see what it was like, we got up as quickly as possible, and of course the natives had no protection in the way of clothes.

When this was over, the *Illpongwurra* rested for an hour by the side of the waterhole, for the day was a hot one, the thermometer registering 110.5° F. in the shade, and 156° F. in the sun, while the ceremony was in progress.

Later on in the afternoon they came into camp and witnessed the last of the ceremonies prior to the final fire ceremony which was to take place in the women's camp. Two men, one a Purula of the emu totem and the other a Kumara of the little bat totem, performed a Quabara belonging to the frog totem of Imanda. Each was decorated on the head and body with longitudinal bands of white down while the Purula man carried a Churinga five feet long on his head. The *Illpongwurra* having put down their shields, boomerangs, and boughs of *wetta*, stood in a long line by the side of the *Parra* facing the *Kauaua*, which they now saw for the first time. Then the two performers came up from the bed of the creek which lay on the opposite side of the ground, the man with the Churinga walking behind the other one and carrying a shield at his back. Both at first adopted the high knee action, but when about thirty feet from the *Kauaua*, the front man suddenly knelt down and then moved forward, jumping on his knees with his hands behind his back. The idea is that the front man was a frog which suddenly jumps out of a tree, the latter being one of the special gum-trees growing at Imanda. When this was over the *Illpongwurra* lay down by the side of the *Parra* for two or three hours.

After dark a dozen or more fires were lighted around the base of the *Kauaua*, and around these the men were grouped, each *ab-moara* amongst the elder men taking charge of and decorating his *protégés*. That night no one in either the men's or the women's camp went to sleep. On the opposite side of the river to the Engwura ground, the light of the women's camp fires could be seen flickering amongst the trees. All night long also the old men kept shouting across to the women, who answered back again, and the scene was one of great excitement. An old man would shout out, "What are you doing?" and the women would answer, "We are making a fire." "What are you going to do with the fire?" to which the reply would come, "We are going to burn the men." Then the old men would dare the women to come across into the

Engwura camp; one ancient Panunga man was especially active in calling to his *Mura* woman, to whom under ordinary circumstances it would not be permissible for him to speak in this way, calling her by name and saying, "Urliwatchera, are you there?" and she would answer, "Yes, I am here; what is it?" and then he would call out to her to come across. The men would ask the women derisively if they were going to send the *Kurdaitcha* after them, and, indeed, this kind of badinage was kept up at intervals all night long. In the women's camp all were gathered together at one spot, and here, side by side, the Panunga and Bulthara women on the one hand, and the Purula and Kumara on the other, dug out, each of them, a shallow pit about two yards in diameter, and in each of these, towards daybreak, they made a fire.

In the Engwura camp it was a busy and also a picturesque scene. The leader had, during the day, consulted the older men who were especially associated with him, and it had been decided what brands should be painted on the various young men. Each brand was distinctive of some special totem, but the most striking point in connection with the painting was that the brand of any particular individual had no relationship of necessity to his own totem, or to that of the man who painted him. It was purely a matter of what the old men, and especially the leader of the Engwura, decided upon. The following cases will illustrate the point:—

A Panunga man of the snake totem decorated an Umbitchana man of the plum tree totem with a brand of the frog totem. A Kumara man of the wild cat totem painted a Bulthara man of the emu totem with a brand of the kangaroo totem. An Appungerta man of the witchetty grub totem painted an Umbitchana man of the wild cat totem with a brand of the Hakea totem.

A Kumara man of the little bat totem painted an Appungerta

man of the bandicoot totem with a brand of the frog totem. A Bulthara man of the wild cat totem painted a Purula man of the native pheasant totem with a brand of the same totem, this being the only instance in which a man was painted with a brand of his own totem, and the old men said that there was no special reason for its being done in this special case. A Purula man of the emu totem painted an Uknaria man of the lizard totem with a brand of the frog totem.

For this strange want of relationship between the totems of the men who did the decorating and those who were decorated, and still more for the total absence of any between the man who was decorated and the totem with a brand of which he was decorated, we could find out no reason whatever. Certainly the natives have no idea why it is so.

The materials used in the painting were charcoal, red and yellow ochre, white pipeclay and wad. In some few cases bands of wad edged with white down were drawn on the chest, but in almost all cases the totemic brand was confined to the back, so that, as the *Illpongwurra* might neither speak to, nor in the presence of, their *ab-moara* men who were doing the painting—a rule strictly observed during the decorating—none of the men, unless they could detect it by the feel, were aware of what design they were personally branded with, though each one could of course see the brands on the other men. The arms of each man were tightly encircled with bands of *kulchia* made of opossum fur-string, which had been specially spun by men and women for the purpose. Every man wore his waist-girdle, and the forehead bands were painted up for the occasion. A characteristic ornament always worn on this occasion was a necklet, called *wupira*, consisting of a single thick strand of well-greased and red-ochred fur-string, one end of which hung down the middle of the back as far as the waist, and terminated in a little tuft of kangaroo-rat tail tips. Tufts of the latter were also suspended over either ear.

It was five o'clock in the morning before the painting was complete. Then, having shouted across to the women that all was ready, the leader of the Engwura went and broke through the middle of the *Parra*, and then through the line of boughs. Each of the *ab-moara* men then led his *protégés* round the *Parra*, all singing out "*whrr, whrr*," as they ran round for the last time. When all had been round, the men grouped themselves at the base of the *Kauaua*,[134] and then, in perfect silence, the whole party walked in single file through the break in the *Parra* and the line of bushes, each *ab-moara* leading his own men, all linked hand in hand. It was a most picturesque scene in the early morning light, for the sun had not yet risen, as the men filed down into the sandy bed of the river, on which they formed a long string reaching across from one bank to the other. On the opposite side they halted about fifty yards from the group of women and children who were standing behind the two fires, which were now giving off dense volumes of smoke from the green bushes which had been placed on the red-hot embers. The women, bending one leg while they slightly swayed the body, and beckoned the men forwards with their hands, kept calling "*kutta, kutta, kutta.*" First of all one *ab-moara* man with his *Illpongwurra* ran forwards, taking a semicircular course from the men towards the women, and then back again. After each of them had done this, then in turn they led their men, running, up to the fires, and on one or other of these the *Illpongwurra* knelt down, the Panunga and Bulthara men on the fire made by the Purula and Kumara women, and *vice versa*, while the women put their hands on the men's shoulders and pressed them down. In this way the performance was rapidly gone through, not a word being spoken when once the ceremony had begun, each man simply kneeling down in the smoke for at most half a minute. In less than half an hour all was over; the women remained for a short time behind their fires and then dispersed, and the men, in silence, marched back to their camp on the Engwura ground, where the newly-made *Urliara* grouped themselves around the *Kauaua*. With this the ceremonies on the Engwura ground came to a close; the *Kauaua* was taken down and dismantled, all traces of the blood being rubbed off; the Churinga were sorted out and returned to their respective owners.

The older men now returned to their camps, but the newly-made *Urliara* men had still to remain out in the bush until the performance of a ceremony at which the ban of silence between them and their *ab-moara* men was removed. The Engwura ground was deserted, and for months afterwards it must not be visited by women and children, to whom it was strictly *ekirinja*, or forbidden.

The fifth phase may be described very shortly. When the old men return to their camps and the newly-made *Urliara* go out into the bush, one or more ordinary dancing festivals take place. A special one associated with this period is a woman's dance. At night the men and women all assemble in the main camp. A few, perhaps six or eight of the men, are painted with bands of ochre, and the dance opens with these men, one after the other, coming out of the darkness into the light of the camp fire behind which a group of men and women are seated, beating time with sticks and boomerangs on the ground and singing a corrobboree song. As each man approaches the fire he looks about him as if in search of some one, and then, after a short time, sits down amongst the audience. After the men have separately gone through this short performance a number of young women, who have been waiting out of sight of the fire, come near. Each one is decorated with a double horse-shoe-shaped band of white pipe-clay which extends across the front of each thigh and the base of the abdomen. A flexible stick is held behind the neck and one end grasped by each hand. Standing in a group the women sway slightly from side to side, quivering in a most remarkable fashion, as they do so, the muscles of the thighs and of the base of the abdomen. The object of the decoration and movement is evident, and at this period of the ceremonies a general interchange, and also a lending of, women takes place, and visiting natives are provided with temporary wives, though on this occasion in the Arunta tribe the woman allotted to any man must be one to whom he is *unawa*, that is, who is lawfully eligible to him as a wife. This woman's dance, which is of the most monotonous description possible goes on night after night for perhaps two or three weeks, at the end of which time another dance is commenced. By the time that this is over, or perhaps earlier still, for there is no fixed time, the final ceremonies commence in connection with the newly-made *Urliara*. Each of them has to bring in an offering of food to his *ab-moara* man. Under ordinary circumstances such a food-offering is called *chaurilia*, but this particular one is called *ertwa-kirra*, that is, man's meat. When the present has been made, the *ab-moara* man either performs, or else requests some one else to perform, a sacred ceremony which belongs to himself. These ceremonies are of the nature of those already described, and the description of one or two will suffice to illustrate the nature of them all. A Panunga man of the lizard totem brought in a wallaby as *ertwa-kirra* to his *ab-moara*, who was a Purula man of the emu totem. It need hardly be said that the food brought in belongs neither to the totem of the giver nor to that of the recipient. The latter in this instance prepared a ceremony of the wild cat totem in a secluded spot amongst the ranges away from the Engwura ground. A remarkable feature in connection with this and other of these special ceremonies concerned with the offering of food was the sprinkling of the older men with blood drawn from the arms of the younger men, not necessarily from the younger man who was making the offering. Early in the morning of the day on which the ceremony was performed, one of the young men had opened a vein in his arm and had allowed the blood to flow out in a thin stream over the bodies of four of the older men who were present, including the *ab-moara* man to whom the food was being given. Some of the blood had been allowed to flow into their open mouths, the idea being to strengthen the older men at the expense of the younger ones, and it had trickled down and over their bodies in thin streams and had dried up. The ceremony itself was of the usual description, and was accompanied by the dancing round of the young men who came running into the narrow defile in which it was held, and where the decorated men were waiting for them. When it was over, the men all grouped themselves close together and began singing, while the elder *ab-moara* man took a bunch of feathers which had been used as part of the decoration and touched with it the mouths of all those present. By means of this action, which is called *Aralkalilima*, the ban of silence was broken. Sometimes, as in this case, a part of the decoration of some individual was used; at others, when one had been used in the ceremony, a *Nurtunja* was brushed against the mouths of the men present, and in many, but not all cases, not only the mouth of the man who was being released from the ban was touched, but also that of all the men who happened to be present. When this part was over, the man who was receiving the food sat down together with the older men, and then the young man, or perhaps two or three together who were making the presentation, went back to the spot at which the food had been deposited, and, bringing it in, placed it before the *ab-moara* man and then sat down close in front of him. After singing for a minute or two the old man took up the food, and holding it, or a fragment of it, in his hands, placed it against the mouth of the young man or men. In this way, after the lapse of some time, the ceremonies of the Engwura were brought to a close.

In another of these ceremonies of *Aralkalilima*, a wild cat Quabara, belonging to a place called Atnyraungwuramunia, was performed by two men, one an Apungerta of the witchetty grub totem, and the other his son, a Panunga of the Irriakura totem, the object being to release from the ban of silence two Purula men, who were *ab-moara* to the first-named man. For use in the ceremony a *Nurtunja* was made, and during the making only the *nakrakia* of the performers were present. The ceremony itself, with the performers squatting at the base of the *Nurtunja*, was much as usual, the crowd who took part in the running round comprising all classes. One of the *ab-moara* men carried his *ertwa-kirra* offering in his hands as he ran round, the other left his some distance away. The performance came to an end by the *ab-moara* men suddenly squatting down behind the performers. All then stood up, and one of the Purula men offered his *ertwa-kirra*, having done which he and all the other Purula and Kumara men moved to one side, forming a group with the two *ab-moara* men in the centre. The old man now lifted out the *Nurtunja*, and all the men belonging to his moiety of the tribe stood in two lines with the *Nurtunja* held horizontally between them, every man supporting it with his hands and lifting it slowly up and down while they sang, and at the same time gradually approached the other group of men. The front rank of the latter now opened out, leaving the two *ab-moara* Purula men in front of the *Nurtunja*. Still singing, and with an occasional "*wah! wah!*" the faces of the two men, but of none of the others, were stroked with the *Nurtunja*, after which the latter was again replaced in the ground, and for some minutes they continued to sing of the *Nurtunja* and *Kauaua* of the Alcheringa. This ceremony is one of those which for some reason has special associations with one moiety of the tribe, and during its performance the separation of the two moieties was most strongly marked.

The following ceremony is of interest in one or two respects. It was performed on the occasion of an offering of *ertwa-kirra* made by two men, one a Panunga and the other an Uknaria, who were *ab-moara* to a Kumara man, and comprised two separate performances. The first of these was concerned with the Unchipera or small bat totem, and the performer personated a man carrying about the body of a dead man which he intended to eat, and which was represented by a semi-circular structure made of grass stalks bound round with fur-string, which is called *Atnuta*, and is supposed to be emblematic of the limp body. The second part of the ceremony was concerned with the Elkintera or white bat totem, and one of the two performers also carried one of these *Atnuta* objects, representing a dead man, on his head. When the two performances were over, the three performers, one of whom was the Kumara man to whom the offering was being made, stood up, and the ceremony of *Aralkalilima* was performed, the *Atnuta* being used to stroke the mouth of the *ab-moara* men. This over, the performers sat round the *ertwa-kirra*, but the difficulty arose that the man to whom the offering was being made was *Gammona* of one of the *ab-moara* men, and for a *Gammona* to receive food from his *Ikuntera* (in this case a tribal father-in-law) is contrary to custom. To obviate this difficulty the *Gammona* man turned his back on the food while his *Ikuntera* came up, tore a small piece of meat off, and with it rubbed the *Gammona's* mouth, and then thrust it into the latter, thus for the time being removing the tabu.

A man is not supposed to come into the presence of his *ab-moara* until such time as he has made an offering of *ertwa-kirra* to the latter, and if it be inconvenient to the *ab-moara* man to perform a Quabara and go through the whole *Aralkalilima* ceremony, he performs a minor ceremony called *Anaintalilima* which, though not releasing a man from the ban of silence, permits him to come into the presence of the *ab-moara*. In this case a messenger is sent to the *ab-moara* asking him to come and receive *ertwa-kirra*. He goes to a certain spot—there is no particular place but it must be out of sight of the main camp so that the proceedings cannot be witnessed by women and children—and there he sits down and powders up some red ochre, which he places beside him on a shield. The man brings up the offering of meat (sometimes there may be more than one man), places it on the *ab-moara's* lap, and then kneels down close in front. Not a word is spoken, but the *ab-moara* gravely rubs him all over with red ochre. The ban of silence is not removed, but he may now go into the presence of his *ab-*

moara, by whom at some future time a sacred ceremony will be performed, and the ban removed in the usual way. This second ceremony will probably, though not of necessity, entail a second offering of *ertwa-kirra* and very often a hint is conveyed from the old *ab-moara* that such an offering will facilitate matters.

Chapter X

Traditions Dealing with the Origin of the Alcheringa Ancestors of the Arunta Tribe and with Particular Customs

The early, middle and later Alcheringa—The early Alcheringa—Transformation of the *Inapertwa* creatures into human beings by the *Ungambikula*—Tradition referring to the *Ulpmerka* of the plum tree totem—The two lizard men kill the *Oruncha* at Simpson Gap—Marital relations not restricted by totem in the Alcheringa—The middle Alcheringa—The Ullakupera men and their stone knives—Introduction by them of circumcision by means of a stone knife—Endeavour of the Utiara men to secure stone knives—Wanderings of the Ullakupera from Atnaturka to Utiara—The Ullakupera transform *Inapertwa* into human beings and give them class names—An old Echidna man disapproves of the use of stone knives—The men of the Elonka totem who had not been circumcised by the *Ungambikula* are operated on and made into *Arakurta*—The Echidna mutilates and kills the last man on whom the Ullakupera were about to operate—He is himself killed, and the spears which were thrown into his body are represented by the spines of the Echidna—In consequence of this there are no more Echidna men and women—The Ullakupera men march on, and another Echidna man murders one upon whon they were about to operate, and is killed—The murdered man comes to life again—End of the Ullakupera wanderings—The wanderings of the Achilpa or wild cat people and the introduction by them of the ceremony of sub-incision—The first group of wild cat people start from the east side and travel north—The wild cat men feed on Hakea flower and drink their own blood—They join a party of plum tree men, die, and come to life again as *Ulpmerka* of the plum tree totem—The second group of wild cat people—Divides into two groups, one of which travels north by way of Imanda on the Hugh River, and then on beyond the Macdonnell Ranges to a spot at which they are all drowned in blood by a wild cat man—The third group travels to the west of the second group, crosses the Macdonnell Ranges, reaches the centre of the continent, and there the men die—The fourth party travels still further to the west, crosses the Macdonnell

Ranges, and journeys on to the north until the Salt Water country is reached—The later Alcheringa—Restrictions with regard to marriage in the middle Alcheringa—Men and women of the same totem living together—The emu people establish the present class system—Outline of stages supposed to have been passed through in the development of the social organisation, &c., according to tradition.

WE have hitherto spoken of the Alcheringa in general terms, using the word to denote the whole period during which the mythical ancestors of the present Arunta tribe existed. In reality the traditions of the tribe recognise four more or less distinct periods in the Alcheringa. During the first of these men and women were created; in the second the rite of circumcision by means of a stone knife, in place of a fire-stick, was introduced; in the third the rite of *Ariltha* or sub-incision was introduced, and in the fourth the present organisation and marriage system of the tribe were established. The second and third periods are, however, by no means sharply defined, and to a certain extent they are contemporaneous, or rather they overlap one another.

We may speak of these periods as the early, the middle (comprising the second and third), and the later Alcheringa.

The earliest tradition with which we are acquainted is as follows. In the early Alcheringa the country was covered with salt water (*Kwatcha alia*). This was gradually withdrawn towards the north by the people of that country who always wanted to get it and to keep it for themselves.[135] At last they succeeded in doing so, and the salt water has remained with them ever since. At this time there dwelt in the *Alkira aldorla*, that is the western sky, two beings of whom it is said that they were *Ungambikula*, a word which means "out of nothing," or "self-existing." From their elevated dwelling-place they could see, far away to the east, a number of *Inapertwa* creatures,[136] that is rudimentary human beings or incomplete men, whom it was their mission to make into men and women.

In those days there were no men and women, and the *Inapertwa* were of various shapes and dwelt in groups along by the shores of the salt water. They had no distinct limbs or organs of sight, hearing or smell, and did not eat food, and presented the appearance of human beings all doubled up into a rounded mass in which just the outline of the different parts of the body could be vaguely seen.

Coming down from their home in the western sky, armed with their *Lalira* or great stone knives, the *Ungambikula* took hold of the *Inapertwa*, one after the other. First of all the arms were released, then the fingers were added by making four clefts at the end of each arm; then legs and toes were added in the same way. The figure could now stand, and after this the nose was added and the nostrils bored with the fingers. A cut with the knife made the mouth, which was pulled open several times to make it flexible. A slit on each side separated the upper and lower eye-lids, hidden behind which the eyes were already present, another stroke or two completed the body, and thus, out of the *Inapertwa*, men and women were formed.

These *Inapertwa* creatures were in reality stages in the transformation of various animals and plants into human beings, and thus they were naturally, when made into human beings, intimately associated with the particular animal or plant, as the case may be, of which they were the transformations—in other words, each individual of necessity belonged to a totem the name of which was of course that of the animal or plant of which he or she was a transformation. This tradition of the *Ungambikula* only refers to a certain number of totems, or rather to a certain number of local groups of individuals belonging to particular totems; in the case of others such as, for example, the Udnirringita or witchetty grub totem, there is no tradition relating to the *Inapertwa* stage. The *Ungambikula* made into men *Inapertwa* who belonged to the following totems:—Akakia or plum tree, Inguitchika or grass seed, Echunpa or large lizard, Erliwatchera or small lizard, Atninpirichira or Alexandra parakeet, and Untania or small rat. In the case of all except the first they also performed the rite of *Lartna* or circumcision by means of a fire-stick.

The same tradition relates that, after having performed their mission, the *Ungambikula* transformed themselves into little lizards called *Amunga-quiniaquinia*, a word derived from *amunga* a fly and *quiniaquinia* to snap up quickly. There is no reason given for this, and in no other tradition do we meet with either the *Ungambikula* or the special kind of lizard into which they changed.

In the case of a group of plum tree men who lived at a spot called Quiurnpa,[137] which is associated with many traditions and in the case also of certain of the Unguitchika (grass seed totem) men, the *Ungambikula* first of all made them into human beings but did not circumcise them, so that they were what the natives call *Ulpmerka*,—the term applied to boys before this rite has been performed upon them. The *Ungambikula*, so the tradition goes on to say, intended to return and complete the work, but they were annoyed by the behaviour of certain *Oruncha*, that is "devil-devil" men, who lived at a place called Atnuraquina, which is near to a gap in the Macdonnell Range now called Temple Bar. These evil beings killed and ate a lot of lizard men and women whom they had made out of *Inapertwa*, so they did not return, and therefore the plum tree people of Quiurnpa, and one or two other groups of men and women, remained in the state of *Ulpmerka* or uninitiated. The same *Oruncha* ate a number of Alexandra parakeet, grass seed and small rat people. Of the lizard men only two survived the slaughter. They were brothers (how they came to be so the tradition does not say) and the younger of the two, together with his wife, was away down south when the slaughter took place. Upon his return he at once saw the tracks of the *Oruncha*, and being frightened he placed his wife, who was also a lizard, in the centre of his *Ilpilla*, which is the large bundle of eagle-hawk feathers worn in the hair-girdle in the middle of the back, and thus concealed her from view. Then he searched for his *Okilia* or elder brother, and at length found his head, to which he spoke, with the result that the man at once came to life and said, "the *Oruncha* killed us but they threw away my head; they will come again, take care of yourself."

Then he pointed to the track which they had made, and the two men, arming themselves with strong *Urumpira*, that is spears of heavy wood such as mulga, all made in one piece and only used for fighting at close quarters, went to opposite sides of a narrow gorge which is now known as the Simpson Gap, and is at the present day an important local centre of the lizard totem. The natives point out special stones which mark the spot where the two men stood.

When the *Oruncha* made their appearance, the two brothers rushed down upon them, and with their good *Urumpira* killed them all. They fell in a great heap just at the entrance to the gorge, and to the present day a great pile of jagged boulders marks the exact spot. After having thus destroyed their enemies, the elder of the two brothers stayed at the gorge, and there finally died, though his spirit remained in the Churinga, which he, like every other Alcheringa individual, carried about with him; the younger brother travelled away to a place a long way to the south called Arumpira not far from Erldunda, where he died, and so, by leaving his spirit behind in his Churinga, together with those associated with other Churinga which he carried, formed there a local Echunpa or lizard totem centre.

The above tradition is of considerable interest; it is in the first place evidently a crude attempt to describe the origin of human beings out of non-human creatures who were of various forms; some of them were representatives of animals, others of plants, but in all cases they are to be regarded as intermediate stages in the transition of an animal or plant ancestor into a human individual who bore its name as that of his or her totem. It has already been said that the tradition only refers to certain totems; we shall see subsequently that in the middle Alcheringa the making of men out of *Inapertwa* was continued by individuals of the Ullakupera or little hawk totem. The reference in the tradition to the *Ulpmerka* men of the Akakia (plum tree), and Ingwitchika (grass seed) totems is of importance, as it serves to throw light upon what had been to us for some time a matter of considerable difficulty, and one for which no explanation had been forth-coming. We were acquainted with numerous ceremonies concerned with a group of individuals who were always spoken of as the *Ulpmerka* of a place called Quiurnpa, and we were also acquainted with ceremonies concerned with certain so-called *Arakurta* men. In each case the men were groups of individuals who belonged to special totems. One man, for example, would be an Akakia or plum tree man, while another would be an *Ulpmerka* of the Akakia totem. In just the same way one man would be an Elonka (a Marsdenia fruit) man, and another would be an *Arakurta* of the Elonka totem. In the above tradition and in those concerned with the middle Alcheringa period, we can see how this is accounted for by the natives. The *Ulpmerka* were certain of the plum tree men who were not circumcised by the *Ungambikula*, and the *Arakurta* were in the same state, but were subsequently operated upon by the Ullakupera and were thus changed from *Ulpmerka* into *Arakurta*.

Attention must also be drawn to the striking fact that there is no reference whatever to any system of organisation apart from the totemic system, and further that this is not described as regulating marriage. The only reference to the latter which occurs is in the case of the younger of the two lizard brothers, who carried his wife in the bunch of eagle-hawk feathers, and it is expressly said of her that she was a lizard woman, that is, she belonged to the same totem as that to which he himself did. In fact, during the Alcheringa period concerning which we have very numerous and full traditions, some of which will be dealt with subsequently, it will be clearly seen that we are dealing with a time in which marital relations were not restricted by totem. We have definite indications of the existence of such relations between men and women of the same totems. We have been constantly on the watch for any tradition which would deal with the regulation of the marital relationship in times past, but though, as will be seen shortly, there are clear indications of a time when the restrictions which now obtain were adopted, there is no indication whatever of a time when a man of any particular totem was obliged to marry a woman of another one. Such indications as there appear on the contrary rather point towards the usual existence of marital relations between men and women of the same totem. There are, however, one or two traditions which deal with the relationship of men and women of different totems, and these will be discussed later; meanwhile it may be said that in the matter of totems and the restriction by these of marital relationship, a sharp line of separation may be drawn between the northern central tribes as exemplified by the Arunta, and the southern central tribes as exemplified by the Urabunna.

We may now pass on to deal with the middle Alcheringa period. Tradition relates that a great *Oknirabata*[138] of the Ullakupera or little hawk totem arose at a place called Atnaturka by the side of a stream now called Love's Creek. He and the men of his group were remarkable for the possession of very fine stone knives, called *Lalira*, with which they performed the operation of *Lartna* or circumcision. Amongst the men of all other totems up to that time stone knives were not used for this purpose, and the operation was always performed with a fire-stick.[139]

One of the Ullakupera men, who was a Purula named Ulpmurintha, flew from Atnaturka to Utiara, a place about ten miles north of Alice Springs, where at an earlier time the *Umgambikula* had made into *Ulpmerka* certain *Inapertwa* creatures of the Untaina or small rat totem. Along with these people there dwelt two Ullakupera men, one a Kumara named Irtaquirinia and the other a Purula named Yirapurtarinia, a Kumara man, both of whom are at the present time represented by living men, who are in fact simply regarded as their reincarnations.

Previous to the arrival of Ulpmarintha the two Ullakupera men had prepared a large *Apulla*, that is a special ground on which the rite of circumcision is performed, and on this they intended to operate on the *Ulpmerka* with the usual fire-stick. When, however, Ulpmurintha appeared upon the scene, the two men went to him and said, "How must we cut these *Ulpmerka* men?" and he replied, "You must cut them with *Lalira*." They replied sorrowfully, "We have no *Lalira* but we will cut them with *Ura-ilyabara*" (that is a fire-stick). The old man said, "No, do not do that, follow me to Atnaturka and I will give you some *Lalira*." Then he flew back quickly to Atnaturka and told two old men of his group what he had seen and said. One of these old men was a Kumara named Intumpulla, and the other was a Bulthara named Ungipurturinia, and these two went and hid away the good *Lalira*, leaving only the poor ones in sight. Shortly afterwards the two Ullakupera men flew across the country to Atnaturka, and there they were given some *Lalira* swathed in bark. After receiving these they, without examining them, at once started back on their return journey, very much pleased with their good fortune in securing the knives. Upon arriving at Utiara they opened their parcels and found, very much to their annoyance, that the stone knives were very rough, and quite unlike those described to them by the old men. After this they paid several visits to Atnaturka with the object of securing some good *Lalira*, but were always treated in the same way, and being very desirous of securing them in some way or another they finally invited the old Ullakupera men to again visit Utiara, where a great number of *Ulpmerka* were ready to be operated upon. Accordingly a party of Ullakupera led by the two old men already named started from Atnaturka taking with them some women and carrying some good *Lalira*. They made their first camp at a place called Urtiacha, where the two streams now called Love's Creek and Todd River unite. They had no *Nurtunja* with them nor any bird's down, but only *Equina*, or white pipe-clay, and *Apirka*, or powdered charcoal, with which to decorate themselves. Here they found an *Apulla* in readiness, at which were assembled a number of men, some of whom belonged to the Ertwaitcha or bell bird totem, and others to other totems. The Ullakupera men here performed the operation upon some of the young men, and afterwards upon a number of the local men who considered the *Lalira* to be a great improvement upon the fire-stick.

Close by the *Apulla* ground there were a large number of *Inapertwa* creatures of the same totem as the local men who had been operated upon. These the Ullakupera, with their stone knives, made into men and women, and at the same time conferred upon them the class names which they ever afterwards bore. It was these Ullakupera men who for the first time conferred upon the Arunta people the names of Panunga, Bulthara, Purula, and Kumara.

The Ullakupera were very quick in performing the operation of circumcision, and an Inarlinga (Echidna or "Porcupine") man who dwelt close by was very angry when he arrived and found that it was all over. He very strongly disapproved of the introduction of the stone knives.

Where the *Apulla* ground had been made a fine clay-pan—
that is a shallow depression capable of holding water for
some time after a rainfall—was formed to mark the spot, and
here several of the Ullakupera men went into the ground with
their Churinga, from the spirits associated with which men
and women, some of whom are now living, have sprung.

Leaving this camp the party travelled a little north of a spot
called Wurungatha, followed by the Inarlinga man. Here again
they operated upon some more men; the Inarlinga man came
up too late, and was angry as before, and another clay-pan
arose to mark the spot. The Inarlinga man did not follow
them any further. Travelling on the party came to a spot
called Iturkwarinia, where they found a number of men of the
Arwatcha totem (little rat), but they did not operate upon
these people, because there was no *Apulla* in readiness, but
they transformed a number of *Inapertwa* into Arwatcha men
and women. At this place one Purula woman and a Kumara
man were left behind, the *Lalira* which the latter carried being
transformed into a Churinga when he went into the ground
and died. Then they went on to the east of what is now
Mount Undoolya, where they came across a number of
Inapertwa of the Alchantwa (a seed) totem, who were
transformed into human beings, and to the present day a fine
group of gum trees marks the spot where they performed the
operation. Thence, crossing the range, they came to
Urwampina, and here they found that the Arwatcha (little rat)
people had prepared an *Apulla*, and therefore they performed
Lartna upon them, and also operated upon *Inapertwa*
creatures. Here also one Purula man remained behind and
went into the ground. He has since undergone reincarnation
in the form of a man who was the father of a woman now
living at Alice Springs.

Travelling on they came to a place called Bulthara, because at
the suggestion of the old Bulthara man, the party divided, the
one half, that is the Panunga and Bulthara, going to one side,

while the other half, that is the Purula and Kumara, went to the other side. Turning their faces towards the east they looked back upon the course which they had come, and as soon as they had done this two hills arose to mark the spots on which they had stood. Then they again mingled together and some *Inapertwa* of the Irritcha (eagle hawk) totem were operated upon, and others also who belonged to the Untaina (small rat) totem. These newly-made beings were divided into two groups and made to stand apart just as the other men had done before. Then they marched on to a place called Ilarchainquila, on the present Jesse Creek, to the north of Undoolya, where they found, and operated on, some more *Inapertwa* of the eagle-hawk totem; at Pitcharnia they found and operated upon some more, and at Chirchungina they met with *Oruncha Inapertwa*, and at Chara there were some belonging to the Arthwarta (a small hawk) totem; on all of these they operated.

At Chara they were met by two men, who came from Utiara, and said, "We have brought back your stone knives which you gave us, they are of no use, why did you not give us good ones?" The old men said, after they had looked at the *Lalira*, "Yes, these are no good, you may take some others." They accordingly took some, and saying, "Come quickly to our *Apulla*," at once returned to Utiara. Some curious looking stones, now regarded as sacred, arose to mark the spot were the *Lalira* were spread out. At Kartathura some *Inapertwa* of the Erlia (emu) totem were operated upon, and then, without camping, the party moved on to Thungumina, which lies some seven or eight miles to the north of Alice Springs, where again more *Inapertwa* of the emu totem were operated upon. At Thungamina they deposited some inferior *Lalira*, which were, however, afterwards picked up by the local people, and being by them regarded as sacred were placed in the store-house or *Ertnatulunga* at Utiara. Then the party travelled on to Thungarunga, and operated there upon *Inapertwa* creatures of the Marsdenia fruit and rat totems, and, having done so, cleaned up and sharpened their *Lalira* with ashes and walked on to Utiara, where they stood waiting to hear the *Lartna* song which would show them that the *Apulla* was ready. As soon as the singing was heard they went on to the *Apulla* ground, a number of stones standing up on end now marking the spot where they stood and waited.

Standing to one side of the *Apulla* they watched while the two local men for the first time operated with stone knives. They were not, as yet, expert in the use of the knives, and after two or three operations the old Ullakupera man named Intumpulla said, "Stand aside, I will do the cutting;" and so he cut all the *Ulpmerka* who had previously been transformed out of *Inapertwa* by the *Ungambikula*. He told them to go away altogether to the Utiara Range where they went into the ground and so formed there an *Oknanikilla* which is called that of the *Arakurta* of the Elonka totem, and which is the only one of this nature in the neighbourhood.

After sending the *Arakurta* away the old man still went on cutting, and when about to operate on the last man, who was *markilunawa*, that is a married man, an old man of the Inarlinga (Echidna) totem rushed on to the *Apulla* ground and said, "I must cut this man with my *Lalira*," and drawing a knife from a socket in his skull just behind his ear, grasped the man's penis and scrotum, and with one savage stroke of his knife cut them off, and the man fell down dead. The old Echidna man at once ran away, but was followed by the Ullakupera and other men, who killed him, riddling his body with spears. Since then no Echidna men or women have ever sprung up in the country, but only animals covered with spines, which represent the spears with which the Alcheringa Echidna man was killed. Before this happened there were Echidna animals, but they had no spines, and this is how the Inarlinga or Echidna came to be covered with spines. By thus killing the man on the sacred *Apulla* ground the Inarlinga "spoilt" himself, and all the totem kindred, and so they cannot rise again except in the form of little animals covered with spines which are simply Alcheringa spears.

When the wives of the murdered man missed him they went to the *Apulla* ground and there they found him dead, and, noticing his mutilated state, they searched for many days for the missing organs. They dug up the *Apulla* ground without success, and were much troubled until one day the younger of the two women, who was *Quitia* or younger sister of the other, found the missing organs under the bank on one side of the *Apulla*; placing them in her *alpara* or *pitchi*, she took them to the body and tried to join them on again, but they would not remain in position, and so she called her elder sister and both tried many times without any success, until finally, placing the organs on the ground, they laid the body on the top of them, face downwards, so that they might rest in the proper position. Then, feeling very mournful, the two women sat down, one on each side of the dead man, and all three then turned into the stones which still exist to mark the spot. A little distance away is another stone which represents the mother of the two women, who came to look for her daughters and would not go away without them. Being *Mura* to the dead man she could not come close up to him and so sat down a little distance away.

At this spot the Ullakupera men left some women, thus forming another *Oknanikilla*, and of these women, one a Purula, called Chitta, has at the present day a living representative.

From Utiara the party flew up into the sky, and travelling northwards descended again to earth at Ilkania, a spot close to what is now known as the Burt Plain, where they found bandicoot, carpet snake and one old Echidna man assembled at an *Apulla* ground. Here they performed *Lartna* with their stone knives, and once more, just as they were about to cut the last man who was an Okranina or snake man, the old

Echidna man rushed up, and, before they could stop him, mutilated the man with a stone knife which he carried, as before, in a socket behind his ear. The Echidna was at once speared, but ran a short distance from the *Apulla* while the spears were pouring in upon him, until, after having run round in a circle, he fell down dead. A circular rock hole appeared to mark the spot. All the men who had been operated upon ran away, followed by their women; the wives of the murdered man remained behind and called to him many times, but received no reply, and as it was night-time they could not see him, and so they sat down and waited anxiously for the daylight. Early in the morning they went to the *Apulla* ground, and there they found him dead and mutilated. For some time they mourned over him, and then they started to search for the missing parts, which, after a time, they found close to the *Apulla*. Then they lifted the body into a sitting position, placing it in a large *pitchi*, and replaced in their position the parts which had been cut off, and then after much crying, being hungry, they went away in search of food. Shortly after their departure the man awoke as if from a dream, perfectly sound, but of course an *Ulpmerka*, for the old Ullakupera man had not operated upon him. He at once found the women's tracks and followed them to where they were eating Okranina, or snake, which was their totem. They were rejoiced to see him, and then all of them went into the earth, carrying their Churinga with them, and three stones arose to mark the spot where they went in.

After killing the Echidna man and leaving behind one little hawk woman, who has no living representative, the party once more took wing and travelled on to Urang-pa, where they found a lot of Kakwa men assembled at an *Apulla* ground. Here the old Intumpulla insisted upon performing *Lartna*. He also transformed a number of *Inapertwa* into human beings, and, so says tradition, being enamoured of the Kakwa women he decided to stay at Urangipa, and accordingly stayed there altogether, together with another

Kumara man named Unchinia. The rest of the party went on under the leadership of the Bulthara man. For some distance they took wing and then came down to earth at the *Mirra* or camp of the Ullakupera, where they found a Yarumpa or honey-ant woman of the Panunga class, who had a *Nurtunja* which she did not wish the strangers to see. She did her best to drive them away, using abusive language, which very much annoyed the old Ullakupera man, who killed her with a spear, but did not interfere with her *Nurtunja*, which is now represented by a large gum tree. At this spot a Panunga man was left behind, and hence they travelled on to Urumbia, which lies to the north of the place which was named Anna's Reservoir by Stuart, the early explorer, during his journey across the continent. This lies within the country of the Ilpirra tribe, and the party changed its language to that of the Ilpirra. Here also they met with a number of extraordinary-looking *Inapertwa* creatures of the honey-ant totem, who were engaged in performing an Engwura ceremony. These they made into men and women, and then, leaving a Panunga woman behind, they went away, flying off towards the west to a place called Ungapirta, where they found *Inapertwa* of the Ullakupera totem, whom they transformed into human beings; and then they all went into the ground, where the Churinga with their associated spirits ever after remained, so that at this place there is a large and important *Oknanikilla* or local centre of the Ullakupera totem.

It will be seen that there are two points of importance so far as these Ullakupera men and the work which they carried out is concerned. In the first place they introduced the use of a stone knife in place of the fire-stick[140] at the ceremony of circumcision. They were apparently not the only men who possessed stone knives, as the Echidna men are distinctly stated to have had them, and in the southern part of the tribe a woman of the frog totem is said to have possessed one. Probably we have in this tradition an indication of a time when a more primitive method of cutting was retained in connection with a sacred ceremony than was used in the case of the ordinary operations of life.[141] In the southern Arunta tradition says that one day the men were, as usual, circumcising a boy with a fire-stick when an old woman rushed up and, telling the men that they were killing all the boys because they were using a fire-stick, showed them how to use a sharp stone, and ever afterwards the fire-stick was discarded.

The second point of importance is the introduction of the class names, but it must be also noticed that there is no mention of any restrictions with regard to marriage connected with them, nor is any reason assigned for their introduction. In fact, as yet, we have no indication of any restrictions on marriage so far as either totems or classes are concerned, such restrictions we shall meet with in traditions referring to a later period in the history of the tribe. It will also be seen that there is no attempt to offer any explanation of the origin of the ceremony of circumcision, and in connection with this subject it may be noticed that, so far as the Arunta tribe is concerned, circumcision is represented as being practised upon men who are already provided with wives, and this, which is the earliest tradition dealing with the subject, gives no indication whatever of the reason for the fact that circumcision is, at the present day, one of the most important ceremonies which must be passed through before any youth is allowed to have a wife.

Concerned with the middle Alcheringa people, but coming at a later date than the Ullakupera men, who introduced the use of the stone knife at *Lartna*, we meet with traditions concerning certain early Achilpa, or wild cat men, who in their turn introduced the ceremony of *Ariltha*, or sub-incision.

Amongst the Achilpa there are four distinct groups, with regard to the doings of whom the natives have traditions as follows.

The first group started from a place called Okira, somewhere to the east of Wilyunpa, which itself lies on the Finke river, out to the east of the present telegraph station at Charlotte Waters. They carried with them a sacred pole called a *Kauaua*, which they erected at various stopping places. To this special ceremonial object, reference is made in the account of the Engwura ceremony, as it is always, and exclusively, used in connection with this. When during the course of their marchings they performed the rite of *Ariltha* or sub-incision they always erected a special *Nurtunja*.

Leaving Okira the men came to Therierita, where they performed *Ariltha*, made Engwura, and left some members of the party behind them. Thence they went on to Atymikoala, a few miles to the east of Love's Creek, and there they performed *quabara undattha*, that is a sacred ceremony concerned with one or other of the totems in connection with the decoration for which *undattha* or bird's down is used. Each of the sacred ceremonies, as performed at the present day, is supposed to be the exact counterpart of one of these ceremonies of the Alcheringa. The Quabara Achilpa of Therierita, as a particular ceremony is now called, is, for example, the special ceremony which was performed on the occasion when the wild cat men visited Therierita, and the ceremony was the special property of one member of the party. It was in this way—by their performance at certain particular spots—that the ceremonies became, each one of them, associated with these spots.

From this resting place they marched on to Achilp-ilthunka, which means where the Achilpa was cut to pieces, and is close to the present Arltunga out in the eastern Macdonnell Ranges.

Here they met a wild cat man who had come down from the salt water country away to the north. He is recorded as having been abnormally developed, and as having ravished and killed women all along his route. He was also *atnarbita* or foul-smelling, and intended going on to Therierita, but the Achilpa being enraged with him on account of his conduct, killed him and mutilated him, and a large stone arose to mark the place where they buried him. Leaving this spot they marched on, driving enormous numbers of mosquitoes on in front of them. Tradition also says that they lived on Unjiamba, or Hakea flower, and that when they were thirsty they drank their own blood, as the natives often do at the present day. As they journeyed on they passed Unchiperawartna, but did not see two women of the opossum totem who lived there, and then they reached a place now called Aurapuncha. Before, however, they came quite close up, they smelt Akakia or plum tree men, and as soon as they came into the bed of the creek they saw a number of men and boys eating plums. With them they stayed for some time, and after performing *quabara undattha* they went into the ground; in other words they died, and after a time arose again, no longer as Achilpa men, but changed into *Ulpmerka* or uninitiated men of the Akakia or plum tree totem. Taking along with them the local *Ulpmerka* of the Akakia totem, the newly arisen *Ulpmerka* went on to a place called Erlua, somewhere in the neighbourhood of the Strangway Range, and leaving at various spots a few members of their party behind them, so as to form *Oknanikilla*, they came at last to Arwura-puncha, where they met a large number of *Ulpmerka* men, who had come up from Quiurnpa under the leadership of a celebrated man called Kukaitcha, and were carrying with them a large *Nurtunja*. The two parties joined forces, and when they had performed *quabara undattha* they left two men behind and proceeded to Urangunja, where they found two women of the Urpura totem (magpie) who had a Nurtunja and owned certain ceremonies which they showed to the men. These women had their arms, heads and necks covered with furstring and the tail-tips of the rabbit-kangaroo, called *Alpita*, which at the present day are always worn as a decoration by women at special ceremonies. The *Ulpmerka* camped here for some time performing sacred ceremonies, which, however, the women were not allowed to see. Leaving here they passed on to Ilchartwa-nynga, where they made a great *Altherta*—that is, an ordinary so-called corrobboree which has no sacred nature and may be seen and taken part in by women and the uninitiated—and here a large number of stones standing up on end arose and still exist to mark the spot where the *Ulpmerka* danced. They are now called *Ulpmerka atnimma*, that is the standing *Ulpmerka*. After this they journeyed on to Alawalla, which lies to the east of Central Mount Stuart, which, as its name implies, is situated in the very centre of the continent, and there they made Quabara. As they did so a curious phenomenon was witnessed—the Akakia trees shed their plums so thickly that it was just as if it were raining plums; the fruit ran along the ground like a flood, and the *Ulpmerka* would have been drowned in them if they had not quickly gone into the ground and so made their escape. They emerged at Incharlinga on the Stirling Creek, where they performed ceremonies, and from here Kukaitcha led them right away north to the country of the salt water.

The second group of Achilpa or wild cat people came from the country of the Luritcha tribe, far away to the south-west of the present Arunta land, and camped at a place called Yungurra to the west of Henbury on the Finke river. The party was led by two *Oknirabata*, or wise old men, who on account of the abnormal development of their organs were called *Atnimma-la-truripa*.

At Yungurra the party divided into two groups, one of the old men going with each of them. Of these two parties one will now be spoken of as the second and the other as the third group of the Achilpa.

The second group crossed the Finke river about twelve miles south of Henbury, and travelled on to Imanda on the Hugh river, where they changed their language to the Arunta tongue. Like the first party they carried a sacred pole or *Kauaua*. On arriving at Imanda they found a large number of Unchichera (frog), Elkintera (white bat), and Unchipera (little bat) men who were engaged in performing an Engwura ceremony in which the new comers joined, the young men amongst the Achilpa being sent out daily into the bush along with those of the other totemic groups. The head of the Unchichera totem at this spot was also *Atnimma-la-truripa*, and his name was Kartuputapa. The Achilpa remained for a long time at a spot close to Imanda, where they left some men behind them and so established an important *Oknanikilla*. When they left Imanda they were accompanied by Kartuputapa, and camped first at a big clay pan called Itnunatwuna in the James Range, where they performed ceremonies and saw a Purula woman of the frog totem whose name was Umbalcha. She possessed a *Nurtunja* and sacred ceremonies which she showed to the Achilpa. This woman had arisen in this spot. Then they travelled to Ooraminna, where they made an Engwura and discovered a number of men who were suffering from *Erkincha*—a disease common amongst the natives and concerning which there are certain traditions to which reference will be made subsequently. They also saw a number of Unjiamba (Hakea flower) men and women who had originated there, and also the two Unjiamba women who had come from Engwurnanunga. After performing *Ariltha* upon the Unjiamba men and also upon some of their own young men, they performed the initiation ceremony called *Atna ariltha-kuma* upon the two women just referred to. At Ooraminna they left three men and here also Kartuputapa, the frog man, left the party and went back to his own country at Imanda. The wild cat men journeyed on to Urthipata, a swamp on the Emily plain, journeying, as they went northwards, close by, but not actually along, the tracks of the Unjiamba women who had travelled in the opposite direction. Here they made Engwura and found a man and woman both of whom belonged to the Unjiamba totem; the man was a Purula and the woman a Kumara. Each of them possessed a

Nurtunja and *quabara undattha*, and when the Achilpa men attempted to interfere with the woman they could not do so because of her *quabara*. Leaving here they were seen by a Purula man of the witchetty grub totem[142] who had originated in the locality, but as he hid himself the Achilpa did not see him.

The next camping place was at a small hill on the Emily Plains on the top of which a stone arose to mark the spot; here they made *Ampurtanurra*,[143] that is a long series of ceremonies concerned with the Achilpa totem, and then they went on to Okirra-kulitha, a depression in the Macdonnell Range a little to the east of the Emily gap. They camped right on the top of the range, performed *quabara undattha*, and also the rite of *Ariltha* on some of their young men, and then went on eastwards for five or six miles to a hill called Irpai-chinga near to the Emily Creek and performed some more ceremonies. Here they noticed plenty of witchetty grubs, feeding on grass, but they did not interfere with them and went on to Achilpa-interninja, a hill about two miles away from the Emily soakage. Owing to the breaking of the string with which a bundle was tied together, they lost a small Churinga, from which sprung afterwards a Purula man named Ultanchika, whose descendant now lives at Alice Springs; then they went on to Okilla-la-tunga, a plain amongst the ranges, and there found a Purula woman of the Unjiamba totem whose name also was Unjiamba, and who possessed a *Nurtunja* and *quabara undattha*, which she showed to the Achilpa men, who danced round her *Nurtunja* and then showed her their *quabara undattha*. Then they went on to Ulir-ulira, which means the place where blood flowed like a creek, and is a water-pool on the Todd Creek. The young men opened veins in their arms and gave draughts of blood to the old men, who were very tired. Ever afterwards the water at this spot was tinted with a reddish colour; indeed it is so at the present day. After again making *Ampurtanurra* they journeyed on and came to a place called Ertua, where they saw two women of the Ertua (wild turkey) totem, one a Purula named Ulknatawa, who had a little boy child, and the other a Kumara. An old Kumara man of the same totem lived with these women, but was out hunting at the time. His name was Arungurpa, and he was the husband of the Purula woman. The women had neither *Nurtunja* nor *quabara undattha*. Passing on, the Achilpa camped at Arapera, a big stone hill to the east of Bond Springs, where they stopped for some time making Engwura and performing *Ariltha*. Here they found a Purula woman of the Achilpa totem whose name was Ariltha-mariltha, and who has a descendant now living. She had a large *Nurtunja* which was erected and stood so high that it was seen by the Achilpa from a long way off. The woman showed her *quabara undattha*, and they afterwards performed *Atna ariltha-kuma* upon her, and then all of them had intercourse with her. At this spot they left one man, a Kumara named Achilpa, whose descendant is now alive. Leaving Arapera they reached Ilchinga and, being tired, camped for a few hours, the old men painting the newly-made *Urliara* with long parallel lines from the feet to the head. Here they found a Bulthara woman of the Unjiamba totem named Cho-urka, who had a *Nurtunja* and *quabara undattha*, and whose *Nanja* was a large stone which can still be seen. With her they did not interfere, but after a short rest marched on to a place called Ungwurna-la-warika, which means "where the bone was struck," because here one of the men while swinging a Churinga accidentally struck another man on the shin with it. At this spot they found two Bulthara women of the Unjiamba totem, one named Choarka-wuka, and the other Abmoara, who possessed *Nurtunjas* and *quabara undattha*, which they showed to the Achilpa. One Purula man was left behind here. Walking on they came to Ilchi-lira, where they made *quabara* and found two men of the Unjiamba totem, one a Bulthara named Wultaminna, and the other a Kumara named Ungarulinga, the last descendant of whom has recently died. There was here another Unjiamba man whom they did not see. They also saw one Unjiamba woman, a Bulthara. All these people had *Nurtunjas* and sacred ceremonies, and had originated on the spot. The Achilpa left behind them one Purula man.

The next stopping place was Ituka-intura, a hill at the head of the Harry Creek, where they found a large number of Achilpa men and women with whom they mixed. These people were of all classes and had sprung up on the spot. After having performed *Ariltha* upon a great number of men and made Engwura they left the local Achilpa behind and marched on to Arara. Here they remained for a long time and made Engwura; when doing this the *Kauaua*, or sacred pole, was always erected and made to lean in the direction in which they intended to travel. Starting on their travels once more they came near to a spot on the Harry Creek where they first smelt, and then saw, some Achilpa men who were suffering from *Erkincha*. These men had no women, but close to them lived two Unjiamba women, both of whom were Panunga. The latter hid themselves on the approach of the Achilpa and so escaped being seen by them. One of them was called Thai-interinia, and has a living descendant. After seeing the men with *Erkincha* the party moved on and camped on a tableland close by, where they found an Unjiamba woman named Ultundurinia, who has now a living descendant. Marching on towards the west, they reached Ungunja and found there a Panunga man of the Unjiamba totem, whose name was Ultaintika, who is now represented by a living descendant. Then they followed the course of the Harry Creek to Apunga, until finally they came out on to the Burt Plain which lies just to the north of the Macdonnell Ranges. Here there was no water and the old men were very thirsty; they dug for water without finding any and the holes which they dug out remain to the present day. The young men again bled themselves, but the blood was too hot to drink, so some of them were sent back to Ituka-intura to bring water which they carried back in their shields. While the young men were away, the old men dug out holes in the sand and lay down in them as wild dogs do. At this spot they found a Purula woman of the Quirra (bandicoot) totem who had a *Nurtunja*, and is now represented by a living descendant. They also found a Panunga man of the same totem named Chimurinia, who also has a living descendant. Hence they moved on northwards to a big clay pan called Ilthwarra, where they performed *Ariltha* upon a number of their young men and made Engwura. While travelling on from here they crossed the Hamm Range at a gap where they saw an old Bulthara man of the Undathirka (carpet-snake) totem named Kapirla who lived entirely upon carpet-snakes. The Achilpa men passed on and camped at Ilchinia-pinna, a little to the north of the range and here they made Engwura and every night heard the sound of distant *Nammatwinnas* (or small bull-roarers). Thence they went to Utachuta, a little to the west of what is now called Ryans Well, where they found a large number of Quirra or bandicoot men who were engaged in making an Engwura. The *Kauaua* which these men had erected was visible from some distance, and it was from this place that the sounds of the bull-roarers had come. The Achilpa and Quirra men mixed together and joined in the Engwura, the old men of both parties sending the young men out into the bush every day. The rite of *Ariltha* was performed on all of the Quirra men and also on some of the Achilpa, and it is stated that the Quirra men consisted of all classes.

When the ceremonies were completed, the Achilpa men journeyed on to Inta-tella-warika and, being too tired to carry it, dragged the *Kauaua* behind them. At this place they found an old Panunga man of the Achilpa totem who had a large *Nurtunja*, and who, on seeing them approach, opened a vein in his arm and thus flooding the country, drowned the Achilpa men in blood; a large number of stones sprang up to mark the spot, and they still remain to show where the men went into the ground. The men carried with them a very large number of Churinga, which are now in the sacred store-house at Inta-tella-warika.

The third party of Achilpa or wild cat people consisted of one division of the original group which came out of the country now occupied by the Luritcha tribe, and split into two after arriving at Yungurra.

Under the direction of a Kumara man who was *Atnimma-la-truripa*, the men took a north-westerly course, crossed the Finke river just where it emerges from the long Finke gorge, through which, hemmed in between lofty walls of quartzite, it passes from north to south across the James Range, and camped at Urapitchera near to a spot now called Running Waters. Here they erected the *Kauaua*, which they carried with them, and made an Engwura. At this place they found a number of Inturrita (plgeon) men and women of all classes who were cannibals. The Achilpa people saw them eating human flesh, and two large round Churinga which are preserved in the sacred store-house at Urapitchera represent the heads of men who were eaten.

The Inturrita killed their victims with long stone Churinga about the size of, and shaped like, the beaked boomerangs of the Warramunga tribe. At this spot the Achilpa changed their language to that of the Arunta people, and, leaving a Purula man behind them, passed on to Itnunthawarra in the present Waterhouse Range, where they camped for a short time and performed ceremonies. Travelling slowly northwards amongst the ranges they came to Iruntira on the Hugh river, where they left one man, a Bulthara whose name was Iruntirinia. Then they came to Okir-okira, a place ten miles to the north-west of the present Owen Springs, and thence travelled on to the junction of the Jay and Hugh where there was a Panunga woman living who showed them her ceremonies. She belonged to the Alk-na-innira (a large beetle) totem. The Achilpa in return showed the woman some of their ceremonies and did not interfere with her. Leaving her, the Achilpa followed up the Jay Creek to Chelperla, where some time was spent in performing *Ampurtanurra*, and where the old leader remained behind. At this spot many of the party developed *Erkincha*. Journeying on they came to Mount Conway, a bold lofty bluff in the Macdonnell Ranges, and close to its base they rested for a few hours before attempting the steep ascent. Then they crossed the mountain and camped at Ningawarta, a little way over on the northern side of the range, and here they performed ceremonies. Their next stopping place was Alla (the nose), a sharply outlined hill in the most northern of the series of parallel ridges which all together form the Macdonnell Ranges. At this place they made Engwura and while the young men, who were being initiated, were out in the bush, they came across a Purula woman of the Ulchilkinja (wattle seed) totem, with whom, contrary to one of the most rigid rules by which the Engwura is governed, and without the knowledge of the old men, they all had intercourse. At Alla, two men who were Kumara were left behind, and the party went on to Kuringbungwa, and as, when they reached there, some of the old men were getting very thin, the younger men opened veins in their arms and, to strengthen them, gave them large draughts of blood, by which treatment they were much benefited. At Enaininga, a waterhole on the Jay Creek, they performed the rite of *Ariltha* upon a number of young men, leaving untouched those who were suffering from *Erkincha*. Further on, at Iranira, they again performed the rite of *Ariltha*, and here they left one man called Unatta who was a Purula. Then they went on to Okinchalanina, where they performed ceremonies, and elaborately painted the backs of all the men. They stayed here a short time making *Okinchalanina* (necklets), *kulchea* (armlets), and *uliara* (forehead bands), and when they again started to march on they left one man, a Panunga, behind them, as he was too ill with *Erkincha* to walk any further. They considered that the unlawful intercourse with the wattle seed woman had spread the disease and increased their sufferings.[144] Still travelling amongst the ranges, they camped at various places, at one of which, called Lilpuririka, which means running like a creek, the old men were again nourished with blood given to them by the young men. Leaving behind them an old Panunga man who was suffering from *Erkincha*, they travelled on to Ilartwiura, a waterhole on the Jay Creek, and erecting their *Kauaua*, they performed sacred ceremonies, a large rockhole now marking the spot where the *Kauaua* stood. Some more men developed *Erkincha* here. At their last stopping place amongst the ranges they stayed some little time, making *Ampurtanurra* and performing *Ariltha*, and then they crossed the most northerly of the rocky ridges amongst the Macdonnell Ranges, and came down on to the Burt Plain which stretches far away to the north. At Alpirakircha they found an old Kumara man of the Achilpa totem named Alpirakircharinia, who had originated there and had a very large *Nurtunja* which they had been able to see from the top of the last ridge which they had crossed. They performed *Ariltha* here upon a number of young men, including the local Achilpa man, and also made Engwura. Leaving the man in his camp, they went on to the west, away down the Burt Plain, and met two Achilpa women who had originated there. One was a Purula and the other a Kumara, and they had a *Nurtunja* which they hid away when they saw the Achilpa men coming. Without interfering with the women, the men camped and performed certain ceremonies, and then went on to Ungatha where a man was left behind named Ungutharinia. This man, like many of the party, was suffering from *Erkincha*; at the present day he is represented by a living descendant whose secret name is, of course, Ungatharinia.

Being now very tired the men went underground and followed a northerly course until they came to Udnirringintwa, where they made a great Engwura. Many of the party died here from *Erkincha*, and a large number of Churinga representing them are in the local store-house. A large sand hill also arose to mark the spot where the *Parra*, that is the long low mound always made on the Engwura ground, was raised, and this hill can be seen at the present day. The surviving members of the party—still a large one—

went once more into the ground and came out again at Alkirra-lilima, where they camped for a long time and made *Ampurtanurra*. They found there an old man of the Panunga class and Unjiamba totem whose name was Alkaiya, and who had a big *Nurtunja* and owned *quabara undattha*. Here again more men developed *Erkincha*. Travelling now above ground, they came to Achichinga in the vicinity of Mount Wells, where dwelt an old Panunga man of the Unjiamba totem, whose name was Achichingarinia. He possessed a large Nurtunja which the leader of the Achilpa men tried to take by force, but the old man clung to it so closely, and made such a very loud *arriinkuma*[145] that he was forced to desist.

The party here made *quabara undattha* and changed its language to Achicha, which is a mixture of the Ilpirra and Kaitish tongues. Turning round they looked back upon their tracks and all said "We have come very far."

Leaving here they passed Parachinta, without seeing the Ullakupera and Quirra people who dwelt there, and camped at Appulya, north of Parachinta, and close by here saw an old Bulthara man of the Irritcha (eagle hawk) totem, who was out hunting and so had not got his *Nurtunja* with him, but when he saw the Achilpa men he ran back to his own country. *Ariltha* was performed upon some of the young men, and an Engwura was made. Then they went on to Arrarakwa, on Woodeforde Creek, where they found a Panunga man of the Achilpa totem who was busily engaged in making a *Nurtunja*. Upon him and others they performed *Ariltha*, and then, for some time, they camped at a spot higher up the creek making *Ampurtanurra*. At this part, the creek has a steep, high bank, which arose to mark the exact spot where the *Kauaua* rested against it before being erected. Here they left a Bulthara man and then went on to a place on the Hanson Creek, to the south-west of Central Mount Stuart, where they found an old Bulthara man of the Yarumpa (honey-ant) totem who was sitting by the side of a *Kauaua*, and they learned that Engwura ceremonies had just been made, and that all the young men were out in the bush. By and by they returned, and then the two parties mixed together, and the Achilpa performed *Ariltha* upon all the Yarumpa, including young and old men, and then commenced another Engwura which they did not wait to complete, but, leaving the Yarumpa people to finish it, they started on their journey and travelled on to Kurdaitcha, a spot to the west of Central Mount Stuart, where dwelt a large number of Achilpa of all classes who had originated there. After performing *Ariltha* upon all of them, the two parties mixed together and made a big Engwura. Going still further on, they met with a number of men and women belonging to all classes and to the Intilyapa-yapa (water beetle) totem, close to whom they camped, but without mixing with them. At a place called Okinyumpa an accident befell them which made them all feel very sad; as they were pulling up the *Kauaua* which was very deeply implanted the old *Oknirabata*, who was leading them, broke it off just above the ground, and to the present day a tall stone standing up above the ground at this spot represents the broken, and still implanted, end of the pole.

Carrying on the broken *Kauaua* they came to Unjiacherta, which means "the place of Unjiamba men" and lies near to the Hanson Creek. They arrived here utterly tired out, and found a number of Unjiamba men and women of all classes. They were too tired and sad to paint themselves, their *Kauaua* in its broken state was inferior to many of those which the Unjiamba people had, so they did not erect it, but, lying down together, died where they lay. A large hill, covered with big stones, arose to mark the spot. Their Churinga, each with its associated spirit individual, remained behind. Many of them are very large and long, and are now in the *Ertnatulunga* or store-house at Unjiacherta.

The fourth party of Achilpa or wild cat people was led by a Purula man who was remarkable for his strength and abnormal development, in which respect he is reported to have exceeded the celebrated *Atnimma-la-truripa*. He came from the country now inhabited by the Luritcha people, far away to the south-west of the Arunta, and brought with him two Panunga women. He had a *Kauaua*, and carried under each arm a large bundle called *Unkapera* which, when he arrived at Erloacha, a place situated to the west of Hermannsburg on the Finke river, he opened. They contained a great number of men of various ages. After the parcels had been opened, a great Engwura was made, in which they all took part, and, after remaining here for a long time, they left two men behind, one a Panunga and the other a Purula, and then they travelled on. The old Purula who was leading them travelled at some little distance to one side of the main party, and his progress was slow owing to the size of his penis, which frequently struck the ground, digging furrows in it as he went along. While travelling they met at Yapilpa, a place now called Glen Helen Gorge, a party of *Unthippa* or dancing women, who were approaching from the west, dancing all the way along. With them the Achilpa men did not interfere but passed on, crossed the range, and then camped at Ulpmaltwitcha, a waterhole lying a little to the west of the position of Mount Sonder. After making *quabara undattha* they went on and crossed Mount Sonder, which is one of the highest peaks in the Macdonnell Ranges. While crossing they saw an old Illuta (bandicoot) man making large wooden *pitchis*, and therefore they called the place Urichipma, which means "the place of *pitchis*."[146] Here they paused and, presumably from the summit from which a very extensive view is to be obtained, looked back to see their tracks and a row of stones arose and still remains to mark the spot. They went on and camped at Kurupma, north of Glen Helen, and after holding an Engwura, they left one man, an old Purula named Kurupmarinia, whose aged descendant now lives there and has charge of the store-house and Engwura ceremonies.

Leaving here they proceeded to Poara, where they performed *Ariltha* and made Engwura, and where they also found a number of women of the Kakwa (hawk) totem, all of whom were Purula and some of whom were called *Illapurinja*.[147] These women had a *Nurtunja* and sacred ceremonies which they showed to the Achilpa men. The old leader of the latter had intercourse with a great number of the women, many of the younger ones dying in consequence. The *Urliara*, that is the fully initiated men who had been through the Engwura, were also allowed access to them. Leaving behind several men of the Kumara and Purula classes the men, being ashamed of their excesses, started before daylight and travelled on to Irpungarthra, a water-hole on a creek running northwards. Here they camped and found a Purula woman of the Arawa totem. She had no *Nurtunja* but was in possession of several wooden Churinga which she hid away on the approach of the party. Here they made *quabara undattha*, which the woman was allowed to see, and afterwards *Ariltha* was performed upon some members of the party. Journeying on, they came to Al-lemma, a water-hole in one of the gorges which are often met with in this part of the country, and here they found a number of Kakwa (hawk) women and men who were all Purula and Kumara, and with whom they did not mix. They camped apart from them and then moved on to Ariltha, where they changed their language to the Ilpirra tongue and camped here for a long time, finding again a number of hawk men and women all of the same classes as before. Here the old leader caused his abnormal development to disappear and he became like an ordinary man, and then the travelling and resident groups mixed together. After the performance of *Ariltha*, a big Engwura was made, the women, as at the present day, making fur-string necklaces and armlets. Thence they went on to a place in the scrub not far from Lake Macdonald, where they found as before another lot of hawk men and women. Here they performed ceremonies and left one Kumara man whose descendant is now living. Then they went to Irincha, a large clay pan, where they found a

Panunga man of the Irpunga (fish) totem who was engaged in catching fish, of which the water was full. They were afraid of the number of fish in the water and did not interfere with the man, whose name was Ungunawungarinia, but camped a little distance away, making *Ampurtanurra*, and stayed here a long time. Then they went on to Alknalilika, a spot lying to the south of Anna's Reservoir, where they found a number of Tulkara (quail) women who had no *Nurtunja* or Churinga and lived entirely on Intwuta, a kind of grass seed. Upon seeing these women the Achilpa men hid away their *Kauaua* and all had intercourse with them. Without performing any ceremonies they went on to Inkuraru, where *Ariltha* was performed upon a number of the party. A number of Churinga were deposited in a mulga tree close to the camp, where they still remain, and a large stone arose at the spot where *Ariltha* was performed. After crossing one range they came to another lying away to the north and called Irti-ipma, where was a large waterhole. Here they camped, made *quabara undattha* and left one man, a Bulthara, and then journeyed on, meeting a woman of the Tchanka (bull-dog ant) totem who was a kind of *Oruncha* ("devil-devil") creature of whom they were much afraid, thinking that she might bite them. She had neither *Nurtunja* nor Churinga, and giving her a wide berth they went on to Kuntitcha, where they camped and found a large number of Quirra (bandicoot) men who were unable to walk, in fact they were creatures like the *Inapertwa*. All of these were killed, and then *Ariltha* was performed and an Engwura held. One man, a Purula named Kuntitcharinia, was left behind whose descendant is still living.

Tradition says that from here they journeyed northwards and finally stopped in the country of the salt water forming *Oknanikilla* or local totem centres as they travelled along.

THE LATER ALCHERINGA

We have already seen that, according to the traditions of the middle Alcheringa, there were no restrictions to marriage such as now obtain. At Urthipita, for example, a Purula man and a Kumara woman, both of the Unjiamba (Hakea flower) totem, are represented as having been found living together by the Achilpa people. Again at Ertua there lived two Ertua or wild turkey women, one of whom is expressly stated to have had a child, and to have been the wife of an old Kumara man of the same totem; and at other places groups of hawk men and women, all of the Purula and Kumara classes, who may not now marry one another, are represented as living together.

The class names had been given in the first place by the Ullakupera men who had traversed the country prior to the advent of the Achilpa. It looks much as if the traditions relating to the middle Alcheringa were concerned with a people whose organisation and marriage system were very different from those of the present Arunta tribe. The traditions as we know them now cannot, in respect to this matter, be simply explained by supposing that the references to the classes and totems are due to the fact that they have grown up amongst a people who have these class and totem names. If it were nothing more than this, then we should not expect to find such specific references to the living together of Purula and Kumara men and women, which is exactly the reverse of what now takes place, and is, by the natives, regarded as having taken place ever since the later Alcheringa times. It seems as if the traditions can only be explained on the supposition that the class names which were given by the Ullakupera men entailed restrictions upon marriage, but restrictions which were of a different kind from those introduced at a later period. What these restrictions were, it does not seem possible to gather from the traditions concerned with the early and middle Alcheringa times, and there do not appear to be any now known to the natives which throw any light upon the matter, though perhaps the constant reference to the class and totem names may be regarded as evidence that restrictions of some nature did exist. One thing appears to be quite clear, and that is, that we see in these early traditions no trace whatever of a time when the totems regulated marriage in the way now characteristic of many of the Australian tribes. There is not a solitary fact which indicates that a man of one totem must marry a woman of another; on the contrary we meet constantly, and only, with groups of men and women of the same totem living together; and, in these early traditions, it appears to be the normal condition for a man to have as wife a woman of the same totem as himself. At the same time there is nothing to show definitely that marital relations were prohibited between individuals of different totems, though, in regard to this, it must be remembered that the instances recorded in the traditions, in which intercourse took place between men and women of different totems, are all concerned with the men of special groups, such as the Achilpa; further still, it may be pointed out that these were powerful groups who are represented as marching across country, imposing certain rites and ceremonies upon other people with whom they came in contact. The intercourse of the Achilpa men with women of other totems may possibly have been simply a right, forcibly exercised by what may be regarded as a conquering group, and may have been subject to no restrictions of any kind.

As to the people with whom the Achilpa came into contact, and whom they found settled upon the land, the one most striking and at the same time most interesting fact, is, as just stated, that a man was free to marry a woman of his own totem (as he is at the present day), and further still we may even say that the evidence seems to point back to a time when a man always married a woman of his own totem. The references to men and women of one totem always living together in groups would appear to be too frequent and explicit to admit of any other satisfactory explanation. We never meet with an instance of a man living with a woman who was not of his own totem[148] as we surely might expect to do if the form of the traditions were simply due to their having grown up amongst a people with the present organisation of the Arunta tribe. It is only, during these early times, when we come into contact with a group of men marching across strange country that we meet, as we might expect to do, with evidence of men having intercourse with women other than those of their own totem.

Turning now to the later Alcheringa period, we find that it was after the time of the *Ungambikula*, the Ullakupera and the Achilpa, that the organisation now in vogue was adopted. The present system of marriage, and a proper understanding of the class system, is traditionally ascribed to the wisdom of the Erlia (emu) people of four widely separated localities. The *Oknirabata*, or great leader of the Thurathertwa group, living near to what is now called Glen Helen in the Macdonnell Range, proposed a system which permitted of Panunga men marrying Purula women, and of Bulthara men marrying Kumara women, and *vice versa*. According to this, men and women who now stand in the relation of *Unkulla*, as well as those standing in the present relation of *Unawa*, could marry each other. His proposal was carried out in his immediate neighbourhood, and he was also supported by the *Oknirabata* of the southern emu people living at a place called Umbachinga.

The *Oknirabata* of the Ulalkira and Urliipma groups, who lived about one hundred miles to the north, were what is called *Charunka*, which means very wise, and they said that it was not good for *Unkulla* to marry. At a meeting between them and the two other *Oknirabata*, it was decided that the plan of the northern men was the better one, and made, as the natives say, things go straight, and it was decided to adopt the new system.

Tradition says that the *Oknirabata* of one of the northern emu groups living at Urliipma, sent out *Inwurra*, that is messengers carrying the sacred Churinga, to summon the people from all directions. They assembled at Urliipma, which is situated in the country of the Ilpirra tribe away to the north of the Macdonnell Range, and were led thence by the *Oknirabata*, whose name was Ungwurnalitha, to Apaura, now called the Belt Range, where a great Engwura was held. After this was over all the people stood up, each man with his wife or wives behind him, and those who were wrongly united were separated, and the women were allotted to their proper *Unawa* men. The old man Ungwurnalitha presided at the Engwura, and he was assisted by old emu men of Ulalkira, Thuratherita, Umbuchinia and other places, all of whom had agreed with him that the change should be introduced.

The intermarrying halves stood in the relationship of *Unawa* to each other, this term being a reciprocal one, while the other halves were *Unkulla* to each other. Thus if we take the case of a Panunga man, under the old system all Purula women were eligible to him as wives, but under the new one only half of the Purula were *Unawa* to him, and half were *Unkulla*; with the former, or rather with those of them assigned to him, he might have marital relations, but the latter were strictly forbidden to him.

Taking all these traditions together we can see in them indications, more or less clear, of the following stages which are supposed by the natives to have been passed through in the development of the tribe so far as its organisation and certain important customs are concerned. We have:—

> 1. A period during which two individuals who lived in the western sky, and were called *Ungambikula*,

came down to earth and transformed *Inapertwa* creatures into human beings whose totem names were naturally those of the animals or plants out of which they were transformed. The *Ungambikula* also performed the rite of circumcision on certain, but not all, of the men, using for this purpose a fire-stick.

2. A period during which the Ullakupera or little hawk men introduced the use of the stone knife during circumcision. In addition they carried on the work commenced by the *Ungambikula* of transforming *Inapertwa* creatures into human beings, and further still, they introduced the class names now in use, viz. Panunga, Purula, Bulthara, Kumara. We may presume that along with the introduction of the class names there was instituted in connection with them some system of marriage regulations, but what exactly this was, there is not sufficient evidence to show.

3. A period, following closely upon the latter, during which the Achilpa or wild cat men introduced the rite of *Ariltha* or sub-incision. It is said of the Achilpa, also, that they arranged the initiation ceremonies in their proper order, first circumcision, then sub-incision, and lastly the Engwura.

4. A period during which, first of all, the marriage system was changed owing to the influence of certain Erlia or emu people, with the result that Purula men might marry Panunga women, Bulthara men Kumara women, and *vice versa*. Secondly, and at a later period, each of these classes was divided into two, so that, to a Panunga man, for example, only half of the Purula women were eligible as wives, the other half being *Unkulla* or forbidden to him.

It is not without interest to note that, according to tradition, the emu men who introduced the division of the classes now in use, lived away to the north, because the adoption of the distinctive names for the eight groups thus created is at the present time taking place in the Arunta tribe, and, as a matter of actual fact, these eight names did originate in the north, and are now slowly spreading southwards through the tribe.

Chapter XI

Traditions Dealing with the Origin of the Alcheringa Ancestors of the Arunta Tribe and with Particular Customs (Continued)

The Udnirringita totem—Alice Springs group consists of forty individuals at the present day—Emily Gap the centre of the totem—Wanderings of Udnirringita people from various places into the Gap—The wanderings of two women—A handicoot woman performs *Ariltha* on an Unjiamba woman, and then changes the totem of the latter—Two women join the wandering *Ulpmerka* men and travel on with Kukaitcha northwards—Wanderings of the wild dogs—Two young men steal the two Churinga of an old man, who pursues them to Mount Gillen—They kill and eat wild dog people—The old man is killed on Mount Gillen—The young men travel to the north and go down into the ground—Wanderings of two Unjiamba women—Travel southwards and stop at Ooraminna—Wanderings of emu, honey-ant and lizard men—The *Unthippa* women—Give rise to deposits of red ochre—Line of hills arise to mark their route—The *Unthippa* dance at circumcision—Tradition of *Erkincha*—Tradition of the snake of Imyunga—The fire totem—Origin of fire—The *Orunchertwa* and the *Oknirabata*—Association of birds with particular totems.

THE UDNIRRINGITA OR WITCHETTY GRUB TOTEM

THE most important group of the Udnirringita totem is located in the neighbourhood of Alice Springs in the northern part of the Macdonnell Ranges, and consists all told—men, women and children—of forty individuals, which is the largest number, in any one local group, with which we are acquainted. The totemic name is derived from that of a grub or larva, which in turn derives its name from a bush called *Udnirringa*, upon which the insect feeds and deposits its eggs. The bush bears a berry of which emus are very fond.

The Udnirringita people in this locality occupy a tract of country which is about 100 square miles in extent, and through the centre of which runs a range of often lofty hills, amongst which occur the gaps or gorges with which they are especially associated. The western boundary of their country is co-terminous with the eastern wall of the gap called by the natives Untariipa, and by the whites the Heavitree Gap. The eastern boundary is formed by the Adnurinia or Jessie Gap.

At various places throughout this district Udnirringita people originated in the Alcheringa from their animal ancestors, and these Alcheringa people deposited Churinga at various spots during the course of their wanderings, or where they originated. The Alcheringa Udnirringita people, both men and women, are supposed to have been full of eggs, which are now represented by rounded water-worn stones, many of which are stored in the *Ertnatulunga* at the various gaps, and are called *Churinga Unchima*. Every prominent, and many insignificant natural features throughout this strip of country—the most picturesque part of the great central area of the continent—has some history attached to it. For example, a gaunt old gum tree, with a large projecting bole about the middle of the trunk, indicates the exact spot where an Alcheringa man, who was very full of eggs, arose when he was transformed out of a witchetty grub. When he died his spirit part remained behind along with his Churinga, and used to especially frequent this tree, and therefore, when that spirit went inside a woman of the local group and was reincarnated in the form of a man who died a few years ago, that special tree was the *Nanja* tree of that man. An insignificant looking splinter of black, gneissic rock, projecting from the ground at another spot, indicates the exact place at which a woman of the Alcheringa arose whose living reincarnation—an old woman—is now to be seen at Alice Springs.

Emily Gap, or, as it is called by the natives, Unthurqua, is, probably, owing to its central position, the most important spot in the Udnirringita country. It is a narrow gorge not more than a hundred yards from end to end and about thirty in width, hemmed in by precipitous rocks of red quartzite, and runs from north to south right across the long ridge which, for some 200 miles, bounds the Horn or Mercenie valley on its southern side. Within a radius of two miles of this gap there are eight or ten holes, varying from three to five feet in depth, which are supposed to have been sunk, in the first instance, by the Alcheringa men. They are called *Ilthura*, and are strictly tabu to women and children, who must not on any pretence go near to them, and their exact locality is well known to all of the members of the local group. Each hole contains, carefully covered over, one large stone called *Churinga Uchaqua*, which represents the witchetty in its chrysalis stage, and a smaller, more rounded stone, called *Churinga Unchima*, which represents the egg stage.

It was just within the northern entrance to the gorge, at a spot marked now by a large stone, close to which stands the trunk of an old and long since dead gum tree, that the great Alcheringa leader of the witchetties, who was named Intwailiuka, sprang into existence. With him and with the people whose leader he was many of the natural features of the gorge are, as we shall shortly see, associated in tradition.

The stone has since been associated with the spirit, not only of the dead Intwailiuka, but also with one or two men who have been regarded as his successive reincarnations, the last of whom was the father of the present Alatunja of the group. A number of smaller stones close by represent men who sat there with him, for during his life he spent much time in this spot, which he chose because, owing to its position, he could easily guard the approach to the gap and at the same time keep watch over the sacred store-house of the Churinga, which was always located in one of the many clefts which he made in the rocks for this purpose.

In the western wall of the gap is situated the sacred cave which is called the *Ilthura oknira*, or the great *Ilthura*, at which he performed the ceremony called *Intichiuma*, the object of which was then, as at the present day, to increase the number of the Udnirringita grub on which he and his companions fed. Directly opposite to this, but low down on the eastern wall of the gap, is the sacred *Ilkinia*, a drawing on the rocks which it is believed sprang up spontaneously to mark the spot where the Alcheringa women painted themselves, and stood peering up and watching while Intwailiuka and his men performed *Intichiuma*. This spot is called the *Erlukwirra*, or camp of the women, in the Alcheringa, and one of the drawings is supposed to represent a woman leaning on her elbow against the rocks and gazing upwards. In this, as in many other instances, we meet with traditions showing clearly that in past times the position of women in regard to their association with sacred objects and ceremonies was very different from that which they occupy at the present day, when, for example, no woman dare to venture near to the sacred spot while *Intichiuma* was being performed there. About 200 feet below the *Ilthura*, a steep, broad belt band of quartzite, less weathered than the surrounding rock, stands out and dips steeply down into the bed of the creek. This is called *Alknalinta*, which means "eyes painted around," and indicates where, in the Alcheringa, Intwailiuka stood in the bed of the creek at the base of the rock. Standing here he threw numbers of *Churinga Unchima*, or eggs, up the face of the rock, just as is now done during the *Intichiuma* ceremony. Here also he used to sit while he pounded up large quantities of the grub. On the northern edge of the rock is a long, deep, ridge-shaped depression, which looks as if the stone had been cut out with a great knife, and this marks the spot where the special *pitchi* of Intwailiuka rested while he poured into it the pulverised grubs. A high precipitous wall of rock rises abruptly from the top of the *Alknalinta*, and in a line with the mass of rock an old pine tree stands and marks the spot where *Churinga Unchima* were stored by Intwailiuka for *Intichiuma* purposes, and where they are still stored by his successors. These special Churinga represent the eggs which the Alcheringa people carried in their bodies, and at the present day every man belonging to the totem has a few of these which he believes were carried thus by his Alcheringa ancestors, and when he dies they are buried with him. Any round pebble found in the vicinity of the gap may be one of these Churinga, but only the old men are able to tell whether it is genuine or not.

Looking south from the spot last referred to, a group of stones can be seen which mark the spot where a group of men coming into the gap in the Alcheringa sat down. At the west side of the northern entrance a great jumble of quartzite boulders, much weather-worn, indicates the spot where the grub men, who marched into this, the headquarters of the totem, from a place called Ulathirka, sat down. Just outside the northern end of the gap a group of gum trees indicates where the people who marched in from Ungunja sat down, and further still up the creek, a large boulder, standing in the bed, indicates where a celebrated old man, the leader of one group of the Alcheringa, sat down. Up on the western bank, a group of gum trees and acacia scrub indicates where the men coming in from Urliipma sat.

The Udnirringita people of this, their central group, did not wander about, and they are not recorded as having had any *Inapertwa* ancestors, but the grubs are supposed to have been transformed directly into human beings. Whilst, however, those who originated at the Emily Gap, according to tradition, remained there, other groups are recorded as having immigrated to the same spot from outside parts of the country.

The first to come were the Udnirringita from a place called Urliipma, which lies twenty miles away to the east of the present telegraph line, where it passes on to the Burt Plain at the northern side of the Macdonnell Ranges. They were led by an old Bulthara man, who was what is called *Erilknabata*, that is, a very wise man of the Alcheringa, his wisdom being commensurate with the length of his name, which was Irpapirkirpirirrawilika. They travelled at first under the ground until they reached Atnamala, a place a little to the east of Painta Springs, where they fed on Udnirringita, painted their bodies with the totemic design, and fixed many *Lalkira*, or nose bones, in their hair. Thence they travelled above ground, and came on south to Okirilla, where they cooked and ate many Udnirringita, and also made *Intichiuma*, and left the *Churinga Uchaqua* stones, which now remain there, in the *Ilthura* which they used. Thence they travelled to Unthurqua, or the Emily Gap, where they sat down on the northern entrance, the old man Intwailiuka warning them to come no further.

The next party to immigrate consisted of men from a place out to the west in the neighbourhood of Mount Heuglin. Unlike the Urliipma people they had some women with them and were led by a Panunga man named Ilpiriiwuka, who, when he found that Intwailiuka would not allow him to come within the sacred precincts of the Emily Gap, became angry and, leaving his party, returned to Ulathirka, where his descendant is now living amongst the Udnirringita of that locality. This party travelled first of all to Atnamala, where, like the first group, they painted their bodies with the *Ilkinia* of the totem and made *Intichiuma*. Thence they travelled south-east to Yia-pitchera, about six miles west of Alice Springs, where again they painted themselves and fed upon the grub, a large waterhole springing up to mark the spot where the grubs were cooked. Thence, after travelling only half a mile to Nang-wulturra, they again painted themselves, ate grubs, and another waterhole was formed. Travelling south they came to what is now called Charles Creek, where they performed sacred ceremonies and left a Panunga woman. Then, following down the creek, they came to Ilpillachilla, where they stopped for a few hours and decorated themselves with the *Ilkinia* designs. Then they went on to Kiula, a clay-pan about three miles to the south of Alice Springs, where they again painted the *Ilkinia* on their bodies and left one man, a Bulthara named Ulaliki-irika, whose last descendant died a short time ago. Then they travelled on to the east along the plain which is bounded on the south by the range through which the Emily Gap runs, and at a spot about three miles further on, which is now indicated by a great heap of stones, they stopped to listen for the voice of Intwailiuka, and presently they heard him singing about the coming of a Panunga man. Leaving behind them a Panunga man named Ilpiriiwuka, whose descendant is now living in the person of a little boy, they travelled on to an *Ilthura* about two miles away from the gap, where they met a number of the local Udnirringita people whom they joined, and then all of them went into the ground and came out again at the entrance to the gap on the western side. They were warned by Intwailiuka not to come any further on, so they sat down and their leader at once returned to Ulathurka. Where they sat down, a large number of black stones arose to mark the spot. At a later time Intwailiuka led the party to the *Ilthura Oknira*, where they assisted him to perform *Intichiuma*.

After this party, there came another from Wulpa, a spot amongst the sand hills west of Mount Burrell on the Hugh River. This was led by an old Panunga man named Akwithaintuya. The men of this party travelled underground to Yinthura passing, but at some miles distant, Imanda, where at that time the Achilpa and Unchichera were making Engwura. Here they made *quabara undattha* and ate

Udnirringita. They then travelled on, above ground, to Nukwia, east of Ooraminna, where they left a Panunga man; thence they came to a large clay-pan on the Emily Plain, made Engwura and then passed on to Intiripita, where they performed ceremonies and left two men, one a Panunga named Urangara, and the other a Bulthara named Irchuangwa. Then they passed on to Ilpirikulla, where a Panunga woman was left, and finally they reached the southern entrance to the Emily Gap where they were stopped by Intwailiuka and sat down, a group of stones now marking the spot. After their arrival they performed *Ariltha* upon some members of their party, the operator being a great medicine man named Urangara.

Another party came from Unthurkunpa, a range about fifty miles away to the east of Alice Springs, where there still exists a witchetty totem centre. They were led by a Bulthara named Intwailiuka, whose living descendant is the present Alatunja of the Alice Springs, or, to speak more correctly, of the Emily Gap group of Udnirringita. The members of this party at first travelled underground to Entukatira, a creek some miles to the east of Undoolya, where they ate witchetty grubs and painted themselves with *Ilkinia*. Thence they went on to Iliarinia, where they again painted and left a Bulthara man named Unchalka. Then they travelled on to the south and, after one or two halts, reached the entrance to the Jessie Gap, where they saw a number of witchetty men, amongst whom was a Bulthara named Kakathurika, who warned them not to approach any nearer to the gap and whose descendant is now the Alatunja of that group of the totem.[149]

Then they journeyed on to Laliknika on the Emily Creek about four miles north of the gap, where they painted *Ilkinia* on their bodies and left one woman, a Panunga, whose descendant is one of the daughters of the present Alatunja of Emily Gap. Thence they travelled on to the Todd River, where some men and women were left, and then, following the banks down to a spot, about half a mile away from the gap, where a Panunga man named Pitcha-arinia was left, they rested for a short time and then went on till they came to the eastern side of the Emily Gap, where they sat down all together and a group of trees arose to mark the place.

The last party of immigrants came from Ungwia in the Hart Ranges. The members of this party were of both sexes, and they travelled underground until they reached Ilpirulcha, a spot on the Emily Creek a few miles to the north of the gap, where they painted themselves with *Ilkinia* and ate witchetty grubs. Then they went on to Achilpa-interninja, the spot at which one of the travelling groups of the Achilpa lost a small Churinga. After painting themselves here and eating some more of the totemic grub, they came to Laliknika, and then on to one of the *Ilthura*, where they halted because they heard the voice of Intwailiuka singing. Here they left one Bulthara man, and going on stopped every now and then to listen for the singing. Camping on the Emily Creek half a mile to the north of the spot called Chalipita, they left here a Bulthara woman named Chantunga, and then going on they performed some sacred ceremonies. Leaving behind one Bulthara man, whose descendant is now living, they came to I-yathika, and found there a Bulthara man of their own totem. Here they could plainly hear Intwailiuka singing of the coming of the men from Ungwia, so they at once went on to the mouth of the gap, a group of trees arising to mark the spot where they stood. Intwailiuka objected to their passing through the gap, so they entered the ground and came up again on the south side at Ertichirticha, where they found the Wulpa people had previously sat down. The only living descendant of this group is a man named Ertichirticharinia, who now lives at Alice Springs. They wished to continue their journey to Wulpa, but Intwailiuka told them to remain, so they sat down and stayed at the gap, and a group of gum trees marks the spot where they sat down.

At the present time there are just forty individuals who are regarded as the descendants of the original resident group of Emily Gap and of the immigrant parties. Of these forty, twenty-six are the descendants of the former and fourteen are the descendants of the latter, and out of the total number only five belong to the Purula and Kumara moiety of the tribe.

THE WANDERINGS OF THREE WOMEN

A woman of the Panunga class and Quirra (bandicoot) totem, left a place called Ilki-ira, lying to the north of Anna's Reservoir, and, carrying with her a *Nurtunja* and Churinga, travelled south to Intita-laturika, where she found another Panunga woman of the Unjiamba totem who also had a *Nurtunja*. She took this woman and her *Nurtunja* with her, and, still travelling south, came to a place called Alkniara, to the east of, and not far from Mount Heuglin. Here they camped and made *quabara undattha*, and the Quirra woman performed the operation of *Atna ariltha-kuma* on her companion, a great gully arising at the spot, and, in the middle of this, a large stone to mark the exact place where, after the performance, the women went down into the ground, underneath which they travelled southwards to Ariltha. Here they made *quabara undattha* and then went on to Arurumbya, where they found erected the *Nurtunja* of a Bulthara man named Akwithaka, of the bandicoot totem. The bandicoot woman here painted her Unjiamba companion with *Quirra undattha*[150] and so caused her to change her totem to Quirra, after which, the tradition says, she fed exclusively on bandicoot. The owner of the *Nurtunja* was absent searching for bandicoot, and they did not see him, but, being afraid lest he should follow their tracks, they entered the ground and went on to Urtiacha in the Waterhouse Range, where they again made *quabara undattha*, and then came on to a spot five miles to the east of Owen Springs, where by means of *quabara undattha* the woman who was originally

Unjiamba and Panunga, changed herself into a Kumara and remained there altogether. Her name was Illapurinja, which means, the changed one.

The remaining woman now went on alone to Urapitchera, near to what is now called Boggy Waterhole on the Finke, where she found a number of Achilpa people making Engwura; she caused blood to flow from her sexual organs in great volume, directing it towards the people, who at once fled to a spot close by which is now marked by a number of stones which sprung up where they took refuge. The blood covered the Engwura ground and formed a fine clay-pan which remains to the present day.

Finding at Urapitchera a Kumara woman of the bandicoot totem, she took her on as companion and started off underground towards the north-east. After making *quabara* at various places they were chased by an old Kumara man of the lizard totem, named Yukwirta, but he could not capture them, and so they went on until they camped at Inkila-quatcha, where they found the *Ulpmerka* of the plum-tree totem who subsequently travelled northwards under the guidance of Kukaitcha and were at that time engaged in making Churinga by means of opossum teeth, which they used to draw the designs with. With the *Ulpmerka* the two women went to Quiurnpa, which was close by, and there Kukaitcha decorated the Kumara woman with sacred down, and thus caused her to change her class from Kumara to Panunga, and thus she became *Quitia*, that is, younger sister of the other woman.

It has been already described in the account of the Engwura how these two women accompanied the *Ulpmerka* as they travelled northwards from Quiurnpa under the guidance of the great Kukaitcha. It was this party of *Ulpmerka* who were camped at Aurapuncha, when one of the wandering parties of Achilpa came and joined them, and finally changed into Ulpmerka men of the plum-tree totem.

WANDERINGS OF THREE WILD DOG MEN

In the Alcheringa there dwelt at Chilpma, about one hundred miles east south-east of Alice Springs, three men of the Ukgnulia or wild dog totem; one was an old Bulthara man named Kaltiwilyika, and two were young men, both Panunga, one named Kalterinya and the other Ulthulperinya. The old man had a string bag, called *Iruka* or *Apunga*, in which he kept two Churinga. The two young men stole this bag and ran away followed by the old man who carried a great stabbing spear called *Wallira*. The two younger ones travelled away towards the north-west, and came to Uchirka, where they found an old woman of the wild dog totem, with a newly-born child, both of whom they killed and ate, leaving some meat for the old man. Here they left a Churinga from which sprang subsequently a man called Uchirkarinia, whose descendant is now living.

Leaving Uchirka they travelled quickly, being afraid of the old man, and during the day passed Therierita, where they saw a large mob of Achilpa. They went on and camped at Itnuringa, where they found some *Oruncha* men with whom they were afraid to interfere and camped at Ulkupiratakima, a rock-hole on the Emily Plain, about eighteen miles to the south-east of Alice Springs. Here they found an old woman of the wild dog totem, whom they killed and proceeded to eat, and while thus engaged, the old man came in sight. They just had time to conceal the bag with the Churinga in it, when he came and sat down a little distance from them without speaking. They gave him meat, but he only ate a very little of it, being sulky. That night they were afraid to sleep lest the old man should kill them, and before daylight they ran away and came on to Pilyiqua, where there are some small rock-holes. Here they camped and found some small wild dog men, some of whom they killed and ate. The old man again overtook them and again they gave him meat, of which he would only eat a little, being still very sulky and on the look-out for an opportunity of killing them. Once more they ran away before daylight and, passing a hill called Irpalpa, about seven miles south of Alice Springs, they travelled on to Okniambantwa or Mount Gillen, where they camped on top of the range and found an old woman of the wild dog totem whom they killed and ate. The old man came up later on, but the two young men had hidden themselves. He saw, however, a lot of wild dog men who had originated here (this lies in a wild dog locality at the present day), and thinking the two might be in their midst he attacked them with his great spear and killed several, after which they all combined together and killed him.

The local men were very angry, and so the two young men being afraid to join them, went up into the sky taking the bag with them. They went away towards the north-west and did not alight until they reached Ulthirpa, which is nearly seventy miles from Alice Springs. Here they camped and found a Bulthara man of the wild dog totem named Ulthirpirinia, whose descendant is now living, and who lived only on wild dog flesh (the animal not the man), of which he consumed large quantities. He had a *Nurtunja* and *quabara undattha*, which he showed to the two young men, who then went on foot to Erwanchalirika, where they found a Bulthara wild dog man whom they killed and ate. He had no *Nurtunja* or Churinga. After eating him their faces became suffused with blood, producing a most uncomfortable feeling, so that they relieved each other by sucking one another's cheeks.

Travelling on they passed the spots now called Johnston's Well and Harding's Soakage, both on the Woodforde Creek, and at the latter found a big *Nurtunja* erected which belonged to an old Panunga wild dog named Kalterinia, who was of remarkable appearance, having a broad white streak down the centre of his face. They joined him and he showed them his *quabara undattha*. At Imbatna, seven miles further north, they found another wild dog man with a *Nurtunja* and ceremonies, and then they turned slightly towards the west and came to

Eri-quatcha, where they opened up the bag and looked at the Churinga which fluttered about in the most extraordinary manner. They closed it up again, and travelling on crossed Hanson Creek at Urumbia, and reach Kurdaitcha away to the west of Central Mount Stuart, where, long afterwards, one of the Achilpa parties camped. Here they deposited the bag containing the Churinga, from which sprung a Kumara man whose name was Kurdaitcharinia. A large stone arose at the spot where the Churinga was deposited. Only one wild dog man can arise, at a time, at the spot which lies in the middle of an Achilpa locality. After they had deposited the Churinga one of the men mounted on to the back of the other and went into the ground, and it is only the far away western people who know where they came out again.

WANDERINGS OF TWO UNJIAMBA OR HAKEA WOMEN

Two women of the Unjiamba totem, named respectively Abmoara and Kuperta, sprang up at Ungwuranunga, about thirty-five miles north of Alice Springs, where they had a *Nurtunja* and Churinga, and dwelt alongside their *Ertnatulunga*. Leaving this place they entered the ground, and came out again at Arapera, where they saw a Purula wild cat woman named Arilthamariltha, who originated here and had a big *Nurtunja*, and whose descendant is now alive. The two women did not join her but camped close by, and ate Unjiamba, on which they always fed. Thence, travelling above ground, they went to Okillalatunga, where they erected their *Nurtunja* and walked about looking for Unjiamba, but did not see another Unjiamba woman, a Purula of that name, who was camped in the locality with a large *Nurtunja*, round which one of the Achilpa parties danced when they passed by. Taking their *Nurtunja* to pieces, they went on to Atnyra-ungwurna-munia, where they camped and ate Unjiamba. Thence they went to Unthipita, where they erected their *Nurtunja* again, played about, and looked for Unjiamba. Then they once more took their *Nurtunja* to pieces and travelled on to the Ooraminna rock-hole, where they went into the earth, and two large stones arose to mark the spot beneath which were their Churinga. The descendant of Abmoara is now living, and one of the two stones is her *Nanja*. The descendant of Kuperta died recently, and it will be some time before she will again undergo reincarnation.

In the following accounts, which refer to the wanderings of Erlia, or emu, Yarumpa, or honey-ant, and Echunpa, or lizard men, we omit the greater part of the details, as these are closely similar to those already given in the case of other totemic groups.

WANDERINGS OF THE EMU MEN

These people originated at a place called Erliunpa, about ten miles to the east of Giles Creek, which is situated eighty or a hundred miles east of Alice Springs. A party of men, accompanied by three women, left this place, travelling nearly due west. They carried *Nurtunjas* on their heads, and their bodies were at first covered with feathers, which they gradually shed along their line of route until at last they had all disappeared. Their first camping place was at Oniara, where they went into the ground. They came out at Ulpira and travelled to Karpirakura, a little west of Soda Creek, where they found a group of emu people of both sexes. Here they left a number of men and travelled on in a general westerly direction, following the trend of the main Macdonnell Ranges and forming totem centres at various spots as they went along, the exact locality of which is known to the natives. About fifty miles to the west of Alice Springs they shed their few remaining feathers, and a short distance beyond what is now called Glen Helen, they entered the earth and did not come out until they reached Apaura in the Belt Range, at the western end of the Macdonnells, where they found and stayed with a local group of emu men and women, forming there an important emu totem centre.

WANDERINGS OF THE HONEY-ANT PEOPLE

The Yarumpa or honey-ant people, who were of all classes, originated at a place called Ilyaba, in the Mount Hay country. From this spot, which is the great centre of the totem, they dispersed in various directions. A great *Oknirabata*, named Abmyaungwirria, started out from Ilyaba to see what the country out northwards was like, and, returning after many days, told his people that he had found another mob of honey-ants far away in the north-east, and that he intended leading a party to them. After performing a lot of ceremonies which the women were allowed to see, he started off with the party, and after finding two or three honey-ant men living in the scrub in various places (it may be noted that the honey-ant is found in mulga scrub), they came to Inkalitcha, where the water-hole by which they camped was dry. They suffered much from thirst, and so opened veins in their arms and drank blood, some of the old men consuming immense quantities. Then they went into the ground, and alternately travelling above and under ground, came to a spot on the Burt Plain, where it is related that they made *Ilpirla* This is a drink made by steeping the bodies of the honey-ants in water, and then kneading them until the honey is pressed out and mixed with the water. The *Ilpirla* was mixed in the hafts of their shields. After drinking some of it the *Oknirabata* left the party, and went on ahead to find the honey-ant people whom he had seen before. He found them at Koarpirla making an Engwura, and, returning at once to his party, he led them to that place. The local people were very angry, and refused to have anything to do with them, and moreover they opened veins in their arms, making such a flood that all the party were drowned except the *Oknirabata* who returned to Ilyaba, where finally he died. A black hill covered with black stones arose where the wanderers perished, and their Churinga are now in the store-house of the local group. A spring of fresh water is said to mark the central spot of the Engwura ground, which lies far out in sand-hill country, and has the natives say, never been visited by white men.

Another party of honey-ant people started out west under the guidance of two *Oknirabata*. At a place called Tanulpma a large *Nurtunja* was erected, and here one of the leaders remained behind with the *Nurtunja*, a large gum tree arising to mark the spot where this stood. At Umpira the party met a honey-ant woman, who, like all those seen along the course of their travels, had a *Nurtunja* and *quabara undattha*. When she died a large stone arose to mark the spot, and this is the *Nanja* of her living descendant. At Umpira *Ariltha* was performed upon some of the party. Then they travelled on to Lukaria, where they found a large number of honey-ant men and women who had many *Nurtunjas*. On seeing the strangers the women were very angry, and assumed a threatening attitude, stamping and beating the air with their palms extended outwards, shouting "*Yalika pira arinilla litchila Churinga oknirra ninunja*" (Stop; don't advance; we have many Churinga). The party, frightened, camped a little distance away, where they erected a *Nurtunja* and performed *Ariltha*. The local honey-ants did not come near to them. They travelled on westwards, camping near Mount Heuglin and on the Dashwood Creek, and forming various totem centres. At a place called Amulapirta they stayed for a few hours performing *Ariltha*, and all the men had intercourse with a Panunga honey-ant woman.

On the north side of the Belt Range they camped by the side of a creek, and here they erected their *Nurtunja*, and were too tired to take it up again. While travelling on they heard a loud *arri-inkuma*—a special form of shouting—and soon found themselves face to face with a large number of honey-ants at a place called Unapuna. The local people resented their coming, and at once drew forth floods of blood from their arms, with the result that all the strangers were drowned, their Churinga remaining behind and giving rise to an important Yarumpa or honey-ant totem centre.

WANDERINGS OF THE LIZARD MEN

In the Alcheringa a man of the Illunja (jew lizard) totem, who sprung up at Simpson's Gap at a spot high up on the eastern wall, now marked by a column called by white men the Sentinel, journeyed away underground to a place called Ulira, east of Arltunja, where there were a number of Echunpa or big lizard people, who originated there, but, unlike the lizards of the Simpson's Gap locality, they always fed on lizards. The Illunja man had brought with him a lot of Owadowa, a grass seed which formed the food of the Simpson's Gap lizard people. Some of this he consumed on the road, and the rest he offered to the Ulira lizard people, who declined it, so he placed it on the ground, a large stone now marking the spot.

Having induced the Echunpa people to accompany him, they all started back for Simpson's Gap, carrying a number of Churinga but no *Nurtunja*. On the way they ate Echunpa, the Illunja man joining them in doing so. Travelling westward, they camped at various places, and at one spot near to the Love Creek the younger men, whose duty it was to provide and cook the lizards for the older ones, only brought in a little to the old men, who were angry and called then *Unkirertwa*, that is, greedy men, and to punish them caused them to become *anchinya*, that is, grey-haired.

At Irulchirtna they made *quabara undattha*, carrying Churinga on their heads, as shown during one of the Engwura ceremonies which represented one of those performed during this march. Here it was that some men of the Thippa-thippa (a bird totem) came and danced round them as they performed, and were afterwards changed into birds, which still hover over the Echunpa lizards and show the natives where they are to be found. Leaving Irulchirtna, they still carried their Churinga on their heads, and the Thippa-thippa ran round looking at them. At a place on the Todd River in the Emily Plain they stayed some time performing *Tapurta*, that is, a long series of lizard ceremonies, and then moving on a little further, the party was divided into two by the Illunja man. One lot went away south to somewhere in the region of Erldunda, and the other kept on a westerly course till Illaba, not far from the Heavitree Gap near Alice Springs, was reached. Here it is said that a Purula man who had a stumpy tail left the party, intending to go away, but changed his mind and returned. Then they went to what is now a large clay pan, called Conlon's lagoon, where *Tapurta* were again performed. Here a thin, emaciated man was left, and where he died arose a stone, the rubbing of which may cause emaciation in other people. This stone is charged with *Arungquiltha*, or evil influence.

At Conlon's lagoon the Illunja man left the rest and went on ahead to Simpson's Gap, where he wanted to muster the Alexandra parakeet, small rat (Untaina), and Ilura (a lizard, a species of Nephrurus) people. The Alexandra parakeet people have, since that time, been changed into the bird which is supposed to inhabit caves underground, out of which it comes every now and then in search of grass seed.

The lizard party came on and camped at Atnakutinga near Attack Gap, and then proceeded to the south of Temple Bar Gap, and from there followed up the Ross Creek where the Illunja man met them. A little further on they found a lizard man whose descendant now lives at Alice Springs. At length they reached Simpson's Gap and then they danced in front of the people who were assembled, and after that a long series of sacred ceremonies was performed. Then the Illunja man and one of the Echunpa returned underground to Ulirra where they stayed altogether.

The lizard people left some of their party at the Gap; three of them being very thin and emaciated died, and the stones which arose to mark the spot are charged with *Arungquiltha*. The rest of the party travelled north, still eating lizards, until they reached Painta Springs on the northern side of the Macdonnell Range and the southern edge of the Burt Plains. Travelling northward they passed Hanns' Range, and at a place called Ilangara they were too tired to go further and so joined the Iwutta (nail-tailed wallaby) people who lived there. Their Churinga were deposited in two spots close to the storehouse of the Iwutta.

THE UNTHIPPA WOMEN

In dealing with the wanderings of the fourth group of the Achilpa people reference was made to some dancing women called *Unthippa* who were met at a place called Yapilpa. The women were *Oruncha*, that is what is usually translated "devil" women, which implies that they were of an evil nature, always ready to annoy human beings, and endowed with special superhuman powers of various kinds. As explained, however, in the case of the *Oruncha* men the word "devil" must not be taken in the sense of their being at all the equivalents of malicious creatures whose one object was to work ill to men and women; they are more mischievous than malicious, and in this instance the term "uncanny" more nearly expresses the idea associated with them.

These women were supposed to have sprung into existence far out in the *Aldorla ilunga*, that is the west country, and as they journeyed they danced all the way along carrying shields and spear-throwers until they passed right through the country of the Arunta people. When they started they were half women and half men, but before they had proceeded very far on their journey their organs became modified and they were as other women.

When they arrived at a place in the vicinity of Glen Helen they found a number of Okranina or carpet snake people who were assembled at an *Apulla* where they were about to perform the rite of circumcision upon some *Wurtjas*, that is boys who had undergone the preparatory painting and throwing up which form the first of the initiatory rites. Such women as were *Unawa* to the boys took the latter on their shoulders and carried them along with them, leaving them at various spots *en route*, after performing *lartna* on them. Women were also left occasionally.

Somewhere out west of the River Jay the women changed their language to Arunta and began feeding on *mulga* seed, on which they afterwards subsisted. Upon arrival at a place called Wankima, about a hundred miles further to the east, their sexual organs dropped cut from sheer exhaustion, caused by their uninterrupted dancing, and it was these which gave rise to well-known deposits of red ochre. The women then entered the ground and nothing more is known of them except that it is supposed that a great womanland exists far away to the east where they finally sat down.

The long ridge of quartzite ranges which forms a marked feature in the surface configuration of the country, in the region of the Macdonnell Ranges, and extends east and west for more than 200 miles, forming the southern boundary of the long narrow Horn or Mereenie valley, arose to mark the line of travel which they followed.

The *Unthippa* dance, which is performed during the ceremonies concerned at the present time with *lartna*, refers to these women. Upon the night when the boy is taken to the ceremonial ground the women approach, carrying shields and spear-throwers, and dance as the *Unthippa* women did in the Alcheringa, while the men sing, time after time, the refrain "the range all along," referring to the march of the *Unthippa* which the women are dancing in imitation of. At a later time also in the ceremony, after the boy has been painted and advanced to the grade of *Wurtja*, and just before the performance of the actual ceremony, one of the women (not, however, as in the case of the *Unthippa* an *Unawa* woman, but one who is *Mura* to the boy), placing her head between his legs suddenly lifts him up on her shoulders and runs off with him, as in the Alcheringa the *Unthippa* women did, but, unlike what happened in the past, the boy is again seized by the men and brought back. Whatever these remarkable *Unthippa* women may have been, the myth concerning them, which has evidently arisen to account for certain curious features in the initiation ceremonies, may be regarded as evidence that there was a time when women played a more important part in regard to such ceremonies than they do at the present time.

TRADITION OF ERKINCHA

In the Alcheringa one of the wandering parties of Achilpa or wild cat men were under the guidance of an old *Oknirabata* named Atnimma-la-truripa, who was renowned for the size of his penis (the native word is *pura*, being the same as that for tail, kangaroo tail, for example, is *okira pura*). He was always gorgeously decorated with down, especially the *pura*. This party camped near to the waterhole at Ooraminna, where they made an Engwura. While there they discovered a group of wild cat men who were suffering from the disease called *Erkincha*, or *Yerakincha*, and smelt most offensively. The southern Achilpa men had intended to settle here, but the presence of these men frightened them and they hurried away northwards.

Shortly after the wild cat men had gone a party of men who belonged to the Arwarlinga (a species of Hakea) totem, who dwelt close by in the sand hills, came in and went to the top of the Ooraminna rockhole and made what is called *abmoara*that is a favourite drink of the natives made by steeping Hakea flowers in water. The water was held in their wooden vessels, and then, opening veins in their arms, they allowed the blood to flow into the vessels and mix with the *abmoara*, until the vessels overflowed to such an extent that the Ooraminna Creek became flooded and all of the *Erkincha* men were drowned. A stone arose at the spot where the diseased men perished, and since the days of the Alcheringa this stone has been known as *Aperta atnumbira* (*aperta*, stone; *atnumbira* signifies a diseased growth issuing from the anus). Ever since this time the *Erkincha* has been prevalent amongst the natives, and it is believed that old men visiting the stone can, by means of rubbing it and muttering a request to the contained *Arungquiltha*, or evil influence, to go out, cause the disease to be communicated to any individual or even group of men whom they desire to injure.[151]

THE SNAKE OF IMYUNGA

About fifty miles north-north-west of Alice Springs there is a gorge opening out from the northern ridge of the Macdonnell Range on to the Burt Plain. In the gorge is a waterfall with a small permanent pool at its base which is said to be inhabited by the spirit of a great dead snake and by some living snakes, the descendants of the former. The spot is called Imyunga, and is in the centre of an Ingwitchika or grass seed locality. Here, in the Alcheringa, there lived a woman of the totem who was very expert in gathering the grass seed on which she fed, but she suffered great annoyance and was very angry because the people of the same totem who dwelt with her were always stealing her grass seed, so she journeyed far away to the south-west beyond Erldunda and brought back with her an enormous snake. She took the latter to her camp at Imyunga and there it ate up all the Ingwitchika thieves, after which it lived in the waterhole. It was long after the Alcheringa before it died, in fact it was seen by the grandfathers of some old men still living, and it was finally killed by a great flood which came down over the waterfall and washed it out of its hole. In the range there are great caverns which are occupied by the spirit of the snake. Some of its descendants are seen occasionally in the waterhole, to the eastern side of which no man dare go except at the risk of being sucked under the ranges—a fate which has, more than once, overtaken men who ventured too near, though it is a long time now since such a thing happened. When approaching the waterfall men always stop and sing out several times to give the snake warning of their approach, for it would make him angry if he were taken by surprise.

Close by the waterfall is the storehouse of the local group in which all the Churinga are of stone. The *Churinga nanja* of the woman referred to is ornamented on one side only with a number of series of concentric circles which are supposed to represent her breasts, her name being Urlatcha (breasts).

THE FIRE TOTEM

In the Alcheringa a spark of fire (*urinchitha*) ascended into the sky at Urapuncha, the place of fire, which lies far away in the north and was blown by the north wind to a spot now indicated by a large mountain also called Urapuncha, or Mount Hay. Here it fell to earth and a great fire sprang up which by and by subsided, and from the ashes came out some *Inapertwa* creatures—the ancestors of the people of the fire totem. These *Inapertwa* were after a time discovered by two wild duck (Wungara) men who flew over from the west and both of whom were Bulthara, one being called Erkung-ir-quilika and the other Mura-wilyika. They came from Ilalil-kirika close to the junction of the Hugh and Jay Rivers, and made the *Inapertwa* into men and women, after which they flew back to their camp in the west. The remains of the great fire still smoulders on the top of the mountain where the sacred storehouse of the totem is located, and at night time, especially if the night be dark and rainy, the fire can be seen from a long distance. Close to the storehouse is a great block of stone which in the Alcheringa was the piece of wood used by the great leader of the fire people, who was called Yarung-unterin-yinga, for the purpose of being rubbed by the *amera* or spear-thrower when he made fire. The *amera* is represented in the storehouse by a Churinga.

THE ORIGIN OF FIRE

In the Alcheringa a man of the Arunga or euro totem, named Algurawartna, started from a place named Ililkinja out in the east in pursuit of a gigantic euro which carried fire in its body. The man carried with him two big Churinga with which he tried to make fire, but could not. He followed the euro as it travelled westwards, trying all the time to kill it. The man and the euro always camped a little distance away from one another. One night Algurawartna awoke and saw a fire burning by the euro; he at once went up to it and took some, with which he cooked some euro flesh which he carried with him and upon which he fed. The euro ran away, turning back along its old tracks to the east. Still trying to make fire, but without success, the man followed until they once more came to Ililkinja, where at length Algurawartna succeeded in killing the euro with his Churinga. He examined the body carefully to see how the animal made fire, or where it came from, and pulling out the penis, which was of great length, he cut it open and found that it contained very red fire, which he took out and used to cook his euro with. For a long time he lived on the body of the big euro, and when the fire which he had taken from its body went out he tried fire-making (*urpmala*) again and was successful, always singing the *urpmala* chant:—

"Urpmalara kaiti
Alkna munga
Ilpau wita wita."

THE ORUNCHERTWA AND THE OKNIRABATA

In the Alcheringa a number of men belonging to the Unchipera (little bat) and the Erlkintera (large white bat) totems set out from Imanda. They were *Orunchertwa*, that is "devil" men, and upon arrival at a place called Etuta they went up into the sky, but not very high up. From this position they killed men who walked about on the earth beneath.

An old *Oknirabata* lay down at Etuta and two boys played about aiming at trees with spears. These two boys heard the *Orunchertwa* sing out and were killed by them. Then the old *Oknirabata* was angry and went to his sacred storehouse which was close at hand, and took out a large stone Churinga; sitting down he held this in both hands, and pointing it towards the *Orunchertwa* he brought them down to earth, and then with the Churinga cut them in pieces.

ASSOCIATION OF BIRDS WITH PARTICULAR TOTEMS

Around each of the *Ilthura*, or sacred holes of the witchetty grub totem, at which a part of the *Intichiuma* ceremony is performed, there are certain stones standing on end which represent special birds called Chantunga. These birds are looked upon as the *ilqualthari*, or the mates of the witchetty people, because in the Alcheringa certain witchetty *maegwa*, that is the fully-grown grub, changed into the birds. The latter abound at the time when the grub is plentiful and are very rarely seen at other times, and they are then supposed to sing joyously and to take an especial delight, as they hop about amongst the Udnirringa bushes all day long, in watching the *maegwa* laying its eggs. The witchetty men will not eat the bird, as they say that to do so would make them "*atnitta takurna irima*" (which literally means stomach, bad, to see) if they were to do so, and they speak affectionately of it.

In the Okira or kangaroo totem the men have as *ilquathari*, grass parrots called Atnalchulpira, who in the Alcheringa were the *Uwinna*, that is the fathers' sisters, of the Okira men, to whom they brought water as the birds do at the present day, according to the native belief, to the kangaroos in the dry country, where they are always found hovering about these animals. Associated also with the kangaroo people are the birds called Kartwungawunga, who are the descendants of certain kangaroo men of the Alcheringa who were always killing and eating kangaroos and euro, and changed into the little birds who are often seen playing about on the backs of these animals.

The Arunga or euro people have as mates the rock pigeon or Inturita, who in the Alcheringa were the *Uwinna* of the euro men, whom they furnished with water just as the natives say that the bird now does for the animals in the dry ranges. The euro men have a second mate in the form of the Unchurunqua, a small beautifully coloured bird (*Emblema picta*), the painted finch, which in the Alcheringa was a euro man. In the Alcheringa these euro men are said to have been great eaters of euro, and their bodies were always drenched with blood which dripped from the bodies of the euros which they killed and carried with them, and that is why the painted finch is splashed with red.

The Yarumpa or honey-ant people have as mates a little bird called Alatipa, which, like the Yarumpa itself (*Camponotus inflatus*), only frequents *mulga* scrub country. They also have as mates another bird called Alpirtaka, which is a small "magpie," which also frequents mulga scrub. Both birds were once honey-ant people.

The emu people have as mate the little striated wren (*Amytis striata*), which they call Lirra-lirra; and the Echunpa or big lizard people have a smaller lizard (*Varanus punctatus*), which they call Ilchaquara.

The Quatcha or water people have the waterfowl as their mate; and the Urliwatchera, a large lizard (*Varanus gouldii*) people, have a small scincoid lizard called Irpanta.

All these mates of the people of various totems are held in affectionate regard by those to whom they are especially related, but except in the case of the mates of the witchetty grubs there does not seem to be any restriction with regard to their not being eaten. Certain totems, such as the wild cat, the Hakea flower and the crow, are apparently without any mates of this kind.

In addition to these birds which are regarded as mates or the members of various totems, there are others which are regarded as representing men of the Alcheringa of particular totems which became extinct. Thus the little scarlet-fronted Ephithanura (*E. tricolor*) which the natives call Ninchi-lappa-lappa were men who in the Alcheringa continually painted themselves with red ochre, until finally they changed into the bird. Again, in connection with the wanderings of a group of lizard men, we meet with a tradition which says that as they wandered across the country in the region of Simpson's Gap in the Macdonnell Ranges they came across a group of people of the Atninpirichira or Princess Alexandra Parakeet totem. For some reason they all changed into the birds, and now they live far underground, only coming up at intervals near their old camping ground to look for grass seed on which they feed—an allusion probably to the fact that this particular bird has a strange habit of completely disappearing out of the district for years at a time and then suddenly appearing in large numbers.

Associated with the lizard people is a small bird called Thippa-thippa. In the Alcheringa these were men of that totem who came and danced round the lizard people as they performed ceremonies, and for some reason were transformed into the birds, which have ever since continued to hover round the lizards, and by doing so often show the natives where the animal is to be found. In one of the ceremonies of the Engwura they were represented by two men who danced around a lizard man.

Chapter XII

Customs Concerned with Knocking out of Teeth; Nose-Boring; Growth of Breasts; Blood, Blood-Letting, Blood-Giving, Blood-Drinking; Hair; Childbirth; Food Restrictions; Cannibalism

Operation of tooth knocking out in the case of males after the performance of the *Quatcha Intichiuma*—Explanation of the ceremony given by the natives—Operation in the case of females—Throwing the tooth towards the mother's camp in the Alcheringa—Comparison of the ceremony with that of other parts of Australia—Nose-boring ceremony—Men painting the breasts of a girl with fat and red ochre after charming it—To be regarded as a ceremony of initiation—Customs concerned with menstruation—Drinking blood when starting on an avenging party—Blood-drinking at meetings of reconciliation—Blood-letting at sacred ceremonies—Painting the *Kauaua* with blood—The blood after the ceremony of *Ariltha* upon a woman in the Kaitish and northern tribes—Deposits of red ochre associated with women's blood—Giving blood to men and women to strengthen them—Charming fat and red ochre and rubbing it over sick people—Part of the reproductive organs of an opossum or kangaroo used to strengthen women—Distribution of human hair—Customs at childbirth, making the umbilical cord into a necklet—Food restrictions—Totemic—The wild cat must not be eaten—Food killed by certain individuals may not be eaten—The projecting of a man's smell into food—Men who have to be supplied with food by any individual man belong to his wife's side of the tribe—Restrictions during pregnancy—Food restrictions for boys and girls with penalties attached—Cannibalism in the traditions—Killing and eating a younger child in the Luritcha tribe.

KNOCKING OUT OF TEETH

THIS is a rite to which individuals of both sexes must sooner or later submit, if they happen to belong to one or other of the various groups which inhabit what is called the *Kartwia Quatcha*, or rain country, which lies in the north-east of the area of the country occupied by the Arunta tribe. It is evident that the rite is one the significance of which, so far as this tribe is concerned, has undergone very considerable change in course of time. As a general rule it is performed before marriage, but not always, and when not done at an early age, the natives give as a reason that the boy or girl was too frightened, an excuse which would not gain a minute's delay if the ceremony were one concerned with initiation, and that such should be made shows that the ceremony is not one to which any very great importance is now attached.

The operation always takes place after the Water *Intichiuma* ceremony has been performed, and in the case of a fully-grown man, it is performed on the *Intichiuma* ground. It is impossible to find out why the ceremony has become so especially associated with the rain or water totem, though at the same time it must be remembered that it is performed, not infrequently, on men and women of other totems; in fact any one, whatever his or her totem be, may undergo the rite at pleasure, but in the case of just the one totem it is obligatory, or practically so, though at the same time the non-observance of the custom would not prevent any man from being admitted to the secrets of the tribe, but it would subject him to what is most dreaded by the native, and that is the constant ridicule of the other men and women, with whom he is in daily contact. The explanation, evidently devised by the natives to account for the special association of the custom with the rain totem, is that the object of the rite is to produce in the face a resemblance to what they call *Alailinga*, which is the name applied to certain clouds, dark with a light margin, which are of peculiar appearance and are said to portend the coming of rain. There evidently was, as will be seen later on, a time when the ceremony had a much deeper meaning than it has at the present day.

If the operation be performed on a man he lies down on his back, resting his head on the lap of a sitting man who is his tribal *Oknia* (elder brother), or else a man who is *Unkulla* to him (mother's brother's son). The latter pinions his arms and then another *Okilia* or *Unkulla* fills his mouth with furstring for the purpose, partly, they say, of absorbing the blood and partly of deadening the pain, and partly also to prevent the tooth from being swallowed. The same man then takes a piece of wood, usually the sharp hard end of a spear, in which there is a hole made, and, pressing it firmly against the tooth, strikes it sharply with a stone. When the tooth is out, he holds it up for an instant so that it can be seen by all, and while uttering a peculiar, rolling, guttural sound throws it away as far as possible in the direction of the *Mira Mia Alcheringa*, which means the camp of the man's mother in the Alcheringa. The man who has been operated upon then gets up and picks up some boomerangs which he throws at a shield which has been fixed upright in the ground some little distance away, throwing them gently so as not to hurt the shield. There is no singing or demonstration of any kind, other than that described, but the mother of the man must provide an offering of *mirna*, that is seed food of some kind, or "yams," and send it to the tribal *Okilia* or *Unkulla* who performed the operation, and he, in his turn, must provide an offering of food for the use of the man on whom he operated, which is a curious reversal of the usual rule, according to which it is necessary, in all other cases with which we are acquainted, for the man who has been operated upon to provide the operator with food.[152]

In the case of boys the operation is performed away from the *Intichiuma* ground near to which they may not go, and at this ceremony women may be present, for with regard to the

Intichiuma ground the same restriction applies to them as to boys. The performance is carried out in the same way as described, and the same rules apply with regard to the offering of food.

When a woman or girl is to be operated on, a little space is cleared near to the main camp where men and women all assemble, except only those who are *Mura* to the girl. A tribal *Okilia* sits down and the girl lies with her head in his lap, and the operation is conducted as in the case of the men and boys, being almost always performed by a tribal *Okilia*. The tooth when taken out is lifted up with the same guttural sound and thrown in the direction of the mother's Alcheringa camp. The girl now springs to her feet, and seizing a small *pitchi* which has been placed close at hand for the purpose, fills it with sand, and dancing over the cleared space agitates the *pitchi* as if she were winnowing seed. When it is emptied she resumes her seat amongst the women. Previous to the operation the *Okilia* places in her hair a topknot of feathers of a cockatoo, which is returned to him later on. The girl, not her mother, must now provide an offering of seed food for the use of the operating *Okilia*, and he in his turn must send her an offering of meat.

Amongst the Kaitish tribe the operation on men is performed by tribal *Okilia*, and on women and girls by tribal *Ungaraitcha* (elder sisters), and in both cases, just as in the Arunta and Ilpirra tribes, the tooth is, when extracted, thrown in the direction of the mother's Alcheringa camp.

The existence as well as the details accompanying the performance of this custom in these central tribes is of considerable interest. As is well known, it forms amongst many of the eastern and south-eastern tribes of Australia the most important initiation ceremony, after passing through which the young men are admitted to the status of manhood. Amongst the central tribes it has no such significance, and it is not even of universal occurrence amongst them. At the same time, the ceremony which accompanies the operation may in all probability be regarded as indicative of a time when it was a more important rite than it is at the present day. Circumcision and sub-incision are amongst these tribes the initiation rites, and they are as characteristic in this respect of the central tribes as the knocking out of teeth is of certain tribes of the east and south-east of the continent. If, however, we examine more in detail the accounts of the ceremony as conducted in the Arunta and certain of the latter tribes, we find unmistakable points of agreement which are difficult to account for on any supposition except that the two have had a common origin in times past.

Blandowskisup[153] in writing of certain Victorian natives, says, that on arriving at manhood, a youth was conducted by three leaders of the tribe into the recesses of the woods, where he remained two days and one night. Being furnished with a suitable piece of wood, he knocked out two of the front teeth of his upper jaw, and on returning to the camp gave them to his mother. Then he again returned to the woods for the same length of time. During his absence, his mother selected a young gum tree and inserted in the bark of the fork of two of the topmost branches the teeth which had been knocked out. This was ever afterwards in some sense held sacred. It was only known to certain persons of the tribe, and the youth himself was never allowed to know where his teeth had been placed. If the youth died, then the base of the tree was stripped of its bark, and it was killed by fire, so that it might remain as a monument of the dead man. It may be remarked, that it would be more likely to remain as a monument if it were not killed, and that probably this was not the real reason for destroying it.

Collins,[154] in an excellent account of the rite as practised amongst the natives of a New South Wales tribe, describes how a throwing stick was made, and with this the tooth was knocked out by means of hitting it with a stone. The last performance before the actual operation consisted in a man standing out with a shield in one hand and a club in the other, "striking the shield with the club, at every third stroke the whole party poised and presented their spears at him, pointing them inwards and touching the centre of the shield. This concluded the ceremonies previous to the operation; and it appeared significant of an exercise which was to form the principal business of their lives, the use of the spear." Further on he says, "The natives when speaking of the loss of the tooth always use the word yor-lahng era-ba-diahng," which "appears to be compounded of the name given to the spot where the principal scene takes place, and of the most material qualification that is derived from the whole ceremony, that is, the throwing of the spear."

Though Collins does not state anything very definite with regard to whom the teeth were given, we can gather indirectly, but at the same time quite clearly, that they came into the possession of certain women. He says, "Ben-nil-long's sister and Da-ring-ha, Cole-be's wife, hearing the author express a great desire to become possessed of some of these teeth, procured them for him;" and again, "one of the boys who had undergone the operation had formerly lived with the principal surgeon of the settlement till that gentleman's departure for England. A female relative of this boy brought the teeth to the author with a request that he would send them to Mr. White; thus with gratitude remembering after the lapse of some years the attention which that gentleman had shown to her relative."

In these accounts we see, certainly modified in detail but yet agreeing in essential points, the two significant features of spear-throwing and of the presenting of the teeth to some female relative of the person operated upon. The idea which evidently lies at the root of the ceremony in both the Arunta and Kaitish tribes on the one hand, and the Victorian and

New South Wales tribes on the other hand, is that the individual operated upon has ceased to be a mere boy or girl as the case may be, and has passed from the control of the mother into the ranks of the men or women, and the tooth is probably given to the mother or female relative as an indication of this. In those tribes in which the ceremony is one of initiation it is not of course practised, at the present day, upon women, but when it ceases to be an important ceremony of initiation, then the same idea is, as it were, carried over to the women along with the ceremony itself.

In the Central Australian tribes for example, the rite has ceased to hold the importance which it still retains, or rather did until the advent of the white man and their consequent extinction, amongst the tribes of the eastern coastal district. In the former it has given place to a new and presumably more recently developed form of initiation ceremony—that of circumcision followed by sub-incision. Whilst this change has been brought about, the original rite has persisted in the form of what we have before spoken of as a rudimentary custom, and, losing its original significance, as applied to men only, has been extended, so that now it is common to both sexes. In its earlier form, the tooth when extracted is given to the mother, or at least (judging from Collins's account) to some female relative. In its rudimentary state, as in the Arunta tribe, we find that the tooth is thrown in the direction of the camp of the Alcheringa mother, which may perhaps be explained as indicating that in the Alcheringa, or rather the early times to which this name is given, the mother was entitled to the tooth. The natives can, as might have been expected, give no reason for the custom, and the performance of this is certainly not now associated with the idea of showing to any living woman that the boy has passed out of her control this idea being, as we have already seen, expressed in one of the ceremonies connected with initiation, as now practised.

Of equal interest with the disposal of the tooth is the curious custom in the Arunta of the erection of a shield at which the man who has been operated upon throws boomerangs, but without hurting it. This is clearly the equivalent of the gentle striking of the shield by the spears in the New South Wales tribe, as described by Collins. In the one case the men assembled touch the shield with their spears, in the other the man who has been operated upon throws boomerangs at it, but in both we have the fundamental idea represented that the individual passing through the ceremony has arrived at the age of manhood when he may use the weapons by which the men both defend themselves and secure their prey.

In the Arunta and Kaitish tribe we find, when the rite is extended to include women as well as men, that the same two fundamental ideas are expressed. The tooth is thrown in the direction of the mother's Alcheringa camp, a feature carried over from the man's to the woman's ceremony, and secondly, we have the curious ceremony of the emptying of the *pitchi* which the girl carries on her head, and which may be regarded as indicative of the fact that she has reached the age when she can enter upon the duties of a woman, not the least important of which is symbolised by the *pitchi* filled with food, gathered in the bush, which she carries daily poised on the top of her head.

It can scarcely be doubted that there is a common origin for these customs in the central and coastal tribes—the details of agreement just referred to are, it seems to us, inexplicable except on this hypothesis. This would seem to imply, inasmuch as in one group of tribes we find tooth extraction the important ceremony, with no trace of the form of ceremonies (circumcision, &c.) practised in the other group, whilst in the latter, side by side with the present initiation rite, we find tooth extraction in the form of a rudimentary custom, that the more ancient ceremony is that of tooth extraction.

We have spoken hitherto as if it might be almost taken for granted that the latter rite was in all cases originally restricted to men, and that when, as in the central tribes, we find it practised by both sexes, it is to be regarded as a custom which, losing its sacred significance, was, as it were, passed on to the women, who then shared in it equally with the men. We do not in reality, by any means, desire to imply that this was of necessity the case. Into the question of what was the origin of the custom it seems hopeless to inquire. Whether it always had a sacred significance as it has at the present day, or whether it is a custom to which in course of time the present sacred nature as an initiation ceremony became, as it were, tacked on to its previous attributes, is a problem which will probably never be settled. What we wish to draw attention to now is the fact that in the traditions of the Arunta tribe we have, so far as they are worth anything as evidence in this direction, the clearest possible indication of a past time when the things now regarded as so sacred that if seen by a woman she would be put to death, were not thus tabu to women. In tradition after tradition we have accounts set out in great detail of how particular women of the Alcheringa carried the sacred *Nurtunja* just as the men did, and of how they had Churinga just as the men had, and further, of how they performed sacred ceremonies exactly as the men did. It can scarcely be held that these traditions are merely fanciful creations of the men; if so it is a curious feature that they have been built up amongst a people to whose ideas of the fitness of things as they are now and probably have been for some time past, any such acquaintance of the women with the sacred objects is utterly foreign. It seems more probable that the traditions do really indicate the former existence of a time when, in this respect, men and women were upon terms of greater equality than they are now. This being so it will be seen that it is at all events unsafe to take for granted that even as a rite of initiation the knocking out of teeth has always been confined to men. There are, it appears to us, two theories, in favour of either of which many arguments might be adduced. According to the first of these the knocking out of teeth may be regarded from the very first as a sacred rite of initiation confined to the men; in those tribes in which it has remained as the rite of initiation it has always been so confined to the men, while in others it has been superseded by more elaborate rites and has been passed on to the women when once its sacred character was lost. A second theory would regard the custom of knocking out of teeth as, at first, unconnected with any rite of initiation, and as practised by both men and women. Starting from this basis the customs, as we find them now developed, may be supposed to have followed one or other of two lines. Along the first, for some unknown reason, the rite came to be associated with initiation to, in the early days, both manhood and womanhood. After a time (and as pointed out it seems certain that changes in this direction have taken place) the rite came to be confined to men, and dropped out so far as women were concerned until, as in the eastern and south-eastern parts, it came to be a sacred ceremony confined to the men. Along the second line the rite came also to be associated with initiation both to manhood and womanhood, but its place, for some also unknown reason, came to be taken by a quite different ceremony in the case both of men and of women; for it must be remembered that in the tribes of the Centre the women have initiation rites just as the men have, only that the same sacredness is not attached to them as to those of the men. With the introduction of the new rites the old one of knocking out of a tooth lost its original significance and persisted as a rudimentary custom, the relationship of it to the same custom, still practised as an initiation rite in other tribes, being unmistakably shown by a remarkable similarity in the details of the ceremony as performed in the different tribes.

CEREMONY OF NOSE BORING

In the Arunta and Ilpirra tribes when a boy's nose has been bored, that is as soon as the operation has been completed, he strips a piece of bark off a gum tree, if possible, and throws it as far as he can in the direction of the Alcheringa camp of his mother, that is where the spirit individual of which his mother is the reincarnation lived in the Alcheringa. This little ceremony is called *ilyabara iwuma* or the bark-throwing, and the boy is told to do it by men who stand to him in the relation of *Arunga, Oknia*, and *Okilia*, who also tell him that the reason for doing it is that it will lessen the pain and promote the healing of the wound. When the nose of a girl is bored, which is usually by her husband very soon after she has passed into his possession, she fills a small wooden vessel with sand, and facing in the direction of the Alcheringa camp of her mother, executes a series of short jumps, keeping her feet close together and her legs stiff, while she makes the *pitchi* move as if she were winnowing seed until she gradually empties it, after which she simply resumes her ordinary occupation. Neglect to perform this ceremony would, so say the natives in explanation of it, be regarded as a grave offence against her mother.

PROMOTING THE GROWTH OF THE BREASTS

To promote the growth of the breasts of a girl, the men assemble at the *Ungunja* or men's camp, where they all join in singing long chants, the words of which express an exhortation to the breasts to grow, and others which have the effect of charming some fat and red ochre which men who are *Gammona*, that is, brothers of her mother, have brought to the spot, as well as head and arm bands of fur-string. These men belong to the other moiety of the tribe to that to which the girl belongs; if she, for example, be a Panunga, then they will be Kumara. At daylight one of them goes out and calls her to a spot close to the *Ungunja*, to which she comes accompanied by her mother. Here her body is rubbed all over with fat by the *Gammona* men, who then paint a series of straight lines of red ochre down her back and also down the centre of her chest and stomach. A wide circle is painted round each nipple and straight lines below each of these circles. Long strings of opossum fur-string are passed across each shoulder and under each arm-pit; numbers of neck-rings are put round her neck, several head-rings are placed on her forehead, and a number of tail tips are fixed so that they droop down over the forehead and ears. All these things have been charmed by the *Gammona* singing over them.

When this has been done the girl is taken out into the bush by her mother, who makes a camp there at some distance from the main one, and here the girl must stay until the *ilkinia* or lines on her body wear off, when, but not until when, she may return to the main camp. The girl wears the charmed necklets and head-rings until one by one they drop off and become worn out. As we have pointed out previously, this is to be regarded as a form of initiation ceremony concerned with women,[155] and may be looked upon as the equivalent of the first ceremony of throwing up and painting the boy.

VARIOUS CUSTOMS CONCERNED WITH BLOOD, BLOOD-LETTING, AND BLOOD-GIVING, &c.

In the Arunta and Ilpirra tribes a girl at the first time of menstruation is taken by her mother to a spot close to, but apart from, the *Erlukwirra* or women's camp, near to which no man ever goes. A fire is made and a camp formed by the mother, the girl being told to dig a hole about a foot or eighteen inches deep, over which she sits attended by her own and some other tribal *Mia*, who provide her with food, one or other of them being always with her, and sleeping by her side at night time. No children of either sex are allowed to go near to her or to speak to her. During the first two days she is supposed to sit over the hole without stirring away;

after that she may be taken out by one or other of the old women hunting for food. When the flow ceases she is told to fill in the hole. She now becomes what is called *Wunpa*, returns to the women's camp, and shortly afterwards undergoes the rite of *Atna-ariltha*, and is handed over to the man to whom she has been allotted. She remains *Wunpa* until such time as her breasts assume the pendent form so characteristic of the native women who have borne one or more children, after which she is spoken of as *Arakutja*, the name for a fully-grown woman.

Blood may be given by young men to old men of any degree of relationship and at any time with a view to strengthening the latter. When it is given to a man of the same moiety of the tribe as the donor it is drawn from a vein in the middle of the arm, and when to a man of the other moiety, it must be taken from a vein at the inner side of the arm. Occasionally it is drawn from the back of the hand, and still more rarely by the painful process of deeply puncturing the finger tips under the nail.

When starting on an avenging expedition or *Atninga* every man of the party drinks some blood, and also has some spurted over his body, so as to make him what is called *uchuilima*, that is, lithe and active. The elder men indicate from whom the blood is to be drawn, and the men so selected must not decline, though the amount drawn from a single individual is often very great; indeed, we have known of a case in which blood was taken from a young and strong man until he dropped down from sheer exhaustion.

In addition to the idea of strengthening the recipient, there is the further important belief that this partaking together of blood prevents the possibility of treachery. If, for example, an Alice Springs party wanted to go on an avenging expedition to the Burt country, and they had with them in camp a man of that locality, he would be forced to drink blood with them, and, having partaken of it, would be bound not to aid his friends by giving them warning of their danger. If he refused to drink the blood, then, as actually happened in one case known to the authors, his mouth would be forced open and blood poured into it, which would have just the same binding influence as if the drinking had been a voluntary one.

Blood-drinking is also associated with special meetings of reconciliation which sometimes take place between two groups who have been on bad terms with one another without actually coming to a fight. In this instance the group which is supposed to have suffered the injury sends a messenger to the old men of the offending group, who says, "Our people want you to come and have a friendly fight." This peculiar form of meeting is called *Umbirna ilirima*, which means "seeing and settling (things)." If the offending group be willing, which they are almost sure to be, then the meeting is held, and at the commencement each party drinks the blood of its own members, and a more or less sham fight takes place with boomerangs, no one being any the worse.

When a young man for the first time takes blood from another man, the latter becomes for a time tabu to him until he chooses to release the young man from the *intherta*, or ban of silence, by singing over his mouth.

Apart from these special occasions, blood is not infrequently used to assuage thirst and hunger; indeed, when under ordinary circumstances a blackfellow is badly in want of water, what he does is to open a vein in his arm and drink the blood.

Blood-letting is a prominent feature of certain sacred ceremonies, such as the *Intichiuma* rite, as practised by the kangaroo men at Undiara, the great centre of their totem, where the young men open veins in their arms and allow the blood to stream out on to, and over, the edge of the sacred ceremonial stone which represents the spot where a celebrated kangaroo of the Alcheringa went down into the earth, its spirit part remaining in the stone which arose to mark the place. In the same way at the *Intichiuma* of the Unjiamba or Hakea flower totem held at Ilyaba, blood from the arm is sprinkled over the stone which represents a mass of Unjiamba.

The sacred pole called the *Kauaua*, which is erected at the close of the Engwura ceremony, is painted all over with blood, and, in all sacred ceremonies, in fact, in many of the ordinary corrobborees down derived from either birds or plants is attached to the human body by blood drawn either from the arm or the subincised urethra.

Women are never allowed to witness the drawing of blood for decorative purposes; indeed, the feeling with regard to women seeing men's blood is such that when a quarrel takes place and blood is shed in the presence of women, it is usual for the man whose blood is first shed to perform a ceremony connected with his own or his father or mother's totem. This is in some manner supposed to be by way of reconciliation, and to prevent the continuance of ill-feeling. The special term given to these ceremonies is *Alua uparilima*, which means "the blood fading away." After a fight which took place recently, one of these ceremonies was performed by an Apungerta man of the witchetty grub totem. He personated a Chankuna (small berry) woman, to which totem his mother belonged, and was decorated with an elaborate head-dress representing the woman's digging-sticks, to which were affixed pendent bunches of feathers representing Chankuna bushes with the berries on them, which the woman was eating. There are also various customs relating to the blood of women which may be referred to here.

In the Kaitish and other northern tribes, when the rite of *Atna ariltha kuma* is performed on a young woman by an

Ungaraitcha or elder sister, the blood is collected in a special *pitchi* which is made for the purpose by an elder brother of the woman, and is taken to the camp, where the *Mia, Uwinna,* and other women both smear their bodies with it and drink some. It has been already described, in the account of the initiation ceremonies, that the blood which flows at the operation of *lartna* on a boy is taken to the women's camp and rubbed over the breasts and foreheads of women who are the elder sisters of the boy and of his mother.

The deposits of red ochre which are found in various parts are associated with women's blood. Near to Stuart's Hole, on the Finke River, there is a red ochre pit which has evidently been used for a long time; and tradition says that in the Alcheringa two kangaroo women came from Ilpilla, and at this spot caused blood to flow from the vulva in large quantities, and so formed the deposit of red ochre. Travelling away westward they did the same thing in other places. In much the same way it is related of the dancing *Unthippa* women that, at a place called Wankima, in the eastern part of the Arunta district, they were so exhausted with dancing that their organs fell out, and gave rise to the large deposits of red ochre found there.

Blood is occasionally given to both men and women to strengthen them when they are ill. When given to a man— and it is only given in very serious cases—it is drawn from the labia minora, and one of the women, taking first of all one of the several kinds of witchetty grubs which are eaten, dips this in the blood and gives it to the man to eat, after which his body is rubbed over with the blood and afterwards with grease and red ochre. When a woman is very ill and weak, one of her male *Umba,* to whom she is *Mia alkulla,* that is, he is the son of one of her younger sisters, may volunteer to strengthen her with his blood, in which case all the women and children are sent away from her. The man draws a quantity of blood from the subincised urethra, and she drinks part of it while he rubs the remainder over her body, adding afterwards a coating of red ochre and grease. If the woman recovers, she must not speak to the man, or to the men who accompany him, until such time as she has sent to him an offering of food. In all cases when a man or woman feels ill, the first thing that is done is to rub red ochre over the body, which may possibly be regarded in the light of a substitute for blood, just as sometimes a ceremonial object may be rubbed over with red ochre instead of blood. We may mention here also certain customs, which are concerned with the curing or strengthening of weak men and women.

In some cases of serious illness women will charm by "singing" it a mixture of fat and red ochre, which they rub into the body of the sick man, all classes taking part in the operation. If the man recovers he must not speak to any of the women, except his own *Unawa*, who took part in the ceremony, until after such time as he has made them an offering of meat. When this is done, the women assemble at some little distance from the *Erlukwirra* or women's camp, while the man, accompanied by his own and tribal *Okilia* (elder brothers) and *Oknia* (fathers), carries the meat, which is most likely kangaroo or euro flesh, and silently places it in front of the women, who then rub him over with red ochre, thus removing the ban of silence. The men and women then return to their respective camps, and the meat is cooked and eaten at the women's camp.

In the northern and western Arunta and in the Ilpirra tribe, for the purpose of strengthening a delicate woman, a part of the internal reproductive organs (called *ertoacha*) is taken from a male opossum, wallaby, euro, or kangaroo. The woman lies down on her back, and her husband placing the *ertoacha* upon the *mons veneris*, "sings" over it for some time after which the woman swallows it whole.

In some cases the same part of the animal is taken by the man and half cooked, after which he coats it with grease, charms it by singing over it, and then presents it to his wife; she has to swallow it whole without having any idea of the nature of the object, which, in this case, is given for the purpose of promoting sexual desire. For the same purpose fluid material from the *ertoacha* may be squeezed into the vulva.

CUSTOMS CONCERNED WITH HAIR

A man's hair always goes to some one who is either *Ikuntera* or *Umbirna* to him. Supposing a man has three sons, then each of them is made son-in-law to some special man whom he calls *Ikuntera-tualcha*. The latter has the first claim to the younger man's hair. Any which there may be to spare goes to the son of an *Ikuntera*, that is to a man who is *Umbirna* of the donor. In this way a man receives hair from (1) his actual mother-in-law (his principal supply), (2) from a *Gammona* or son-in-law, (3) from an *Umbirna* or brother-in law, while (4) under certain circumstances, already described, he receives a special supply from a particular *Umbirna* to whom he stands in the relationship of *Ungipinna*. In addition to these, which may be called his normal sources of supply, he will sometimes receive hair-string as a return for some favour rendered. For example, a man who belongs to a different totem from his father inherits the Churinga of the latter, but they still remain in the store-house of the father's local totemic group. A suitable present of such a valuable article as hair-string will often persuade the head man of the father's group to allow the son to remove, for a time, the Churinga of the former to the store-house in which his, *i.e.* the son's, Churinga is kept.

A man when cutting or having his hair cut, which he must do periodically, as it is his duty to present it to certain individuals, always squats facing the direction of the Alcheringa camp of his mother. If he fails to do this some great calamity will befall him.

At the close of the initiation ceremony of *Ariltha*, in the case of the Northern Arunta, the elder sisters of the boy cut off a few locks of his hair, which they keep for themselves.

The distribution of a dead man's hair has been already alluded to, as well as the fact that in these tribes the remarkable customs according to which a man's hair must be given to certain individuals have of necessity prevented the existence of the feeling, so strongly developed amongst many other Australian tribes, that on no account must a stranger be allowed to secure even the smallest fragment of hair.

CUSTOM AT CHILD BIRTH

When a child is born, the fact is notified to the father by his actual or a tribal *Mia*.

Before the child is born, the woman goes to the *Erlukwirra* or women's camp. If there be any difficulty in childbirth the husband, who is at his own camp, without saying anything strips off all his personal adornments, and empties his bag or wallet of knick-knacks on to the ground. Then a man who is *Mura* to him, without in any way referring to the matter, takes the hair-girdle, and proceeding to the *Erlukwirra*, near to which as a general rule no man may go, ties it tightly round the woman's body just under the breasts, and then returns to the husband's camp. Not a word is spoken, but if after a time the birth of the child is not announced, the husband, still quite unadorned, walks once or twice slowly, at a distance of about fifty yards, up and down past the *Erlukwirra* with a view to inducing the unborn child to follow him, which it is said rarely to fail to do.

After birth the umbilical cord is cut with a stone knife, or sometimes with the pointed end of a digging-stick at a distance of some inches from the body of the child. There is no ligature, but the cut end is frequently dressed with hot ashes. The afterbirth is burnt. After a few days the attached part of the cord is cut off by the mother, who by swathing it in fur-string makes it into a necklace called *Akurlaitcha*, which is placed round the child's neck. The necklace is supposed to facilitate the growth of the child, to keep it quiet and contented, to avert illness generally, and it also has the faculty of deadening to the child the noise of the barking of the camp dogs.

The painting of a black line over the eyebrow in imitation of the mark on the *Erathippa* stone has already been alluded to.

FOOD RESTRICTIONS

In the Urabunna tribe, as in the great majority of Australian tribes with regard to which we have information relating to their totemic systems, each individual is strictly forbidden to eat the animal or plant, the name of which he bears, as that of his totem. That is, for example, an emu man or woman must not in any way injure an emu, nor must he partake of its flesh even when he has not killed it himself.

The exact restrictions vary, however, to a certain extent in different tribes, in some apparently, such as the Urabunna, it applies at all times, in others, as described by Sir George Grey in the case of certain West Australian natives, the rule is observed at some but not at all times. Thus he says,[156] "a certain mysterious connection exists between a family and its *kobong*, so that a member of the family will never kill an animal of the species to which his *kobong* belongs; should he find it asleep, indeed he kills it reluctantly, and never without affording it a chance of escape. This arises from the family belief that some one individual of the species is their nearest friend, to kill whom would be a great crime, and carefully to be avoided. Similarly, a native who has a vegetable for his *kobong*, may not gather it under certain circumstances, and at particular times of the year."

In the Arunta and other Central Australian tribes, restrictions as to not eating the animal or plant because it bears the name of the individual's totem may be said to agree in actual practice with those just described with, however, this difference, that the Arunta native does not imagine that the animal or plant, or some particular one of the species, is his nearest friend. A man will eat only very sparingly of his totem, though there are certain special occasions on which, as a sacred ceremony, he partakes of his totemic animal or plant.

To this reference has been made elsewhere,[157] meanwhile it may be said here that, in broad outline, the Central Australian agree with the majority of Australian tribes in the general restriction according to which the totem is tabooed. That this has not, however, always been the case appears to be indicated by certain traditions in which we see very distinct references to the eating of the totem by the members, in fact the latter are represented as having a kind of prior claim to it for this purpose.

The only case in which there is any general restriction applying to the eating of an animal is in regard to the Achilpa, or "wild cat," but in this instance there is something of a very special nature, as the restriction not only applies to members of the Achilpa totem but extends to every member of the tribe except the oldest men and women.

Apart from restrictions concerned with the totems, there are others which relate on the one hand to food which has been killed by special individuals, and on the other to food which may not be eaten by particular individuals at certain times of their lives.

Under the first series of restrictions we find that a man may not eat the flesh of any animal which has been caught and killed, or even handled, by his *Ikuntera* (father-in-law), *Umba* (children of his sisters), female *Mura* and *Ipmunna*, nor by the man who is the father of his mother-in-law. On the contrary he must share his food with his *Ikuntera* or actual and tribal fathers-in-law, and it is his duty on killing game to ascertain if any of them are in want of food. As a matter of practice a man will never go out hunting with either his *Ikuntera* or *Umba* men, as they will appropriate everything which he kills while he is with them, so that he takes care to keep out of their way as much as possible. In the distribution of food he gives a portion first to his *Ikuntera*, then after feeding himself and his own *Unawa* and children, he gives any which he does not require to his *Umba*, and after that to his *Mura* and *Ipmunna* women. It may be added that this giving away of food according to well-established rules is not a custom more honoured in the breach than the observance, but is actually carried out. The Australian native cannot be accused of a lack of generosity; what he has he distributes freely to those to whom tribal custom tells him that he ought to, and, it may be added, that he obeys to the letter the injunction of taking no heed for the morrow.

Not only must a man supply the individuals named with food, but he must also take care that, when he is eating, none of them is sufficiently near to distinguish what he is eating, lest they should spoil it by what is called *Equilla timma*, which means "projecting their smell into it." Should a man eat meat which has been killed or seen by any of these persons, the food would disagree with him, and he would sicken and suffer severely, a belief which has the result of securing the observance of the custom.

If we take the case of a particular man, say a Panunga, and refer to the table already given, it can be seen at a glance what are the classes to which the individuals concerned with this restriction belong. They are Kumara men and women. Bulthara women, Uknaria women, together with the Uknaria man who is the father of the man's actual mother-in-law. The association in this respect is clearly that between a man and, what we may call, his wife's side of the tribe, and it is somewhat instructive to note that in the Arunta and other Central Australian tribes, in which descent is counted in the male line, a man continues, as it were, to pay a kind of tribute to his wife's group during his lifetime, which may perhaps be regarded as an early form of what obtains in so many other tribes under the different custom of paying, as it were, a lump sum down at the time of marriage.

This is, further, the one important feature, so far as the Arunta and other tribes akin to it are concerned, which appears to indicate in any way a former condition in which a man owed allegiance to the group of his wife; in no Australian tribe, so far as we know, is it the custom for a man to take up his abode with the family of his wife and to work for them, but in this custom we see, clearly expressed, the idea that a man owes something to the group from which his wife comes.

The second class of restriction is of an entirely different nature, and is associated with the idea, firstly, of reserving the best things for the older people, secondly, of reserving certain things for the men as opposed to the women, while, thirdly, there are restrictions which deal with the food of individuals at particular times.

We may take the third series first. When a youth is circumcised, and until he has undergone and recovered entirely from the rite of *ariltha* or sub-incision, he is forbidden to eat of the flesh of a number of animals; if he were to transgress this rule then his recovery would be retarded and his wounds would become much inflamed. The forbidden animals are—snakes, opossums, echidna, all kinds of lizards, mound birds or their eggs, bandicoots, wild turkey and their eggs, eagle-hawks and their eggs. The idea underlying this is evidently that of disciplining the novice, in just the same way as, during the Engwura, the younger men are not allowed to eat much food of any kind, but have to bring in the greater part of any game which they may secure and present it to the older men who remain in camp.

There are certain restrictions as to food connected with the early stages of pregnancy. A woman may, if she likes to do so, eat meat, but the unborn child is supposed to resent this by causing sickness, and therefore the woman at first only eats vegetable food. Further still, during the first three or four months, the husband does not kill any large game necessitating the use of spear or boomerang, but only catches rats, opossums and other small game. It is supposed that the spirit of the unborn child follows him about and gives warning of his approach to large game. Should the man attempt to throw a spear or boomerang at any animal, then the spirit child will cause the weapon to take a crooked course, and the man will know that he has lost his skill in the chase and that the child is angry with him. If, however, despite this warning, the father persists in trying to kill large game, then the sickness and sufferings of the mother would be very largely increased. There is, however, nothing to prevent the man from eating game which has been killed by other men. The natives can offer no explanation of this custom, and it may be pointed out that the restriction with regard to killing game does not appear to have the slightest reference to anything which has to do with the totems.

The list of foods which an *Ulpmerka*, that is a boy who has not been circumcised, may not eat is of considerable length. We append it with the list of penalties following on transgression of the rules. The idea throughout is evidently that which obtains so largely in savage tribes of reserving the best things for the use of the elders, and, more especially, of the elder men. The forbidden foods are as follows:—

Kangaroo tail (*Okirra purra*); penalty, premature age and decay.

Wild turkey and its eggs (*Ertua*); penalty, premature age. Female bandicoot (*Quirra*); penalty, probably bleed to death at circumcision.

Large lizards (*Ilchaquarra* or *Parenthie*); penalty, become *Arro-iwama*, that is, one with an abnormal and diseased craving for sexual intercourse, an individual held in much contempt. Emu fat (*Erlia inga*); penalty, abnormal development of the penis.

All kinds of parrots and cockatoos; penalty, development of a hollow on the top of the head and of a hole in the chin. Large quail (*Tulkara*) and its eggs; penalty, non-growth of beard and whiskers and general stoppage of growth. Eagle-hawk (*Irritcha*), except the legs; penalty, premature age and leanness; the leg is supposed to impart strength and generally to improve the growth of the limb. Boys are often struck on the calf of the leg with the leg bone of an eagle-hawk, as thereby strength passes from the bone into the boy's leg.

(*Achilpa*); penalty, painful and foul-smelling eruption on head and neck. This restriction applies until very old age is reached. Podargus (*Aurainga*) and its eggs; penalty, an ugly enlargement of the mouth.

The following restrictions and penalties concern girls and young women until after they have had a child, or until their breasts begin to be pendent, in the characteristic way of the native women. They may not eat:—

Female bandicoot (*Quirra*); penalty, continual flow of the menses.

Large lizards; penalty, become *Arro-iwama*, that is, one with an abnormal craving for sexual intercourse; such a woman would be always tempting men irrespective of tribal laws with regard to class, and would thus, sooner or later, meet with severe punishment, probably with death.

Large quail and its eggs; penalty, non-development of the breasts.

Wild-cat (*Achilpa*); penalty, the same as in the case of the men.

Kangaroo tail (*Okirra pura*); penalty, premature age, baldness, non-development of the breasts.

Emu fat; penalty, malformation of the vulva.

Cockatoos and parrots of all kinds; penalty, development of a hollow on the top of the head, and of a hole in the chin. Echidna (*Inarlinga*); penalty, general malformation of the genital organs.

Brown hawk (*Hieracidea orientalis*, native name *Irkalanja*); penalty, absence of milk from the breasts, which will also swell until they burst. Young women are only allowed to eat the young nestlings. The customs connected with this particular bird are curious. Not only is it *ekirinja* or forbidden to the young women, but, if one of them be suckling a child and she sees one of these birds, she at once makes haste to turn so that her breast cannot be seen by the bird, because, if the bird should catch sight of it, or worse still, if its shadow were to fall on it, then the milk would fail and the breast would swell and burst. The women also believe that if they eat the old birds their sons will be afflicted with varicose veins (*ulurkna*) on the forehead, causing much disfigurement. While the *Arrakurta* is out in the bush the actual *Mia*, that is, his mother, may not eat opossum, large carpet snake, large lizard, and fat of any sort, or else she would retard her son's recovery.

A curious restriction applying to women during the time of pregnancy, and also during the menstrual period, is that they may not, during the continuance of either of these, gather *Irriakura*, the bulb which forms, together with Munyeru (*Portulaca* sp.), a staple vegetable food; the breaking of this rule would result in the failure of the supply of *Irriakura*. With this exception, there are no restrictions with regard to vegetable food, except in the case of individuals whose totem is one of them.

CANNIBALISM

There is very clear evidence that during a former stage cannibalism was a well-recognised custom. We have already described certain ceremonies performed at the Engwura which can only be regarded as pointing back to the existence of a different state of affairs from that which now obtains. For example, in the *Quabarra Ingwurninga inkinja*,[158] two men had their bodies decorated with circles of white down which were supposed to represent the skulls of slain and eaten men. The performers themselves represented the *Ulthana* or spirits of the dead men wandering about in search of those who had killed and eaten them. In another ceremony two Achilpa men were engaged in cooking the body of a third; in another, concerned with the white bat totem, one of the performers carried on his head an object representing a limp, dead body; and in the traditions dealing with the wanderings of the wild dogs, the men are continually referred to as killing and eating other wild dog men and women.

These ceremonies may be regarded as probably indicative of what took place in past times amongst the ancestors of the present Arunta tribe, and of what still takes place amongst the Luritcha tribe where enemies are eaten. Care is always taken at the present day, amongst the latter, to destroy the bones, as the natives believe that unless this is done the victims will arise from the coming together of the bones, and will follow and harm those who have killed and eaten them. It is regarded as especially essential to destroy the skull—an existing belief which may be compared with the tradition referring to the early lizard man, whose head was not destroyed, and who therefore came to life again when his brother spoke to the head.

In the Luritcha tribe also young children are sometimes killed and eaten, and it is not an infrequent custom, when a child is in weak health, to kill a younger and healthy one and then to feed the weakling on its flesh, the idea being that this will give to the weak child the strength of the stronger one. As usual, in regard to customs such as this, it is by no means easy to find out exactly what takes place, as the natives of one part of the country will assure you that they do not indulge in the habit, but that they know that those of other parts do. When the accused are questioned, they in turn lay the same charge against their accusers and so on, often from group to group.

Chapter XIII

The Customs of Kurdaitcha and Illapurinja and the Avenging Party or Atninga

No idea of natural death—Death of one individual must be avenged in the normal condition of the tribe by the death of another—Organisation of a Kurdaitcha party—The ceremony of dislocating a toe before a man becomes entitled to wear the so-called Kurdaitcha shoes—The Kurdaitcha man accompanied by a Medicine man—Decoration of the two men—Killing the victim and operations of the Medicine man—Another form in which the Kurdaitcha man goes alone—The shoes do not serve to hide the tracks, and can only prevent who made them from being known—The Illapurinja—A form of female Kurdaitcha—The decoration of the woman—How the enemy is killed—Object of the Illapurinja is to punish a woman who has not mourned properly on the death of a daughter, blood or tribal—The Atninga or avenging party—Account of the proceedings of a party—Offering the use of women to the party—Agreement between the avenging party and the old men of the attacked party to kill three of the latter—A special fire is built at each camp—Spearing the victims—The actual slayers must not touch the bodies—Seizure of a woman—*Immirinja* who actually slew the men and *Alknalarinika*, the on-lookers—Return to the home camp—Precautions to prevent the *Immirinja* being injured by the spirits of the dead men—The women strike the shields—The spirit of the dead man assumes the form of a bird which must be watched for as it flies over the camp, otherwise it will produce paralysis.

AMONGST the Central Australian natives there is no such thing as belief in natural death; however old or decrepit a man or woman may be when this takes place it is at once supposed that it has been brought about by the magic influence of some enemy, and in the normal condition of the tribe the death of one individual is followed by the murder of some one else who is supposed to be guilty of having caused the death. Not infrequently the dying man will whisper in the ear of a *Railtchawa*, or medicine man, the name of the man whose magic is killing him. If this be not done then there is no difficulty, by some other method, of fixing sooner or later on the guilty party. Perhaps when digging the grave a hole will be found leading out of it on one side, which at once shows the direction in which the culprit lives; or this may be indicated, perhaps as long as a year after the death, by a burrow made by some animal on one side of the grave. The identity of the guilty man is always revealed by the medicine man.

When it is known who the culprit is a Kurdaitcha party may be arranged to avenge the death. This custom is, so the natives say, much less frequently carried out at the present day than in former years, and in the southern parts of the tribe seems to have died out altogether.[159] When it is decided who is guilty, a council of the old men of the group to which the dead man belonged is held and, if it be decided that vengeance is to be exacted by means of a Kurdaitcha party, then the man who is to play this part is chosen. The name Kurdaitcha is applied to the latter[160] and he wears the shoes to which by white men the name of Kurdaitcha shoes has been given. In the north the native name for them is *Interlinia* and in the south *Intathurta*.

These shoes have the form of a thick pad of emu feathers matted together with human blood drawn from the arm of some young man. They are so ingeniously made however that the use of anything like blood in their construction would never be suspected; indeed it is difficult to detect, even with the shoes in one's hands, how the feathers are matted into such a compact mass without apparently the use of anything like stitching. On the upper surface is a network of human hair string made from the hair of any living man or woman— it does not in the least signify who the individual is—and in the middle of the network is a hole through which the foot passes and across which stretches a cord made of several strands of hair string twisted together. As we have said, it is is by no means an easy matter to make the shoes and, as usual, in the manufacture of any special article, there are certain individuals who are famed for their skill in making them. No woman or child may see them and they are kept wrapped up in skin or else placed for safety in the sacred store house along with the Churinga. It is said that they may be used more than once, but the nature of the shoe is such that it could not last more than one journey over the hard ground characteristic of the interior.

Before a man may wear the shoes he has to submit to a most painful ordeal. A stone is heated to redness and then applied to the ball of the small toe of either foot, it does not matter which, until, as the natives say, the joint is softened when with a sudden jerk, the toe is pulled outwards and the joint is thus dislocated. There is no doubt that some such ordeal as this is passed through, as we have examined feet of men who claim to be what is called *Ertwa Kurdaitcha* at Charlotte Waters, Crown Point on the Finke River, Owen Springs and Alice Springs amongst the Macdonnell Ranges, all of which show the remarkable peculiarity of the dislocation. In correspondence with this is the fact that the true Kurdaitcha shoe has, at one side, a small opening made in the hair network through which the toe is thrust.[161]

Each Kurdaitcha man when going on his errand is accompanied by a medicine man and the two men are rubbed over with charcoal—black being in the Arunta tribe the colour associated with magic—and decorated with bands of white down. The hair of both men is tied up behind and a small conical helmet of twigs is fastened on with hair string. The Kurdaitcha himself has lines of down passing across the front of the helmet, down the side of the face and front of the body and legs as far as the knees. The medicine man has a median line running from the top of the helmet to the tip of his nose; another curved line meeting this at both ends encloses the eye of each side; and on the body a broad band of charcoal runs across from shoulder to shoulder and downwards till, at the level of the sternum, it divides into two, one passing on either side of the mid line and so on as far down as the knee. The bands are outlined with white down, and, as the pattern is a constant one, the Kurdaitcha man can always be distinguished from the medicine man.

Both of the men wear the *Interlinia* or shoes which, when thus in use, are decorated with lines of white and pink down, and, while they are being put on and attached to the feet and legs with human hair string, the Kurdaitcha sings—

"Interlinia turlaa attipa
Interlinia attipa."

which literally translated means "*Interlinia* to me hold fast, *interlinia* hold fast." There is not, either at the making or at the putting on of the shoes, anything in the way of an incantation beyond this simple one.

Like the man who is on any particular occasion acting as a Kurdaitcha, the doctor himself must be an *Ertwa Kurdaitcha* who has qualified by passing through the ordeal by fire in which the toe is dislocated. Both men carry shields and spears, and also one or more Churinga, which are supposed as usual to impart to them strength, courage, accuracy of aim, and also to render them invisible to their enemies, and in addition they act as charms to prevent their wearers being wounded. Around his waist each one wears the *Kirra-urkna*, or girdle, made from the hair which has been cut from a warrior after his death and which is supposed to add to the wearer all the war-like virtues of the dead man.

Followed by the medicine man the Kurdaitcha takes the lead until the enemy is sighted. Then the medicine man falls into the rear while the Kurdaitcha stealthily creeps forward towards his quarry and suddenly rising up, spears him before he is aware of the presence of an enemy. Both medicine man and Kurdaitcha have meanwhile put the sacred Churinga between their teeth and when they are thus armed the spear cannot fail to strike the victim. As soon as this is done the Kurdaitcha man goes away to some little distance from the fallen man and from which he cannot see the operations of the medicine man who now approaches and performs his share in the work. By aid of his magic powers and by means of the *Atnongara* stones he heals the victim. These *Atnongara* stones are small crystalline structures which every medicine man is supposed to be able to produce at will from his own body throughout which it is believed that they are distributed—in fact it is the possession of these stones which gives to the medicine man his virtue. Into the spear wound he rubs a white greasy substance called *Ernia* which he obtains by pressure of the skin glands on the outside of the nostril. After all external traces of the wound have disappeared he goes quietly away and, together with the Kurdaitcha man returns to his own country. Having been touched by the *Atnongara* stones, the victim returns to life, but is completely ignorant of all that has taken place. He returns to camp and in a short time sickens and dies. His death is attributed to Kurdaitcha or to some other form of magic influence, but no one will be able to trace the tracks of the Kurdaitcha.

Another form of Kurdaitcha which has not the sanction of the council of elders but is said to be the more favourite method of procedure is for the Kurdaitcha to go alone without the medicine man accompanying him. After killing his enemy he allows the body to lie out in the sun for an hour or two and then he makes an incision in the tongue through which he sucks away the blood which is supposed to have accumulated internally. Then he plugs up the spear wound with the *Alpita* (a rat tail tip ornament worn as a conventional covering) and leaves it there a short time while he sings a magic chant. Then the *Alpita* is removed and a small fire stick is held close to the wound so that the skin contracts and the wound closes up and heals. Sometimes instead of sucking the tongue, the Kurdaitcha catches a special kind of slender, smooth bodied lizard (*Rhodona bipes*) which frequents the roots of Mulga trees and inserts the head of the animal into the wound through which it is supposed to suck up all the blood. Finally he either bites the tongue of the victim or else presses a charmed bone called an *Injilla* under it, the effect of either of which actions is to cause the victim to completely lose all recollection of what has taken place when, a short time afterwards, he comes to life again. The man who has thus been killed returns to his camp having no idea of what has happened, and soon sickens and dies.

Whilst there is much of a mythical nature about the Kurdaitcha it is quite possible that there is a certain amount of truth underlying a good deal that is, of course, a matter of pure imagination. It is very possible that the shoes, if not actually used at the present day, have been used in past times for the purpose of aiding in secret killing and, to the present day, the fear of the Kurdaitcha man lurking around is always present with the native. We have met several Kurdaitcha men who claim to have killed their victim and many more men who are perfectly certain that they have seen Kurdaitcha One group of men will tell you that they do not go Kurdaitcha but that another group does do so, and if you then question the latter they will tell you that they do not, but that their accusers do. It is in fact a case of each believing the other guilty and both being innocent. At the same time many will at once confess that they do go Kurdaitcha, when as a matter of fact they do not.

As to the question of tracking, the idea which has been generally held, that the shoes are used to prevent the tracks being seen will not be regarded as at all satisfactory by those who are acquainted with the remarkable power of the Australian native in this respect. They will neither hide the track nor, though they are shaped alike at each end, will they even suffice to prevent any native who cares to look from seeing at a glance which direction the wearer has come from, or gone towards. Any even moderately experienced native will, without the slightest difficulty, tell from the faintest track—from an upturned stone, a down-bent piece of grass or a twig of shrub—not only that some one has passed by but also the direction in which he has travelled. The only way in which they can be of use in hiding tracks is by preventing it from being recognised who was the particular individual, and in this way they might be of service, for when once an experienced native—almost incredible though it may sound to those who have not had the opportunity of watching them—has seen the track of a man or woman he will distinguish it afterwards from that of any other individual of his acquaintance.

Most probably the explanation is, not that the native cannot follow the track, but that either he persuades himself that he cannot, or, what is still more likely, that the fear of the magic power of the dreaded Kurdaitcha causes him, if he catches sight of such a track, to avoid as much as possible the spot where he has seen it, in just the same way in which an ordinary European peasant will avoid the spot haunted by a ghost.

Our impression with regard to the Kurdaitcha is that at the present day it is merely a matter of myth, though at the same time every native is firmly convinced that some other native does actually "go Kurdaitcha," and is quite prepared, as a general rule, to allow others to think that he himself does; he will even go to the length of suffering the pain of having his toe dislocated in order to "prove" that he is a genuine *Ertwa Kurdaitcha*. To those who are personally acquainted with the Australian native there will not appear to be anything at all improbable in this. He delights in mystery, and for the purpose of standing high in the estimation of his fellow men will submit to inconveniences and discomforts which perhaps appear to a white man to be ludicrously out of all proportion to the advantages to be gained, but to him it is far otherwise, and the mystery which surrounds and lends importance to the individual who has actually, for example, "gone Kurdaitcha," is just what appeals to the imagination of the Australian native. At the same time it is not by any means improbable that at some time past some such custom associated with secret killing was even largely practiced, and formed a kind of endless vendetta. Possibly some old *Oknirabata* whose superior wisdom had gained for him great repute (just as it would do at the present day), perceiving the endless deaths which it entailed, introduced the curious and painful ordeal of dislocation of the toe as a means of checking the practice.

During the Engwura which we witnessed a special ceremony was performed which had reference to the Kurdaitcha custom. This was called the *Ininja*, the word being the name applied to a small party of men sent out by the older men of any group to kill some special individual. The ceremony was in the possession of the Alatunja of a group of Ullakupera (little hawk) men and had been received by him from a group of natives living out to the east. In connection with the performance five men were decorated with bands of charcoal edged with white down, a line of the latter running straight from the top of the helmet along the bridge of the nose and then over the upper lip and beard, which was tied back upon the face with hair string. A semi-circle of white down, each end of which touched the median line surrounded the eyes. Every man carried a shield, and was either armed with a spear-thrower or boomerang, while one of them carried a long spear, the pointed end of which was decorated with down.

One by one the men ran out with exaggerated high knee action from the group of natives who were assembled at one side of the Engwura ground. Crouching down in various spots, each man lay on the ground with his shield over his head and his body huddled up so as to occupy as little space as possible. They all lay perfectly still while an old man armed only with a fighting club came and walked about, wandering here and there as if he were looking for some track. Then the Kurdaitcha men arose and one after the other crept stealthily up to him from behind. Suddenly he turned round and caught sight of the Kurdaitcha who were just about to kill him with a boomerang or spear. Then a mock fight took place, in which the Kurdaitcha was always worsted and tumbled down, the old man each time giving him a final tap with his club, which particularly pleased the audience, for in these performances there are certain conventional actions which must be observed by the actors. One after another the Kurdaitcha men came up, and each was worsted in his turn. When apparently all had been killed the old man still went wandering about, and the same performance was again gone through. After about fifteen minutes had been spent in this way the old man leisurely walked back to the group of spectators, once more killing each of the men before he got there. When close home a combined attack was made upon him, but with no success, as he killed them all and the performance ended with him standing, brandishing his club over their dead bodies, which were heaped together in front of him. The actions of the old man and of the Kurdaitcha men might have been copied from a stage fight.

Tradition relates that the incident to which the performance refers actually took place in the far past when a noted warrior slew five Kurdaitchas who followed him as he went out tracking animals for food.

THE CUSTOM OF ILLAPURINJA

Illapurinja, a word which means "the changed one," is the name given to a woman who may be spoken of as, in a modified form, a female Kurdaitcha, and whom we may regard, at all events at the present day, as being entirely a mythical personage, whose existence in the mind of the native is concerned mainly with the observance of certain customs in connection with mourning for dead relatives. The natives' idea with regard to her is as follows.

On very rare occasions a woman may, at her own request, be sent out by her husband to avenge some injury done, or supposed to be done, to one of her own kindred. There is no such thing as any consultation of the old men in connection with this; in fact, if they knew of its being prepared, they would prevent her going, so that the affair is a secret one, known only to the woman and her husband. It seems as if the Illapurinja has never been a very popular form of avenging an injury, and is very rarely mentioned except when a medicine man discovers that one of his patients, who has been seized with sudden and unaccountable illness, is suffering from the attack of an Illapurinja. As usual, the natives when questioned on the subject said that though they knew all about it, yet it was a custom which they did not practise, or, rather, had not practised for many years, but that it was prevalent out to the east. It is only a few years since a man was out hunting euros near to Alice Springs, and was attacked by an Illapurinja who had come from an outlying group. He was picked up insensible (the day was a very hot one, and in all probability the case was one of sunstroke), and brought into camp in a dazed condition. Under the treatment of an able medicine man, whose services were fortunately available, he recovered, after the extraction from his body of a number of pieces of a wooden Churinga.

When being prepared, the Illapurinja is rubbed all over with grease and red ochre and decorated with white down, which is fixed on to her body with blood drawn from her husband, this being the only occasion known to us on which a woman is thus decorated. Her head is ornamented with head rings and tufts of tail tips. In one hand she carries a long fighting club, the ends of which are decorated with down, and in the other a large wooden Churinga, which has been specially made for the occasion by her husband.

When the decoration, which is done in perfect secresy, is complete, no one but just the man and woman knowing anything whatever about it, the husband takes one of her digging sticks, fixes it upright in the ground, and ties on to the upper end a small tuft of *Alpita* or rat tails. This he carefully watches while she is away. Should she be killed, then the *Alpita* at once falls to the ground of its own accord; and the husband, understanding what this means, will immediately destroy his camp and everything in it which belonged to the Illapurinja, and move to a new spot, leaving, however, the digging stick and *Alpita* untouched.

It is always night time when the woman sets out, and after having been decorated, she first of all lies down in the camp as if nothing unusual were about to happen; but when her husband is asleep she steals quietly away quite alone, and goes to the place where she hopes to find the man or woman whom she is in search of. It it be a man, then she lies down concealed, and waiting her opportunity, which comes when his attention is occupied in stalking a kangaroo or emu. If a woman be her quarry, then she hides close to some favourite "yam" ground, and when the former is busy digging up the tubers she creeps up. In either case the Churinga is thrown from behind so as to hit the victim's neck, when it enters the body, becoming, as it does so, broken up into a number of small pieces.

The victim at once becomes insensible, and remains so for some little time, and, when consciousness is once more recovered, suffers great pain. In the case of an old woman death is sure to follow, but in that of a man or younger woman, recovery is possible with the aid of a clever medicine man, who, after much trouble and by dint of long-continued rubbing and sucking, may succeed in extracting the broken bits of Churinga from the patient's body.

If successful, the Illapurinja returns at once to her husband's camp, always waiting, however, till it be dark before she comes close up to it. During her absence he has made, and kept burning, a small fire at some little distance. By the side of this she lies down quietly until her husband discovers her presence, when he goes and takes her by the arm and leads her into his camp, where both of them sit down without speaking a word, while he removes all traces of the decorations and rubs her with fat and red ochre. The woman then takes up the stick to which the *Alpita* is tied, and sits down, while the man asks questions to which she replies, but she must not volunteer any information.

The special breach of custom, with the punishment of which the Illapurinja is associated, is the omission of a *Mia* to cut herself as a mark of sorrow on the death of an *Umba*, that is, a daughter blood or tribal. Such an omission is a grave offence against a dead *Umba*, and the dread of punishment at the hands of an Illapurinja must act as a strong inducement to secure the proper carrying out of the ceremony. If one *Mia* omits to cut herself, then some other one will go in search of her, and, failing the chance of killing her, will strike one of the offending woman's brothers. There is now living at Alice Springs a man who was thus injured by an Illapurinja, and whose life was only just saved, so the natives believe, by the exertions of a medicine man. When his death does occur, it will undoubtedly be attributed to this attack, certain parts of the Churinga—so it will be said—not having been extracted.

This is the only case which has come to our knowledge in which a woman is decorated with down fixed on with blood, and in which she actually handles a Churinga. The latter, of course, is not one of the ancestral Churinga, but it is regarded as being a sacred stick, and is spoken of as a Churinga just as are certain other similarly shaped sticks which are used in various ceremonies, for which they may be specially made. All that the woman is told is that the stick has been sung over, and is what is called *Arungquiltha*, that is, charged with magic and evil influence.

The whole affair is a superstition kept alive to make some women believe that they, or their brothers, will suffer if certain ceremonies are not duly attended to, and it is worthy of notice that in this instance the victim belongs to the same group as the avenger.

THE ATNINGA OR AVENGING PARTY

Very often one group of natives, that is, the members of the tribe inhabiting a particular locality, will quarrel with the members of some other group either belonging to the same or to some other tribe. The quarrel is usually due to one of two causes: either some man has stolen a wife from some other group, or else the death of a native is attributed by the medicine man to the magic of some member of a distant group. When this is so, the aggrieved party will arrange to make an attack upon the men who are regarded as the aggressors. Most often the attackers, armed with spears and spear-throwers, boomerangs, and shields, will march up to the enemies' camp, and the quarrel will be confined to a wordy warfare, lasting perhaps for an hour or two, after which things quieten down, and all is over; but in some cases a regular fight takes place, in which severe wounds may be inflicted. In other cases the attacking party will steal down upon the enemy, and, lying in ambush, will await an opportunity of spearing one or two of the men without any risk to themselves.

The following incident which happened recently will serve to show what often takes place.

The men living in the country round about Alice Springs in the Macdonnell Range were summoned by *Inwurra*, that is, properly accredited messengers carrying Churinga, who had been sent out by the Alatunja of the group to assemble for the purpose of making war upon the Iliaura tribe, which occupies the country between eighty and a hundred miles to the north of the Ranges.

For a long time the northern groups of the Arunta tribe had been in fear of the Iliaura, who had been continually sending in threatening messages, or at least it was constantly reported that they were doing so, for it must be remembered that imagination plays a large part in matters such as these amongst the natives. Several deaths, also, which had taken place amongst the Arunta, had been attributed by the medicine men to the evil magic of certain of the Iliaura men. When the messengers and the men summoned had assembled at Alice Springs a council of the elder men was held, at which it was determined to make a raid on the Iliaura, and accordingly a party was organised for the purpose. Such an avenging party is called an Atninga.

When all was prepared the Atninga started away for the north, and, after travelling for several days, came upon a group of Iliaura men, consisting of about a dozen families, near to whom they camped for two days.

As usual on such occasions, the Iliaura sent some of their women over to the strangers' camp, but the fact that the use of the women was declined by the visitors at once indicated that the mission of the latter was not a friendly one. The women are offered with a view of conciliating the Atninga men, who, if they accept the favour, indicate by so doing that the quarrel will not be pursued any further.

In the Iliaura community were two old men, and with them matters were discussed by the elder men amongst the Arunta at a spot some little distance from the camp of the latter. After a long talk extending over two days, during which the strangers set forth their grievances and gave the Iliaura men very clearly to understand that they were determined to exact vengeance, the two old men said, in effect, "Go no further. Our people do not wish to quarrel with your people; there are three bad men in our camp whom we Iliaura do not like, they must be killed. Two are *Iturka* (that is men who have married within the forbidden degrees of relationship); the other is very quarrelsome and strong in magic and has boasted of killing your people by means of Kurdaitcha and other magic. Kill these men, but do not injure any others in our camp, and we will help you."

These terms were accepted by the Arunta, and it was agreed between the old men of the two parties that an attempt should be made to kill the three men on the next day. At daylight the old men of the Iliaura went some little distance away from their camp, and there made a fire, and called up the other men of their party. This special fire, at which it is intended to surprise and kill the men who have been condemned and handed over to the tender mercies of their enemies, is called *Thara* (the ordinary word for fire being *Ura*). At the Atninga camp another fire, also called *Thara*, was lighted at the same time. Shortly after daylight a number of the Arunta, led by an old man, went over to the *Thara* of the Iliaura, all of them being unarmed, and here they took special care to engage the condemned men in conversation. The remainder of the Atninga party in full war-paint, with whittled sticks in their hair, their bodies painted with red ochre, carrying spears, boomerangs, and shields, and each one wearing the magic *Kirra-urkna* or girdle made of a dead man's hair, crept up unseen and, suddenly springing up, speared two of the condemned men from behind. The third man—one of the two *Iturka*—had grown suspicious during the night and had accordingly decamped, taking his women with him.

A large number of spears were thrown into the bodies of the men who were killed. When they were dead the Atninga party danced round the bodies, and taking the whittled sticks or *Ilkunta* from their heads, broke them up and threw the pieces on to the bodies. These *Ilkunta* are always worn by certain groups of the Northern Arunta when they really mean to fight, and amongst the same natives also under these circumstances little curved flakes are cut by means of flints on their spears about a foot from the pointed end.

The Iliaura men looked on quietly while the killing took place, and when all was over, the spears were taken out of the bodies by the men of the Arunta who had acted as decoys, and were handed back to their respective owners. It is supposed that if the latter themselves removed them some great evil would befall them, as the body and anything in contact with it of a victim killed in this way is strictly tabu to the killer.

When this had been done, the Arunta went to the main camp of the Iliaura and took the *Unawa* of one of the dead men, and she became and is now the property of the old man who seized her, she being a woman of the class into which he could lawfully marry. One girl child was annexed by one of the younger men, who carried her on his back for the greater part of the return journey for about a hundred miles. The two women who belonged to the *Iturka* man were away, but no attempt was made to capture them, as being themselves *Iturka*, they would not be taken as wives by the men of the avenging party. They would when captured meet with severe punishment at the hands of the Iliaura men and in all probability would be put to death. Had they been the proper *Unawa* of the dead man, they would, if present, have been appropriated by men of the Atninga party to whom they were also *Unawa*. The special name of *Immirinja* is given to the men who actually took part in the spearing, those who acted as decoys and who thus merely took a passive part, being called *Alknalarinika* which means "onlookers."

Travelling back to the Arunta country, the Atninga party separated into various contingents, each of which went to its own locality, upon arrival at which certain ceremonies had to be observed. The Alice Springs contingent, which will serve to illustrate what took place in each instance, halted some distance away from the main camp and decorated their bodies, painting them all over with powdered charcoal and placing on their foreheads and through the septum of the nose small twigs of a species of Eremophila. As soon as they came in sight of the main camp they began to perform an excited war-dance, approaching in the form of a square and holding and moving their shields as if to ward off something which was being thrown at them. This action is called *Irulchiukiwuma* and is intended to beat off the *Ulthana* or spirit of the dead man.

The *Immirinja* men were in the lead and, upon arrival within sight of the camp, they separated from the others and formed a single extended line with spears at rest and their shields held in front of them with the convex side outwards. Not a word was spoken and the *Immirinja* stood perfectly still looking straight ahead. The *Alknalarinika* men, who now formed an irregular square in the rear, shouted out, with evident enjoyment, the result of the expedition. Then a number of old women approached carrying fighting clubs and performing, as they came along, a kind of exulting skip movement. Each one with her club struck the shield of every one of the *Immirinja*, and when this had been done the men who did not go on the expedition followed suit, using their boomerangs.

The striking of the shields is called *ulquita atuma* (*ulquita* shields, *atuma* to strike). This is a ceremony of very considerable importance, and every one listens intently to the sound which is produced by the blow. It it be hollow (*atalya*), the owner of the shield is under some malignant influence and he will not live long; if, on the other hand, the the sound is firm and strong (*elatilkima*), then he is safe and is not a victim of magic.

After the shield striking was over the women and children returned to their camp and the Atninga party marched to the corrobboree ground, the *Immirinja* men remaining perfectly silent. There, all sat perfectly silent, the *Immirinja* in the front and the *Alknalarinika* behind them. After singing and beating of boomerangs had gone on for some time two of the *Immirinja* jumped up and, making a wide circuit of the gathering, ran round with exaggerated knee action and went through a performance in which they imitated the different attitudes of attack and defence. They then halted with spears at rest and shields held as before, until all of the men who had not been with them came up and struck their shields with a boomerang, after which they walked back to the party and sat down. The same performance was passed through by all the *Immirinja* two at a time. It is supposed to be very effective as a means of frightening the *Ulthana*, that is the spirit of the dead man. One of the shields gave out a hollow sound at which all appeared to be much distressed, while some shouted out telling the man to hold it straight up. After slightly altering the position it was again struck and to the apparent relief of the listeners gave out the right sound. While this ceremony was in progress the *Alknalarinika* men were vying with each other in relating the details of the expedition, only stopping to listen when the shields were struck.

Shortly afterwards the men separated and went to their respective camps. During that night, and for some days afterwards, none of the *Immirinja* would speak of the incidents of the expedition, and they continued to paint their bodies with charcoal and to decorate their foreheads and noses with green twigs; finally they painted their bodies and faces with bright colours and became free to talk about the affair. Their troubles were not yet over however. The *Ulthana* or spirit of the dead man is supposed to follow the party in the form of a little bird called *Chichurkna* and is constantly on the look-out to injure the *Immirinja*. While flying it makes a noise like a child crying in the distance, and, should any one of the men fail to hear this, he would become paralysed in his right arm and shoulder. At night time especially, when the *Chichurkna* is flying over the camp, they have to be wakeful, and, when lying down, are always careful to conceal the right arm and shoulder lest the bird should look down upon and injure them, and every man wears *Alpita* in his hair which is supposed to help him to keep awake, the rabbit-kangaroo from which it comes being a nocturnal animal and so acts as a charm against his being surprised by the *Chichurkna*. When once the voice has been heard there is no further fear, because the *Ulthana* recognises that it has been watched for and detected and is therefore powerless to do any harm.

Some little time afterwards the shields of all the men were again tested to see that they were sound.

This killing of *Iturka* men by strange blacks belonging to other groups has been a common practice amongst the tribes. When a case of this kind arises, the old men of the group to which the offender belongs hold a meeting to discuss the matter, and if all of them vote in favour of the death of a man or woman, a neighbouring group is asked to come and carry out the sentence. Sometimes it is agreed that the offending parties are to be punished in some less severe way, perhaps by cutting the man's legs or by burning the woman with a fire-stick, and then if after this the two still continue to live together, the death penalty will be carried out.

Sometimes, but only rarely, a man is strong enough to resist, but even if he be successful his life is at best a miserable one as he dare not come anywhere near the camps, but is forced to live in inaccessible parts in constant fear of being surprised and put to death. At Charlotte Waters, for example, there has been in recent years a case of this kind. One of the finest men of the group carried off a woman who was not his lawful *Unawa*, both the man and the woman belonging to the Purula class.[162] For two or three years the two led a wandering life away from the usual haunts and several attempts were made to kill them, the woman being very severely wounded on one occasion. The man, however, was a formidable antagonist of well-known prowess, and after having killed two of the men who attempted to punish him and nearly killing the proper husband of the woman, it was thought best to leave him alone, though up to the present day when quarrels occur in which he is concerned he is often taunted with being *Iturka*.

Chapter XIV

Customs Relating to Burial and Mourning

Earth burial in the Arunta tribe—Depression made on the side of the grave facing the place from which the spirit of the individual came originally—Hair cut off a man—As a general rule nothing buried with the body—Burning of the camp—Amongst the Warramunga and northern tribes the body is placed on a platform in a tree until the flesh has shrivelled up—Degrees of silence to be observed by different individuals in regard to mentioning the name of the dead—Special restrictions on the sons-in-law of a dead man—The widow paints herself with pipeclay, and at first remains in camp, silent, speaking by means of gesture language—Ceremony to remove the ban of silence—Widow and younger brothers—Ceremony of *Urpmilchima* at the grave—Wearing of the bone chaplet—The women cutting themselves upon the grave—*Urpmilchima* of a woman—No man allowed to attend the ceremony at the grave—The object of painting the body white is to attract the attention of the spirit.

WITHIN a very short time of death the body in the Arunta tribe is buried. It is placed in a sitting position with the knees doubled up against the chin, and is thus interred in a round hole in the ground, the earth being piled directly on to the body so as to make a low mound with a depression on one side. This is always made on the side which faces towards the direction of the dead man or woman's camping ground in the Alcheringa, that is the spot which he or she inhabited whilst in spirit form: the object of this is to allow of easy ingress and egress to the *Ulthana* or spirit which is supposed to spend part of the time until the final ceremony of mourning has been enacted in the grave, part watching over near relatives, and part in the company of its *Arumburinga*, that is its spiritual double who lives at the *Nanja* spot.

In the case of a man the hair is cut off from his head and his necklaces, armlets and fur string used for winding round his head are carefully preserved for further use. In the Eastern Arunta it is said that sometimes a little wooden vessel used in camp for holding small objects may be buried with the man, but this is the only instance which has come to our knowledge in which anything ordinarily used is buried in the grave. Amongst the Udnirringita (witchetty grub) people one or more of the round stone Churinga which are supposed to represent the eggs of the grub in the Alcheringa may be buried with the man, but this is the only instance in which we can find that anything of a sacred nature is buried with him.

As soon as burial has taken place, the man or woman's camp in which death occurred is at once burnt down, and all the contents are then destroyed—in the case of a woman nothing whatever being preserved—and the whole of the local encampment is shifted to a new place. Earth burial directly after death occurs from the Urabunna tribe in the south as far north as the Warramunga at Tennant's Creek. Amongst the latter the body is at first placed on a platform made of boughs in a tree until such time as the flesh has disappeared, when the bones, with the exception of the smaller ones from the arms which are used for the purpose of making pointing bones, are taken down and buried.

It is generally supposed that amongst Australian natives the name of a dead man is never mentioned. This is not however strictly true as regards the Arunta tribe. There are various degrees of silence to be observed by different persons and these are dependent upon the mutual relationship which existed between the dead and living individual. During the period of mourning which follows immediately upon the death of a man and occupies a period of from twelve to eighteen months, no person must mention the name of the deceased except it be absolutely necessary to do so, and then only in a whisper for fear of disturbing and annoying the man's spirit which in ghost form, or as they call it, *Ulthana*, walks about. If the *Ulthana* hears his name mentioned he comes to the conclusion that his relatives are not properly mourning for him—if their grief were genuine it would cause them too much pain to hear his name mentioned to allow them to do so—and so he will come and trouble them in their sleep, to show them that he is not pleased with them.

All individuals who are *Okilia Oknia, Mia, Ungaraitcha, Uwinna*, or *Mura* of the dead man or woman may never mention his or her name, nor may they ever go near to the grave when once the ceremony of *Urpmilchima*, shortly to be described, has been performed. Those who were *Allira, Itia, Umbirna, Umba, Unkulla, Unawa, Ikuntera, Chimmia*, or *Arunga* may, when the time of mourning is over, speak of the dead and mention his name without fear of incurring the anger of the *Ulthana*. As a matter of fact the grave is very seldom indeed visited by any one for a long time after the burial; no camp will be formed close to where a grave has been made for at least two years' time for fear of disturbing the *Ulthana*.

The *Gammona* of the deceased, that is the men who may lawfully marry his daughters—whether they actually do so or not makes no difference—must not only never mention his name, but they neither attend the actual burial, nor do they take any part in the subsequent mourning ceremonies which are carried on at the grave. It is their duty to cut themselves on the shoulder when the man who is their *Ikuntera* or father-in-law dies. If a son-in-law does not well and faithfully perform this cutting rite, which is called *Unangara*, then some *Ikuntera* will punish him by giving away his special *Unawa* or wife to some other man to appease the *Ulthana* of the dead father-in-law.

The name of the latter is strictly tabu to the *Gammona*, and if by any chance he should hear the name mentioned in camp, he will at once rattle his boomerangs together so as to prevent his knowing what is being said.

Every man bears on his shoulders, as will be seen clearly in many of the illustrations, the raised cicatrices, which exist as the permanent record of the fact that he has fulfilled his duty to a dead father-in-law.

When a man dies his special *Unawa* or *Unawas* smear their hair, faces and breasts with white pipeclay and remain silent for a certain time until a ceremony called *Aralkililima* has been performed.[163] The widow is called *Inpirta*, which means the whitened one in reference to the pipeclay. Some times she smears over the pipeclay ashes from a fire, in which case she is called *Ura-inpirta*, *ura* meaning fire. In some of the more northern tribes, as for example amongst the Warramunga living on Tennant's Creek, the widows are not allowed to speak for sometimes as long a period as twelve months, during the whole of which time they communicate only by means of gesture language. In the latter they are so proficient that they prefer, even when there is no obligation upon them to do so, to use it in preference to speaking. Not seldom, when a party of women are in camp, there will be almost perfect silence and yet a brisk conversation is all the while being conducted on their fingers or rather with their hands and arms, as many of the signs are made by putting the hands, or perhaps the elbows, in varying positions. Many of the positions assumed by the fingers are such that it is not at all easy for a white man to imitate them, and yet by long practice the native can place his fingers in the most wonderful variety of positions with regard to one another and at the same time move them about in a way which no white man can, except with extreme difficulty and very slowly.

When among the Arunta the widow wishes the ban of silence to be removed, she gathers a large wooden vessel, called a *Tirna*, full of some edible seed or small tuber and smears herself afresh with white pipeclay at the *Erlukwirra*, or women's camp, where she has been living since her husband's death. Carrying the *Tirna*, and accompanied by the women whom she has gathered together for the purpose, she walks to the centre of the encampment midway between the two sections of the community, that is to the creek or whatever natural feature it may be which serves to divide the Bulthara and Panunga moiety from the Kumara and Purula. Here they all sit down and cry loudly, whereupon the men who were the *Allira* and *Itia*, that is the sons and younger brothers of the dead man (blood and tribal), come up and join the party. The men take the *Tirna* from the hands of the widow and, as many as possible taking hold of it, they shout loudly "*Wah! wah! wah!*" The women except the widow stop crying and join in the shout. After a short time the *Tirna* is held close to, but not touching, the face of the widow and passes are made to right and left of her cheeks, while all again shout "*Wah! wah! wah!*" The widow now stops her crying and utters the same shout, only in subdued tones. After a few minutes the *Tirna* is passed to the rear of the men who now, squatting on the ground and holding their shields in both hands, strike them heavily on the ground in front of the women who are standing. The widow springs to her feet and joins in the shouts of "*Wah! wah! wah!*" which accompany for some minutes the striking of the shields. When this is over the men disperse to their camps and eat the food brought in the *Tirna* by the widow, who is now free to speak to them, though she still continues to smear herself with pipeclay. The meaning of this ceremony, as symbolised by the gathering of the tubers or grass seed, is that the widow is about to resume the ordinary occupations of a woman's life, which have been to a large extent suspended while she remained in camp in what we may call deep mourning. It is in fact closely akin in feeling to the transition from deep to narrow black-edged paper amongst certain more highly civilised peoples. The offering to the sons and younger brothers is intended both to show them that she has properly carried out the first period of mourning and to gain their goodwill as they, especially the younger brothers, are supposed to be for some time displeased with a woman when her husband is dead and she is alive. In fact a younger brother meeting the wife of a dead elder brother out in the bush, performing the ordinary duties of a woman such as hunting for "yams" within a short time of her husband's death, would be quite justified in spearing her. The only reason that the natives give for this hostile feeling is that it grieves them too much when they see the widow because it reminds them of the dead man. This however can scarcely be the whole reason, as the same rule does not apply to the elder brothers, and very probably the real explanation of the feeling is associated, in some way, with the custom according to which the widow will, when the final stage of mourning is over, become the wife of one of these younger brothers whom at first she has to carefully avoid.

After the lapse of perhaps twelve or eighteen months the ceremony of *Urpmilchima* is performed at the grave. The meaning of this term is "trampling the twigs on the grave."

Previously to this the widow has been saving up small bones of any animal such as the jaws of opossums or rabbit-kangaroos, or leg and arm bones of various small animals. She also procures the same from her tribal sisters. From the female *Itia, Allira* and *Umba* of the dead man she obtains short locks of hair to which by means of *Atcha*, the resin obtained from the porcupine grass, she attaches firmly the bones, which are then hung on, in little groups, to one of the hair head rings which are commonly worn by women. In addition she procures *Alpita* and makes plumes out of the tail feathers of the ring-necked parrot or of the black cockatoo. In this way a hideous and bulky chaplet is made which the women call *Aramurilia* and the men *Chimurilia*—why they should have separate names we cannot say, but they are both applied to the same chaplet and have nothing to do with whether it is concerned with the *Urpmilchima* of a man or woman.

When these preparations have been made the widow is invited by a younger brother of the dead man to visit the grave or *Ulkna* and there to take part in the ceremony of *Urpmilchima*. The date is determined by the tribal brothers and sons of the dead man and on the appointed day the widow is painted all, or nearly all over, with fresh pipe-clay.

Probably in different parts of the tribe the ceremony varies to a certain extent in details, and it may also vary somewhat according to whether the dead man was held in great or little esteem. The following is an account of the *Urpmilchima* as it was celebrated in the case of the brother of the present Alatunja of the Alice Springs group. The women, on the appointed day, were assembled at the *Erlukwirra* painting the widow; the men were sitting a few hundred yards away on the line of route from the camp to the grave. The *Oknia, Okilia, Itia,* and *Allira,* were decorated on the front of the body with a Y-shaped figure, painted of course in pipeclay, white being the colour of mourning. The *Gammona* sat apart with bent heads and nearest to them were their *Allira,* that is their sons blood and tribal. When the painting of the widow was complete, the women approached from the *Erlukwirra* uttering their peculiar mournful wail, a weird sound well-known to all who have spent the night camped near to a group of natives amongst whom a death has occurred at all recently. The lead was taken by the widow who was carrying the *Chimurilia* in a wooden *pitchi*. They came on until the spot was reached at which the *Gammona* were seated and approached in such a way as to come up behind the latter. Then, standing behind each man, the widow thrust the *pitchi* under the arms and on to the lap of each one in turn. There it was allowed to remain, held by the man for some minutes, the women crying loudly and the men with bent heads shedding tears but uttering no sound. As the *pitchi* rested on the lap of each man, the widow and other men who were *Unawa* with the dead man and who were in consequence *Mura* to the *Gammona*, embraced the latter from behind. These women were, it must be remembered, those who are strictly prohibited from speaking to or having any intercourse with the men in question, to whom they were tribally mothers-in-law, which will account for the fact that they approached them from behind as if in recognition of this mutual relationship of *Mura*. After this was over the sons of the *Gammona* were treated in just the same way, and then these two sets of men remained seated on the ground while all the other men, followed by the women, started off for the grave. About midway the party was met by the eldest son of the deceased's eldest brother and a halt was made. Taking the *Chimurilia*—two in number—from the *pitchi* he approached each man who was *Oknia, Okilia, Itia, Ikuntera, Umbirna*, and *Allira* of the dead man and embraced them all in turn, pressing as he did so the *Chimurilia* against their stomachs. Then he placed one *Chimurilia* on the head of the widow, and the other on that of a younger sister of the dead man, and taking from the *pitchi* some *Okincha-lanina* or fur string rings, he tore the string tags off and placed the rings on the heads of women who were *Allira* or *Umba* of the dead man. The tufts of feathers of the ring-necked parrot were stuck in the hair behind the ears over which hung *Alpita* or tail tips.

When the putting on of the *Chimurilia*, &c., was complete, the party, led by the man who had superintended this part of the proceedings, went on, each man carrying a shield and spear-thrower. No words were spoken, and the only sound was the wailing of the women. A visit was first paid to the camp where the man died, and, dancing round the charred remains (when a native dies his camp is at once destroyed by fire) they all shouted "*Wah! wah! wah! wa-a-ah!*" the men as they did so beating the air with their spear-throwers, which were grasped in the centre instead of at one end, and held with their hollow side outwards—suggestive somewhat of the reversed arms at a military funeral. The shields were held at rest in the left hand. The women joined in the dancing and shouting, beating the air with the palms of their hands, which faced away from the body with the fingers widely distended, the idea being to drive the spirit away from the old camp which it is supposed to haunt. Those women who were *Mia, Uwinna*, and *Mura* of the dead man did not join in the shouting, or make any movement with the arms, but wailed loudly and threw themselves on to the ground. When the dancing, which lasted about ten minutes, was over, the whole party proceeded to the grave at a run, the leader making a circuit away from the main party, shouting loudly with very prolonged intonation "*Ba-au! ba-au!*" The idea of the leading man making a circuit was, perhaps, though the natives could give no explanation, to prevent the spirit from doubling back to the camp from which they were supposed to be driving him. The idea is that the spirit is frightened when he hears the noise and sees the widow coming on wearing the *Chimurilia*, and being driven on takes refuge at the bottom of the grave. The main party went on shouting in suppressed tones "*Wah! wah!*" the men keeping time by beating the air with their spear-throwers, held as previously described, while the women followed behind.

The leader, who had been running more rapidly than the rest, arrived at the grave just before the others, and with a final and much prolonged "*Ba-au!*" jumped on to the grave into which the spirit was supposed to have fled and began dancing wildly. He was quickly followed by the others, all of whom, except the *Mia, Uwinna*, and *Mura* women, who lay down on the ground close by, began to dance backwards and forwards on and around the grave shouting "*Wah! wah!*" and beating the air downwards as if to drive the spirit down, while with their feet they stamped upon and broke the twigs with which a newly made grave is always covered. When these were thoroughly broken up the dancing ceased, the men separated from the women and went to one side, while the widow and other women cleared up the *débris* which was carried a little distance away from the grave, immediately around which a space was cleared for a few yards. When this had been done the *Mia, Uwinna,* and *Mura* women, who had meanwhile been lying prostrate, wailing at the top of their voices, and now and again striking the ground with their bodies, got up and approached the grave. Gathered around this, they struck and cut their heads with fighting clubs, inflicting on themselves often severe wounds from which the blood flowed on to the grave. After a little time the cutting ceased and they moved away. The men stood solemnly on one side while the widow came forward with her sisters, blood and tribal, and scratched a hole in the top of the grave When this was deep enough the widow and the younger woman took the *Chimurilia* off their heads and, while all the women cried loudly, tore them to pieces, and, kneeling over the grave, deposited the remains in the hole. This done the fur string rings were treated in the same way, the feather tufts and *Alpita* were placed in the hole, above these was put the *pitchi*, in which the *Chimurilia* had been carried, and then the earth was heaped up. When this had been done the men prostrated themselves for a few minutes on the grave. When they got up their place was taken by the widow and other *Unawa* women, and lastly the *Mia, Uwinna,* and *Mura* women came and lay down.

After this was over, the widow, standing by the grave, rubbed off the white pipeclay from her body, thus showing that her mourning was at an end. She may still, if she likes, paint a narrow white band on her forehead, which is regarded as an intimation that she is not anxious to marry at present, as she still mourns, though to a less degree than before, for the dead man.

The spirit of the dead man was supposed to have been watching all these proceedings as he lay at the bottom of the grave. From the fact of the widow's having painted herself with white, and having made and worn the *Chimurilia*, he knows that he has been properly mourned for, while the fact of her wearing in her hair the gay feathers of the ring-neck parrot shows him that her period of mourning has come to an end. Having had similar experiences during his own lifetime he recognises that, with the *Chimurilia*, she buries the sorrow of herself and of his relatives and friends. The loud shouting of the men and women shows him that they do not wish to be frightened by him in his present state, and that they will be angry with him if he does not rest. Should he at any time forget the wishes of the survivors, then the presence of the broken up *Chimurilias* will remind him of them. He may still watch over his friends, guard them from harm, and visit them in dreams, but he must not come in such a way as to frighten them.

In the case of every grave, it may here be noted that the earth is always especially heaped up on one side; the side on which it is less heaped up, or on which sometimes a slight depression is left, is always the one facing towards the place at which, in the Alcheringa, the ancestor of the man lived and at which place the spirit double of the man has lived ever since with whom the *Ulthana* will now, for the most part, live.

In the case of the *Urpmilchima* of a woman the proceedings are somewhat different, and the following describes what took place at one which was held some twelve months after the death of a woman at Alice Springs.

All the women in the camp assembled at the *Erlukwirra* shortly after sunrise. The actual mother of the deceased was painted deeply all over with pipeclay, the tribal *Mias* were painted with the same material, but to a lesser extent, the *Ungaraitcha* had bands of white across the foreheads and chests, the *Uwinnas* were painted with dry yellow ochre on the body and head, and had also white bands across the forehead. After about ten minutes had been spent in embracing one another, while a continuous wailing was kept up, a start was made for the grave. After going a short distance they were met by a man who was a blood brother of the dead woman, and was accompanied by a number of his tribal brothers. Every one sat down and the lamenting again began. The *Ungaraitcha*, who carried the *pitchi* containing the *Chimurilias*, handed it to the brother, who bowed his head over it while he pressed it against his stomach for a minute or two, after which he removed one of the *Chimurilias* and placed it upon his mother's head. After it had been worn by the woman for a short time she replaced it in the *pitchi*, which was then taken by the *Ungaraitcha* and pressed against the stomach of each man in turn, the idea being to assuage their sorrow. The *Chimurilias* were then taken by the brother and placed on the heads of two tribal *Ungaraitcha* of the dead woman, and the party started for the grave, led, but only for a short distance, by the brother, all the other men remaining behind. No man is allowed to attend the *Urpmilchima* of a woman.

On the way to the grave the actual mother often threw herself heavily on the ground and attempted to cut her head with a digging stick. Each time she did so she was picked up by two women, whose duty it appeared to be to prevent her from hurting herself too much; but by the time that the grave was reached her body was a mass of bruises and covered over with sharp, three-cornered prickles. At the grave she threw herself upon it, tearing up the earth with her hands and being literally danced upon by the other women. Then all the *Mias* and *Uwinnas* threw themselves on the grave, the *Mias* cutting and hitting each other about the body until they were streaming with blood. Each of them carried a digging stick, which was used unsparingly on its owner's head and on those of the others, no one attempting to ward off the blows which they even invited. Amongst the *Mias* was an aged cripple, who was carried to the ground, and was one of the most keen participators in the ceremony. The *Uwinnas* though hard hit were not cut as were the *Mias*. After some time the other women dragged the *Mias* and *Uwinnas* away and then the

Ungaraitcha scraped a hole in the earth in which, after tearing them up, the *Chimurilias* were deposited. Once more the *Mias* threw themselves on the grave cutting each other's heads. The weeping and wailing of the women who were standing round seemed to drive them almost frenzied, and the blood, streaming down their bodies over the white pipe-clay, gave them a ghastly appearance. At last only the old mother was left crouching alone, utterly exhausted and moaning weakly on the grave. The *Ungaraitcha* approached her, and, rubbing off the pipe-clay, lifted her up. After this the ceremony came to an end and the grave was smoothed down and left.

No *Mia* would think of being absent from an *Urpmilchima* ceremony, which, though the Australian native cannot be supposed to feel pain as acutely as the average white man does, must yet involve no small amount of physical suffering. The women seem to work themselves up into a perfect frenzy, and to become quite careless as to the way in which they cut and hack themselves about, with, however, this restriction, notable on all such occasions, that however frenzied they apparently become no vital part is injured, the cutting being confined to such parts as the shoulders, scalp, and legs.

To those who have had no personal contact with savages, such as the Australian natives, and have never seen them at times when they are excited by the performance of ceremonies, the carrying out of which forms a most important feature in their lives, the above account may appear to be exaggerated. It is not for a moment to be supposed that the self-inflicted pain and the loud lamentings are to be taken as a measure of the grief actually felt. To a certain extent, perhaps to a very large one, the excessive display is due to the fact that it is a tribal custom, and as such has a very strong hold upon the imagination of a people whose every action is bound and limited by custom. There is nothing to which a blackfellow is so sensitive as to the contempt and ridicule of his fellows, to which non-compliance with a custom such as this will expose him. Partly, also, must be taken into account the fear which a native has that, unless a sufficient amount of grief be displayed, he will be harmed by the offended *Ulthana* or spirit of the dead man. In many respects the mind of the Australian native is like that of a child amongst ourselves. One moment he will be in a passion of grief or rage, and the next, if anything attracts his fancy, his humour will rapidly change and tears will give place to laughter. At the same time, he is certainly capable of genuine grief and of real affection for his children.

It may finally be pointed out that, in connection with the custom of painting the body of the mourner with white pipe-clay, there is no idea of concealing from the spirit of the dead person the identity of the mourner; on the other hand, the idea is to render him or her more conspicuous, and so to allow the spirit to see that it is being properly mourned for.

Chapter XV

The Iruntarinia and Arumburinga, or Spirit Individuals

The spirit part of an Alcheringa individual and the *Nanja* tree or rock—From the *Nanja* issues a second spirit, which is the *Arumburinga*—The spirit individuals are collectively the *Iruntarinia*—They are aggregated into local groups just as the living members of the tribe are—When a spirit goes into a woman there remains the *Arumburinga* which is its double—Relationship between an individual and his *Arumburinga*—When a man dies his spirit is called *Ulthana*—This goes finally to the *Nanja* spot and joins the *Arumburinga*—Certain gifted individuals can see the *Iruntarinia*—Habits of the *Iruntarinia*—Carrying off women—Presenting sacred ceremonies to particular men—Native feeling with regard to them.

IN the Arunta tribe there is a firm belief in the existence of spirit individuals, between whom and the individual members of the tribe there exists a very definite relationship.

As we have already seen when dealing with the Churinga, every individual is supposed to be the reincarnation of an Alcheringa being. Now these Alcheringa beings are very closely indeed associated with the animals or plants whose name they bear; indeed, some of them are regarded as having remained in the form of animals, such, for example, as the celebrated kangaroo called Ultainta. We can distinguish three forms of Alcheringa individuals, (1) those who were the direct transformations of animals or plants into human beings; (2) those who were at first *Inapertwa*, and who were transformed into men and women by the *Ungambikula*; and (3) those who, like the kangaroo mentioned, were never actually transformed into human beings, but were endowed with powers not possessed by the ordinary animal, and were practically animal-men. In all cases the Alcheringa individuals were possessed of powers far greater than those exercised by living men; they could travel on, or above, or beneath the ground; by opening a vein in the arm each of them could flood whole tracts of country or cause level plains to arise; in rocky ranges they could make pools of water spring into existence or could make deep gorges and gaps through which to traverse the ranges, and, where they planted their sacred poles, there rocks or trees arose to mark the spot. In regard to one point of fundamental importance they all agreed— each of them carried about some sacred object, a stick or stone called Churinga, with which was associated their spirit part. When, as happened to all of them sooner or later, they died and went into the earth, that Churinga remained behind and along with it the spirit part. At the same time there always arose some natural object, a rock or tree, to mark the spot where the Alcheringa being went into the earth, and this natural object was henceforth the *Nanja* rock or tree of the spirit of that particular individual whom it represented. From that *Nanja* there issued another spirit being whom the natives speak of as the *Arumburinga* of that particular individual. The spirit of each Alcheringa individual, when resident in the Churinga, is thus closely associated with, indeed watched over by, an *Arumburinga*, so that at each *Oknanikilla*, or local totem centre, we have a group of what are called the *Iruntarinia*, each of whom is either a spirit associated with a Churinga or else the *Arumburinga* of one of these spirits.

The *Iruntarinia* are especially given to wandering during the summer time, as they do not like the cold of the winter nights; in fact, during the latter period they spend most of their time in underground caves, where are streams of running water and perpetual sunshine, the two great desiderata of the Arunta native, as the one implies a plentiful food supply, and the other the warmth of which, being himself fond, he naturally supposes that the spirits are so too. Each local group has its group of *Iruntarinia* who are supposed to be associated with that special locality and its inhabitants, and of course bear the name of the Alcheringa individuals with whom they are each one associated, that is, the *Iruntarinia* are aggregated in local totemic groups just as the living members of the tribe are. Close to Alice Springs is an ancient hollow tree which is supposed to form a favourite entrance of the *Iruntarinia* of that district to the caves, which, according to native belief, stretch out for many miles underground.

When a spirit individual goes into a woman there still remains the *Arumburinga*, which may be regarded as its double, and this may either dwell along with the *Iruntarinia*, of whom it is of course one, or may at pleasure follow the spirit which is within the woman, or may attend the woman's husband as he goes out hunting. The *Iruntarinia* are, indeed, supposed to have their likes and dislikes as regards the human members of the group to which they belong. Some men who are popular amongst them will often be followed as they go out hunting by perhaps two or three of the spirit people who will assist them by driving prey towards them. A man's *Arumburinga* is not, however, supposed to watch over him continuously, but only in a more or less general kind of way. The idea in this respect is a vague one; but if, say, to take a special example, a man be out hunting and has his eye fixed on his prey, and for some reason, apparently without any cause, he suddenly looks down and sees a snake just where he was about to tread, then he knows at once that his *Arumburinga* is with him and prompted him to look down suddenly. The *Arumburinga* can of course travel over long distances with ease, and though they spend most of their time at the *Nanja* tree or rock, still if their human representative lives far away, as he may do, they will frequently visit him, and if he be gifted with the power of seeing spirits, will make themselves visible to him, or if not, then they sometimes send him a message through a man who is thus gifted.

When a man or woman dies and the body is buried, there remains the spirit part or *Ulthana*, that is, practically what may be called the equivalent of the ghost of the dead person, which is supposed to haunt the burial place and at night time to come into the camp, or it may go back to its old *Nanja* rock or tree; but at all events for a period it is supposed to spend a considerable time either around the grave or in the camp. The name *Ulthana* is given to the spirit until such time as the *Urpmilchima* ceremony has been performed and it has ceased to regularly haunt the camp and burial ground. The *Ulthana* is supposed to be capable, like other spirits, of hurting its enemies, and the sure sign of an attack by one of them is the presence of human teeth in the body of the victim. Medicine men will sometimes extract these, which are regarded as an infallible indication of an attack by an *Ulthana*.

Finally, when all the mourning ceremonies have been carried out, the *Ulthana* is supposed to leave the grave and to return to its *Nanja*, where it rejoins and lives along with its *Arumburinga*. After a time it gets itself another Churinga, with which it becomes associated, just as before it was associated with the Alcheringa Churinga, and then, after the lapse of some time, but not, it is supposed, until even the bones have crumbled away, it may once more be born again in human form.

To sum up the Arunta belief we have (1) the spirit part of an Alcheringa being in connection with a Churinga; (2) the *Arumburinga* which arises from the *Nanja* tree or rock, which marks the spot where the Alcheringa being went into the earth; and (3) the *Ulthana* or spirit part of the dead man or woman, and which is, in reality, identical with (1). The *Arumburinga* is changeless and lives for ever; the spirit part of the Alcheringa individual also lives for ever, but from time to time undergoes incarnation.

There are certain ideas with regard to the spirits or *Iruntarinia* with which we may conveniently deal here.

In addition to the medicine men, who have the power of seeing and communicating generally with the *Iruntarinia*, there are others to whom this privilege is granted. It is believed that, so say the natives, children who are born with their eyes open, or, as it is called, *alkna buma* (*alkna*, eye; *buma*, open), have this power when they arrive at maturity, provided always that they grow up sedate, for the *Iruntarinia* much dislike scoffers, frivolous people, and chattering men and women, and will not show themselves to such on any account. Men and women who are what is called irkun oknira (*irkun*, chattering; *oknira*, much) are supposed to annoy the spirits. Children who are born with the eyes closed, *alkna bunga*, cannot communicate with the spirits when they grow up unless they become medicine men.

In general appearance the *Iruntarinia* are supposed to resemble human beings, but they are always youthful looking, their faces are without hair, and their bodies are thin and shadowy. They are fond of decorating themselves with down or *undattha*, of which they are supposed to have unlimited supplies, some of which, as it is highly prized amongst the natives, they every now and again present to specially favoured individuals.

As a general rule they only go about at night time, and only make themselves visible when men or women are alone. They are fond of prowling about the camp, and sometimes, when successful in evading the notice of the camp dogs, who have the gift of seeing them at all times, they steal hair and fur string, or other material, which after a time is as mysteriously returned to its owner as it disappeared in the first instance. It is, so the natives say, no uncommon thing for a man to wake in the morning, or even after a sleep in the middle of the day, and find that his spare string has disappeared. He looks around for tracks, but finds none, and at once concludes that the *Iruntarinia* have been visiting him. He must not be angry or else he would offend them, and, moreover, he feels that his *Arumburinga*, who has most likely taken the string, needed it for some special purpose, and will return it safely when done with. Sooner or later he will awake to find it by his side. What may be the real meaning of this belief it is difficult to see, unless, what is not by any means impossible, the explanation lies in the fact that one of the so-called *Iruntarinia* men has cunningly taken the articles, and then after a time returned them, his object being to keep up the belief in the existence of the spirits, owing to his supposed power of interviewing whom he is held in considerable respect.

The spirits kill and eat all manner of game, but always uncooked, for they are not supposed to have any fires, and not seldom they steal game which has been wounded, but not killed on the spot, by men. For instance a kangaroo which has been speared but not killed will perhaps run away out of sight of the hunter, who tracks it up for some time and then loses all trace of it, and when this is so he knows that the *Iruntarinia* have taken it.

It is a matter of tradition that now and again they have carried off women who have wandered too far away from their camp after dark; in fact, it is not considered safe for a woman to go about too much alone, as there is always the danger of the *Iruntarinia* seizing her and carrying her away to be imprisoned in the depth of a cave. This fear, which is ever present with the women, acts as a wholesome check upon their wandering about alone too much. Not very long ago at a place called Undoolya, a woman strayed some distance from her husband's camp in the dusk, and he was only just in time, when attracted by her cries, to prevent her being carried off by the *Iruntarinia*, who had seized upon and were dragging her away when he came upon the scene.

There is a tradition that long ago, before any of the oldest men now living were born, a party going to the south from the Macdonnell Ranges was met at the Edith Range, near to Ooraminna water-hole, about twenty-five miles distant from Alice Springs, by a host of *Iruntarinia*, who drove the party back with great slaughter.

The *Iruntarinia* are also supposed to possess a number of Churinga, which are of both wood and stone, and occasionally they present one or two to specially favoured individuals. The men amongst the natives who, in addition to the medicine men, can communicate with them are held in considerable esteem, and to some of them the spirits impart sacred ceremonies. An example of one of these ceremonies, which is associated with the eagle-hawk totem, is described in connection with the Engwura. Another very characteristic *Iruntarinia* ceremony may be described here, as it is concerned with one of the important features in regard to the character of the spirits and their relation to men. This particular ceremony was shown to a medicine man of the witchetty grub totem by the *Iruntarinia* of a Hakea tree totem, for, as we have already said, the *Iruntarinia* naturally have their totems just as the men do whose doubles they in reality are, though at the same time, unlike the men, the *Iruntarinia* are endowed with the powers characteristic of the Alcheringa individuals.

The important feature of the ceremony consisted of a cross, each of the two arms of which were about six feet in length, one being fastened across the other at a distance of eighteen inches from what was the upper end when it was fixed upright in the ground. There were three performers, decorated as usual with lines of down, and each one of them wore in his head-dress two pointing sticks or *Ullinka*, arranged as if they were horns projecting in front. The curious cross is called *Umbalinyara*, and when the *Iruntarinia*, whose totem was the same as that of the medicine man's mother, showed it to the man, he told the latter to go and show it to his companions, and to tell them that no medicine man, however clever he might be, could possibly extract the cross if once the *Iruntarinia* had placed it in the body of a man. At first only one of the performers sat beside the cross and moved about, quivering in the usual way; then he stood to one side and from some little distance the other two were seen approaching, while the onlookers sang of how the *Iruntarinia* walked about in the Alcheringa and kept hiding out of sight, as the two performers pretended to do. They were performing all kinds of antics, causing the audience much amusement; finally they reached and sat down by the cross, round which they shuffled with their legs bent under them; after a short time the third man joined them, and then the audience rushed round and round them, shouting "*Wah! Wah!*" until, with a final prolonged quiver, the performance came to a close.

It is not at all necessary for the *Iruntarinia* to give the ceremony to a man of any particular totem; but, if the recipient wishes to hand it on as a compliment to some other man, which he frequently does, then that man must belong to the totem to which the ceremony refers.

It is again the *Iruntarinia* who are supposed frequently, but not always or of necessity, to communicate in dreams to the Alatunja of any group the time at which it is right for him to perform the ceremony of *Intichiuma*. They themselves perform similar ceremonies; and if a plentiful supply of, say, witchetty grub or emu appears without the performance of *Intichiuma* by the peoples of the respective totems, then the supplies are attributed to the performance of *Intichiuma* by friendly *Iruntarinia*.

To the native the *Iruntarinia* is a very real personage, who, as a general rule, is a beneficent being, though at times capable of great cruelty; he is in fact a man of the Alcheringa endowed with all the powers possessed by such an one. If he be offended, then he may place in the body of the offender one of his pointing sticks, or *Ullinka*, which as a general rule is a barbed stick a few inches in length and attached to a string, the malicious pulling of which causes severe pain, and the stick can only be removed by the aid of a very skilled medicine man.

There is always the feeling that it is well to be careful not to offend the *Iruntarinia*, or to tempt them by going out too much after dusk, when there is almost sure to be an odd spirit or two in search of lonely wanderers on whom they may at least play some unpleasant prank. On the other hand, the *Arumburinga* is supposed to keep a general watch over his human representative, and though he does not personally do the latter any harm, quite in fact the reverse, yet he cannot always shield him from the capricious malice of some other individual spirit.

Chapter XVI

The Making and the Powers of Medicine Men; Various Forms of Magic

Three methods of making medicine men—Those made by the *Iruntarinia*—Those made by the *Oruncha*—Those made by other medicine men—Description of the ceremonies attendant upon the initiation in each case—Functions of the medicine men—Pointing a bone or stick—Various forms of pointing sticks—*Injilla—Irna—Ullinka*—The methods of using them—Charming a spear—"Singing" a wound made with such a weapon—The hair of a dead man—Fur string ornaments of a dead man—Distribution of the hair girdle, armlets, etc., of a dead man—*Ililika* or knout—The *Tchintu*, supposed to contain the heat of the sun—Obtaining wives by magic—*Namatwinna*, a small Churinga which is swung round, the sound being supposed to reach the woman—Charming a forehead band—Instance of this—Only women whom the man can lawfully marry must be charmed—A man will be assisted by particular individuals in retaining a woman obtained by charming—Use of the *Lonka-lonka* as a charm—Use of the "trumpet" or *Ulpirra*—Churinga of a rat totem used to secure growth of beard—Churinga of a fly totem used to cure bad eyes—"Poison" stones of the Kaitish—Women and magic—Punishment of a man who has charmed away a woman and of the woman by means of magic—Sympathetic magic—*Arungquiltha* of various forms—Blowing spittle.

THE individuals to whom the name of medicine men is usually given—though perhaps the term magic men or wizards would in certain respects be better—have a very considerable influence in the tribe. Before dealing with their powers we may first of all describe the way in which a man is admitted to the status of medicine man.

In the Arunta, and the same holds true of the Ilpirra tribe, there are three distinct schools of medicine men—(1) those made by the *Iruntarinia* or spirits, (2) those made by the *Oruncha* who are in reality only a special class of spirit individuals of a mischievous nature, and (3) those initiated by other medicine men. Sometimes the three kinds of practitioners practise side by side, but the two first are more highly thought of than the third. In the northern groups of the tribe the medicine man is called a *Railtchawa*, on the Finke River *Nung-gara*, and in the south at Charlotte Waters, *Ingwalara*.

As an example of the making of medicine men by the *Iruntarinia* in the northern groups as well as in the Ilpirra tribe, we will describe what is said to take place in connection with the initiation of a man of the Alice Springs group.

About fourteen miles to the south of Alice Springs there is a cave in a range of hills which rises to the north of a wide level stretch of country, now called the Emily plain. This cave, like all those in the range, is supposed to be occupied by the *Iruntarinia*, or spirit individuals, each one of whom is in reality the double of one of the ancestors of the tribe who lived in the Alcheringa, or in other words of some living member, as each one of these is but the reincarnation of one of these ancestors. Amongst other powers possessed by the *Iruntarinia* is that of making medicine men.

When any man feels that he is capable of becoming one, he ventures away from the camp quite alone until he comes to the mouth of the cave. Here, with considerable trepidation, he lies down to sleep, not venturing to go inside, or else he would, instead of becoming endowed with magic power, be spirited away for ever. At break of day, one of the *Iruntarinia* comes to the mouth of the cave, and, finding the man asleep, throws at him an invisible lance which pierces the neck from behind, passes through the tongue, making therein a large hole, and then comes out through the mouth. The tongue remains throughout life perforated in the centre with a hole large enough to admit the little finger; and when all is over, this hole is the only visible and outward sign of the treatment of the *Iruntarinia*. How the hole is really made it is impossible to say, but as shown in the illustration it is always present in the genuine medicine man. In some way of course the novice must make it himself; but naturally no one will ever admit the fact, indeed it is not impossible that, in course of time, the man really comes to believe that it was not done by himself. A second lance thrown by the *Iruntarinia* pierces the head from ear to ear, and the victim falls dead and is at once carried into the depths of the cave, which extends far under the plain and is supposed to terminate at a spot beneath what is called the Edith Range, ten miles distant.

The name of the cave, of which the natives have a superstitious dread, is Okalparra, and in it the *Iruntarinia* are supposed to live in perpetual sunshine and amongst streams of running water—a state of affairs which we may regard as the paradise of the Arunta native. Once, not very long ago, two natives, so says tradition, not knowing the nature of the cave, entered it in search of water, and were never more heard of.

Within the cave the *Iruntarinia* removes all the internal organs and provides the man with a completely new set, after which operation has been successfully performed he presently comes to life again, but in a condition of insanity.

This, however, does not last long, and when he has recovered to a certain extent the *Iruntarinia*, who is invisible except to a few highly-gifted medicine men and also to the dogs, leads him back to his own people. The spirit then returns to the cave, but for several days the man remains more or less strange in his appearance and behaviour until one morning it is noticed that he has painted with powdered charcoal and fat a broad band across the bridge of his nose. All signs of insanity have disappeared, and it is at once recognised that a new medicine man has graduated. According to etiquette he must not practise his profession for about a year, and if during this time of probation the hole in his tongue closes up, as it sometimes does, then he will consider that his virtues as a medicine man have departed, and he will not practise at all. Meanwhile, he dwells upon his experiences, doubtless persuading himself that he has actually passed through those which are recognised as accompanying the making of a medicine man by the *Iruntarinia*, and at the same time he cultivates the acquaintance of other medicine men, and learns from them the secrets of the craft, which consist principally in the ability to hide about his person and to produce at will small quartz pebbles or bits of stick; and, of hardly less importance than this sleight of hand, the power of looking preternaturally solemn, as if he were the possessor of knowledge quite hidden from ordinary men.

In addition to providing him with a new set of internal organs the *Iruntarinia* is supposed to implant in his body a supply of magic *Atnongara* stones, which he is able to project into the body of a patient, and so to combat the evil influences at work within. So long as these stones remain in his body he is capable of performing the work of a medicine man, but sometimes they are for some reason withdrawn, in which event they are supposed to return to the *Iruntarinia* from whom they came, and with their departure the man feels at once that his powers have also departed. What causes the man to become convinced that the *Atnongara* stones have gone from him cannot be said; but every now and again an erstwhile medicine man is met with who tells you that they have gone away from him. There are certain foods from which the medicine man must abstain at risk of losing his powers. He may not for instance eat fat or warm meat, neither must he inhale the smoke from burning bones, nor go near to the nest of the large "bull-dog" ant (a species of Myrmecia), because if he were bitten by one of these he would lose his powers for ever. The loud barking of the camp dogs will sometimes also cause the *Atnongara* stones to take flight.

With regard to the second school of medicine men—those made by the *Oruncha*, that is, by the *Ulthana* or spirits of *Oruncha* men of the Alcheringa—the plan of procedure is essentially similar to that of the *Iruntarinia*, the only difference being that instead of being taken by the *Oruncha* into a special cave, he is taken down into the earth at the spot at which the *Oruncha* lives. Close by Alice Springs, for example, in a rough rocky hill lives the *Oruncha* of Chauritji, as the spot is called, and occasionally he seizes upon a man, takes him into the earth and makes him into a medicine man.

Women doctors, though of rare occurrence, are occasionally met with, and are usually made by *Oruncha*, but sometimes by *Iruntarinia*, the method of initiation being precisely similar in the case of the women to that of the men.

In the case of the third school, that is, the medicine men made by other medicine men, the method of procedure is naturally quite different, and the following is an account of what took place at the making of one on the Upper Finke River.

The young man who desired to be initiated spoke to two old medicine men, one of whom had been initiated by the *Iruntarinia* and the other by an *Oruncha*, and told them what he wanted; and on the following morning the latter, who are here called *Nung-gara*, took him along with another man to a secluded spot, and there they first of all made him stand up with his hands clasped behind his head, and told him that whatever happened he was to maintain perfect silence. The *Nung-gara* then withdrew from their bodies a number of small clear crystals called *Ultunda* (the equivalents of the *Atnongara* of the Alice Springs and other parts in the north of the tribe), which were placed one by one as they were extracted in the hollow of a spear-thrower. When a sufficient number had been withdrawn, the *Nung-gara* directed the man who had come with them to clasp the candidate from behind and to hold him tightly. Then each of them picked up some crystals, and taking hold of a leg, gripped the stones firmly and pressed them slowly and strongly along the front of the leg and then up the body as high as the breast-bone. This was repeated three times, the skin being scored at intervals with scratches, from which blood flowed. By this means the magic crystals are supposed to be forced into the body of the man, who was now told to lie down at full length on his back. The *Nung-gara* then went some little distance away, and, striking an attitude, pretended to project some of the crystals into the man's head. While doing this the left hand holding some of the crystals was placed on the palm of the right one, and in this position was jerked rapidly backwards and forwards several times. When this was over they came up again and once more subjected the legs and abdomen and this time the arms also to scoring with the stones, after which each of them pressed a crystal on the head of the novice and struck it hard, the idea being to drive it into the skull, the scalp being made to bleed during the process.

The next operation consisted in one of the *Nung-gara* taking a "pointing stick," and after having tied some hair string round the middle joint of the first finger of the man's right hand he forced the pointed end of the stick under the nail and for a considerable distance into the flesh, making thus a hole into which he pretended to press a crystal. The man was then told to keep a finger pressed up against the hole so as prevent the stone from coming out, after which he was told to remain perfectly quiet and go to sleep. In the middle of the day the scoring was repeated and again in the evening; after which the *Nung-gara* gave the man meat to eat in which they told him were *Ultunda* and after this he was given water, which actually did contain a few small crystals, which he was told were *Ultunda*, and which, without any hesitation, he drank straight off. On the day following his body was again scored, and he eat meat and drank water containing crystals, and in addition was given native tobacco[164] to chew, which also contained the same.

On the third day the scoring and eating and drinking were repeated, and he was told to stand up with his hands behind his head and to put his tongue out. One of the *Nung-gara* then withdrew from his skull just behind his ear (that is he told the novice that he kept it there) a thin and sharp *Ultunda*, and, taking up some dust from the ground, dried the man's tongue with it, and then, pulling it out as far as possible, he made with the stone an incision about half an inch in length. After a short rest one of the *Nung-gara*—the one who had been initiated by an *Oruncha*—rubbed the body of the man over with grease, and then placing him on his back proceeded to paint a special design upon his chest, abdomen and forehead. This design is called *Marilla*, and it is the *ilkinia* or sacred drawing of the *Oruncha*, the mark on the forehead representing what is called *orunchilcha*, which means, literally translated, "the devil's hand," the *Oruncha* being the evil or at least the mischievous spirit of the Arunta. A long black line in the centre of the drawing on the body represents the *Oruncha* himself, and the marks around it are supposed to represent the magic crystals which he carries in his body. When the drawing was complete the man's fur string bands were placed on his head, and leaves of a gum tree were fixed so as to hang down from beneath them over the forehead, partly hiding the drawing of the *Oruncha's* hand. The newly made medicine man was then told that he must remain at the *Urgunja*, that is the men's camp, and maintain a strict silence until the wound in his tongue had healed. He was also told that he must keep his thumb pressed up against the wound in his finger, until this also was healed, or else the magic stone would pass out. For a very long time also he must abstain from eating fat of any kind, nor must he touch the flesh of wild dogs, fish or Echnida. He might eat the marrow of the bones of different animals, but only if the bones were broken and were voluntarily given to him by other men.

When all was over he returned to the camp and remained at the *Ungunja* for about a month, during which time his *Unawa, Mia* and *Ungaraitcha* (but not his *Quitia* or younger sisters) sent him food. When he had recovered, and the treatment to which he had been subjected left him really in a low state, the *Nung-gara* men told him that he might go to his own camp; but that for some little time yet, about a month, he must talk very little and must in every way be abstemious. At night time he always slept with a fire between him and his *Unawa*, the idea of which was to render him visible to the *Oruncha* and to make it clear to the latter that he was holding aloof from every one, even his *Unawa*. Should he fail to do this, then the *Oruncha* would cause the magic power to leave him and to return to the old *Nung-gara*, and thus his powers as a medicine man would disappear for ever.

So far as his functions are concerned the medicine man may be regarded as partly, perhaps in the main, what this name implies, and at the same time as a wizard. His chief function is undoubtedly that of curing the natives; but as all ailments of every kind, from the simplest to the most serious, are without exception attributed to the malign influence of an enemy in either human or spirit shape, the method of curing takes the form of an exhibition of what is really sleight of hand, the object being to remove from the body of the patient something, such as a pointing stick or the broken pieces of a Churinga, which has been placed in it by the enemy. In many Australian tribes the equivalent of the medicine man amongst the Arunta is the one individual who can hold intercourse with the spirits; but in this tribe this is by no means the case, as there are men who, without being medicine men, are especially favoured in this respect. In many tribes also it is only the medicine men or their equivalents who have the power of, for example, securing by means of special incantations the illness or death of the individual whom it is desired to harm, and therefore to secure this end recourse must be had to a medicine man. In the Arunta, Ilpirra and other of the Central Australian tribes, this does not hold true; every man may have recourse to what is usually spoken of as sorcery, by means of which he may work harm of some kind to an enemy, and this power is not in any way confined to the medicine men, though on the other hand they are the only men who can counteract the evil influence of an enemy. At the same time there are certain of the very old medicine men who are supposed to be endowed by the *Iruntarinia* with the special power of bringing disease down upon not only individuals, but whole groups of men and women.

In cases of sickness the natives have implicit faith in the medicine man, and in serious cases two or three if they be available are called in, in consultation.[165] No reward of any kind is given, or expected, nor is any blame attached in case of non-success, the latter being attributed to the malignant action of superior magic on the part of some hostile spirit or individual, though it is sometimes said, as we have heard on different occasions, that if a particular medicine man had been present he would have been able to counteract the influence of the enemy when the individual who was present was unable to do so and the patient died. Just as amongst ourselves certain medicine men are regarded as better qualified and more able than others.

In ordinary cases the patient lies down on the ground while the medicine man bends over and sucks vigorously at the affected part of the body, spitting out every now and then supposed pieces of wood, bone or stone, the presence of which is believed to be causing the injury and pain. This suction is one of the most characteristic features of native medical treatment, as pain in any part of the body is at once supposed to be due to the presence of some foreign body which must be removed. Amongst especially the Western Arunta the medicine man in addition to the *Atnongara* stones is supposed to have a particular kind of lizard distributed through his body, which endows him with great suctorial power, such as the natives attribute to the lizard itself. In serious cases the action is more dramatic, and the medicine man needs a clear space in which to perform. The patient, perhaps too ill to sit up, is supported by some individual, while the medicine man who has been called in and may have come a long distance, gravely examines him and consults with other practitioners who may be present, and with the more immediate relatives of the patient, as to the nature of the illness. The diagnosis may occupy some time, during which every one maintains a very solemn appearance, all conversation being carried on in whispers. As a result the medicine man will perhaps pronounce that the sick man is suffering from a charmed bone inserted by a magic individual, such as a *Kurdaitcha*; or perhaps, worse still, the verdict is that one of the *Iruntarinia* has placed in his body an *Ullinka* or short barbed stick attached to an invisible string, the pulling of which, by the malicious spirit, causes great pain. If the latter be the case it requires the greatest skill of a renowned medicine man to effect a cure. While the patient is supported in a half-sitting attitude, the medicine man will first of all stand close by, gazing down upon him in the most intent way. Then suddenly he will go some yards off, and looking fiercely at him will bend slightly forwards and repeatedly jerk his arm outwards at full length, with the hand outstretched, the object being to thereby project some of the *Atnongara* stones into the patient's body, the object of this being to counteract the evil influence at work within the latter. Going rapidly and with a characteristic high knee action from one end of the cleared space to the other he repeats the movement with dramatic action. Finally, he comes close again, and, after much mysterious searching, finds and cuts the string which is invisible to every one except himself. There is not a doubt amongst the onlookers as to his having really done this. Then once more the projecting of the *Atnongara* stones takes place, and crouching down over the sick man he places his mouth upon the affected part and sucks, until at last either in fragments or, very rarely, and only if he be a very distinguished medicine man, the *Ullinka* is extracted whole and shown to the wondering onlookers, the *Atnongara* stones returning, unseen, once more into his own body. When this is over, unless it is simply a case of senile decay on the part of the patient, in which case the medicine man is too acute to take so much trouble when he knows pretty well that there is no chance of effecting a cure, the chances are strongly in favour of the latter, but if death ensues it is simply because the magic stick has been inserted in some vital part, or because the aid of the medicine man had not been called in early enough, or because his efforts had been maliciously thwarted by some *Iruntarinia*.

The functions of the medicine man as a wizard or sorcerer are associated with, first, bringing ill upon other people, and second, ascertaining who is responsible for the death of a native.[166]

We have already mentioned that certain very old medicine men are able to bring disease down not only on individuals but upon whole groups of men and women, but this is only, in reality, a further extension of the power possessed by each man of working harm by magic. Amongst, however, certain tribes such as the Mungaberra, living out to the west of the Macdonnell Ranges, the medicine men are supposed to have special powers. They can and often do assume the form of eagle-hawks, and when thus disguised, travel long distances at night time, visiting camps of other tribes, amongst whom they cause much suffering and even death by their habit of digging their sharp claws into people. Only recently, in the presence of one of the authors, a medicine man extracted parts of eagle-hawk claws from a native of the Arunta tribe who had been maliciously attacked in this way at night time by a Mungaberra medicine man.

However, as a wizard, the function of the medicine man is mainly associated with finding out the particular individual who is responsible for the death of any native. Sometimes when a man is dying he will whisper in the ear of the medicine man the name of the culprit, but even if he does not do so, the medicine man will often state as soon as death has taken place the direction in which he lives and very probably the group to which he belongs. It may perhaps be two or three years before he discovers the actual man, but sooner or later he does so. During the progress of the Engwura, which we witnessed, news was brought in to the camp that a very celebrated old man had died far away out to the west. His death was due simply to senile decay, but along with the news of his decease word was brought that he had been killed by a charmed stick pointed at him by a man of a distant group, the locality of which was stated with certainty.

Another duty of the medicine man is, as already described, to accompany the *Kurdaitcha*, and to assist him by magic power in rendering the victim unconscious of what has befallen him.

In what has just been described in connection with the medicine men, as well as in the account of the *Kurdaitcha* and *Illapurinja*, certain forms of magic have been dealt with. There remain however certain other customs which may be grouped under the general designation of magic, and which may be conveniently dealt with together.

The first of these, which is one of the commonest forms of magic in many savage tribes, and is indeed world-wide in its distribution, is the pointing of a bone or stick at some individual with the idea of injuring him. Amongst the Arunta tribe these pointing sticks or bones are known under various names, such as *Injilla, Irna, Ullinka, Ingwania,* and *Takula*, of which we will describe the nature and uses of the first three as typical examples.

The *Injilla* is a small bone about six inches long, at one end of which is a small lump of resin procured from the porcupine grass, and round this a few strands of human hair string are wound. It is used by a *Kurdaitcha* man who places it under the tongue of his victim, its special virtue when thus employed being that it renders the injured man perfectly oblivious of what has befallen him at the hands of the *Kurdaitcha*. It may also be used for the same purpose as the *Irna* now to be described.

The *Irna* is a small piece of wood perhaps as much as nine inches in length, though it may be less than this. At one end it tapers to a point and at the other is tipped with a small lump of porcupine grass resin. The stick is further ornamented with a series of notches which are apparently made with a fire-stick. The *Injilla* or *Irna*—both being equally effective—are charmed, that is, are sung over, and thereby endowed with magic power in the following way. The man who has made one goes alone into the bush to some unfrequented spot at a distance from the main camp, taking great care that he is seen by no one. After making quite sure that he is not being watched he chooses a hidden spot for his incantations and places the *Injilla* or *Irna* in the ground. Then he crouches down above it and in muttered tones hisses out the following curses:—

"*I-ta pukalana purutulinja appinia-à*" (May your heart be rent asunder).

"*Purtulinja appinaa intaapa inkirilia quin appani intar-pakala-à*" (May your backbone be split open and your ribs torn asunder).

"*Okinchincha quin appani ilchi ilchaa-a*" (May your head and throat be split open).

When this has been done he returns to his camp leaving the *Injilla* or the *Irna*, as the case may be, in the secret spot for three or four days, after which he removes it to within a short distance of the camp. Here he carefully conceals it until it is dark, and then while the natives are sitting chatting round the camp fire he steals out into the darkness, procures the *Injilla* or *Irna*, and stealthily approaches the camp until the features of his victim are clearly discernible by the fire light, he himself, of course, keeping carefully out of view. He now turns his back upon his victim and stooping down jerks the *Injilla* or *Irna* towards him several times muttering the curse already quoted as he does so in a subdued tone. When this has been done he once more conceals the implement and returns to camp. The victim is within a short time—a month at most—supposed to sicken and die, unless his life be saved by the magic of a medicine man. When the charm takes effect and the victim becomes ill, the man secretly takes away the implement which he has used, and in the case of the *Injilla* burns the hair string while expressing the wish that the destruction of his enemy's life may be as surely brought about as has been that of the string.

It is common to attribute almost all deaths, or at least a majority of them, to the use of a "poison" bone or stick, and the performance of "pointing" has to be conducted in strict secrecy, as, were any man caught in the act, he would be most severely punished and most likely put to death.

The *Ullinka* which is always used by the *Iruntarinia* is a special form of *Irna* with a hooked end instead of a lump of resin, and is supposed to be a favourite charm used by malevolent spirits to annoy and often to kill men against whom they have some special grudge. The *Ullinka* is projected into the body of the victim, and the string to which it is attached is every now and then maliciously pulled by the *Iruntarinia* so as to add to the annoyance and pain of the man. As we have already said, it requires a very able medicine man to abstract one of these so as to make quite sure that there is no part of it left in the body of the victim.

In addition to procuring death by giving an enemy a bone or stick it is a very common thing to charm a spear by singing over it.

Any bone, stick, spear, &c., which has thus been "sung" is supposed to be endowed with what the natives call *Arungquiltha*, that is magical poisonous properties, and any native who believes that he has been struck by, say, a charmed spear is almost sure to die whether the wound be slight or severe unless he be saved by the counter magic of a medicine man. There is no doubt whatever that a native will die after the infliction of even a most superficial wound if only he believes the weapon which inflicted the wound had been sung over and thus endowed with *Arungquiltha*. He simply lies down, refuses food and pines away. Not long ago a man from Barrow Creek received a slight wound in the groin. Though there was apparently nothing serious the matter with him, still he persisted in saying that the spear had been charmed and that he must die, which accordingly he did in the course of a few days. Another man coming down to the Alice Springs from the Tennant Creek contracted a slight cold, but the local men told him that the members of a group about twelve miles away to the east had taken his heart out, and believing this to be so he simply laid himself down and wasted away. In a similar way a man at Charlotte Waters came to one of the authors with a slight spear wound in his back. He was assured that the wound was not serious, and it was dressed in the usual way, but he persisted in saying that the spear had been sung, and that though it could not be seen yet in reality it had broken his back and he was going to die, which accordingly he did. As a result of this a party was organised among the members of his group to avenge his death, and the man who had wounded him with the charmed weapon was killed.

Instances of occurrences such as these could be multiplied, and though of course it is impossible to prove that death would not have followed under any circumstances, that is whether the native had or had not imagined the weapon to have been "sung," yet, with a knowledge of what wounds and injuries he will survive if he does not suspect the intervention of magic, it is not possible to explain death under such circumstances except as associated directly with the firm belief of the injured man that *Arungquiltha* has entered his body, and that therefore he must die.

It will be noticed in these cases that the medicine man does not intervene. Wounds from charmed spears or other weapons are of a different nature from injuries due to the placing of a pointing stick in the body of the victim. In this latter case there is something tangible which the medicine man can remove, but in the former there is simply an intangible form of *Arungquiltha*. A case which occurred recently during a fight at Alice Springs will serve to illustrate the matter. An Arunta native was hit by a boomerang which inflicted a wound by no means dangerous as such, but the difficulty was that the wounded man declared that the weapon, which had come down from the Ilpirra tribe which lives away to the north of the Arunta, had been "sung" by an Ilpirra man. An Arunta medicine man was of no use under such circumstances, but fortunately there was an Ilpirra man in camp and he was brought and "sang," that is, went through the usual pantomime of making passes, sucking and muttering over the wound. As he belonged to the same locality as the man who had originally "sung" the boomerang it was supposed that he could counteract the influence of Illpirra *Arungquiltha*, which he successfully did.

Another form of magic instrument is made from the hair of a dead man. When a man dies his hair is cut off by his sons, if he has no sons then by his younger brothers or by their sons, or, failing them, by the sons of his elder brothers. While the hair is being cut off, the women and children retire out of sight. Some time after the burial of the man the hair is taken to a secluded spot safe from the intrusion of women, and here the sons and younger brothers of the deceased make it up into a hair-girdle which is given to a son of the dead man, the eldest son having the first right to it, or, failing him, to a younger brother. If neither son nor younger brother be alive then it goes to the eldest son of an elder brother. The *Okilia* or elder brother cannot himself inherit the girdle, which is called a *Kirra-urkna* and must always descend to a man who is tribally younger than the dead man. This girdle is a valued possession, and is only worn on such occasions as a tribal fight, or when a man is going out as a *Kurdaitcha*. It is supposed to be endowed with magic power and to add to its possessor all the war-like attributes of the dead man from whose hair it was made. It ensures accuracy of aim and at the same time destroys that of an adversary. In the same way a small piece of a dead man's hair—cut from the body after death—is sometimes placed in the inside of one of the ordinary hair necklets, and worn as a charm by men. To even place by the side of a woman or child one of these magic girdles or necklets would be productive of serious evil to her.

A dead man's *Immitnia* and *Kulchia*, that is his opossum fur-string girdle and head-bands, are also held in high esteem. When a man dies these are carefully preserved, and when the *Urpmilchima* ceremony has been performed at the grave they are made up into what are called *Okinchalanina irrulknakinna*. The first of these two words is the name given to the ordinary necklet made of opossum fur-string, which is well greased and red-ochred, and worn on ordinary occasions. The second is compounded of the words *Irra*, he, *Ulkna*, grave, *kinna*, from, which will serve to show that the ornaments worn by the dead man are supposed to be endowed in some way with the attributes of the dead man.

When these necklets have been made, it is then decided to whom they shall be given. While the hair of the dead man himself must go to some member of his own moiety of the tribe, that is to his father's side, the *Irrulknakinna* must be given to some member of the other moiety, that is to his mother's side, and not only this, but they must go to a member of another local group. They are what is called *ekirinja*, or tabu, to men of the same local group as that to which the dead man belonged.

When the necklets are ready, the men of a neighbouring group are summoned by messengers sent for the purpose and assemble at the men's camp to which the women may not come, and here the son or younger brother of the dead man places the *Irrulknakinna* round the necks of the chosen recipients by whom they are very highly valued.

In the central and northern groups of the Arunta tribe this special form of necklet is made of perhaps four or five circles of hair-string each about half an inch in diameter, but in the western Arunta there is but one circle, or rather horse-shoe shaped structure forming a coil about an inch and a half in diameter, the two ends of which are tied together by strands of opossum fur-string.

A form of string implement also associated with magic is called *Ililika*. This consists of about fifty or sixty comparatively thin strands of tightly strung string, made of vegetable fibre. From their use they may be spoken of as knouts, and though seldom seen, most of the men carry one about in their wallet. The sight of one is alone enough to cause the greatest fright to a woman who has offended her blackfellow, while the stroke is supposed to result in death, or at least in maiming for life. In addition to this use, the *Ililika* is sometimes unwound and cracked like a whip in the direction of any individual whom it is desired to injure when the evil influence is supposed to travel through the air, and so to reach the victim. Though in use amongst the Arunta, Ilpirra, Kaitish and Warramunga tribes, they are only actually manufactured and endowed with their magic power by the members of the latter tribe, and it is the knowledge of this fact which causes them to be viewed with such peculiar dread by the women. Magic of a distant group has a very potent influence on the average native mind.

Away out to the west on the internal border-land of Western Australia is a tribe known as the Wyingurri. Amongst these the name of the sun is *Tchintu*, and the same name is also applied to an object of magic which consists of a small pear-shaped lump of porcupine grass resin, into one end of which are affixed two incisor rat-teeth, and at the other end is attached a stout piece of hair-string about two feet in length. The string is covered with red down, and the whole is carried out of sight, wrapped up in thin pieces of bark of the paper-bark tree. The specimen which is figured we owe to the kindness of Mr. C. E. Cowle, who obtained it from a Luritcha man living away to the west of the Arunta tribe, and to him it had again been given by an old medicine man of the Wyingurri tribe, the members of which are reported to be very expert in matters of magic. In connection with this statement it may be remarked that all distant groups are, as a general rule, supposed to be especially fond of, and powerful in, the practice of magic. This *Tchintu* is supposed to contain the heat of the sun, and it is believed that by placing it on the tracks of an individual the latter will be seized by a violent fever which will rapidly burn him up. When examining the specimen in the presence of the Luritcha man to whom it belonged, a little of the down fell off, and it was with evident fear pushed aside and then covered over with sand.

We may now deal with various forms of magic which are concerned with the procuring of wives, though it must be remembered that women obtained, or supposed to be obtained, by the aid of these magic means, must belong to the proper class into which, and into which only, a man may marry. That is, for example, a Panunga man can only legitimately use magic to help him to secure a Purula woman.

The first of these methods is used when the woman, whom it is desired to charm, lives in some distant group. When a man is desirous of securing such a woman for himself, and it makes no difference whether she be already assigned or not to some other man—indeed she is perfectly sure to be so—he takes a small wooden Churinga about six or eight inches in length, or, if he has not got one, then he will manufacture one for the occasion, marking it with a design of his own totem. This particular form of Churinga is called a *Namatwinna*[167] from the words *nama*, grass, and *twinna*, to strike, because when using it, it is struck against the ground. Armed with it he goes into the bush accompanied by two or three friends whom he has asked to come, and who may be of any relationship to him. All night long the men keep up a low singing of Quabara songs together with the chanting of amorous phrases of invitation addressed to the woman. At daylight the man stands up alone and swings the Churinga, causing it first to strike the ground as he whirls it round and round and makes it hum. His friends remain silent, and the sound of the humming is carried to the ears of the far-distant woman, and has the power of compelling affection and of causing her sooner or later to comply with the summons. Not long ago at Alice Springs a man called some of his friends together and performed the ceremony and in a very short time the desired woman, who was on this occasion a widow, came in from Glen Helen about fifty miles to the west of Alice Springs, and the two are now man and wife, the union being regarded as a perfectly lawful one as they belonged to intermarrying classes.

This custom is a well-recognised one. If, by its means, a man obtains the wife of another blackfellow and the latter comes armed, as he most likely will, to resent the interference, then the men who belong to the group of the aggressor will stand by the latter and support his claims, if necessary, by fighting. The woman naturally runs some risk, as, if caught in the act of eloping, she would be severely punished, if not put to death. Under no circumstances would a man be aided in securing a woman of a class into which he might not lawfully marry, nor would he, even if successful in doing so, receive any assistance from his friends in the event of a quarrel arising, as it certainly would, in connection with the abduction.

The custom is by no means confined to the Arunta tribe, but exists at all events among the Ilpirra, Walparri, Kaitish and Warramunga tribes, all of whom use Churinga which are the equivalents of the *Namatwinna* of the Arunta.

Another method of obtaining a wife by magic is by means of a charmed *Chilara* or head-band. The latter consists of a number of strands usually made of opossum or euro fur-string placed side by side so as to form a flat band which stretches across the forehead from ear to ear. On special occasions, such as dancing festivals this will be decorated with designs drawn in red ochre and pipeclay. When a native is desirous of charming a woman he will make one of these *Chilara* out of euro fur-string and whiten it with pipeclay, or else, so it is said, by rubbing it against the white bark of *Eucalyptus terminalis*. Then in secret he charms it by singing over it, and placing it on his head, wears it about the camp so that the woman can see it. By some mysterious means her attention is drawn to it, and she becomes violently attracted to the man, or, as the natives say, her internal organs shake with eagerness. At night, if possible, when all is quiet she creeps into his camp. Sometimes two men who are friends will decide upon making and wearing *Chilara* so as to charm two women. After wearing them they will depart to their own camps and the women, while pretending to go out hunting, will in reality follow the men and probably not be missed till the evening, when the unlucky husbands will return to find their respective camps empty. How often this method is resorted to it is difficult to say, but it certainly is employed at times. At Alice Springs recently a man named Urkaitcha purinia, when visiting a spot about seventy miles away, to the east, his wife being with him, was attracted by a woman living there who was called Thunginpurturinia, who was the wife of another man. While out hunting during the day he made *Chilara*, and having charmed it by singing over it wore it when coming into the camp, where he took care to show himself to the woman, who in her own words became *Okunjepunna oknirra*, the equivalent of our expression "much infatuated." That night she went to his camp and talked with his wife, and the next day when he left for Alice Springs she followed him, and has ever since been living with him, though the elopement has been the cause of very much ill-feeling between the two groups concerned.

In another case known to us a man named Allapita charmed by means of a *Chilara* a woman named Irriakura, who was afterwards captured and killed by her previous husband and his friends, who went in search of her and her charmer.

Whilst it is an undoubted fact that these methods of obtaining possession of a woman are actually practised it is not probable that they are of very frequent occurrence, for the simple reason that everything depends on the acquiescence of the woman, and with the sure and certain knowledge that, if caught in the act of deserting the man to whom she has been assigned, she will meet with very severe punishment and in all probability be put to death, while, even if not caught, she is almost certain to come in for rough handling during the course of the quarrel which is bound to ensue, the woman is not very easily charmed away from her original possessor. Still, as we have said, she sometimes is, and this method allows of the breaking through of the hard and fast rule which for the most part obtains, and according to which the woman belongs to the man to whom she has been betrothed, probably before her birth.

It may be as well to note that these "runaway marriages" which are seemingly irregular are not so in reality. Certain men and women are *Unawa* to one another, that is they may lawfully marry, and so long as the contract is entered into between two who are thus entitled tribally to enter into it there is no irregularity. It is a breach of manners but not of custom, and it then comes to be merely a test of strength between the local friends of the two men who are both *Unawa*, that is tribal husbands, of the girl. It is also worthy of note as contrasted with what takes place in other parts of the continent, that the men to assist a particular man in a quarrel are those of his locality, and not of necessity those of the same totem as himself, indeed the latter consideration does not enter into account and in this as in other matters we see the strong development of what we have called the "local influence" when dealing with the Engwura ceremony. The men who assist him are his brothers, blood and tribal, the sons of his mother's brothers, blood and tribal. That is if he be Panunga man he will have the assistance of the Panunga and Ungalla men of his locality, while if it comes to a general fight he will have the help of the whole of his local group. This division of the tribe into local groups with the consequent development of a more or less strong local feeling is one of the leading features of the Arunta tribe.

Another means of charming women is found in the much valued shell ornament which is traded down through the centre of the continent from the tribes living away on the north coast who manufacture it out of the shell of *Melo ethiopica* or *Meleagrina margaritifera*. This is often worn, especially at corrobborees, suspended from the waist-girdle.

If a man desires to charm a particular woman he takes the *Lonka-lonka*,[168] as the ornament is called, to some retired spot and charms it by singing over it "*Ma quatcha purnto ma quillia purtno*," which words convey an invitation to the lightning to come and dwell in the *Lonka-lonka*. After the charming has taken place it is hung on a digging-stick at the corrobboree ground until night time, when the man removes it and ties it on to his waist-belt. While he is dancing the woman whom he wishes to attract alone sees the lightning flashing on the *Lonka-lonka*, and all at once her internal organs shake with emotion. If possible she will creep into his camp that night or take the earliest opportunity to run away with him.

A woman will also be charmed by the use of a native horn of very primitive construction called an *Ulpirra*. A small fire is lighted and a body of smoke made by placing green bush on it; the *Ulpirra* is then held over the fire so that the smoke passes through it while the man charms it by singing, whilst he thrusts his head into and swallows some of the smoke. That night at the corrobboree ground while the dance goes on he blows the horn and at once the woman becomes *Okunjepunna oknirra*, or much infatuated, she alone feeling the influence of the charmed *Ulpirra*.

Amongst the Churinga there are certain special ones which are used for special magic purposes, the latter having an intimate relationship to the totem to which they belong. One of these is called *Churinga Unginia* and belongs to a rat totem, the animal being distinguished by the possession of very long whiskers. Unlike any other Arunta Churinga with which we are acquainted, this one has a lump of resin attached to one end and is painted with alternate stripes of red and black. It is in special request by the young men, as it has a remarkable power of increasing the growth of the beard. The ceremony is a very simple one, the chin of the young man is first of all pricked all over with a pointed bone and then carefully stroked with the Churinga. During the rubbing it is supposed that a stimulus resulting in the growth of whiskers, the most striking feature of the animal represented by the Churinga, passes from the latter to the chin which it rubs.

Another Churinga which belongs to the Amunga or fly totem is used as a charm in the case of eyes, which, as not unfrequently happens in Central Australia, become completely closed up by inflammatory growth consequent upon the bites of the innumerable flies which form one of the most objectionable pests of the Centre. In the case of the whisker stone, as we have seen, it is supposed to put some of its virtues into the man who uses it, whereas in the case of the fly stone the idea seems to be exactly reversed, as the stone is supposed either to withdraw something out of the eyes which has been put in by the flies, or possibly to supply something which will act as an antidote to what the animals, one of which it represents, have put in.

Amongst the Kaitish and other tribes curious small stones called by the former *Mauia* are met with. They are supposed to be highly charged with magic power, and amongst other uses to which they are put, is that of causing the victim, to bring about the death of whom they are used, to die whilst asleep. One method of securing this result is to place a tiny fragment of the stone on a long stick or the blade of a spear, and then to carefully drop it on to the face of the victim while he sleeps, for if this be done then he will never awake. The Arunta natives, though they have no *Mauia* stones themselves, are aware and extremely frightened of them, and on one occasion one of them was brought to one of the authors to be examined. The parcel in which it was carefully wrapped was the size of an ordinary pillow, but wrapper after wrapper was taken off until the dreaded contents were exposed to view, and proved to be a minute stone, which subsequent analysis showed was a fragment of magnesium limestone.

Amongst the Kaitish and Warramunga tribes a stone object, identical in form with the Churinga which they use, is devoted to magic purposes. It is somewhat pear-shaped and flat, and at the narrow end, as is characteristic of the Churinga of these tribes, is a small lump of resin to which a strand of human hair-string is attached. The stone is held in the palm of the right hand, the thumb of that hand is linked with the little finger of the left, and the two hands, thus linked together, are held in front of the face and jerked three times towards the person whom it is intended to kill, an incantation being uttered at the same time.[169]

Amongst the Arunta tribe, women, while not dealing with magic as a general rule, or at any rate not to anything like the extent that the men do, are still supposed to be able to exercise peculiar powers in regard to the sexual organs.[170] To bring on a painful affection in those of men, a woman will procure the spear-like seed of a long grass (*Inturkirra*), and having charmed it by singing some magic chant over it, she awaits an opportunity to point and throw it towards the man whom she desires to injure. Shortly after this has been done the man experiences pain, as if he had been stung by ants, his parts become swollen, and he at once attributes his sufferings to the magic influence of some woman who wishes to injure him. A woman may also charm a handful of dust which she collects while out digging up "yams" or gathering seeds, and having "sung" it brings it into camp with her. She takes the opportunity of sprinkling it over a spot where the man whom she wishes to injure is likely to micturate. If he should do so at this spot he would experience a scalding sensation in the urethra and afterwards suffer a great amount of pain. Women may also produce disease in men by singing over and thus charming a finger, which is then inserted in the vulva; the man who subsequently has connection with her will become diseased and may lose his organs altogether, and so when a woman wishes to injure a man she will sometimes, after thus "poisoning" herself, seek an opportunity of soliciting him, though he be not her proper *Unawa*. Syphilitic disease amongst the Arunta is, as a matter of fact, very frequently attributed to this form of magic, for it must be remembered that the native can only understand disease of any form as due to evil magic, and he has to provide what appears to him to be a suitable form of magic to account for each form of disease.

As love-charms women will sometimes make and "sing" special *okinchalanina* or fur-string necklets, which they place round the man's neck, or they may simply charm a food such as a witchetty grub or lizard and give this to the man to eat.

Just as we find magic used in connection with the securing of a wife who is already the property of another man, so we find also a special form of magic employed in the punishment of the individual who is guilty of the theft. The western and south-western Arunta are famed for their skill in magic, and especially in various forms of *Arungquiltha*.[171] To punish a man who has stolen a wife and who belongs to a distant group, or to one which is too powerful to make it advisable to allow matters to come to an open fight, two men, perhaps the former husband and another man to whom the stolen woman is *Unawa*—but they need not of necessity be either of them *Unawa*—prepare a special implement of magic. A thin flake of flint or quartzite, in fact a miniature knife blade, is made, to the blunt end of which a lump of resin is attached, and to this a miniature spear is fixed. Then a very small spear-thrower is made, and into this a bole is bored so that the end of the spear fits tightly into it. To this implement the name of *Arungquiltha* is applied. It is painted all over with red ochre and when this is dry, cross bars of white, yellow and black are added along the whole length.

It is now sung over and left in the sun for some days at a secluded spot, the men going to it every day and singing to it a request to go and kill the man who stole the woman, the words of the request being "Go straight; go straight and kill him." Finally the two men come to the spot, and after singing for some time one man kneels down, huddling himself together with his forehead touching the ground in front of his knees, while the other man takes up the magic implement, and, standing between the feet of the first man, throws the thing with all his force in the direction in which his enemy lives. When he has done this he kneels, huddled up in the same position as the other man, and with his head between the latter's feet. In this position they remain in perfect silence until they hear the *Arungquiltha*, which is regarded in this instance as an evil spirit resident in the magic implement, saying, "Where is he?" Upon hearing the voice—and sometimes they have to remain in this most uncomfortable position for several hours—they get up and return to camp, where they abstain from talking and are always listening. By and by if the *Arungquiltha* be successful—and it is generally supposed to be so—they hear a noise like a crash of thunder, and then they know that, in the form of a great spear, it has gone straight to the man, mutilating and thus killing him. This form of *Arungquiltha* is frequently seen at night, and sometimes even during the daytime, streaking across the sky like a ball of fire. Quite recently a man out west was found mutilated and dead, and certain men living at Henbury on the Finke River are accused of having projected the *Arungquiltha*.

Another form of *Arungquiltha* which produces comets is brought about in the following way, and is only used for punishing women. If a woman runs away from her husband and he is unable to recover her, he and his friends, that is men of his local group, assemble at a secluded spot where a man skilled in magic draws upon the surface of a small patch of ground, which has been cleared and smoothed down for the purpose, a rough diagram, of which the accompanying sketch (Fig. 107) is a copy. This drawing is simply marked out on the ground with the finger and is intended to represent the figure of the woman lying down on her back. It is called

Aura, a term which has much the same significance as the word emblem.[172] While the drawing is being made, and throughout the whole proceedings, low chants are sung, the burden of which is an exhortation to the *Arungquiltha* to go out and enter her body and dry up all of her fat. When the drawing is done a piece of green bark is placed at the spot marked with an asterisk. This is supposed to represent the spirit part of the woman, and then all the men who are present stick into it a number of miniature spears, which have been made for the purpose and have been "sung." The spears with the bark into which they are fixed are then flung as far as they can be thrown in the direction in which the woman is supposed to be. The party now returns to camp, and sooner or later, very often after the lapse of a considerable time, the woman's fat dries up, she dies, and her *ulthana*, or spirit, appears in the sky in the form of a shooting-star.

We have already, in the account of Undiara, referred to the old man Ungutnika who plucked boils from his body, each of which turned into one of the group of stones which are still to beseen at Undiara and are called *Aperta tukira*, that is stone sores. Men who desire to harm others in one particular way make a number of small wooden imitation spears and go to these stones, at which they throw the spears, taking care that the points strike the stones. Then the spears are picked up and thrown one by one from a spear-thrower in the direction of the man, whom it is desired to injure. The spears are supposed to carry away with them *Arungquiltha* from the stones, and this produces an eruption of painful boils in the individual or individuals towards whom they are thrown. Sometimes a whole group of people can be afflicted in this way by a skilful magic man.

Yet another form of *Arungquiltha* is associated in tradition with the story of an emaciated emu. In the Alcheringa a very thin and emaciated emu came from the far north-east, from a mythical place called Atnangara. It carried on its head a

Nurtunja, and a Churinga under its armpit. Its body was covered with feathers and inside it carried some eggs. The creature was in fact half emu and half man, and belonged to the Panunga class. Unlike other Alcheringa individuals it did not perform sacred ceremonies as it travelled along. The first known camping place was at Ilpma in the Strangway Range, and its only food consisted of Udnirringa berries which form a favourite food of the emu. From Ilpma it travelled south to Udnurringunia, where two eggs were deposited which turned into stone, and are now represented at the spot by two large round black stones. Then it went on to Uknurulinga in the Strangway Range, and thence travelled on till it came to Iralta, where it passed a lot of emu men and women, but being ashamed of its poor condition it did not go near to them. They had *Nurtunjas* which they carried on their heads. Then it passed Narpipa without seeing the Unjiamba people who dwelt and had sprung up there. Walking on across the Burt Plain, which lies to the north of the Macdonnell Ranges, it came to what is now called Bond Springs, where a number of emu men and women were met who had originated there and with whom it fraternised for a time. These people, however, did not like it because it was so thin and miserable-looking, so they at length drove it away, and going on it camped halfway between Bond Springs and Undoolia, a slender column of stone rising to mark the spot where it camped, and this may be seen to the present day. Travelling on amongst the Ranges it came to a spot a little to the east of the Jessie Gap, where it deposited its solitary Churinga, from which a Bulthara man named Untwarntwa now living is descended. At this spot the poor creature became still more emaciated and finally changed into a large stone, which became charged with *Arungquiltha*, or evil influence, for in some curious way thinness seems to be especially associated with the latter.

Any one wishing to injure another person may perform a simple ceremony here, which consists merely in rubbing the stone with the hands while muttering an exhortation to the evil influence to come forth and afflict the person whom he desires to harm. After this has been done the person will gradually grow thinner and thinner until he withers away altogether.

Another stone close to a large clay pan not far from Alice Springs marks the spot where a lizard man died in the Alcheringa. He also was thin and emaciated, and so the stone is charged with *Arungquiltha*, which by rubbing and muttering, as just described in the case of the emu stone, may be projected into the body of an enemy.

Amongst other forms of magic the following may also be noticed. Just as the stones marking the spot where the thin animals or men died are associated with magic, so we find the same to hold good in the case of other trees and stones which are associated with special individuals of the Alcheringa. Near to Charlotte Waters, for example, is a tree which sprung up to mark the spot where a blind man died. This tree is called the *Apera okilchya*, that is the blind tree, and the spot where it stands the *Mira okilchya*, or blind camp. Should this be cut down it is supposed that the men of the locality in which it grows will become blind: or if any one wishes to produce blindness in an enemy, all that he has to do is to go alone to the tree, and while rubbing it mutter his desire and an exhortation to the *Arungquiltha* to go forth and afflict his enemy. Along by the side of the Hugh River in the Macdonnell Ranges close to Mount Conway is a stone which marks where a blind man of the wild duck totem died; and here again the same ceremony may be performed. Close also to Temple Bar, a gap in the ranges, is another similar stone.

We may refer here also to the *Erathipa* stones which are supposed to be full of spirit children, and by means of rubbing which a man can cause them to go out and enter women. These have been fully described elsewhere.

To cause a person to become thin and weak, spittle is put on the tips of the fingers, which are then bunched together and jerked in the direction of the former. This is called *Puliliwuma* or spittle-throwing. Amongst the Ilpirra tribe especially, a very simple method consists in merely charming a finger by singing over it, and then pointing it at an enemy who is supposed to waste away. In the Ilpirra also a form of magic called *Tchinperli* is practised. A short stick is sharpened at both ends and then a number of little bits of flint are fixed on to it all round with resin. The object thus made is charmed by being "sung," and is then pointed at the enemy, who either wastes away or becomes blind. The same tribe also brings about death by placing a tiny flake of flint which has been charmed under the finger nail. In this position it is carried about until the opportunity occurs of dropping it quietly on to the person whom it is desired to kill.

To produce blindness the Arunta native will sometimes merely point one of the ordinary *Injilla* or pointing sticks, or he will charm a *Chilara* or forehead band, and then present it to his enemy, who after a time loses his sight.

Amongst the Kaitish, Illiaura and Warramunga tribes who bury their dead in trees, before placing them finally in the ground, the small bones of the arm are used for making the magic *Injilla* or pointing bones, and are carried about with them on fighting expeditions.

In connection with the question of magic it may be noticed in conclusion that a special form, which is widely met with in other Australian tribes, is not practised amongst these. We refer to the attempt to injure an enemy by means of securing and then practising some form of charm upon some part of his person, such as hair or nail clippings. As we have already seen, images or representations of individuals are made with the idea that any hurt done to them is sympathetically felt by their human representative, and the absence of the particular form of magic referred to is to be associated with the fact that for some reason in these tribes, unlike what usually takes place, human hair is regarded as a most valuable form of gift, and, as we have described elsewhere, the disposal of it is regulated by fixed rules. Under these circumstances the idea of the Arunta native on this subject is entirely different from the one met with amongst many other savage tribes.

Chapter XVII

Methods of Obtaining Wives

Four methods of obtaining wives—Charming by magic—Capture—The rarest method of obtaining a wife—Capture of a woman by an avenging party—Method of allotment of a woman thus captured—Elopement—Punishment after elopement—Instance of a method in connection with this—Custom of *Tualcha mura*, the most usual way of obtaining a wife—Custom of *Unjipinna*, when a man waives his right to a woman allotted to him—Example of the establishment of the relationship of *Tualcha mura*—No absolute necessity for a man to marry out of his own local group.

THE methods of obtaining wives may be classified under four heads, so far as the Arunta and Ilpirra tribes are concerned. These are: (1) charming by means of magic; (2) capture; (3) elopement; and (4) the custom of *Tualcha mura*, by means of which a man secures a wife for his son by making an arrangement with some other man with regard to the latter's daughter.

Taking these in order we may pass over the method of charming by means of magic, as this has been already dealt with under the head of magic in connection with the description of the use of the *Lonka-lonka, Chilara, Ulpmira*, and *Namatwinna*. The use of these objects is a well recognised method of obtaining wives, as is shown by the fact that a man's right to a woman, secured by means of one or other of them, is supported by the men of his own local group, provided always that the woman stands to the man in the relationship of *Unawa* or lawful wife.

The second method, that of capture, is of much rarer occurrence, a fact which is to be associated with the existence of the custom of *Tualcha mura*, according to which practically every man in the tribe is provided with at least one woman, to whom he is lawfully entitled. Indeed, the method of capture which has been so frequently described as characteristic of Australian tribes, is the very rarest way in which a Central Australian secures a wife. It does not often happen that a man forcibly takes a woman from some one else within his own group, but it does sometimes happen, and especially when the man from whom the woman is taken has not shown his respect for his actual or tribal *Ikuntera* (father-in-law) by cutting himself on the occasion of the death of one or other of the latter relations. In this case the aggressor will be aided by the members of his local group, but in other cases of capture he will have to fight for himself.

At times, however, a woman may be captured from another group, though this again is of rare occurrence, and is usually associated with an avenging party, the women captured by which, who are almost sure to be the wives of men killed, are allotted to certain members of the avenging party. The following which occurred not long ago in the case of a party sent out by the northern groups of the Arunta to take vengeance on the tribe living away to the north of them, on account of some real or supposed hurt done to the Arunta people, will serve to illustrate what takes place with regard to women captured on such an occasion. Shortly before arriving at their destination, the men who formed the party halted, and the old man, who was acting as leader, sitting in front of the others, scraped two long shallow holes in the ground. To these the name of *Aura* is given, and they represented, one the man whom it was intended to kill and the other the woman; had there been more than one woman, then there would have been one hole to represent each of them.[173] The meaning of the holes was explained by the leader, and pointing to the one which indicated the woman he asked who wanted to have her. Two or three men said, "I do;" and then the leader, after a short pause, during which he made up his mind what to do, taking a handful of earth out of the hole, presented it to the man to whom he decided to allot the woman saying, "She belongs to you." When captured, as she was shortly afterwards, she became the property of that man, no one of the others disputing his right, nor, it may be remarked, was there any question of the other men having the right of access to the woman. In all such cases the woman is allotted to a man who is *Unawa* to her, for, even when she belongs to a different tribe to the man, the equivalent groups in the two are well known and regulate marriage just as if the man and woman belonged to the one tribe.

The third method, that of elopement, is to a certain extent intermediate between the method of charming on the one hand and that of capture on the other. It differs from the first of these in that no magic element comes into play, though in reality, of course, there may be no difference whatever between the two so far as this is concerned. In the case of charming, however, the initiative may be taken by the woman, who can of course imagine that she has been charmed, and then find a willing aider and abettor in the man whose vanity is flattered by this response to his magic power, which he can soon persuade himself that he did really exercise; besides which, an extra wife has its advantages in the way of procuring food and saving him trouble, while if his other women object the matter is one which does not hurt him, for it can easily be settled once and for all by a stand-up fight between the women and the rout of the loser. From capture it differs in the fact that the woman is a consenting party.

Not infrequently the elopement of a woman with some man is the cause of serious trouble between the members of different local groups. When an elopement takes place and the man succeeds in getting safely away, some time may elapse before the aggrieved husband takes any action, though at times the eloping couple are at once followed up and then, if caught, the woman is, if not killed on the spot, at all events treated in such a way that any further attempt at elopement on her part is not likely to take place. If the man and woman succeed in getting away to a distant part, then the chances are that sooner or later the original husband of the woman will, accompanied by his friends, go in search of her and the man who has run off with his property. As a general rule the upshot of the matter is a fight between the two interested parties; but at times the result may be that the friends get restive and interfere, in which case the fight becomes more serious and leads to a general quarrel between the two local groups, the men of the resident group, to which the man who has taken away the woman belongs, making common side against the men of the other group. There are certain men who are bound to help any given man in a quarrel of this nature, and these are those who stand to him in the relationship of *Okilia*, or elder brothers, *Witia*, or younger brothers, and *Unkulla*, that is mother's brothers sons. If, for example, a man is a Panunga, then the men of his local group, but only of the latter, who are Panunga and Ungalla, will assist him. The question of totem has nothing whatever to do with the matter in the case of these Central Australian tribes; the sons of his mother and father's brothers, blood and tribal, will stand by him to see that, at least, he gets fair play. The fighting may be of two kinds; in the one case, if the aggrieved man wishes to regain the woman, the latter will go to the victor of a real fight, in which both freely use their weapons, but if he be content to hand her over to the other man, then the latter will have to defend himself against the spears and knife of the first man without using his own weapons or attempting to retaliate. He will simply be allowed a shield with which to ward off spears. In either case the chances are that the woman will fare badly.

The following, which is an account of what actually took place during a recent case, will serve to illustrate the matter A man belonging to a group about forty-five miles away to the west of Alice Springs persuaded a woman belonging to a man of the latter group to run away with him from her husband, and the latter, though he gave chase, could not capture the runaway wife. The elopers went away to the south and lived for a year in a distant group, returning finally to Alice Springs, accompanied by some of the man's friends. On arrival at the latter place the man went to the *Ungunja*, or men's camp, and the woman to the *Erlukwirra* or women's camp. At the *Ungunja* a long discussion took place, during which the *pros* and *cons* of the case were discussed, the two men most interested remaining silent. After some time the man who had taken the woman got up, and taking with him some spears and a shield walked out to a clear space some little distance away from the camp and shouted to the aggrieved man who remained sitting, "*Arakutja thale iknukunja yinga iltai*,"[174] which meant, "I took your woman, come and growl." Thereupon the man got up, and standing some distance off threw spears and boomerangs at the first man, who skilfully guarded himself with his shield but made no attempt to retaliate. When all had been thrown he rushed in to close quarters with his enemy and began attempting to cut the thighs of the latter and his back also with a large stone knife, the attacked man doing his best to guard himself but not again attempting to retaliate. After a time the onlookers thought that enough had beendone, and calling out loudly "*kulla impara*," which means "enough, leave him" dragged the two apart. The women meanwhile had all assembled; and the aggrieved man walking over to where his erstwhile wife was standing caught hold of her and cut her about the legs and body avoiding however any vital part. Then leaving her he waved his knife in the air and started off for the camp, shouting "*Untantimma atnina, ipminja kuta, ipminja kuta*," "You keep altogether, I throw away, I throw away." After having renounced her in this way she became the property of the man with whom she had eloped.

The fourth and most usual method of obtaining a wife is that which is connected with the well-established custom in accordance with which every woman in the tribe is made *Tualcha mura* with some man. The arrangement, which is often a mutual one, is made between two men, and it will be seen that owing to a girl being made *Tualcha mura* to a boy of her own age the men very frequently have wives much younger than themselves, as the husband and the mother of a wife obtained in this way are usually of approximately the same age.

When it has been agreed upon between two men that the relationship shall be established between their two children, one a boy and the other a girl, the two latter, who are generally of a tender age, are taken to the *Erlukwirra* or women's camp, and here each mother takes the other's child and rubs it all over with a mixture of fat and red ochre in the presence of all the other women, who have assembled for the purpose of watching the ceremony. At the same time some of the girl's hair is cut off and given to the boy to signalise the fact that when grown up it will be her duty to provide him (he will be her son-in-law) with her own hair from which to make his waist-girdles. The arrangement is of course only made between boys and girls who stand in a definite relationship to one another. The girl must be one who is *Mura* to the boy, that is one whose daughters belong to the class from which his wife must come; but whilst in common with all the women of her particular class she is already *Mura* to him she now becomes *Tualcha mura*, that is, she is his actual or prospective mother-in-law. This relationship indicates that the man has the right to take as wife the daughter of the woman; she is in fact assigned to him, and this, as a general rule, many years before she is born. Not infrequently a woman's daughters will be allotted to brothers, the elder brother taking the elder daughter, the second brother the second daughter and so on, but it is only in the case of the eldest daughter that the relationship of *Tualcha mura* exists.

It is quite possible for a man to have more than one woman standing to him in the relationship of *Tualcha mura*, in which case he will not infrequently hand on his right in the case of one woman to some younger blood or tribal brother. In doing so he does not necessarily hand over his right to the mother-in-law's hair, but will continue to receive this.

Sometimes a man without passing on his *Tualcha mura* right will waive this if he happens to have a wife already, or does not want for any reason to take the girl assigned to him. It frequently happens that the woman whose daughter is thus allotted to him may have a son and no daughter born, and in this case without waiting on the chance of a girl being born the man may agree to take the boy as what is called his *Unjipinna*. This establishes a relationship between the boy and the man, as a result of which the former has, until he becomes *Ertwa-kurka*, that is circumcised, to give his hair to the man who, on his part, has to, in a certain way, look after the boy; for example, he must grease his body occasionally and paint the sacred designs upon him at the ceremony of throwing-up, the first of the initiatory rites. At the ceremony of *Lartna*, or circumcision, the man has to tie the hair of the boy up with fur-string and place the hair-girdle round his waist.

Whilst accepting the *Unjipinna*, and so waiving his right to the girl, the man still retains his right to the hair of the *Tualcha mura* woman.

It very rarely happens that a man is not allowed to take the daughter of his *Tualcha mura* woman, but occasionally, when a serious quarrel has arisen between the contracting parties an attempt is made to give the girl to some one else, though the latter may feel quite sure that he will not be allowed to retain her without a struggle sooner or later.

The following is one of many instances within our personal knowledge of the establishment of the relationship. A Panunga man and a Purula woman living at Alice Springs had a daughter who was of course an Appungerta girl. About the same time a Bulthara man and a Kumara woman had a son born who was of course an Uknaria. The two fathers consulted, and the result was that the little girl was made *Tualcha mura* to the infant boy. The latter is the prospective husband of the prospective daughter of the Appungerta girl, who will be an Ungalla, that is a woman of the proper class from which the boy's wife must come.

It will be seen from the above that in these tribes there is no necessity for a man to marry out of his own local group, as each of the latter includes men and women of various classes; but as each local group is mainly composed of men of one moiety of the tribe it very often happens that a man's wife belongs to another group. For instance most of the men at Alice Springs are Panunga and Bulthara, and they must marry respectively Purula and Kumara women, so that in the majority of cases they must get them from other local groups in which the Purula and Kumara predominate.

Chapter XVIII

Myths Relating to Sun, Moon, Eclipses, Etc.

The sun regarded as female, the moon as male—Tradition with regard to the origin of the sun—Sacred ceremony connected with the sun totem—Myths with regard to the moon—Names applied to phases of the moon—The evening star a woman whose *Nanja* stone lies to the west of Alice Springs—Eclipses associated with *Arungquiltha*—The Magellanic clouds—Pleiades.

THROUGHOUT the Arunta tribe the sun, which is called *Alinga* or *Ochirka*, is regarded as female and the moon as male. At Alice Springs there is a tradition that in the Alcheringa the sun came out of the earth at a spot now marked by a large stone in the country of the Quirra or bandicoot people at Ilparlinja, about thirty miles north of Alice Springs. It was in the form of a spirit woman, accompanied by two other Panunga women, who were sisters and were called *Ochirka*, just as the sun itself is. The descendants of these two women are both now alive, though one of them, when undergoing reincarnation, having chosen an Appungerta mother, is now an Ungalla. We have before drawn attention to the fact that the spirit individual is regarded as free to enter any woman, though as a general, but by no means invariable, rule, as shown in the present instance, a woman of the right division is selected.

The elder of the two women is represented as carrying with her an *Ambilyerikira*, or newly-born child. Leaving the women at Ilparlinja the sun ascended into the sky, and has continued to do so every day, though at night time it pays a visit to the old spot whence it rises in the morning. In that spot it may be actually seen at night time by very gifted persons such as clever medicine men, and the fact that it cannot be seen by ordinary persons only means that they are not gifted with sufficient power, and not that it is not there. The women remained in the country of the bandicoot people, by whom however they were not seen, being very careful to hide themselves, and these two women gave rise to a local centre of the sun totem to which they belonged.

The sun is regarded as having a definite relationship to each individual member of the various divisions. Thus to a Bulthara it is *Uwinna*, to a Panunga it is *Ungaraitcha*, to a Kumara *Mia*, and to a Purula man *Unawa*—terms which simply imply that it is regarded as belonging to the Panunga division, as did the spirit individual whom it represents.

The following ceremony called the *Quabara Alinga* of Ilparlinja is associated with the two women and the newly-born child left at Ilparlinja by the sun when she came out of the earth at that spot in the Alcheringa. The performers were two old men who were brothers, one being a Panunga of the lizard totem and the other a Panunga of the bandicoot totem. Their father was a bandicoot man and their sister is the living representative of one of the two women with whom the ceremony is concerned. The two performers, while decorating, were assisted by an old Panunga man and several Purula and Kumara men of the same locality, and during the decorating they sang of the *Ambilyerikira*, The performers sat facing each other; the lizard man representing the elder woman, held between his thighs an oblong bundle made of grass and hair-string and decorated with alternate red and white circles of down. This represented the child. From his head hung long strings, made of many strands of fur-string and covered with rings of down with a bunch of tail-tips at the end. These strings were supposed to represent the kidneys and fat of the bandicoot upon which the women fed. The bandicoot man represented the younger sister and carried on his head a weighty, disc-shaped bundle made of twigs, which were covered with many yards of hair and fur-string and decorated with a design of alternate red and white circles of down. This was supposed to represent the sun itself. The performance consisted of the usual quivering and swaying about of the bodies of the two men, while the others present ran round. When it was over the head-dress was removed and pressed against the stomach of all the Panunga and Bulthara men, but not against any of the other moiety, though several were present. It was then handed back to the old man who had worn it during the ceremony, and the latter called up a young Ungalla man of the locality, who had not been present at the decorating, and, while telling him about the woman, kept the head-dress pressed up against the young man's stomach.

THE MOON

The following two myths refer to the moon which, as above stated, is regarded as of the male sex, and is spoken of as *Ertwa Oknurcha*, or a big man, its name being *Atninja*.

The first of these describes how, before there was any moon in the heavens, a man of the Anthinna or opossum totem died and was buried, and shortly afterwards arose from his grave in the form of a boy. His people saw him rising and were very afraid and ran away. He followed them shouting, "Do not be frightened, do not run away, or you will die altogether; I shall die but shall rise again in the sky." He subsequently grew into a man and died, reappearing as the moon, and since then he has continued to periodically die and come to life again; but the people who ran away died altogether. When no longer visible it is supposed that the moon man is living with his two wives who dwell far away in the west.

The second myth describes how in the Alcheringa a black-fellow of the opossum totem carried the moon about with him in a shield as he went out hunting for opossums to eat.

All day long he kept it hidden in a cleft in the rocks. One night another blackfellow of the Unchirka, a seed totem, came up by chance to where he saw a light shining on the ground. This proved to be the moon lying in the man's shield, which he had placed on the ground while he climbed up a tree in search of an opossum which he had seen in the branches. The Unchirka man at once picked up the shield and the moon in it and ran away with them as hard as he could. The opossum man came down from the tree and ran after the thief, but he had got such a start that he could not catch him. When he found that pursuit was hopeless and that he could not get the moon back again, he was very angry and shouted out loudly that the thief should not keep the moon, but that the latter was to go up into the sky and give light to every one at night time. Then the moon went up out of the shield into the sky and there it has remained ever since.

The following distinctive names are applied to the different phases of the moon—

The new moon is *Atninja quirka utnamma*.
Half moon is *Atninja quirka iwuminta*.
Three-quarter moon is *Atninja urterurtera*.
Full moon is *Atninja aluquirta*.

THE EVENING STAR

The name of the evening star is Ungamilia. Amongst the natives of the Alice Springs district the evening star is supposed to have been a Kumara woman in the Alcheringa who had a *Nurtunja* and lived alone. She is associated with a large white stone which arose at a place near to what is now called Temple Bar—a gap in the Macdonnell Ranges—to mark the spot where she went into the earth and left behind, along with her Churinga, her spirit part. Every night the evening star is supposed to go down into this stone which lies away to the west of Alice Springs. It is situated in the middle of a strip of country which belongs to the big lizard totem. If a woman believes that she conceives a child when at this stone, then the child belongs to the Ungamilia or evening star totem, but if it be conceived anywhere in the adjoining country, even close at hand but not actually at the stone, then it is an Echunpa or big lizard. Ungamilia is supposed to have fed in the Alcheringa upon *Owadowa*, a kind of grass seed, just as did the group of lizard people amongst whom she dwelt. There is, as usual, a special performance connected with this woman which is now in the possession of an Uknaria man of the lizard totem, the woman's Churinga being kept in the storehouse at Simpson's Gap which belongs to the lizard totem. Ungamilia has at the present time a living descendant, and during the Engwura the ceremony was performed by the man in whose possession it now is.

ECLIPSES, ETC.

Eclipse of the sun is called *Ilpuma*, and is attributed to the presence therein of *Arungquiltha*, the general term used in reference to an evil or malignant influence, which is sometimes regarded as personal and at other times as impersonal. This particular form of *Arungquiltha* is supposed to be of the nature of a spirit individual living away to the west who has the power of assuming the form of any animal. The natives have a very great dread of eclipses, they have naturally no idea of the distance away of the sun, believing it to be close to the earth, and the visible effects of *Arungquiltha* so close at hand, and so patent, cause them great fear. They believe that the eclipse is caused by the periodic visits of the *Arungquiltha*, who would like to take up his abode in the sun, permanently obliterating its light, and that the evil spirit is only dragged out by the medicine men who on this occasion withdraw the *atnongara* stones from their bodies and throw them at the sun while singing magic chants—always with success.

The Magellanic clouds they regard as endowed with *Arungquiltha*, and believe that they sometimes come down to earth and choke men and women while they are asleep.

Mushrooms and toadstools they will not eat, believing them to be fallen stars and endowed with *Arungquiltha*.

The Pleiades are supposed to be women who in the Alcheringa lived at a place called Intitakula, near to what is now called the Deep Well. They went up into the sky and there they have remained ever since.

Chapter XIX

Clothing, Weapons, Implements, Decorative Art

General remarks on implements—Absence of carving—Use of red ochre—Materials with which the work is done—Clothing and personal adornments—Weapons and implements—Spears, spear-throwers, shields, boomerangs, stone knives, stone. hatchets, adze, fighting club—Musical instruments—*Pitchis*—Wallets and bags—Spindle for spinning fur or hair-string—Rock paintings, ordinary rock drawings and sacred drawings—Decorations during corrobborees—Decorations concerned with sacred ceremonies—The *Nurtunja* and *Waninga*—The *Kauaua*—Churinga—Pointing or poison sticks.

THE Central Australian native, while he has not reached the stage of decorative art of the inhabitants, for example, of New Guinea, still shows more artistic capacity than has generally been granted, or indeed shown to exist, amongst the various Australian tribes.

His rock paintings are closely similar to those described as occurring in different parts of the continent, but, in addition to them, the designs and decorations concerned with his ceremonies are of a very definite and often elaborate description, revealing considerable appreciation not only of form but also of colour.

His weapons and implements are of a very simple nature, and as a general rule while their form is good and their workmanship, so far as it goes, is often excellent, but little trouble is taken in the way of ornamenting them either with painted or incised patterns, or with raised carvings. We have never met in Central Australia with any attempt to take advantage of natural peculiarities in the material out of which the object is fashioned. A peculiarly shaped knot or the root end of a stick out of which he is making some implement, does not serve to him as a means of embellishing his weapon with some design or rudely outlined carving to represent some natural object which is familiar to him. The graceful curves and the symmetry of outline of many of his common implements, such as the *pitchis*, shields and spear-throwers, often strike the eye at once, but without exception any excrescence is carefully smoothed down and the only ornamentation takes the form of a coating of red ochre, with perhaps a rude design in black lines and spots of white, black and yellow. The most striking feature with regard to decoration amongst the Central natives is the constant and plentiful use of red ochre and grease. It may perhaps be that this is due to the fact that for ages past the native has been accustomed to regularly rub this material over his most sacred objects, the Churinga, which are stored in hiding places amongst the rocks, and this again may be associated with the fact that they are thereby protected to a certain extent from the ravages of insects such as the white ant. From the sacred objects the practice may have been passed on to the everyday implements, and so to some extent, as any raised carving would prevent easy rubbing, this may have acted as a deterrent to the development of ornament of this nature. At any rate whatever be the reason, no implement or weapon is ever really carved, or has painted upon it anything but the simplest form of design. This is all the more strange because the native is capable of such work as may be seen by an examination of work of this kind which he does in imitation of what he sees the white man doing; but it must be remembered that in their natural condition the members of the Central tribes do not make anything in the way of carved ornamentation. This should be borne in mind as various objects, such as sticks with knobs, carved so as to resemble natural objects, are occasionally manufactured by members of some of the very tribes with which we are here dealing, who have been in contact with white men, and are even finding their way into museum collections.

Very rarely even are their rock paintings much more than rude and conventional outlines of the animals amongst which they live. Cut off from contact with outside peoples there has been no stimulus leading to the development of decorative art beyond a certain point, and most probably their most elaborate decorations are the much modified representatives of designs which once had a very definite meaning. But to this we shall return at a later time.

So far as the material with which they have to work is concerned their means are very limited. All cutting must be done with chipped bits of flint or quartzite,[175] which are firmly fixed into the end of a curved or straight piece of wood or into the handle of a spear-thrower, the cement used in this part being the resin which is obtained from the leaf stalks of a species of Triodia commonly known as porcupine-grass. Their colouring material consists of charcoal, kaolin or calcined gypsum when white is required, red and yellow ochre, and wad, an oxide of manganese, which, when finely divided up, yields a grey powder. For decorating the body and ceremonial objects the down obtained from the involucral hairs of species of Portulaca, and more especially the down of eagle hawks, is largely used.

In the following account we include a description of the native implements, as it is in the form of these that the Central Australian native principally shows his artistic capacity. We will deal with the subject under the following divisions—

        1. Clothing and personal ornaments
        2. Weapons and implements
        3. Rock paintings
        4. Decorations concerned with ceremonial objects and performances.

CLOTHING AND PERSONAL ORNAMENTS

There is very little scope for the display of artistic capacity in the matter of clothing or personal ornaments. Except for waist-bands, forehead-bands, necklets and armlets and a conventional pubic tassel, shell, or in the case of the women, a small apron, the Central Australian native is naked. The waist-band of the men, and armlets and necklets of men and women, have already been described,[176] and the only real attempt at decorative work is in connection with the *Chilara* or forehead-band of the men, for in this part almost all the decorating is done by the men and practically little by the women. The *Chilara* consists of a good sized skein of opossum fur-string flattened out so as to form a band perhaps two or three inches in greatest width and tapering at each end. The whole surface is plastered over with kaolin or gypsum, so that the strands of string adhere to one another, and a flat surface is produced on which a design can be drawn in red or yellow ochre. These designs take the form of series of concentric circles, curved lines, straight lines or spots. The four of them which are figured were in use by natives in the north part of the Arunta tribe. The patterns do not appear to have any definite meaning, but are evidently suggested by those commonly drawn on various sacred objects, indeed the resemblance between the decorated *Chilara* when laid flat down and the Churinga is most striking, though there is no real relationship between the two objects, one of which is the most ordinary and everyday article of clothing, and the other the most sacred object.

Sometimes instead of having a pattern drawn in ochre the *Chilara* will have a coat of white bird's down. Amongst women ordinary fur-string bands are worn round the head, or sometimes a flat band which is really identical in form with the *Chilara*.

The pubic tassel is a diminutive structure about the size of a five shilling piece made of a few short strands of fur-string flattened out into a fan shape and attached to the pubic hairs. As the string, especially at corroboree times, is covered with white kaolin or gypsum, it serves as a decoration rather than a covering.[177]

Amongst the Arunta and Luritcha the women normally wear nothing, but amongst tribes further north, especially the Kaitish and Warramunga, a small apron is made and worn, and this sometimes finds its way south into the Arunta. Close set strands of fur-string hang vertically from a string waist-girdle. Each strand is about eight or ten inches in length, and the breadth of the apron may reach the same size, though it is often not more than six inches wide.

Sometimes, and especially during corroborees, the men wear as ornaments suspended from the waist-girdle a bunch of the black and white tail-tips of *Peragale lagotis*. These tail-tips are called *Alpita* and are a very favourite form of ornament amongst men and women alike. Women usually wear them suspended over the ears. Another form of ornament amongst the men is the *Lonka-lonka*, to which reference has already been made in connection with magic. This is made out of the shell of *Melo athiopica*, or the pearl shell oyster *Meleagrina margaritifera*, and hangs pendent from the waist-girdle. It is traded down from the north and is widely used throughout the Centre. We have never seen any design incised on the *Lonka-lonka* found amongst these tribes, but on similar articles from West Australia the characteristic zig-zag line pattern is sometimes present.

In the Arunta and Luritcha tribes the men frequently wear a pad of emu feathers which varies in size, the largest being about ten inches in length, five in width, and two in thickness. The pad is made by stabbing the feathers together by means of bone pins and is called *Imampa*. It is worn on the back of the head and is fastened on, partly by fur-string which is wound round it and the hair beneath, and partly by means of bone pins. Into each of the upper corners is fixed a tuft of feathers of some bird such as the eagle-hawk, owl or cockatoo, attached to a pointed stick about six or eight inches in length. Sometimes long white down is used, or tail-tips of the rabbit-kangaroo. Very often the tufts of feathers, when no emu feather pad is used, are fixed into the matted locks.

Occasionally amongst certain groups curiously flaked sticks, called *Inkulta*, are used as head ornaments, though amongst other groups exactly the same objects, and worn in just the same way, are used as an indication that the wearer is bent on fighting. Each of these is about a foot or eighteen inches in length. By means of the flint fixed into the end of a spear-thrower, small curved flakes are chipped, one after the other, so that they follow a roughly spiral line, the first flake being cut at the lowest end. These are worn by men only, fixed in the hair just like the feather tufts.

When an avenging party kills a man, those who spear the latter take the *Inkulta*, which they wear on such an occasion, break them up and throw the broken fragments on the dead body, leaving them there.

A man intent on fighting will chip some flakes, like those on the *Inkulta*, close to the end of the spear, which is an indication that he will not stop until blood has been shed.

Amongst the Kaitish and Warramunga tribes especially, the women wear as an ornament on the forehead a small mass of porcupine-grass resin, into which from six to twelve incisor teeth of a kangaroo are fastened in a radiating manner along the lower edge. A strand of human hair-string, fastened into the resin, serves to attach it to the hair of the wearer, over whose forehead it hangs down. Sometimes, instead of the teeth, a number of small bright red seeds are fixed into the mass of resin over its whole surface.

Nose bones, called *Lalkira*, are frequently worn, every native having his, or her, nasal septum pierced. The most common form is a bone, sometimes the fibula of a kangaroo pointed at one end and measuring as much as 40 cm. in length, or it may be the radius of a large bird such as an eagle-hawk. In this latter case one end of the hollow bone is filled with a small plug of resin and the other ornamented with a tuft of feathers or tail-tips. Occasionally a hollow bone is split longitudinally, and one-half of it with the ends and sides carefully smoothed down is used as a nose bone. In this case the concave surface is usually decorated with roughly cut lines, which run across from side to side, and there may be a few odd lines scratched on the convex side.

WEAPONS

The most characteristic weapons of the native are spears, spear-throwers, shields and boomerangs, all of which he habitually carries about with him when on the march. In addition to these, though they are much more rarely seen, he has stone knives, and still more rarely, stone hatchets. As we have before said the trading propensities of the Australian natives have led long ago to the dispersal far and wide over the continent of the iron tomahawk of the white man, and within the past few years there has been, so far as the Central tribes are concerned, a rapid diminution in the number of stone hatchets made. As in the case of most of their weapons and implements, one group of natives is especially skilled in making one article, and another in making something else, and the one group barters what it makes for the products of another, living, it may be, a hundred miles away. Recently Mr. Roth has called special attention to this in his work.[178]

The spears are of various forms, and in different districts at least six distinct kinds will be met with, of which the first two are confined to the north, and never apparently reach as far south as the Macdonnell Ranges: they may be briefly enumerated as follows: (1) those with stone-flake heads; (2) wooden spears with one or more barbed prongs; (3) wooden spears with barbed heads, the main part being made of Tecoma or some other light wood; (4) spears similar to the latter but without the barb; (5) heavy, wooden unbarbed ones made out of one piece; (6) short, light, hand-spears for catching fish.

The spears with stone-flake heads are made amongst the Warramunga, Walpari, Bingongina and Chingalli tribes, and are met with from Powell Creek northwards. The flake is similar to that of the stone-knife, being trigonal in shape and measuring, in the case of the one figured, 14 cm. in length and 4 cm. in greatest width. It is attached to the spear by means of resin, round which, while it was soft, string made of vegetable fibre was wound. The mass of resin and string is completely covered with white kaolin, or, in other cases, it may be ornamented with dots of the same, and occasionally a band of red ochre, or of yellow ochre with red spots, is painted round the stone itself, at some little distance from the tip. So far as the shaft is concerned these stone-headed spears fall into two groups, in the first of which the shaft is all in one piece and in the second it is composed of two pieces. In either case the main part is composed of some light wood which is very liable to split. In the specimen figured the total length of the spear is 2 m. 89 cm. The handle end has the usual small depression into which fits the point of the spear-thrower, and in three places tendon is wound round to prevent splitting. The whole is covered with red ochre. The total weight of this spear is 538 gm., which will give some idea of the lightness of the wood, as it is nearly three metres in length and the stone and resin are included. In an example of the second form the total length is 3 m. 13 cm.; of this 93 cm. at the handle end is made out of a hollow reed, into one end of which the solid part of the shaft is inserted; a little resin is used to help in fixing, and then tendon is wound tightly round the junction. The hollow end of the reed is plugged with a little mass of dry fibrous material. Sometimes a little ring of hair-string with a small amount of resin so as to attach it may be wound round the very end in order to prevent the reed from splitting. The solid part of the shaft is covered with red ochre, the reed being uncoloured. The total weight of the one described, everything included, is 397 gm. The first form of wooden spear, only met with in the north, has one or more wooden prongs which take the place of the stone head. In the variety with only one prong the latter is attached to the shaft just as the stone flake is; it is possible that a slit may be made in the end of the shaft, but at all events the main attachment consists of a mass of resin round which string is tightly wound, and then this is again covered with resin so that it may be completely hidden from view. The prong has a varying number of backward pointing, hook-like barbs cut out in a row along one side, the whole prong being slightly flattened in the plane in which the barbs lie. The number of the latter varies on the spears in our possession from five to fourteen. The total length of one is 3 m. 12 cm., the prong measuring 52 cm. The end has the usual slight depression and there is a little ring of resin surrounding it with tendon wound round. The shaft is all of one piece and the whole weapon is red-ochred, with lines of white and yellow added on the prong, the attaching mass of resin being painted white. The total weight is 340 gm. In the second variety there are two prongs attached, evidently one to each side of the shaft and so that the two planes along which they are flattened lie parallel to one another with the barbs on opposite sides. The total weight is 368 gm. The second form of wooden spear is the one most commonly met with throughout the Urabunna, Ilpirra, Luritcha, and Arunta tribes. The main part of the shaft may be made of one piece of a light wood such as the shoots of *Tecoma Australis*,[179] but it is more usual to have the terminal part made from a separate piece. In the specimen figured (110A) the total length is 2 m. 90 cm., and the short terminal part measures 40 cm.; this is spliced on to the main part and round the splicing resin is placed, and then tendon is wound firmly round this. The Tecoma shoot has to be carefully straightened by heating in the fire and then by pressure of the hands before it is suitable for the shaft, and there is great difference amongst various specimens in regard to the care with which this is done. When sufficiently straight all excrescences are smoothed down with a flint. The blade is always *lanceolate* in shape and made out of *mulga*: it is spliced on to the shaft, resin wound round with tendon being used to secure the two parts together. In the one figured the length of the blade is 21 cm. and at a distance of 5 cm. from the point a recurved barb is firmly attached by tendon. There is the usual concavity in the end which is in contact with the spear-thrower. The width at the splicing of the blade is 2 cm., and it tapers to 1 cm. at the other end. The total weight is 595 gm. The third form of wooden spear is identical with the one just described, with the exception that there is no barb. It is a characteristic feature of these two forms of spears that they are never red-ochred.

The fourth form of wooden spear is much rarer than the two latter, and is made out of a single piece of dark hard wood, which may be derived from some species of acacia, or, so the natives say, from the Desert oak (*Casuarina Decaisneana*). One in our possession has evidently been cut out of a long straight piece of wood, the surface being quite smooth and rubbed over with red ochre. It is very probable that spears of this form are traded from some distance and they are more frequently met with in the south than in the north. The total length is 2 m. 91 cm.; at a distance of about 70 cm. from the point the blade commences and is distinct from the rest, owing to its being flattened from side to side, its greatest width being 3 cm., while the greatest diameter of the handle part is 2.5 cm. The extremity is bluntly rounded and there is no concavity, as this form is not thrown with the aid of the spear-thrower.

There are three distinct types of spear-throwers in use amongst the various central tribes. The first is called *Wanmyia*, and is made by the Warramunga and other northern tribes. The particular specimen now described consists of a flattened piece of wood 105 cm. in length; at the end held in the hand it is 4.8 cm. in width, and, with the exception of a notch cut on either side so as to form a handle, it continues of this width for about 55 cm., after which it gradually tapers till, at the end to which the point is affixed, it is only 15 mm. Its greatest thickness is 15 mm.; at the handle end it is about 12 mm. and at the point only 8 mm. At a distance of 13.5 cm. from the broad end a notch about 3 cm. in length is cut on either side so that the width is here reduced to slightly less than 3 cm. By means of this notch a handle is formed. At the opposite end a bluntly pointed piece of wood is affixed by means of a lump of resin, in such a way that it slopes at a slight angle to the flattened surface, along which the spear lies when the point fits into the little hole made for this purpose at the extremity of the spear. Round the resin before it had set, human hair-string was wound, so that it is now fixed in the resin. The whole implement is red-ochred, and at corresponding positions on both of the flattened sides, white, roughly circular patches of kaolin have been added by way of ornament, and the end to which the blunt knob is attached has been completely coated with kaolin for a length of 16 cm.

The second type which is called *Nulliga* and is made by the Wambia tribe which inhabits a district out to the east of the telegraph line, consists of a smooth, rounded stick about 87 cm. in length. It tapers slightly towards one end, at which the point is affixed, measuring here 4.5 cm. in circumference and at the opposite end 6.5 cm. The broader end, which is the one held in the hand, has wound round it, at a distance of 5 cm. from the end, what is really a fringe of human hair-string. In making this, a piece of fur-string is taken and then twisted strands of human hair-string are looped round it, as shown in Fig. 112, where however they are represented as pulled apart from one another so as to show the method of construction.

In reality the pendent strands are so close together as to completely hide from view the string, from which they hang vertically downwards. Each pendant is from 12-14 cm. in length, and there may be a hundred or more of them forming the fringe. When the fringe is in place it has the appearance of a tuft of human hair pendants and it is only on taking one to pieces that the existence of the fringe is evident. The construction of the fringe is exactly the same as that of the apron worn by the women of the Warramunga tribe, as described by Dr. Stirling, the only difference between the two lying in the fact that in the apron, opossum fur, and in the spear-thrower, human hair-string is used in the manufacture of the pendants. At each end of the pendent strands a short length of the main fur-string is left projecting, and the method of attachment to the stick is as follows. The fur-string projecting at one end is placed on the stick and then human hair-string is tightly wound round it, and this is encased in resin (Fig. 113, *a*), so that the end is firmly bound on to the stick; then the fringe is wound, in the specimen examined, three times round the stick in the small space marked (*b*), and then the other projecting piece of fur-string is firmly attached to the stick by another circle of resin, no human hair-string being used to tie round as in the first instance. The result is that when the spear-thrower is held upright the fringe forms a tassel completely enclosing the end, while the upper and larger of the two circles of resin affords a firm grasp to the hand, preventing the stick from slipping through. At the opposite extremity is a bluntly rounded knob of wood fixed on with a mass of resin. The third type is one which is widely distributed over the central area of the continent, and is used at all events by the

Urabunna, Arunta, Luritcha and Ilpirra tribes. In the Arunta tribe it is called *Amera*, but amongst white men the word *Wommera*, which was originally only used in a limited area on the east coast, has been generally applied to spear-throwers wherever found in Australia, though it must be remembered that the natives themselves, in the majority of tribes, use quite a different word.

The *Amera* is perhaps the most useful of the implements possessed by the native. It serves not only as a spear-thrower but as a receptacle in which blood and various objects such as red ochre, kaolin, &c., can be placed and carried about during the preparations for a ceremony, and more important still, the flint, which is usually attached to one end, serves as the chief cutting implement of the native by means of which he fashions all his wooden weapons and implements of various kinds. It is used also in the making of fire, and, at times, as a very primitive form of musical instrument, though we have not ourselves seen it employed for the latter purpose.

Each one has the shape of an ovate leaf, the sides of which are more or less turned up so as to produce often a considerable concavity. In the depth of the latter they vary to a considerable extent, some being almost flat but none completely so, as is the case in the Western Australian spear-thrower, which otherwise has much the same form. Unlike the latter, which is often, indeed typically, decorated with the zig-zag lines, the *Amera* has very rarely any trace of ornament; now and again some native will perhaps incise a few lines arranged irregularly, but we may safely say that on not more than one in a hundred is there any attempt to draw or incise any design. One end tapers gradually so as to form a handle, the other tapers suddenly and is produced into a blunt process to allow of the fixation of the point. The total length of a very typical and well-formed concave specimen is 76 cm., the greatest breadth 12 cm., and the least breadth, at the extremity of the handle just above the terminal lump of resin, is 2 cm. The depth of the concavity is 4 cm., and in various specimens every variation between this and even less than 1 cm. may be found. As a general rule, but not always, they are made out of *mulga*, and in the better ones the two faces are smoothed down until the thickness of the wood is not more than 3 mm. In those which are less carefully finished off, the marks of the flint used in cutting them can be distinguished. Sometimes, but only comparatively seldom, they are covered with red ochre, but this, owing to their constant use, is rarely noticeable, and as a matter of fact the spear-thrower, like the ordinary spear, is one of the few things which are not habitually covered with red ochre.

At the distal end and on the concave side, a sharply pointed piece of hard wood is attached facing towards the opposite end. This is, in all, about 3 cm. in length, but only one centimetre projects beyond the small mass of resin which is used to attach it to the blunt process on the body of the weapon. The amount of resin used for this purpose is far less than in the case of the two types already described, which is to be associated with the fact that it is wound round with the strong tendon taken from the leg of some animal such as an emu or kangaroo, by which, as well as by the resin, the point is firmly attached to the body of the spear-thrower.

At the opposite, that is the handle end, is a mass of resin always more or less flattened in the plane of the breadth of the *Amera*, which serves both to give a firm grip to the hand and to hold a sharp-edged piece of quartzite which projects from the resin for a short distance, usually less than 1 cm. This flint, which is rarely absent, has always a definite form. On the side corresponding to the convex surface it has a single conchoidal face, the outline of which is almost always convex; the face corresponding to the concave side has always a number of small facets. It is by means of this definite shape of the flint that the characteristic groove-shaped markings on the surface of such implements as the *pitchi* are formed; in fact the flint of the spear-thrower may be regarded as the most important cutting weapon of the Central native, and is used both in fashioning his Churinga, spear, shield, spear-thrower, *pitchi* and fighting club, and also in cutting open and, when cooked, in carving the bodies of the animals on which he feeds.

On one or two of the spear-throwers in our possession both edges in the part where the broad blade is narrowing to the handle, are marked by very definite crenations, and the crenated surfaces have been rubbed smooth. Though we have never seen it employed for this purpose, it appears that sometimes the implement is used as a rude form of musical instrument, the sound being produced by rubbing the crenate edge over a piece of hard wood such, for example, as another spear-thrower.[180]

A very important use, lastly, of the spear-thrower is that of fire-making. When this is in process a shield made of soft wood is placed on the ground and then two men, one squatting on either side, take hold of the spear-thrower, and rapidly rub one of the edges of the blades backwards and forwards upon the shield; in a short time the light wood is charred, then it glows, and with judicious blowing the glow is fanned into a flame. Many shields such as one of those figured show rows of these charred grooves, for this is the principal method of obtaining fire amongst the Arunta, Ilpirra and Luritcha tribes.

All the shields used by the Arunta, Ilpirra, Luritcha, Warramunga, Waagai, and indeed all the Central tribes, are made of the light soft wood of Sturt's bean tree (*Erythrina vespertilio*). They vary much in size, the smallest one in our possession measuring 62 cm. in length and the longest one 85.5 cm They are all of an elongated oval shape with the outer surface convex and the inner concave the concavity varying much in different shields. The greatest width of the smaller of the two mentioned is 16 cm., and the hole hollowed out for the hand is 9 cm. in length and 10 cm. in width; the depth of the concavity, that is to the under surface of the longitudinal bar, which is left running across the hole, is only 1.8 cm. The greatest width of the large one is 30.5 cm.; the hole for the hand is 11 cm. in length and 10.5 cm. in width, and the depth of the same is 2 cm.

Together with the *pitchis* made out of the same wood, the shields afford evidence of very considerable manipulative skill, and no small appreciation of beauty of form and symmetry of line on the part of their makers. It may be mentioned here that these shields, or rather the best ones, are the work of men of the Warramunga tribe which inhabits the district in the neighbourhood of Tennant Creek. They are also made by the northern Arunta, the Ilpirra and Kaitish people. In regard to these Central natives it is a striking feature that men who live in particular districts are famous for making particular forms of implements and weapons, and that this is by no means wholly dependent upon the fact that suitable material for their construction is only to be found in the districts occupied by them. Thus the best *pitchis*, made of the bean tree, are the work of groups of natives who live out to the west of Alice Springs; the best shields, as we have just said, are those made away to the north, the best spear-throwers are made in the south-west, the best boomerangs away to the east and north-east, and the best spears in the north part of the Arunta tribe, in the Alice Springs district. The western men, for example, though they have the bean tree and make *pitchis* out of it, get their shields by exchange from the north; the Alice Springs blacks in like manner exchange their spears for the boomerangs of the eastern natives, and so on. Even in the old traditions we find reference to the excellence of the *pitchis* made by the western natives; in fact, according to tradition, one of the wandering ancestral groups named what is now called Mount Sonder, Urachipma, or the place of *pitchis*, because here they found an old bandicoot man engaged in making them. The tradition may at any rate be regarded as indicative that this distribution of work is of very old standing. It seems generally speaking, to be independent of the existence in any particular locality of the material necessary for the manufacture of any particular article. It also shows that great care must be taken in dealing with the various implements which are commonly found amongst any particular tribe. Every Arunta man is sure to have one of these shields, and yet the majority of them have not been made in the tribe, nor, indeed, within a hundred miles of the district occupied by it, but by a tribe speaking a quite different language. Why certain things, such as shields and boomerangs, should be traded over wide areas and be common to a number of tribes, and why certain other things, such as the spear-throwers, for example, should be local in distribution, it is difficult to understand.

To return however to the form of the shields. The figures drawn will afford some idea of their nature; but in all of them, especially in the case of the larger ones, the symmetry is perfect, and with only a flint as a cutting agent, the workmanship is astonishing. In the largest one figured the edges on either side curve over in the middle of the length, and then fall away towards either end, so that, at the latter, the inner surface of the shield in transverse section is slightly but distinctly convex. The surface on both sides is furrowed by shallow grooves, forty-eight on the outer and thirty-five on the inner, which run with perfect regularity from end to end. They are always present on these shields, and indicate the curved cutting edge of the flint with which they are made. As a general rule the shields are covered with a thick coating of red ochre, though this may occasionally be absent. Sometimes, and especially when used during performances, they may be decorated on the outer side. Two of these forms of decoration are figured. In the larger one (Fig. 115), there is a broad sinuous band of charcoal with three double black lines running across the breadth of the shield, while a very large number of white spots are painted along the course of all the grooves. In the smaller one (Fig. 116), the sinuous band and the little median one have simply been indicated by an additional coating of red ochre, and they are made to stand out by the painting of white spots all over the surface, except along their course, which is thus outlined by the spots. If, as often happens, the shield gets broken, then it is carefully mended by boring holes and through these lashing the broken parts together with tendon which is first of all damped so that it can be drawn tight. In some cases, apparently for no purpose unless it be with the idea of ornamentation, star-shaped, or sometimes irregular-shaped, patches of resin are let into the wood. There is never, either on shield or any implement with which we are acquainted, any mark, the object of which is to indicate the owner, though of course there are marks, such as particular cracks or damaged parts, by which, if necessary, a man can recognise his own property.

We find two types of stone axes or hatchets (Fig. 117), in use amongst the natives of the Centre, though even now they are comparatively rarely met with owing to the wide distribution, by means of barter, of the iron tomahawk. In fact in the Arunta tribe the manufacture of them has completely died out, and though stone knives are more often seen, the manufacture of the hatchet may even now be considered as a thing of the past.

The first type has the form of a flattened, usually oval, pebble of diorite, one edge of which is rounded and ground down, the pebble being then fixed into a wooden handle. This form is known by the name of *Illupa*, and is, or was, made by the Arunta, Kaitish, Warramunga, and other tribes living to the north. In the case of the Arunta tribe the stones were procured in special localities, which were the property of local groups of men without the permission of whom the stone could not be removed.[181] One favourite quarry lies out to the north-east of Alice Springs.

In the case of these ground axes the head is fixed in between the two halves of a piece of wood bent double. In the one figured (Fig. 117, 1), a mass of soft resin was evidently first of all attached to one end of the stone, and then the wood was bent round this, the outer surface of the wooden lath being almost completely free from resin, which still shows the pattern of the ridges in the skin of the fingers which were used to push the resin tightly down, so as to fill up completely the space between the stone and the wood. The two halves of the flexible haft are bound round by two circles of human hair-string, one placed close to the stone, while the other lies close to the free ends. In the case of this specimen the total length of the stone is 12 cm., the width 9 cm., and the greatest thickness 2.2 cm. Of two other unmounted and ground stones, the surfaces of which are not nearly so well ground as that of the one just described, one measures in greatest length 18 cm., in width 8.5 cm., and in thickness 4 cm.; the second measures in length 14 cm., in width 11.4 cm., and in thickness 3.5 cm.

The second type is a pick-shaped weapon, the blade of which is a lanceolate and, in section, trigonal flake of quartzite. The longest blade in our possession measures 22.5 cm. in greatest length, and 6 cm. in greatest width, tapering to a sharp point, and is a beautiful example of native work in chipped stone, the material employed being the quartzite of the Desert Sandstone formation, which is widely spread over the interior of the continent. It must be remembered that, though this form of stone implement would not usually be regarded as indicating so advanced a stage in the use and application of stone for the purpose of manufacturing axes as would the ground axe-heads already described, yet, on the other hand, it must be said that it is far more easy to grind down a stone than to produce a beautifully flaked axe-head such as the one now described. In the Central Australian tribes we find, existing side by side in the one tribe, stone weapons, the majority of which are more or less roughly chipped flints, while others again are ground stones or flakes of excellent workmanship. The very man who makes the ground axe-heads makes, and also uses as his principal cutting weapon, a small chipped flint, which he embeds in the lump of resin at the end of his spear-thrower or his adze. To a certain extent the matter is simply one concerned with the nature of the material, the quartzite being pre-eminently adapted for chipping and flaking, and the diorite for grinding down, and with both materials at hand the manufacture of both ground, chipped, and flaked implements has been carried on side by side.

The flaked quartzite head is hafted in one of two ways. In the first it is fixed in position between the two halves of a flexible piece of wood bent double, the head of the flake being embedded in a mass of resin which surrounds the wood enclosing the flake. The two halves of the handle are further bound together by means of two circles of human hair-string which are enclosed in resin. In the second method, a stick, which in the specimen figured (Fig 117, 5), measured about 52 cm. in length (owing to the terminal mass the exact end of the stick cannot be seen), is split open at one end, the blunt end of the flake is inserted in the slit and then secured in position by a large knob of resin. The handle is roughly cut with grooved markings so that it can be firmly held in the hand. In order to preserve the fragile pointed tip of the flake a sheath is always made of bark, sometimes of a gum tree, at others of a Melaleuca, and the pieces of bark are held together by means of winding them round with fur-string. By way of embellishment a coating of white kaolin is added, and a tuft of emu feathers, coloured with red ochre and attached to a short stick so that their stiff quill ends radiate outwards, is fixed into the end of the sheath.

This form of flaked axe which is used only in fighting at close quarters is called *Kulungu*, and is, or rather was, made by the Warramunga, Bingongina, and other northern tribes from whom it has been traded over various parts of the Centre.

The stone knife is of two forms, but the difference between them refers only to the nature of the haft, the flake being practically, except so far as size is concerned, the same in all of them. This weapon is evidently very widely distributed, as it has been described from many localities. Lumholtz figures one in his work[182] which is identical in form with those met with in the Centre, while again those figured by Roth are such as might have been collected amongst any of the tribes extending through the northern territory. One of the better class of these knives is also figured and described by Dr. Stirling in his work.[183]

As a general rule the blade is trigonal in section for its whole length, but in the case of some of them there is a fourth surface close to the head end, and extending for a short distance down the blade, parallel to the plane of the single surface which forms what may be called the back of the blade. It is not possible, however, to draw any valid distinction between those with and those without this fourth surface, indeed it is probable that with the removal of the resin a fourth face would not unfrequently be discovered close to the head end, though when the knife is finished it is hidden by the resin haft. It is simply a matter of how, exactly, the quartzite flakes. What the native aims at is the making of a blade which, for the main part of its length, shall be trigonal, tapering to a sharp point. The longest free blade which we have measured is 13 cm., and in the case of the larger knives from 10 to 12 cm. may be regarded as the limits of size within which all of them fall. These larger ones may be divided into two sets according to the hafting. In the simpler form the head of the flake is embedded in a somewhat flattened rounded mass of resin. In the one figured, the length of the blade itself was 13 cm. and that of the haft 9 cm.; the resin is always rubbed over with red ochre and a sheath is made precisely similar to that used in the case of the flaked axe. In the second form, the handle is divided into two parts; just as before the flake is inserted into a mass of resin, but, in addition, a flat piece of wood as broad, and about as long, as the resin is fixed into the latter so as to add to the length of the handle. In the one figured, the free blade measures 12 cm., the resin 6.5 cm., and the wooden part 6.5 cm. also. The resin is, as usual, red ochred, while the addition of the wooden handle gives the opportunity of a little bit of decoration in the form of lines and dots drawn in charcoal and kaolin on a ground-work of yellow ochre. In the case of this knife again there is made a sheath precisely similar to that of the first form.

In addition to these large knives, which are but very rarely indeed seen, there are smaller ones made for ordinary use which, so far as their form is concerned, are simply small and often roughly made specimens of the first kind described. The blade is trigonal, though amongst a large number doubtless a few would be met with which would show a trace of a fourth surface. Sometimes the blade is made of more opaline quartzite than is usual, but this appears to depend merely upon the local peculiarity of the stone, as these smaller and much rougher knives are evidently made in various parts, whereas the better class are, as usual, made in limited areas by the members of groups who are traditionally expert in this particular work. The one figured may be taken as a fair specimen; its length is altogether 15 cm., of which the blade takes up 7 cm. (Fig. 117, 9.)

The large knives with wooden hafts are made by the Kaitish and Warramunga tribes, while the Arunta tribe only make those without the wooden part. The smaller ones are made universally. As Dr. Stirling has said, there is not usually to be seen on the larger ones any stain or disfigurement consequent upon their having been used, but that they are used during fights is undoubted, and it may be added that the same remark applies to the smaller ones which are in constant use.

In addition to these definite knives, the natives use for ordinary purposes chipped stones made of any material that can be chipped to an edge. Sometimes, by the side of a water-hole, or on the top of a hill where the suitable material exists, there will be found numbers of these rude chips which are made as occasion requires, and only the better ones amongst which are kept for use in the making of the cutting surface of the adze or spear-thrower.

A weapon which may be called an adze is found in very many parts of Australia. This consists of a straight or curved piece of hard, heavy wood, such as *mulga*, to one or both ends of which a sharp-edged piece of opaline quartzite is attached by means of porcupine-grass resin. The curved form is evidently more common than the straight one, though here again a sufficiently large series would doubtless show all variations between the most curved and the straight ones. We may really divide these adzes into two groups, first those with the cutting flint at only one end, and, secondly, those with the flint at both ends. Amongst the first group we find that, as a general rule, the wooden handle is more or less curved. An almost straight one in our collection which was obtained from a Luritcha woman who had, before this was found in her possession by one of the authors, never seen a white man, measures in total length 76 cm.; the handle is of dark-coloured heavy wood, the diameter (3.3 cm.) being almost the same throughout the whole length with but a slight tapering at either end. The greater part of the length is marked with fairly regular grooves, each about 4 cm. in width. At the free end, which has been bluntly rounded, there is a space free from the grooves and ornamented with circular scratched lines. At the opposite end there is a space of 6 cm. also free from grooves and marked with irregularly arranged spiral cuts. The whole surface of the handle, and especially this lower portion which is grasped by the hand during use, is smooth and polished by constant handling. The lump of resin is 7 cm. in length, 5 cm. in width (that is in the plane of the cutting face), and 2.8 cm. in depth. The embedded chip of opaline quartzite projects about 1 cm. beyond the resin (rather less on the cutting side) and has a distinct cutting edge. One surface—that which is held away from the person during use—has a single flat facet, while the other is formed of a series of chips carefully made so as to produce a serrated edge. As Dr. Stirling has already remarked, this particular weapon differs from the great majority of the implements of this nature in having the handle straight, and also in the straight edge of the cutting surface.

In the second form the implement is a double one, having a flint inserted into a mass of resin at each end of the curved stick. This form is called *Ankura* or *Chalunka*, and is common amongst the Arunta, Ilpirra, Kaitish, and Warramunga. The total length of the one figured is 58 cm., and of this the free part of the wood measures 44 cm.; the greatest diameter is 3.5 cm., and there is a slight tapering especially towards one end. The wood is heavy, but light in colour, and has been ornamented in a somewhat unusual manner by charring with fire the surface of five rather irregular rings. Each lump of resin is 6-7 cm. in length and about 5 cm. in width, and the embedded chips have a characteristic shape. The cutting edge of each, and the surface formed by a single facet lying in the plane of the convexity of the implement, are both of them strongly convex. The other surface is made by a series of small chips so that a chisel-like edge is produced, and, during use, the concave side is held towards the person using the implement. Adzes such as this are found amongst the Arunta, Ilpirra, Kaitish and Warramunga tribes.

The common form of boomerang found amongst the Central tribes has a flattened and more or less curved form measuring from 60–90 cm. in length along the curve. The latter is always an open one and may be symmetrical, though, most often, it is not so, and one part of the weapon will be slightly curved or even straight, while the main curve is confined to the other part. In some cases one end will curve very distinctly in one direction while the other will have a slight but unmistakable curve in the opposite direction. The blade is always of approximately uniform width along its whole length. The twist, which is characteristic of what are called the "return boomerangs," is quite wanting in all the Central weapons, which are not made with the object of their returning to the thrower. The workmanship of the weapon varies to a large extent; the better ones are made in the north-east of the Arunta tribe and these are marked by regular grooves running, side by side, along the length of the curve on the more convex side; the other surface is marked by wider and more uneven grooves. In the poorer specimens the grooves are less even and the whole weapon is more clumsy in make and appearance. The Luritcha boomerangs are undoubtedly rougher than those of the Arunta and northern tribes,[184] there being but little attempt to smooth down the flatter side, while the grooves on the other face are roughly cut. In one of these the end held in the hand is narrower than the opposite one, and the grooves terminate abruptly at a distance of 12 cm. from the extremity. This part of the weapon has a roughly scratched series of lines to allow apparently, of a better grip being secured.

As a general rule the boomerangs are coated with red ochre and, in addition, they may be ornamented at the end which is not held with a few rings of white kaolin or yellow ochre. Some of them are certainly made of *mulga*, but others of a wood both lighter in colour and weight. It is apparently this form of boomerang which Roth refers to as the "fluted" form and which he says is introduced into the Queensland tribes, with whom he deals, from the west. In just the same way, whilst the ornate boomerang is the characteristic one of the Queensland natives, it is, amongst the Central tribes, but rarely met with, and then as a general rule only in the southern parts. It evidently travels from the interior of Queensland by way of a trade route which follows down the courses of the streams which flow from the interior of Queensland southwards to the Lake Eyre basin, just as in early times the natives themselves did, when they spread over the country.

This ornate boomerang is met with largely amongst the Urabunna tribe, and now and again one is seen in the hands of a man belonging to the southern Arunta. The length of one of these is 88 cm. along the curve which is a very open one, and there is neither a sharp bend nor any twist in the blade, in both of which respects the weapon agrees with the first described. The width of the blade varies from 6 cm. in the middle, from which it tapers off at either end, to 3 cm. in its narrowest part. One surface is always more convex than the other, and it is in fact more distinctly rounded than the grooved form. There is no trace on the convex surface of any grooves, but, from end to end, run series of incised patterns shaped like the figure 8 laid on its side, the interior of each loop being filled in with slanting lines. From end to end of the boomerang there run three rows of these, each row containing nine figures. In addition short curved lines are incised along the margin of the blade corresponding in position to some, but not all of the lines of figures. At each end on the part free from the latter, irregular scratches have been made so as to afford a better grip, and along the convex margin nineteen crosses have been roughly cut, but these are apparently not part of the original design. The flat side is somewhat roughly cut, and no red ochre, such as is never wanting in the case of the first form found in the Centre, has been used, the wood employed being *mulga*.

We now come to deal with a weapon which has sometimes been described as a two-handed sword or club, but which in reality is simply a large boomerang used for fighting at close quarters, and of such a size and weight, that it requires the use of both hands. Of the boomerangs of this description, the great majority which are found amongst the Arunta and Ilpirra tribes, undoubtedly, judging by their ornamentation, are importations from the internal parts of Queensland, just as in the case of the small ornate boomerang, and though they are fairly often seen in the south of the tribe they are rare in the northern districts of the Arunta. The largest one measured had a length of 125 cm. and a width of 8 cm. in the middle tapering gradually to 5 cm. at a distance of 10 cm. from the end. Its greatest thickness was 3 cm. In one specimen the design is very similar to that on the smaller ornate one, except that in the centre a series of parallel curved lines runs across from side to side, having the form of a W placed on its side with the angles rounded off. On either side of this are four bands of 8-shaped loops, those lying immediately to either side of the median line being longer than the others and measuring 18.5 cm. On one side the number of loops in each band, starting from the central line, is 5, 4, 4, 4, and on the other side 5, 6, 4, 4. The cross lines in the half of the loop of each figure slant in opposite directions, and in those on either side of the central line the direction of the slant is reversed. One end is evidently that which is always held by the hand, for here the design is partly obliterated by constant handling, and the space between the end of the design and the tip of the boomerang (6.5 cm.) is greater than at the other end (4 cm.). The opposite side of the weapon is very irregularly grooved, and there are traces of red ochre having been once rubbed over it, but the dark colour of the wood, which is *mulga* or some acacia, is not concealed by these traces.

It will be noticed that in all the forms of boomerangs there is a clearly marked difference between the two sides not only in the degree of curvature but also in the ornamentation. In the one case we have regular grooves on the more convex side, and in the other we have the incised design confined to it. The grooved, or ornate side as the case may be, is always the upper one if the boomerang be held horizontally with the concavity towards the body.

In another of the same size the design is much more roughly and carelessly incised. In the centre are three of the 8-shaped loops lying one above the other, but one of them, that on the concave side of the weapon, has an extra loop. At either side the lines of the loops are continuous with two parallel lines which run along the length of the boomerang, and between which are somewhat roughly arranged series of cross lines slanting alternately in opposite directions. It appears as if the designer had purposely run all the loops into one another, the slanting cross-lines representing those within the original loops. The result is a complete loss of curved lines and the development of a pattern which, though very rough and badly executed, calls to mind the designs characteristic of many West Australian implements.

We have said that the majority of these large boomerangs found amongst the Central tribes are importations from the east, but this does not appear, again judging by the style of ornamentation, to be true of all of them. In what is evidently an old boomerang obtained from a native on the Finke River, the design is very different from that described already. It consists of two curved bands of parallel lines one on either side of the central line, and on either side of these, groups of parallel bands of straight lines, which vary in length, run along towards either end of the weapon. The opposite side has been roughly smoothed, and the nature of the pattern, from which the characteristic loop and the slanting cross-lines are absent—and still more the fact that it has evidently, time after time, been rubbed with red ochre, which the eastern boomerangs do not seem to be, or, at least, not to anything like the extent that is characteristic of those of the centre—appears to make it at all events possible that this one is actually made in either the southern Arunta or in the Luritcha tribe (Fig. 118A.)

Another distinct type of boomerang which is met with all over the Centre from the Gulf of Carpentaria in the north, to at all events Charlotte Waters in the south, and probably two or three hundred miles to the south even of this, is of a somewhat remarkable shape. The blade has the flattened form of the Arunta weapon, but, in addition, it is provided at the distal end with a long beak or hook. The curvature of the blade varies considerably, and the beak, which is flattened like the body, comes off from the convex side, the whole being made out of one piece of wood which is derived from some such tree as a *mulga*, in which a branch or root was given off at a suitable angle from the main part out of which the blade has been made. In the blade there are the same variations in shape which have already been described in the case of the ordinary grooved boomerang. The beak varies a good deal in length and width. In one specimen of which the total length is 80 cm., the beak is 26 cm. long and fully 8 cm. wide where it passes off from the blade, tapering rapidly to 3 cm. In another specimen which is 76 cm. in length, the beak is 26 cm. long and only 4 cm. at its base. The convex side of the weapon is ornamented with the characteristic grooves which follow in their direction the outline of the concave edge of the beak. They are made with considerable regularity, and in the larger ones may be present on both sides, though they are never so well marked or regularly made on the flatter as on the more convex side. Sometimes they may be entirely wanting on the former which may be merely roughly smoothed down. The beak itself and the end from which it springs, may, in addition to the coating of red ochre which covers the whole, be ornamented with bands of white, black and yellow, and lines of spots. It is a curious and constant feature that, in each one, the concave line bounding the curved side of the beak is not directly continuous with that bounding the convex side of the blade. The curve ends abruptly at a small but clearly marked projection which is placed at a little distance down the blade; from this projection there is a little fall of, in some cases, 1 cm. to reach the edge of the blade itself. So far as the making of the weapon is concerned it would be just as easy to make the two curves perfectly continuous and it has all the appearance of being done in order to emphasise the idea of there being a head something like that of the flake axes. The decoration also, when any is present, is always on this head end, and in some a single band of black is painted running round the part where the notch occurs, as if again to indicate the junction of the head and handle parts.

In his description of the weapon Roth[185] gives a very ingenious explanation of the way in which this curious modification of a boomerang is especially useful. The beak catches on the stick or boomerang with which the native at whom it is thrown defends himself, and by its means the weapon, instead of being simply warded off, as in the case of the common boomerang, swings round on the beak and strikes the man at whom it is thrown. We have never seen this occur in the Arunta tribe, but we have on one occasion seen it thrown in the ordinary way with the result that the beak inflicted a very nasty wound on the neck of the man whom it hit. As might be expected, the beak is liable to be broken off, and we have seen such broken ones trimmed so as to cut off the remains of the beak, after which they were used for throwing, just like the ordinary curved ones. We have also seen them used in hand to hand fights after the fashion of a pick.

Roth states that they are made amongst the tribes inhabiting the Upper Georgina district which lies on the western side of the interior of that part of Queensland with the natives of which his work especially deals; in the Centre they are made by the Kaitish tribe, amongst whom they are called *Wialka*, by the Warramunga who call them *Wartilkirri*, and they are also found amongst, and probably also made by, some of the following tribes—Walpari, Bingongina, Waagai, Chingali, and Wambia. The Arunta obtain theirs from the Warramunga and call them *Ilya ilporkita*.

Fighting clubs are met with amongst all the tribes, but are made by the Kaitish and Warramunga and traded down to the Macdonnell Ranges and right away to the south of the Arunta and Luritcha; how much further it is impossible to say. Each one has the form of a long, straight, heavy bar of wood which is sometimes mulga, at others of a lighter colour, but always heavy. Each end is bluntly rounded as a general rule, and the one which is held in the hand can always be distinguished, because it is either grooved or cut in some way so as to afford a firm grip for the hands. In the one represented in the upper figure the total length is 115 cm. and the diameter 4.5 cm. At one end is a series of shallow grooves running parallel to the length of the club and extending for a distance of 21 cm. from the bluntly rounded tip. This one has apparently been made out of some species of eucalypt and has been red-ochred. In the one immediately below it we have a slightly different form. The length is 125 cm. and the diameter 4.5 cm. The end grasped by the hands has a series of shallow grooves extending for a distance of 19 cm. from the end, and across them a number of scratches run in various directions. Close to the end is a circle, 2.5 cm. in width, of porcupine-grass resin to aid in grasping. The third represents again a somewhat different type. It is made of mulga or some heavy dark wood. The two ends are decidedly less bluntly rounded than in most of the clubs, and the whole surface is covered, except about 12 cm. at one end, and 6 cm. at the other, with longitudinally arranged grooves. The end grasped by the hands has a few circularly disposed scratches upon it.

These clubs are used in close fighting, and though employed by both men and women are most frequently used by the latter. They are often met with and are always seen in the hands of women when a fight is going on, in which they either are, or may become at any moment, interested parties. They are grasped with two hands, and with them blows are given such as would at once disable any ordinary white man, especially as they are, according to etiquette, given, and received, mainly on the head, but, as this is the least vulnerable portion of the body of a native, the damage done is merely of a temporary nature. Occasionally bones are broken, and we have seen one old woman gallantly continue to fight with one arm hanging broken and useless by her side.

MUSICAL INSTRUMENTS

The musical instruments are of a very simple nature. The most elementary method of producing sound to accompany the chanting during the performance of ceremonies consists in striking the ground with a shield, spear-thrower, boomerang, or a simple piece of wood. Very often boomerangs are rattled together. In one particular ceremony two short and bluntly rounded pieces of wood are used which, as they fall on one another, each being held in one hand, produce a clunk, clunk, which closely imitates, as it is supposed to do, the sound of the croaking of a particular frog. This particular instrument is only used in one ceremony and is not allowed to be seen by the women, but there are instruments made of almost precisely the same form, but simply more carefully finished off, which are in common use. The latter are called *Trora*,[186] and are more frequently met with in the south than in the north of the tribe. The simplest of them consists of two carefully rounded pieces of wood, the larger of which measures 23 cm. in length and 4.5 cm. in width in the middle. At one end it is ornamented with a circular groove with a shorter groove running close to it, and at the other end with a spiral groove. The shorter piece is 21 cm. in length and 3.2 cm. in diameter, and both have a coating of red ochre.

In a second form one piece of wood has two prong-like projections from one end. The total length is 26 cm. and of the prongs 7 cm.; the greatest width is 3.5 cm. The other piece measures 25 cm. in length. When in use the blunt end of the prong is held in the left hand, and the striker is allowed to fall on to the pronged end.

A third form is of a curious shape. One end of it has just the shape of the pronged piece of the last described, while from between the two limbs of the prong passes forwards a piece which is very similar in shape to the simple rounded portion. The whole is cut out of a single block of wood, but tendon is bound round the narrow part of the projection which passes between the prongs, evidently with the idea of strengthening this, which is undoubtedly the weak part of the instrument. The prongs in this particular position are simply meant as ornament, and do not serve to vary the nature of the sound produced by the instrument. The total length is 32 cm., and the width across the prongs 3 cm., the length of the simple striker being 28 cm.

The first described and roughly made form is simply one of this kind of instrument made for use in a particular ceremony; still the fact that it is so made and used is sufficient to make it representative of that one sound which it is supposed to imitate, and it therefore receives a special name, becomes associated with that ceremony and with nothing else, and is tabu to the women.

The wood employed in their manufacture is usually that of a species of eucalypt, in which case the instrument appears to be always red-ochred; in one specimen, however, the wood is dark *mulga*, and there is no red ochre, a somewhat remarkable feature in regard to a Central Australian instrument.

The only other musical instrument known to us is the rudimentary trumpet called *Ilpirra*. The use of this in connection with obtaining wives by means of magic charm has already been described. Each is simply a hollowed out piece of the branch of a gum tree. The hollowing out has probably been done by some insect such as a white ant, but the external crust which the insect left is very hard. Of two in our possession the length of each is about 60 cm. and the diameter slightly more than 5 cm. The external surface has been first of all smoothed down with a flint leaving shallow longitudinal grooves. Then a coat of red ochre has been painted over the whole length, and at each end the rim has been covered with a circle of resin so as to make the margins smoother. In the one case the exterior is decorated with alternate circles of yellow ochre and white kaolin, between which narrow circles of the underlying red ochre can be seen; in the centre is a space measuring 7 cm. in length, and between the yellow circles at either end of this, yellow lines run across each in a slightly spiral direction.

In the other specimen two rings of white kaolin, about 11 cm. distant from each other, are painted at each end, and between these run five longitudinal lines of the same colour.

When used the trumpet is simply placed to the mouth, and by singing through it the sound is intensified. Trumpets such as these are, apart from the interesting use concerned with magic, generally used in corrobborees such as the *Atnimokita* which has been described by Dr. Stirling.[187]

PITCHIS

So far as the material out of which they are made is concerned we can distinguish two different kinds of *pitchis*, which is the name given by the whites to the receptacles in which the natives carry food and water, and at times even babies. So far as their shape is concerned we can distinguish at least five well marked varieties.

The two materials used are, first, the soft wood of the bean tree (*Erythrina vespertilio*), and secondly, some hard wood which is some species of eucalypt, often, at all events, the red gum (*E. rostrata*) which grows on the banks and in the beds of the creeks.

Of the hard wood *pitchis* there is, in reality, only one form so far as the shape is concerned, though they vary much in size. Each one is, however, only a more or less shallow trough the edges of which never bend over, though the concavity may be of considerable depth and so great as to render the *pitchi* useful for carrying water in. Very often the edge of the trough is sinuous in outline, and it is always cut out of a solid piece of wood entailing a great amount of labour. The surface, both internally and externally, is marked with grooves running along the length of the *pitchi*, those on the interior being in some cases much smaller, more numerous, and much more carefully made than those on the exterior. In the one figured (Fig. 121, 1) there are in the broadest part forty-eight grooves on the external and one hundred and forty-six on the internal surface, and the execution of the latter must especially have cost the maker a very great amount of trouble. A *pitchi* such as this has a certain value, as is shown by the way in which, when a slit has been accidentally made in the rim, the two edges are carefully lashed together with tendon so as to prevent further splitting.

There is every gradation in form to be met with between the well-shaped and carefully-finished *pitchi* of considerable size and the small roughly fashioned and shallow concave piece of wood less than a foot in length, which serves mainly as a shovel or scoop with which to throw out the earth dug up by the native women when hunting after vegetable food or small animals, and which is called an *Apmara*.

Of the soft-wood *pitchis* we can distinguish four different forms. The first of these has an unmistakable boat shape. The one figured (Figs. 121, 2, and 120, 2*a*) measures 91 cm. in length, 29 cm. in height, and 22 cm. in greatest width. The figure will serve to indicate the general shape. The internal surface is rough, showing the grooves made by the flint which have no regular arrangement, but, on the other hand, the external surface has been carefully ornamented with a number of small grooves measuring not more than 2 mm. in width which run parallel to one another from end to end.

The larger ones of the second form reach the length of the one just described, but they differ strikingly from it in the fact that their outline is rounded both in transverse and longitudinal section, and also in the fact that, whilst the internal surface is rough, the external one is marked by broad grooves measuring about 8 cm. in width which have been made with great care and regularity.

The third form may perhaps be considered as a variant of the one just described, as it differs from this only in the fact that in longitudinal section the two ends are not inturned. In addition to this also the external grooves seem to imply that the maker recognised the fact that he was dealing with a different shape, as, instead of the broad grooves running parallel to one another along the whole length, there are two series: (*a*) one which runs from end to end, and (*b*) another on each side which runs along the broad part of the *pitchi* and cuts the first series at an angle (Figs. 121, 4, and 120, 4*a*).

The fourth form is a very well-marked one, and has the shape of a long hollow trough without incurving sides. It is much like an elongated hardwood *pitchi*, but is, owing doubtless to the more easily worked nature of the material, of more regular shape than the majority of the latter. The largest one in our possession measures 97 cm. in length, 26 cm. in width, whilst its greatest concavity is only 8 cm. The sides are not incurved and, like the boat-shaped *pitchi*, the external surface is ornamented with a large number of very narrow grooves running from end to end. Just as in the hard wood *pitchis* of this form, so in this we meet with rudely fashioned specimens in which the external surface is devoid of the narrow groovings and is merely marked by the irregular ones made by the flint, and which have not been afterwards smoothed down before the addition of smaller ones.

WALLETS AND BAGS

It is only in the southern part of the Arunta and in the Urabunna tribe, that anything like a bag made of knitted twine, the latter made of fur or vegetable fibre, is manufactured. These bags used to be traded through as far north as the Macdonnell Ranges, but, as a general rule, the native carries his valuables about in a wallet made sometimes out of the skin of some animal, sometimes out of pieces of bark tied round with fur-string. Another form of receptacle is a primitive skin pouch made by cutting a flap of skin with the fur attached from the back of such an animal as a marsupial, and then, after stretching it in the centre with pressure of the hand, it is filled out with sand to the desired shape and allowed to dry in the sun. A skin pouch such as this is called *Ilarntwa*, and is used both by Arunta and Luritcha men.

In an ordinary skin wallet, procured at Mount Olga out in the desert region to the south of Lake Amadeus, and consisting simply of a piece of skin of a marsupial of some kind, were found a bunch of emu feathers, a tassel of Peragale tail-tips, a spare flint with chipped edge such as is used for the spear-thrower, tendon with which to mend broken weapons or splice on to the main shaft the tip of a spear, a nose bone and lumps of red and yellow ochre. A more capacious wallet, belonging to a native in the northern Macdonnell Ranges, and manufactured simply out of small slabs of bark tied round with fur-string, contained a bunch of eagle-hawk feathers, an emu feather chignon, a stone knife in its sheaf, three knouts, a woman's ornament of resin with teeth fixed into the mass, a piece of pearl shell for a pubic ornament, a nose bone, several armlets and necklets, and two strands of human hair carefully enclosed in fur-string and evidently used as charms.

In the southern Arunta and the Urabunna bags which are as well formed and skilfully knitted as those in use amongst highly civilised peoples, are often met with.[188] In many cases the string used is made out of the fibres obtained from the reeds which grow around the margins of the mound springs which exist especially in the district occupied by the Urabunna tribe. The one figured (Fig. 119, 1) came from Charlotte Waters, and the art of making these bags does not appear to have been acquired by any of the northern tribes, such as those living north of the Macdonnell Range throughout the central area. Around the rim of the bag runs a strand on to which the loops are fixed; the first loop is a short one, the second a long one, measuring 10 cm., while all the others are at most 1 cm. in length. It is worth noting that the manner of attachment of the third to the second, varies in alternate loops; in one, the upper string of the third loop is twisted round the lower one of the second, and in the other the lower string of the second is twisted round the upper string of the third, and so on alternately. The loops are so close together that the arrangement is not noticed until the structure is carefully examined, and as there is no particular reason, structurally, why this method should be adopted, it shows that the maker of the bag probably derived a certain amount of pleasure from varying the design. The handle is made of a number of strands of string continuous with certain of the loops on either side; these strands are again enclosed by two layers of string wound round and round them. The upper edge of the bag for a depth of 7 cm. is coloured red with ochre, and below this four red rings, each about 2 cm. broad, run round. At first sight it looks as if the red had simply been rubbed on after the bag had been made, but closer examination shows that this is not the case, but that the maker used two kinds of string, one uncoloured and one which had been well rubbed with red ochre. The series of long, and the first two of short, loops are made with red string, then follow eight made with white, then one made with red, which forms the first of the narrow red bands running round the bag, then follow ten series of white and again a single red series, then eight white and a single red, then ten white and a single red forming the lowest coloured band, below which there are eight white series. Owing to the diamond shape of the loops the darker bands have the appearance of shading off at their upper and lower edges.

SPINDLE

For spinning fur or human hair into string a simple form of spindle is used. Two curved, thin sticks, each about 14 or 16 cm. in length, are taken, and a slit is made through the centre of each one. They are then placed at right angles, and through the slits a straight rounded stick about 35 cm. in length is passed. The two curved pieces are much nearer to one end than the other, and their concavities are directed towards the nearer end. When in use, the native squats in the usual way with his legs bent under him; with one hand, usually the left, he holds the spindle against his thigh, causing it to rotate rapidly as he rubs his hand up and down the thigh; in the other hand he holds the raw material which with his fingers he continually serves out, as the string becomes spun into a strand which is wound round the spindle. The accompanying figure (Fig. 123) represents a man who was engaged in making opossum fur-string, of which large quantities were made during the Engwura, by men and women alike, for the purpose of making what are called *Kulchia* or armlets for the men to wear who were passing through the ceremony. As the spindle was moving rapidly there appears to be only one cross piece, and in some of the spindles, especially amongst the Luritcha, this is actually the case.

ROCK PAINTINGS

The rock paintings may be divided into two distinct series, (*a*) those which may be spoken of as ordinary rock drawings and (*b*) certain other drawings, in many cases not distinguishable from some of the first series, so far as their form is concerned, but which belong to a class of designs all of which are spoken of as *Churinga Ilkinia*, and are regarded as sacred because they are associated with the totems. Each local totemic group has certain of these especially belonging to the group, and in very many cases preserved on rock surfaces in spots which are strictly tabu to the women, children, and uninitiated men.

If we were dealing with the various drawings simply from the point of view of decorative art we could divide the whole series into two more or less distinct groups. The first of these would contain those which are zoomorphic or phytomorphic in form and origin, and the second would contain those which may be called geometric in form. In both of the series we find examples of the two groups just described, but in the case of the second series, that is the sacred drawings, the geometrical ones greatly preponderate.

We will deal first with the ordinary drawings. Amongst these the zoomorphic and phytomorphic designs are similar to those which are found in many parts of the continent, and represent, often in very rude form, outlines of animals and plants; they are indeed sometimes so rudely executed that, whilst their zoomorphic or phytomorphic nature is evident, it is yet wholly impossible to tell the animal or plant from which the artist has drawn his inspiration. Those represented in Fig. 124 will serve to give a good idea of the nature of these drawings, and there is practically but little variation in them from place to place. The majority of those represented exist on the roof and walls of shallow caves lying around the base of Ayers Rock far out in the desert region away to the south of Lake Amadeus.[189] The materials used are red and yellow ochre, charcoal and some white material such as kaolin or calcined gypsum.

Number 1 represents most probably a dingo, and is drawn merely in outline in charcoal; Number 2 is evidently a somewhat conventionalised drawing of a bird with a long tail; the whole is outlined in red ochre and the body and head drawn solid with charcoal; the tail is of some length, and what are evidently the legs are joined together for some reason; the meaning of the red bands crossing the body is difficult to see. Numbers 3 and 4 represent conventional drawings of lizards. Number 5 is not infrequently met with in various parts of Australia, and represents a snake coming out of a hole in the rock, a natural hole being often utilised for the purpose. Number 6 is probably zoomorphic in origin, but so conventionalised that it is perfectly impossible to say what it represents. Number 7 is evidently a series of human heads drawn in outline with charcoal; they are placed in a group close to one another, and, were it not for the fact that the lower ones are included in the same group as the two upper ones, it would be difficult to suggest what they were intended for. Number 8 is a more complicated drawing, and shows considerable originality on the part of the artist. It is painted on an exposed rock surface at the base of the George Gill Range, and a native described it to us as an attempt to represent, as if seen from below, an emu sitting on its eggs. The neck is a stout black line edged with white, the legs are also black and end in the characteristic toes, the eggs are black oval patches each enclosed in a white line, and the feathers are indicated with white lines. Number 9 represents the frond of a Cycad which grows in fair abundance on certain of the Rocky Ranges, though there are none within eighty miles of Ayers Rock. So far as we have seen this is the only example of a phytomorphic drawing.

Number 10 is drawn in a different way from all the others, but in one which is practised by the natives all over the continent. The method consists in placing the hand flat up against the rock and then blowing over it from the mouth fine dust of red ochre or charcoal, which remains attached to the rock, and so the outline of the hand is stencilled in red or black as the case may be.

In addition to drawings such as those described there are others which are not geometrical and may in all probability be regarded as zoomorphic in origin, though the resemblance to the animal is but faintly if at all discernible, and the artist has further embellished his work with lines which make it still more difficult to trace the origin of the design. Such an one is represented in Number 11, which is copied from a drawing at Ayers Rock. The main outline is probably the modified form of the body of an animal such as is drawn in Number 3, the part which, if this be so, represents the head, almost merges into the blunt prominences which indicate the front limbs, while the two hind ones are only indicated by the swellings at the opposite end. The alternate lines of red and yellow ochre which radiate from the whole surface are evidently intended as an embellishment to the design, and may be regarded as a further development of the radiating lines which occur only at the head end of the body of the lizard represented in Number 3. It may be added that both drawings occur close together at Ayers Rock.

Number 12 is of a different nature and represents apparently one of the stone knives with a resin haft such as is used by the natives, though the attachment of the blade to the haft is somewhat different from that of the real object. There can be, however, little doubt as to what the drawing is meant to represent.

One thing may be noticed with regard to these rock paintings, and that is, that we nowhere amongst these tribes, so far as we know, meet with any of the more complicated drawings depicting scenes such as a kangaroo chase, or men spearing emus, or a corrobboree dance, such as are found amongst other tribes in the south and east parts of the continent, though the Central Australian is by no means, in art matters, inferior to the coastal tribes; nor again, it may be stated here, do we meet with any attempt to sculpture the outlines of animals or plants on the rock surface.

Passing now to the geometrical designs it may be noted that, so far as their form, and indeed that of certain of the zoomorphic and phytomorphic drawings is concerned, there is no distinction between them and certain of the drawings associated with ceremonial objects. They are dealt with separately because, as we have said, the latter have definite associations in regard to the totems and have, what the ordinary geometrical rock-drawings do not appear to have, a definite significance. By this we mean that the artist who drew them had no definite purpose in doing so. The natives when asked the meaning of certain drawings such as these will constantly answer that they are only play-work and mean nothing; but what are exactly, so far as their form is concerned, similar drawings, only drawn on some ceremonial object or in a particular spot, have a very definite meaning. That is, the same native will tell you that a special drawing in one spot has no meaning, and yet he will tell you exactly what it is supposed to signify when drawn in a different spot. The latter, it may be remarked, is always on what we may call sacred ground, near to which the women may not come. It can scarcely be doubted that these ordinary and, in form, geometrical rock-paintings which are drawn in his spare time by a man who is frequently seeing and using objects marked with the sacred symbols, are due to his remembrance of the latter. He is making a drawing the inspiration of which is, in reality, a totemic design, though, as it is not drawn upon a sacred spot or on a ceremonial object, it does not "mean" anything.

In speaking of these as geometrical designs we use the term only in reference to the present form of the design, and not at all as implying that they are merely geometrical figures. All the sacred drawings, the greater number of which are geometric in nature, are associated with the totems, and to the natives each one has a definite meaning, and in all probability, though very much modified, these drawings are to be regarded as derived from zoomorphs. This, however, is a subject of much difficulty, and will be further dealt with in connection with the sacred drawings.

A few of the ordinary rock-drawings of this form are represented (Numbers 13–17), which will serve to indicate their general nature. It will be noticed that in many of them the concentric circle pattern is conspicuous. In regard to this it will be shown later that there is good ground for the belief that the concentric circle pattern which figures so largely on the various ceremonial objects of the Central Australian native has been derived from an original spiral. A glance at the totemic designs will show clearly what we mean by saying that the idea of particular drawings, such as some of those represented in Fig. 124, was derived from the former, though, in regard to them, the natives assure us that they have no definite significance.

DECORATION DURING ORDINARY CORROBBOREES OR ALTHERTA

During the ordinary dancing festivals, or *Altherta*, which are usually spoken of as corrobborees, the principal feature of the decoration is usually a more or less elaborate headdress. This is always made by first of all bunching the hair on the top of the head and then surrounding it with small twigs, so as to form a helmet-like structure of the desired shape. This often measures as much as 2 feet in height, and may run up to a point, or have the summit flattened or bluntly rounded off. Human hair-string is then tied tightly round so as to preserve the shape and to fix it firmly on to the head. The top of the helmet is often further decorated with a bunch of eagle-hawk feathers, or, as in one corrobboree, a semicircular structure, made of grass stalks bound round with hair-string and with a tuft of tail-tips at each end, is fixed through the helmet. On the latter there is always some design drawn in down, which is made from the involucral hairs of a species of Portulaca, and has been coloured red, white, or yellow. Almost always the design includes a band passing across the bridge of the nose and enclosing the eyes. This down is affixed, as usual, by means of human blood, and some of the most characteristic designs are represented in the Fig. 125–128.

On the body various designs are drawn, some of the more frequent of which are also shown in the figures. For each *Altherta* there is a regular series of helmets and body patterns of a particular design which are always made and drawn. The lines of decoration are almost always made of a series of spots placed closely side by side, and, very frequently, the space between two parallel lines will be filled up with a band of down of a different colour from that of the lines. The most elaborate design is perhaps that used in the case of one of the rain dances (Fig. 128), in which a flat piece of wood, in shape resembling a large Churinga, is fixed into the top of the helmet and ornamented with lines and concentric circles of spots. In some of the corrobborees decorated objects, such as sticks carried in the hand, are used, or, as in the Atnimokita corrobboree,[190] a pole of special form is erected, after having been carefully painted with spiral lines of yellow and spots of white and yellow on a red ground. A very frequent decoration takes the form of twigs of green tree tied on to the leg just above the ankle (Fig. 127).[191]

It is impossible to assign any meaning to these designs; in the first place there is, as shown also by Mr. Roth in the case of the same festivals held amongst the Queensland natives, a constant circulation of these corrobborees from group to group and from tribe, with the result that even the meaning of the words chanted is quite unknown to the performers in whose possession the festival may be, at any given time, after it has been passed on by its original owners. All of the corrobborees performed at Alice Springs, for example, are derived from the north, and gradually filter through to the south. The only thing which seems evident with regard to the body designs is, that they are drawn so that, as a general rule, they serve to accentuate the outline of the curves of the body, and beyond this it is very possible that they have no special significance of any kind.

DECORATION DURING SACRED CEREMONIES OR QUABARA UNDATTHA

The characteristic feature of the decorations in all of the sacred ceremonies is that in them birds' down, which the natives call *undattha*, is employed; indeed, the importance of this feature may be gauged by the fact that these performances are commonly spoken of as *quabara undattha*, and such no woman or uninitiated youth is allowed to see, except on extremely rare occasions, and then only at a considerable distance and indistinctly.

In these ceremonies also only a limited number ever take part as actual performers, and, instead of occupying a long time in their performance, they usually last only a few minutes. Unlike those of the ordinary dances, also, the design always has a definite significance, and is supposed in many cases to have been handed down from the Alcheringa, while in others the decorations have been shown to the owner of the *quabara* by the *Iruntarinia*, or spirits. These ceremonies, again, are never passed on from tribe to tribe, but are in the possession of certain individuals who have received them by right of inheritance, that is, they may be regarded as private property, and each one is, save those given by the *Iruntarinia*, associated with some special man or woman of the Alcheringa. All of them are connected with the totems.

The various forms of design may be seen by reference to the figures illustrating the Engwura. Almost always, as in the ordinary dances, special attention is paid to the head-dress. The hair is tied up, and a helmet is made out of twigs or grass stalks wound round with human hair-string. In the case of one of the emu performances (Fig. 73), it forms a slightly tapering column about five feet in height, the end being ornamented with a tuft of emu feathers. Owing to the flexibility of the column, the end droops somewhat, and moves about as the performer walks, imitating well the continuous up and down movement of an emu's head, while the bird walks aimlessly about. In these emu ceremonies the lines of down run along the length of the body, arms and legs, a design which may perhaps have been suggested in the beginning by the very distinct longitudinal markings on the body of the young bird.

In the ceremonies of the frog totem there are two very characteristic styles of decoration; one consists of alternate circles of white and red down running round the head-dress, which sometimes forms a wide disc-like structure. The circles may be continued round the body and limbs, broken by perhaps a few longitudinal lines. Another form frequently met with in this totem consists of small patches of red, each of which is surrounded by a circle of white down. The headdress, with the Churinga which is fixed into it and is also decorated with alternate circles of red and white, represents a large tree; the longitudinal lines indicate roots, and the smaller circular patches represent frogs. This is indicative of the fact that, as is very characteristic of frog life in Central Australia, the animals spend the dry season, or, in some cases the day time, burrowing in the sandy ground amongst the roots of the red gums which grow in the beds and along the banks of the creeks, which latter, it must be remembered, only contain water at rare intervals of time.

Reference to the illustrations concerned with the account of the Engwura will serve to indicate the elaborate nature of some of the decorations, and, as we have said before, while it takes, as in this particular instance, between five and six hours to decorate the performer, the ceremony itself lasts only a few minutes. The whole of the body, back and front, was in this case covered with representations of frogs of various sizes; from the head-dress tufts of eagle-hawk feathers, attached to short sticks, projected, and the whole was surmounted by a long Churinga completely swathed with circles of down and tipped with a bunch of brown owl feathers. The roots of the tree, represented by the Churinga and head-dress, were in this instance indicated by a large number of strings hanging down from the head-dress all round the body. Each string was completely covered with alternate red and white rings and tipped with a tuft of tail-tips, the whole decoration almost completely concealing the man from view (Figs. 72 and 74).

In the case of a ceremony connected with the sun totem, one of the two performers wore as a head-dress a large flat disc with alternate concentric circles of red and white down, the disc being supposed to represent the sun (Fig. 108).

Circles of white down enclosing a central bluish grey or black patch are made to represent the skulls of men who have been killed and eaten (Fig. 80).

A long cord, made of a number of human hair-girdles, is sometimes stretched across between the heads of two or three performers sitting at some distance from each other, and, when so used, is supposed to represent the path followed by certain of the ancestors of a totemic group, such as the wild cat, in the Alcheringa (Fig. 47). At other times a precisely similar cord may be used to unite a number of men standing in a line while the cord passes from the waist girdle of one man to that of the next man, and so on all along the line. In this instance it represents the roots of trees, which are indicated by certain of the men.

An entirely different form of decoration is seen in the little tufts of the red-barred tail feathers of the black cockatoo, which are fixed on to short sticks and have their tips decorated with masses of red or white down. These tufts of feathers, some of which are placed in the ground, where they are then supposed to be growing, while others adorn the heads of the performer, represent the Irriakura plant in flower (Fig. 62).

In a large number of the ceremonies we meet with a very important ceremonial object which has already been referred to, and is called a *Nurtunja*. In certain others we meet with an equally important object, which is called a *Waninga*. The *Nurtunja* is typical of the northern, and the *Waninga* of the southern, part of the Arunta tribe. There are various forms of the *Nurtunja*, the principal ones of which are represented in the figures illustrating the Engwura ceremony. The most usual form is made of from one to twenty spears; round these, first of all, long grass stalks are bound by means of the hair-girdles of the men, and then rings of down are added, and perhaps, but not always, a few Churinga will be suspended at intervals. The top is almost always decorated with a large tuft of eagle-hawk feathers. More rarely the down, instead of being in rings, will be fixed on in long lines running parallel to the length of the *Nurtunja*, or, as in one case, there may be rings at intervals, and between these there will be longitudinal lines of down. Occasionally from the top end of a large *Nurtunja* a small second one will hang pendent; at other times the *Nurtunja* may be in the form of a cross or it may be T-shaped. At times, again, it may have the appearance of a torpedo resting on the head, or, finally, it may be in the form of a huge helmet firmly attached to the head, and of various shapes, according to what it is supposed to represent. This form (Fig. 61) differs from all the others in the fact that one end of the *Nurtunja* is actually continuous with the head-dress, instead of being, as in all other cases, a structure independent of the head-dress and affixed after the completion of this.

The *Waninga*, like the *Nurtunja*, varies much in shape and size; some are so small that they can easily be worn in the head-dress. The fundamental point in the structure of the *Waninga* is that it consists of a main vertical support, which may be merely a stick but little more than a foot in length, or, as is more usually the case, a long spear, across which is fixed a shorter arm or two arms. According to whether there be one or two of the shorter transverse arms we can distinguish two main types. The first has the form of a cross, so far as the supporting structures are concerned, and fur string passes diagonally across the spaces between the central and cross bars, with the result that a lozenge-shaped plate of strands of fur string, placed closely side by side, is formed. In the second type the strands of string run from one cross bar to the other, parallel to the length of the spear, and as one of the cross bars is placed close to either end of the spear, there is formed a long oblong-shaped structure, at each end of which the strands of string pass diagonally across to the central spear at a very obtuse angle. At the upper end there may be a third, and in this case short, transverse bar, close to the tip of the spear, and strands of string, as in the one shown in Fig. 39, may pass to this from the upper of the two larger cross bars. When this is so the *Waninga* is really a double one, the small upper part representing a small one placed at the top of the main larger one in much the same way as, in certain of the *Nurtunjas*, we have seen a small one attached to the large one, only that, in the case of the *Waninga*, owing to its form, the connection between the two is of necessity more intimate.

The fur-string is apparently always of more than one description, part of it being made of opossum and part often of bandicoot fur, while in the larger ones, human hair-string is employed as well. By means of these different coloured strings a definite design can be produced; for example, in one of the smaller ones the central space is made with red-ochred opossum string, the outer part consisting of grey bandicoot string; in another the central part is red, then follows a band of grey, and then, on the outside, another band of red. In the larger ones bands of red, black and grey alternate in various ways, the exact pattern being always definitely determined by tradition. Especially in the case of the larger ones the surface formed by the string may be further ornamented with white down, which in some cases may be laid on so thickly as almost to hide the string from view.

So far as both *Nurtunja* and *Waninga* are concerned we are dealing with objects of a sacred nature, the origin of which it is impossible to conjecture. The mere form apparently means nothing, that is we may find in two perfectly distinct ceremonies that two *Nurtunjas* or two *Waningas* are used which are, respectively, quite identical in form, and yet in the one case, one, say of the *Nurtunjas*, will represent a kangaroo, and in the other a wild cat. The part of one *Waninga* which represents in one ceremony a head of a kangaroo may, in another represent the tail of a lizard. All that can be said in regard to these two characteristic objects is that in whatever ceremony either of them be used, then, for the time being, it represents the animal or plant which gives its name to the totem with which the ceremony is concerned. In a kangaroo ceremony, a *Waninga* or *Nurtunja* means a kangaroo, in an emu ceremony it means an emu. The decoration is, so far as can be seen, perfectly arbitrary and has at the present day no significance in the sense of its being intended to have any special resemblance to the object which the *Nurtunja* or *Waninga* is supposed to represent.

We come now to the remarkable structure which is called a *Kauaua*. The nature of this has already been described. It is the most sacred ceremonial object of the tribe, and its origin is evidently of very early date indeed. The striking features in regard to it are, (1) that it must be cut down and brought into camp without being allowed to touch the ground; (2) that it is completely smeared all over with human blood, though it is not without interest to note that the natives say that occasionally red ochre may be used as a substitute for the blood; (3) that its decorations consist of the various ornaments which are worn on the head of a man when fully decorated, so that it is really a wooden pole the upper end of which represents a human head; and (4) that it is only crested towards the close of the Engwura when the men gather together round it and the painting of the backs of the younger men with designs of various totems is done by the old men.

Unlike the *Nurtunja* and *Waninga*, of both of which there are various forms, there is only one form of *Kauaua*, and this is common to all the totems.

The exact significance of this can only be a matter of conjecture, for the natives have not, so far as we can find out, any idea with regard to its origin or meaning. The decoration evidently points to the fact that it has some relation to a human being, and possibly we may have in the *Kauaua* the expression of the idea of the association of a spirit individual with a tree. We find, it must be remembered, amongst the Arunta tribe that trees are intimately associated with particular celebrated individuals of the Alcheringa whose spirits especially frequent those which are their *Nanja* trees, and, whilst there is no such thing as any offering being made to the tree or to its spirit inhabitant, we may perhaps regard ceremonies in which trees are represented, such as the celebrated ones at Imanda which are associated with men of the frog totem, as an early form of tree worship.

The *Kauaua* is certainly suggestive of an early stage of development corresponding to the stakes or stone columns the upper parts of which are carved into the semblance of the human head, and which, in a stage of culture very considerably in advance of that reached by the Arunta people, are associated with rites paid to special individuals of whom each is regarded as the representative.

In some way which is not very clear to the mind of the native the *Kauaua* is regarded as a something common to the members of all the totems, and in connection with this it may be remembered that it was while sitting round the base of the *Kauaua*, that the young men were painted with the various totemic designs. Possibly it is to be regarded as emblematic of some great ancestor of the tribe who was associated with the origin of the various totems, so that it is an object, and most naturally the most sacred one which they possess, which is common to all the totems.

We can see at all events an interesting gradation in regard to the sacred objects of the Arunta tribe; there is first of all the Churinga which is representative of the individual; secondly, the *Nurtunja* or *Waninga* which is representative of a number of individuals who collectively form the totemic group; and thirdly, there is the *Kauaua* which represents, as it were, the totems collectively, or it may be the great ancestor from whom they all originated and around the representative of whom they all group themselves on the only occasion on which the *Kauaua* is ever used.

The name *Churinga Ilkinia* is given to certain rock-drawings which are found in the neighbourhood of the *Ertnatulunga* or sacred storehouse of the different local groups. These drawings are regarded as peculiarly sacred and are not allowed to be seen by women and children, to whom their locality is known and who carefully avoid the spot.

For those which are represented in Fig. 131, Numbers 1-5, we are indebted to Dr. E. Eylmann, who, at our request and at considerable trouble to himself, most kindly paid a special visit to the spot which lies some distance away from Barrow Creek, and took careful copies and measurements of the designs. At the spot in question, which lies in the country occupied by the Warramunga tribe, there is a small cave at the end of the Crawford Range in the high, steep, sandstone bank of a small creek. Dr. Eylmann says, "It is 1m. 10cm. high, 3m. 59cm. wide, and 4m. 80cm. deep. The bottom is covered with sand and pieces of charcoal. The ceiling is blackened with smoke. Opposite to the cave in the bed of the creek is a small rock hole, which never gets dry because a spring is at the bottom of it. A little further up the creek are some more rock holes. Most of the drawings are outside of the cave, on the smooth sandstone close to the inlet, inside are only some little circles. All drawings are painted on a red ground (artificial) with a white or black pigment. Besides the drawings near and in the cave there are traces of older ones in the neighbourhood of the other rock holes. This place must be a favourite camping place in dry seasons, because I saw many old fireplaces, huts and a broad path leading to the rock holes."

Whilst we have not been able to ascertain the meaning of these drawings beyond the fact that they are sacred and are associated with the honey-ant totem, they are here reproduced because they serve to show the wide distribution of this form of *Churinga Ilkinia*, though at the same time the broad band of white which intersects the series of circles in the two most important designs is a feature which we have not met with amongst those of the Arunta tribe.

The other designs which are represented belong some to the Udnirringita, or witchetty grub, and others to the *Ulpmerka* of the plum tree totem of a celebrated spot called Quiurnpa, to which we have very often had to refer. The former are painted on the precipitous rocky sides of the Emily Gorge and the latter on what is called the Pirkintilia rock at Quiurnpa, a spot which is especially associated in tradition with the *Ulpmerka* men. In both cases we have drawings some of which, such as Fig. 132, Numbers 1-7 amongst the Udnirringita, and Numbers 2 and 14 amongst the *Ulpmerka* ones, are clearly zoomorphic or phytomorphic in origin. Of the two larger drawings of the Udnirringita the curved band of bars near to the centre is supposed to represent the shoulders of some of the Alcheringa ancestors, and in the other one the space between two of the white lines which slant off towards the right hand, is supposed to represent an Alcheringa woman, with her hand up to her head, peering upwards as she watches Intwailiuka, one of the great leaders of the men in the Alcheringa, performing the ceremony of *Intichiuma*.

Of the *Ulpmerka* designs several of them, such as Fig. 133, Numbers 3-8, &c., are those which are painted on boys at the ceremony of throwing them up, the first of the initiation ceremonies. Others, such as Numbers 18 and 20, represent the *Nurtunja* which Kukaitcha, the leader of the *Ulpmerka*, carried on his head; Number 14 represents a plum tree and Number 16 is supposed to be an unripe plum. The explanation of the figures is the one given by the natives at the present day. In the case of these, as in that of the sacred drawings of all other totems, it is not possible to find out anything with regard to their origin. They are supposed to have been handed down from the times of the Alcheringa ancestors, and a knowledge of what they indicate is handed on from generation to generation, but no one has any idea of how this particular meaning came to be attached to them.

We have already, when dealing with the Churinga, described in detail the meaning of the designs on certain particular ones, and have pointed out how, on one Churinga, a spiral or series of concentric circles will mean one thing and on another a similar design will mean quite another thing.

It is important to notice that the spiral and concentric circles will appear in the design on one and the same Churinga, and not only this, but that, on the one Churinga, as, for example, in the case of the frog totem, a large gum tree will be represented in the one instance by a spiral, and in the other by a series of concentric circles. Sometimes the design will, in the case of the smaller ones, be very clearly a spiral, but in the larger ones, while at first glance they may appear to be a series of circles, on closer examination it will often be found that the very central part is a spiral, but that sooner or later two of the raised lines separating the grooves will run into one another, and then on the outside of this there will be drawn a series of concentric circles. It is much more easy to imagine a series of concentric circles originating out of a spiral than to imagine a spiral originating out of a series of circles. Amongst a very large number examined we have not found one in which the central part is a series of circles and the outer a spiral. The internal is the first part drawn, and, taking the facts stated into consideration, we are probably right in regarding the spiral as the more primitive and the series of concentric circles as derived from an original spiral in the case of the designs now used by the Arunta and other Central tribes.

In connection with the description of the Engwura ceremony an illustration is given (Fig. 87) showing the backs of a group of the younger men who had just passed through the concluding ceremony of the Engwura, and on whom were painted, without the slightest reference to the particular totem of the individual, various of the totem *Ilkinia*, that is, the designs characteristic of the totems. It will be seen that while concentric circles with radiating lines preponderate, yet in some the design is much simpler and consists, as in the case of two of those in the foreground, of straight lines running across the back. The materials used for drawing these designs are white kaolin, red and yellow ochre and charcoal, and the effect of the designs standing out on the chocolate-coloured skin of the natives was in many instances far from unpleasing.

It is perhaps hopeless to speculate as to the origin of the totemic designs; if they are derived from what were once zoomorphs, then all that can be said is that in lapse of time they have been modified beyond recognition. At the same time with regard to the very strongly marked spiral and concentric circle design which may be said to be the one characteristic feature of the Central Australian scheme of design, it is perhaps worth noting that amongst the natives of the Papuan Gulf district of New Guinea, Haddon in dealing with the shields has described designs consisting of concentric circles and spirals, which are clearly derivatives of drawings of the human face. In his monograph[192] the drawing of a shield (Pl. 6, Fig. 92) is strikingly suggestive in this connection. Not only is this the case, but he describes the Papuan bull-roarers and ceremonial tablets which, just like the Australian Churinga, are shown to the young men for the first time when they are being initiated, as being decorated with designs representing the human face. We do not mean to imply that there is any direct connection between the present Australian and the Papuan bull-roarer, but that the meaning of the designs on the latter may perhaps afford a clue to the significance of the designs on the former. In the Papuan implement, in which the various stages of modification can be traced, it is seen that circles and spirals are derivatives of drawings of the human face, and it is possible that the circles and spirals which are so characteristic of the Central Australian implement may have had a similar origin.

The question is a most difficult one to deal with, and is rendered all the more so because we have in Australia at least two distinct types of these so-called bull-roarers. Mr. Howitt has described, amongst the natives of the south-east, a triangular-shaped form which is very distinct from the Churinga of the interior parts, as well as from that of the west, all of those from these localities agreeing fundamentally in shape. Apart also from the striking difference in form, that described by Mr. Howitt is quite devoid of the incised ornamentation which is such a characteristic feature of the Churinga of the interior and west. It is quite possible that we have in Australia at least two entirely different types of sacred implements of this particular nature. This is rendered all the more likely when it is taken into account that the bull-roarer of the eastern and south-eastern coastal tribes has, in certain respects, a quite different significance from that of the Central tribes, or, to put it more correctly, the latter has a certain meaning which is quite wanting in the case of the former.

Very different though, at first sight, the concentric circles of the Central Australian Churinga may appear to be from the zig-zag lines characteristic of the Western ones, yet it is not difficult to see how the one may have been derived from the other. In a Churinga of the bell-bird totem which was obtained amongst the western Arunta, and for which we have to thank Mr. Cowle, the concentric circles have become changed into squares with the angles slightly rounded off. In this way curves could be imagined to give way gradually to straight lines, and the patterns characteristic of Western Australian implements generally may be derived from a modification of the designs in which the leading feature was at first a spiral and then a series of concentric circles. At all events the Central and Western bull-roarers, both in form and design, are evidently allied to one another, and are very different from the *Tundun* or bull-roarer of the south-east.

Made in the USA
Lexington, KY
18 October 2016